THE
NUCLEAR
TIPPING
POINT

THE NUCLEAR TIPPING POINT

Why States Reconsider Their Nuclear Choices

Kurt M. Campbell

Robert J. Einhorn

Mitchell B. Reiss

editors

BROOKINGS INSTITUTION PRESS
Washington, D.C.

ABOUT BROOKINGS

The Brookings Institution is a private nonprofit organization devoted to research, education, and publication on important issues of domestic and foreign policy. Its principal purpose is to bring knowledge to bear on current and emerging policy problems. The Institution maintains a position of neutrality on issues of public policy. Interpretations or conclusions in Brookings publications should be understood to be solely those of the authors.

Copyright © 2004
THE BROOKINGS INSTITUTION
1775 Massachusetts Avenue, N.W., Washington, D.C. 20036
www.brookings.edu

Library of Congress Cataloging-in-Publication data
The nuclear tipping point : why states reconsider their nuclear choices /
Kurt M. Campbell, Robert J. Einhorn, and Mitchell B. Reiss, editors.
p.   cm.
Includes bibliographical references and index.
ISBN 0-8157-1330-4 (cloth : alk. paper) —
ISBN 0-8157-1331-2 (pbk. : alk. paper)
1. Nuclear nonproliferation. 2. National security. 3. Security, International.
I. Campbell, Kurt M., 1957– II. Einhorn, Robert J. III. Reiss, Mitchell. IV. Title.
JZ5675.N848 2004
327.1'747—dc22   2004010941

9 8 7 6 5 4 3 2 1

The paper used in this publication meets minimum requirements of the American National Standard for Information Sciences—Permanence of Paper for Printed Library Materials: ANSI Z39.48-1992.

Typeset in Sabon with Myriad display

Composition by Cynthia Stock
Silver Spring, Maryland

Printed by R. R. Donnelley
Harrisonburg, Virginia

Contents

Part Three: Prospects for a Nuclear Future

Foreword

In the celebrated 1932 correspondence between Albert Einstein and Sigmund Freud, Einstein asked the Viennese psychoanalyst if it would be possible to inoculate human beings against the "psychoses of hate and destruction" that lead to war. Freud's response—that aggression is the polar opposite of love, and therefore necessary for survival—did little to assuage Einstein's concerns about the scourge of armed conflict. When the atomic age dawned, in no small measure because of Einstein's own path-breaking theorizing, his concerns were magnified along with the threat. He concluded, ruefully, that "it is easier to denature plutonium than to denature the evil spirit of men" and likened the technological progress reflected in the unleashed power of the atom to an "axe in the hand of the pathological criminal." This powerful axe, he famously lamented, had "changed everything, save our modes of thinking, and thus we drift toward unparalleled catastrophe."

It was in the mid-1980s, under the leadership of then president David Hamburg, that Carnegie Corporation of New York first focused on efforts to change prevailing modes of thinking and prevent the drift that Einstein warned against. Through its Avoiding Nuclear War program, the Corporation invested in people and institutions seeking to advance nuclear nonproliferation and arms control. Developments in the Soviet Union under Mikhail Gorbachev combined with Ronald Reagan's bold, if undeveloped, policy pronouncements had created new opportunities for creative thinking about reducing nuclear dangers and, if not putting the nuclear genie back in the bottle, at least limiting its range of operation. Up to that point, the world had somehow managed to escape a post-Hiroshima blow from Einstein's axe. Hundreds of thousands had still died in conflicts fought with a lethal array of conventional (and, at times, as the Kurds and Iranians could attest, less conventional) armaments, but atomic and, more advanced and lethal, nuclear weapons had not been used again in warfare. During this period, Carnegie supported grantees who worked to craft new approaches and strategies to take advantage of the evolving geopolitical environment.

In the years that followed, the "nuclear club" of declared and undeclared states remained thankfully and, in many ways, surprisingly exclusive. But the specter of nuclear war did not dissipate. Indeed, one of the lamentable developments of the post–cold war world was the "nuclear amnesia" that allowed many to consider the possibility of nuclear conflict as an atavism, of little concern in a "New World Order" in which the absence of a superpower standoff would reap peace dividends through the conversion of latter-day swords into plowshares. The New World Disorder that was soon to erupt from Bosnia to Rwanda would be a grim reminder that the "psychoses of hate and destruction" were as deep and lethal as ever.

In response, the Corporation developed a major grantmaking initiative, the Carnegie Commission on Preventing Deadly Conflict, that sought "to address the looming threats to world peace of intergroup violence and to advance new ideas for the prevention and resolution of" such conflict through a range of scholarly and policy relevant publications. But the Corporation also refocused its efforts in the nuclear arena. While other crises proliferated, cold war nuclear arsenals and the material to produce them remained largely intact and, in the case of the former Soviet Union, increasingly vulnerable. To help address this "new-old threat," the Corporation supported the development of what became the Cooperative Threat Reduction program, commonly known as Nunn-Lugar in recognition of its two congressional sponsors, the estimable senators Sam Nunn and Richard Lugar. Nunn-Lugar has played, and continues to play, a crucial role in securing and dismantling nuclear weapons and fissile material from the former Soviet Union. Over the course of the next decade, and into the new century, the Corporation continued refining its approach to nuclear nonproliferation and arms control through grantmaking on a range of related issues, including export controls, space weaponization, and "Track II" diplomacy. Building on this work, the International Peace and Security program also addressed the growing challenge posed by biological weapons, as well as other threats, from global water scarcity to conflicts within states over contending claims for national self-determination.

Three years ago, the program funded a collaborative project between the Center for Strategic and International Studies (CSIS) and the Reves Center for International Studies at the College of William and Mary to examine factors in the international system that might trigger non-nuclear countries to reconsider their nuclear abstention. At the time, the question was an intriguing one with broader, if somewhat distant, implications for the future of the nuclear nonproliferation regime. Neither we nor CSIS and the Reves Center could have anticipated how developments in the world since the inception of the project—most searingly, the events of September 11 and its aftermath—could have raised the salience of this question even further. Not only did the fate of the nonproliferation regime undergo rapid change during this period, but also countries previously considered pillars of the non-nuclear community were presented with strategic possibilities in which nuclear capability seemed increasingly desirable. Added to this combustible mix was the specter of catastrophic nuclear terrorism. In such circumstances, the prospect of the global security environment slipping toward a nuclear "tipping point" became more than a theoretical possibility. As events unfolded over the course of the project, many of the participants came to believe that while the overall chance of a new kind of nuclear breakout remained unlikely, it was far more likely than it had been three years earlier.

This volume's examination of the nuclear calculations involved in eight cases—Egypt, Syria, Saudi Arabia, Turkey, Germany, Japan, South Korea, and Taiwan—contains insights into ways that the United States and the international community can create a buffer against a cascading spread of nuclear weapons and technology. By focusing on states whose military capabilities cannot compete with those of the United States, Russia, and China and who have been, in many cases, vocal nonproliferation advocates for decades, the findings and recommendations provide a prevention strategy that is at once forward looking and immediately relevant. In doing so, this project not only buttresses a major objective of Carnegie's International Peace and Security program, but also reflects Einstein's abiding and deceptively simple and related hope, notwithstanding his pessimism, that "the discovery of nuclear chain reactions need not bring about the destruction of mankind any more than did the discovery of matches."

VARTAN GREGORIAN
Carnegie Corporation of New York

Acknowledgments

This volume grew out of a three-year-long collaboration between the Center for Strategic and International Studies (CSIS) and the Reves Center for International Studies at the College of William and Mary. It is our collective hope that this volume will help illuminate a relatively unexamined dimension of nuclear politics in the twenty-first century and in the process provide insights for how to diminish the chances of a new and dangerous nuclear tipping point on the horizon. As with every effort of such magnitude, the production of this collection of case studies on rethinking nuclear options is the work of many dedicated people. The editors of this volume would like to acknowledge the enormous efforts of the following, without whom this project would not be possible.

The editors and authors are particularly grateful to Carnegie Corporation of New York for its initial interest in and support for this effort. In this regard, we would like to publicly thank David C. Speedie, Stephen J. Del Rosso, and Patricia Moore Nicholas for their patience and enduring support for our project. The volume has benefited enormously from the hard work and enterprising research of several key personnel at both CSIS and William and Mary. Jessica Cox, an able project coordinator, provided unflagging support and constant reminders of deadlines. Austin Carson helped both in the research for several chapters and with the preparation of our regular authors meetings. Mary Beth Nikitin, Richard

Weitz, and Sarah Banner all helped in the production of various chapters and in the overall construction of the volume. James Steinberg and Michael O'Hanlon, both of the Brookings Institution, provided comments on earlier versions of these chapters. Vinca LaFleur served as an outstanding editor and commentator on various drafts. Margaret Cosentino played an indispensable role in shepherding the project across the finish line. We are also thankful to Bob Faherty and his excellent staff at Brookings Institution Press for helping these disparate chapters to come together into an integrated and coherent whole. To these people, we offer our most sincere gratitude for their able efforts and unflagging support throughout the entire process.

PART 1

Nuclear Past and Present

CHAPTER 1

The Nuclear Tipping Point: Prospects for a World of Many Nuclear Weapons States

MITCHELL B. REISS

In 1946 the English poet W. H. Auden penned *The Age of Anxiety,* in which he lamented the hopelessness and universal disorder in the world. Auden was responding to the wholesale carnage and bleak aftermath of the Second World War, as well as to the recent introduction of an entirely new weapon of mass destruction. For Auden and others living in the shadow of the atomic bomb, the future was uncertain, fearful, and dangerous.

Today, more than five decades after the dawn of the nuclear age, we once again find ourselves living in an age of anxiety. And again, a major reason is the potential unbridled spread of nuclear weapons. But now the risk is not that one or two countries might test a nuclear device every decade or so, thereby giving the international community time to accommodate and integrate new nuclear powers into the existing order. Rather, the danger is that *many* countries might view nuclear weapons as useful, even essential, instruments to maintain security in a Hobbesian world where life is "poor, nasty, brutish, and short."

In this environment, any number of events could spark countries into a headlong dash to acquire independent nuclear arsenals. For example, a single new entrant to the nuclear club could catalyze similar responses by others in the region, with the Middle East and Northeast Asia the most likely candidates. Actual use of chemical and biological weapons could also prompt countries to seek nuclear weapons as a deterrent. Perhaps most disturbingly, even a vague, generalized sense that proliferation was inevitable and self-restraint futile—that "everyone is doing it"—could persuade countries that non-nuclear virtue was a "mug's game" that they cling to at their peril. Under these and other easily imaginable circumstances, previous pledges of nuclear abstention would be quietly or openly abandoned, as countries engaged in the nuclear equivalent of *sauve qui peut*.

Or it may be that countries would not sprint to cross the nuclear finish line but rather hedge their bets by working quietly and methodically to acquire the technology and materials necessary to build nuclear bombs on short notice once a political decision was made. Today, many of the building blocks for a nuclear arsenal—the scientific and engineering expertise, precision machine tools, computer software, and nuclear design information—are more readily available than ever before. And what is unavailable on the open market can be purchased on the black market due to the flourishing illicit trade in nuclear technology and materials between and among rogue (or what used to be termed pariah) states. A hedging strategy would allow a state to gradually increase its nuclear competence and shrink the period of its greatest strategic vulnerability: the time between a decision to acquire nuclear weapons and the actual possession of a usable nuclear arsenal. States that adopt this approach could remain poised on this non-nuclear precipice for months or even years, awaiting a political decision to tip them over the edge.

In other words, in ways both fast and slow, we may very soon be approaching a nuclear "tipping point," where many countries may decide to acquire nuclear arsenals on short notice, thereby triggering a proliferation epidemic.[1] Should current proliferation trends continue, within the next decade there may be more declared nuclear weapons states, more undeclared nuclear weapons states, and more states developing nuclear weapons than ever before. President John F. Kennedy's nightmare vision of a world with fifteen, twenty, or even twenty-five nuclear powers may yet occur. As Director of the CIA George Tenet testified before the Senate Select Intelligence Committee on February 11, 2003, "The desire for nuclear weapons is on the upsurge. Additional countries may decide to seek nuclear weapons as it becomes clear their neighbors and regional rivals are already doing so. The 'domino theory' of the twenty-first century may well be nuclear."[2] Should this occur, few would take comfort in the assurances of some academic theorists that "more may be better."

How did we arrive at this point? The spread of nuclear weapons has moved to its own rhythm, with long periods of nonproliferation success punctuated from time to time by resounding failure. The history of nuclear proliferation offers some guidance, with its failed policies, cautionary tales, good intentions gone awry, and, to be sure, useful lessons and periodic success stories.

The early years of the nuclear age quickly set the tone for much of what was to follow. The bone-chilling prospect of a hundred Hiroshimas prompted policymakers to give serious thought to dispersing America's population to the countryside and even building cities underground. The world-renowned British philosopher and pacifist Bertrand Russell was so alarmed by the nuclear peril that he recommended in 1946 that the United States launch an atomic attack against the Soviet Union if Moscow refused to help form a world government.

Initially, hopes ran high that atomic energy could be placed under international control. "Let us not deceive ourselves," Bernard Baruch, the U.S. representative to the United Nations Atomic Energy Commission, declared in June 1946. "We must elect either world peace or world destruction." But the possibility of success at the United Nations retreated before growing Soviet-American tensions. Stalemate soon gave way to failure and stilled talk in the U.S. scientific community about "one world or none."

The future spread of civilian nuclear power and the dissemination of scientific and technical skills raised concern over the potentially apocalyptic consequences of many states armed with nuclear weapons. As German physicist Werner Heisenberg warned in February 1947, the development of atomic bombs was "no longer a problem of science in any country, but a problem of engineering."

The Soviet Union tested a nuclear device in 1949. The following year, tens of millions of people signed the Stockholm Appeal, a petition demanding that atomic bombs be outlawed as "weapons of terror and the mass destruction of whole populations." Great Britain became the third member of the nuclear club in October 1952. By this time, the United States had mastered a new level of destructiveness, testing a ten-megaton "superbomb" that gouged out a crater three miles wide and half a mile deep. Less than a year later, the Soviet Union exploded its own crude H-bomb. Complementing these hydrogen weapons at the other end of the spectrum was the development of atomic artillery shells, demolition mines, and short-range missiles for tactical use on the battlefield. As the arms race heated up in earnest, the hands on the "doomsday clock" from the *Bulletin of the Atomic Scientists* were moved to a mere two minutes to midnight.

Radioactive fallout from atmospheric nuclear testing in the mid-1950s multiplied fears around the world. American H-bomb tests in the Pacific accidentally doused the crew of a Japanese fishing trawler, the *Lucky Dragon*, that chanced to be in the area; one of its crewmembers subsequently died of radiation sickness. Forty million Japanese signed petitions calling for the abolition of nuclear weapons. Popular culture reflected and reinforced global fears, with novels like *On the Beach*, which described the extinction of the human race by radioactive contamination, and films like *The Day the Earth Stood Still*, about the dangers of a spiraling arms race, and *The Seventh Seal*, Ingmar Bergman's nuclear allegory about mass death.

France became the fourth member of the nuclear club in February 1960 with its test in the Sahara. Later that year, the British scientist C. P. Snow, extrapolating from the rate of nuclear proliferation, predicted that "within, at the most, ten years, some of these bombs are going off. . . . That is the certainty." As if confirming these fears, China tested its first nuclear device the following year. By this time, every country that was technically competent to build nuclear arms, save Canada, had done so, validating policy studies that predicted that all countries with appreciable military strength would develop tactical or strategic nuclear arsenals, or both.

With French help, Israel developed a nuclear capability by the end of the 1960s. Indian leaders concluded in 1964 that China's nuclear blast had left them no option but to permit research on "peaceful" nuclear explosives. On May 18, 1974, the Indians got their bomb, with Prime Minister Indira Gandhi receiving news of the successful test with the code words "the Buddha smiles." From China and India, the chain reaction led to Pakistan. Prime Minister Zulfikar Ali Bhutto had already vowed that his country would acquire nuclear weapons if India did, even if his people had "to eat grass or leaves, even go hungry" to free up the necessary resources. New Delhi's nuclear test energized Islamabad's quest for an "Islamic bomb." South Africa around this time decided that it, too, needed nuclear arms to prevent the overthrow of its apartheid regime by the "total onslaught" of black Africa. The mid-decade oil crisis and the resulting insecurity over oil supplies prompted a renewed interest in nuclear power, leading some observers to worry that research reactors and civilian power programs could be used for building nuclear bombs. The dimensions of this threat were considerable; by the end of the 1970s, civilian nuclear programs existed in over forty-five non-nuclear weapons states. Making matters worse, in 1979 an American journal published the blueprints for the H-bomb, rationalizing that only through greater understanding of this technology could the arms race be brought to a halt.

By the start of the 1980s, the world appeared well on its way to fulfilling Kennedy's nightmare vision. Nuclear terrorism captured the public's imagination with the best-selling international spy thriller *The Fifth Horseman,* in which Libya's Muammar Gadhafi tries to force the United States to support a Palestinian state by threatening to blow up New York City. "The world is moving inexorably toward the use of nuclear weapons," wrote a commentator during the early 1980s, expressing a widely held view.[3] Visions of "nuclear winter," a new nightmare scenario of how the world would slowly die in the aftermath of a nuclear war, terrified the public.

And then, suddenly, it was over. The cold war ended not with the expected bang but a whimper—or at least a long, exhausted exhalation. The ideological competition between fascism, communism, and democracy was over. History had ended with an undisputed champion. President George H. W. Bush triumphantly declared a "new world order." U.S. officials talked about a "peace dividend," where funds from defense would be redirected to social and educational programs. The United States and Russia negotiated sweeping arms control agreements that would significantly reduce their nuclear stockpiles. Global nuclear anxieties abated.

But the good news in superpower relations did not translate into enhanced regional stability. During the first part of the 1990s, efforts to control the spread of nuclear weapons received a series of body blows. In spring 1990, India and Pakistan once again squared off over the neuralgic issue of Kashmir. Amid strikes, bombings, and assassinations by Muslim separatists and religious fundamentalists in Kashmir, the Indian prime minister accused his Pakistani counterpart of fomenting tensions in the region. Words quickly led to military maneuvers along the Indian-Pakistani border. In May, U.S. intelligence concluded that Pakistan had assembled nuclear bombs. Only urgent American intervention defused the crisis.

Other countries also tried to develop nuclear weapons during this time; some may have succeeded. From the allied victory in the 1991 Persian Gulf War came the sobering discovery that Saddam Hussein's Iraq was well advanced on a secret project to build an atomic bomb. That the International Atomic Energy Agency (IAEA) and U.S. intelligence services had either missed entirely or vastly underestimated the sophistication of Baghdad's covert nuclear ambitions reassured no one that they would be able to detect other nuclear aspirants in the future.

And even if nuclear aspirants could be detected, could they be stopped? An answer, of sorts, was provided in late 1992 when the IAEA uncovered, with the help of U.S. satellite imagery, another case of nuclear deceit. North Korea had misrepresented its nuclear activities, secretly separating plutonium from spent fuel, and then prevented international inspections that might have disclosed the scope of its nuclear weapons program. As the crisis on the Korean peninsula heated up, the United States defused the threat by striking a nuclear deal with North Korea in October 1994. The nonproliferation price was high: a multilateral consortium would deliver $5 billion of energy to the North, and Pyongyang would be allowed to delay comprehensive IAEA inspections for as long as a decade, perhaps longer. Critics contended this unhappy precedent rewarded nuclear cheaters; it would encourage other countries to build nuclear weapons as bargaining chips to evade sanctions and resist outside pressures.

Other nuclear anxieties contributed to this new and less certain international environment. In 1993 the director of the CIA, R. James Woolsey, warned that although the Soviet bear was slain, "now we must live in a jungle filled with a bewildering variety of poisonous snakes."[4] It was feared that the sprawling nuclear archipelago of the former Soviet Union, involving laboratories, facilities, and bomb-grade material, would become a fertile breeding ground for new nuclear snakes. Poverty and unemployment among the 1 million former Soviet physicists, chemists, metallurgists, engineers, and technicians raised concern over a brain drain of nuclear expertise. Worse, lax internal security in the former Soviet Union prompted fears that "loose nukes" could find their way to the black market for sale to aspiring nuclear powers and terrorist groups.

It appeared the post–cold war world had ushered in less order and more chaos than previously imagined. The phrase "ethnic cleansing" entered the lexicon with the wholesale slaughter in central Africa and the former Yugoslavia. The AIDS pandemic claimed millions of lives. Environmental degradation, transborder crime, refugee problems, and narcotics trafficking all seemed to grow. Samuel P. Huntington's *The Clash of Civilizations* and Robert D. Kaplan's *The Coming Anarchy* painted dark visions of a future world mired in endless conflict and widespread misery.

Yet from another vantage point, the situation did not appear so hopeless or even desperate, at least with respect to the spread of nuclear weapons. By the mid-1990s, there were important nonproliferation successes. The strategic nuclear weapons inherited by Ukraine, Kazakhstan, and Belarus after the demise of the Soviet Union had all been returned to Russia. There they were secured in part by a unique U.S. program, referred to as "Nunn-Lugar" after its two Senate sponsors, which sought to reduce the nuclear threat through cooperative efforts with Russia. Civilian governments in Argentina and Brazil officially renounced their nuclear weapons ambitions and jointly accepted comprehensive IAEA safeguards. South Africa confessed it had built during the 1980s a small nuclear arsenal of six nuclear bombs—but not before it had unilaterally dismantled them; soon thereafter it formalized its non-nuclear stance by joining the Non-Proliferation Treaty (NPT). Iraq's clandestine nuclear program had been thwarted; it was forced to submit to intrusive and rigorous inspections. North Korea's declared nuclear program was frozen and under international supervision; Pyongyang even pledged to go beyond its NPT obligations by agreeing to eventually dismantle its reprocessing and other facilities. France and China formally joined the NPT. Nuclear supplier states tightened controls on exports of nuclear materials, equipment, and technology. In 1995 the NPT was extended indefinitely. A comprehensive test ban treaty, a long-standing symbol of nonproliferation efforts, was concluded. Nuclear weapons–free zones were established in Southeast Asia and Africa, to join those already in place in Latin America and the South Pacific. By mid-decade the proliferation problem appeared to be under control.

In comparison to the first five decades of the nuclear age, the proliferation battle now assumed a different, more optimistic perspective. To be sure, there had been some casualties: five states had nuclear arsenals, and another three—Israel, India, and Pakistan—were suspected of having covert weapons programs, with "bombs in the basement." But this litany was nowhere near the nightmare levels feared by President Kennedy. No one had tested a nuclear device since 1974. A significant number of nuclear dogs had not barked. By the mid-1990s, an influential report by the Carnegie Endowment for International Peace could confidently state that "the rate of nuclear proliferation was slowing, the geographic scope of proliferation was shrinking." And the collapse of the Soviet Union suggested a powerful nonproliferation lesson: the acquisition of tens of thousands of these weapons could not ensure a regime's prosperity, influence, or even existence.

Yet relief was short lived. In May 1998, India conducted five nuclear tests in the Rajasthan desert. Pakistan quickly followed suit with five nuclear tests to equal what Delhi had done a few weeks earlier, plus a sixth test to match India's 1974 peaceful nuclear explosion. Although both countries had long been suspected of having "recessed" nuclear arsenals, these nuclear tests now infused their long-standing rivalry with new dangers. Questions were raised about each country's ability to establish secure command and control over its nuclear arsenal; their proximity, hostility, domestic instability, and almost daily violence along the Line of Control in Kashmir would, it was claimed, lead to misunderstanding and perhaps fatal miscalculation. These fears were almost realized in spring 1999 over yet another conflict along the border with Jammu and Kashmir; Pakistan's president Nawaz Sharif withdrew his troops from the Kargil region only after intense U.S. pressure. In October 2002, North Korea admitted it was pursuing nuclear weapons through a covert uranium enrichment program, in violation of the 1994 Agreed Framework, its IAEA and NPT obligations, and a 1991 bilateral denuclearization accord with South Korea. And in early 2003, Iran publicly confessed to secretly building a gas centrifuge facility that had the potential to enrich uranium for nuclear bombs. The nuclear nonproliferation regime seemed powerless to stop these developments.

Wishing to diversify their lethal portfolios, countries also pursued chemical and biological weapons and ballistic missiles. Leading suspects here included Iran, Iraq, North Korea, Syria, Libya, and Sudan. By January 2001, according to the Office of the Secretary of Defense, "In virtually every corner of the globe, the United States and its allies face a growing threat from the proliferation and possible use of nuclear, biological and chemical (NBC) weapons and their delivery systems."[5]

Moreover, the likelihood that terrorist groups might acquire or develop weapons of mass destruction increased in the first decade after the end of the cold war. The extreme religious sect Aum Shinrikyu tried unsuccessfully to enrich uranium and spread anthrax spores from city rooftops in Japan; in 1995 it succeeded in killing a dozen Japanese commuters and contaminating over 300 miles of the Tokyo subway system by releasing sarin gas during the morning rush hour. Fears that Osama bin Laden's al Qaeda organization was developing chemical weapons prompted the Clinton administration to launch a cruise missile attack in August 1998 against a pharmaceutical plant in Sudan. Al Qaeda videotapes showing chemical weapons experiments on dogs confirmed these fears. And during the 1990s there were periodic media reports of terrorists trying to smuggle fissile material from the former Soviet Union; some of these episodes were independently corroborated.

The deteriorating international environment during the 1990s was further reflected by increasing doubts about the central theoretical underpinning of the cold war and the reintroduction of two previously discredited security concepts. Deterrence—the idea that the United States could prevent a nuclear attack by the credible threat to retaliate with a devastating nuclear second strike—was widely credited with preserving the cold war's nuclear peace. Yet during the decade, deterrence gradually fell from favor. Instead, support for national missile defense moved from the far-right margins of the American political spectrum to the center, where it was embraced on a bipartisan basis. (Indeed, public opinion polls confirmed that a majority of Americans believed a missile defense system was already in place.) Washington's dedicated—and expensive—pursuit of national missile defense was an implicit acknowledgement that deterrence, while useful against the Soviet Union during the cold war, no longer worked against the full spectrum of threats now confronting the United States, especially those from rogue states and terrorists. This logic culminated in the announcement on December 2001 that Washington would formally withdraw from the 1972 Anti-Ballistic Missile Treaty in order to pursue missile defenses unconstrained by international legal agreements.

Almost a decade earlier, the Pentagon had unveiled its counterproliferation initiative. Although it encompassed support for diplomacy, arms control, and export controls, counterproliferation policy appeared to emphasize the launching of preemptive strikes against adversaries harboring, or suspected of harboring, weapons of mass destruction. In the wake of September 11, 2001, and a much greater appreciation of America's vulnerability, the Bush administration raised high the counterproliferation banner. "I will not wait on events while dangers gather," President Bush warned in his January 2002 State of the Union Address. "I will not stand by as peril draws closer and closer. The United States of America will not permit the world's most dangerous regimes to threaten us with the world's most destructive weapons." Critics, especially among America's European allies, viewed this muscular response as a unilateral impulse that overemphasized a military solution to the proliferation problem, violated international law, undermined the nonproliferation regime, and could lead to more, not less, nuclear weapons states. They complained that the United States was establishing a Star Chamber with itself as "judge, jury, and executioner." The Bush administration un-apologetically dismissed these arguments, instead publicly elevating and enshrining preemption as a military option. "The greater the threat, the greater is the risk of inaction," stated the United States National Security Strategy, released in September 2002, "and the more compelling the case for taking anticipatory action to defend ourselves."

Critics also alleged that some of the very steps the United States adopted to address the terrorist threat and restore order to an unruly world could unwittingly spur nuclear proliferation. The Bush adminis-tration's emphasis on military preemption, interest in both low- and high-yield nuclear weapons to destroy underground bunkers housing weapons of mass destruction (WMD), and preparations to shrink the time needed to resume underground nuclear testing have all raised the sta-tus of nuclear weapons and lowered the threshold for their use, or so the argument runs. In addition, one of the unintended "demonstration" effects of the U.S. war against Iraq was that chemical and biological weapons proved insufficient to deter America; only nuclear weapons, it appeared, could do this job. The aggregate result of these actions was that other countries would now find these weapons more desirable.

Despite these policy differences, there is something approaching con-sensus among the authors of this volume and our colleagues both in and out of government that we now stand on the verge of a new nuclear age, one that may be characterized by more nuclear weapons states and a much greater chance that these weapons will be used. How could this dark future come to pass? Under what circumstances could some of the main supporters of the nonproliferation regime rethink their original non-nuclear bargain? What could cause them, individually or collec-tively, to "tip"?

Powerful reasons have always existed for states to obtain nuclear weapons. These reasons have included the desire to intimidate and coerce rivals, the search for enhanced security against regional or inter-national rivals, the status and prestige associated with mastering nuclear technology, and domestic politics and bureaucratic self-aggrandizement.[6] These incentives, singly and in combination, were responsible for the proliferation that occurred during the cold war. They persist today.

At the same time, numerous disincentives to acquiring nuclear arsenals over the past fifty years prevented more countries from joining the nuclear club. These include financial cost, technical difficulty, domestic opposition, damage to important bilateral relationships or collective security alliances, and global nonproliferation norms. These disincentives persist today as well.

Yet there is widespread concern that the calculus of incentives and disincentives has shifted during the past decade, with incentives increasing and disincentives declining. New threats have arisen while the nuclear taboo has weakened. And it is not just a single factor in this new strategic landscape that gives pause. Rather, it is the accumulation of multiple factors and their interplay and mutual reinforcement that account for many of these new dangers. For instance, there have always been terrorist groups, but never before has there been the simultaneous concentration of terrorist groups, diffusion of bomb design information, and poorly secured or unaccounted for nuclear material from the former Soviet Union.

In the following chapter, Kurt M. Campbell outlines transnational influences on nuclear policy, including local, regional, and international economic, political, military, and even cultural factors. As a complement to this sweeping overview, Robert J. Einhorn then sets out a methodological framework for understanding why certain countries may have originally decided to renounce nuclear weapons acquisition. He also lists country-specific factors that have arisen since the original renunciations that may lead decisionmakers to reconsider their non-nuclear bargain.

Many of our colleagues have written excellent studies on the relatively small number of countries that possess nuclear weapons or on the current "suspects" that already are pursuing a nuclear arsenal. Much work, both theoretical and historical, has already been performed in these areas, producing a rich and diverse literature of case studies, technical reports, and personal memoirs. Foreign policy experts both inside and outside of government have devoted, and continue to devote, much time and attention to particular countries and discrete threats. It is not our intent here to duplicate these efforts.

Instead, this volume examines a different collection of countries: those states that are currently members in good standing of the nonproliferation regime. Many have long possessed the technical, scientific, and engineering competence to build nuclear bombs but resisted the temptation. These countries struck a formal non-nuclear bargain, publicly swearing off the development of nuclear arms. Over the years, some of them have been among the most ardent supporters of the NPT and global denuclearization efforts.[7] Countries that fall into this category include Japan, South Korea, Taiwan, Saudi Arabia, Egypt, Syria, Turkey, and Germany.

The countries chosen for case study in part two have been selected because they serve as a barometer of the health of the international non-proliferation regime and as an early warning system measuring the pressure for independent nuclear arsenals. Should any one of them decide to publicly abandon its NPT and IAEA commitments or, as is more likely, quietly hedge its bets to reduce the time needed to acquire nuclear weapons, it would have a destabilizing impact on regional and global security. Needless to say, the defection of any one of these countries from the non-nuclear to the nuclear ranks would also deal a severe, perhaps even fatal, blow to over five decades of U.S. and international efforts to halt the spread of nuclear weapons.

To be sure, other countries could have been included in this study, such as Argentina, Brazil, South Africa, Indonesia, Australia, and Algeria. They have not been selected because of space and time constraints and because we believe that the eight countries chosen encompass a sufficiently broad range of technical capabilities and political motivations to illustrate the major themes of this volume.

Authors with specific expertise and long experience with our eight countries, as academic researchers or as foreign policy practitioners for the U.S. government, or both, have been chosen to explore their potential nuclear aspirations and detail the circumstances under which they might reconsider their non-nuclear bargain.

All three of our East Asian countries are influenced by at least two common variables: their relationships with the United States and North Korea's nuclear weapons program. Kurt M. Campbell and Tsuyoshi Sunohara illuminate Japan's attitude on nuclear issues and the durability of the U.S. security guarantee; they also reveal Tokyo's recent thinking about the possibility of a nuclear-armed Japan. Jonathan D. Pollack and I examine the case of South Korea, which had attempted to acquire a nuclear arsenal. Under a variety of scenarios, we imagine the factors that could propel Seoul to revisit its previous decision. Taiwan also invested heavily in its own nuclear weapons program in the 1970s before the United States intervened. Derek J. Mitchell looks at Taipei's earlier motivations and then explains what new factors, including the burgeoning independence movement on the island and a growing military threat from the mainland, might cause Taiwan to once again attempt to go nuclear.

In the greater Middle East, four diverse countries—each differing in scientific and technical competence, domestic political systems, and security relationships—pose a potential threat to acquire nuclear weapons. Saudi Arabia's interest in nuclear weapons is unveiled by Thomas W. Lippman, whose detective work provides new information and insights into Riyadh's flirtation with Pakistan and the "proliferation by purchase" path it might contemplate. Egypt is the political, cultural, and economic leader of the Arab world, as well as the neighbor of a suspected nuclear weapons state—Israel. Thus it might naturally be expected to gravitate to nuclear status; but so far, it has firmly resisted that impulse, according to Robert J. Einhorn. Syria faces an even more acute security challenge than Egypt, especially after Operation Iraqi Freedom and removal of its fellow Ba'athist regime from Baghdad. Ellen Laipson seeks to understand Damascus's worldview and how a nuclear arsenal might improve its parlous national security. And Turkey faces a rapidly evolving strategic environment at the crossroads of Europe and the Middle East. Leon Fuerth discusses the importance of Turkey's continued relationship with NATO and the United States and reveals troubling scenarios that could push Turkey toward nuclear reconsideration.

In our one study of a European power, Jenifer Mackby and Walter B. Slocombe analyze the case of Germany, the original "nth" nuclear power that generated so much proliferation concern in the 1950s and 1960s. Noting that Berlin today is the least likely candidate among our group to acquire nuclear weapons, Mackby and Slocombe highlight the importance of alliances and how an alternative conception of security can be manufactured over time.

Building on the analytical framework in part one and the findings in part two, part three is a concluding chapter that explores the implications for international nonproliferation efforts and U.S. policy. What do our case studies reveal about the health of the nonproliferation regime, such as the IAEA and NPT? Can the integrity of these mechanisms be restored and reinvigorated? Or are wholly new institutions and arrangements needed to cope with the new strategic environment of the twenty-first century?

Important elements in this new landscape include biological and chemical weapons and ballistic missiles. How will the promiscuous spread of these weapons affect a country's decision to go nuclear? Do they degrade a country's security so that it might seek refuge by acquiring nuclear weapons? Or do they channel feelings of insecurity into the desire to acquire a similar biological and chemical deterrent that, along with ballistic missiles, may be technically easier to develop or purchase than a nuclear weapons capability?

Are changes needed on the demand side, by offering additional security guarantees and resolving regional disputes? If so, the recent example of secret Anglo-American diplomacy that led to Libya's renouncing publicly its WMD programs, specifically including its nascent nuclear weapons program, might serve as a model for other would-be proliferators. Or are changes needed on the supply side, by tightening up export controls and seeking greater support for the Proliferation Security Initiative? In this case, Saddam Hussein's regime could serve as the poster child for what happens when a country seeks WMD. Or will the motivations lie elsewhere, for example, with local and domestic factors less susceptible to outside influences?

Perhaps the most important factor in the nuclear calculations of the countries examined here is the fate of North Korea's and Iran's nuclear ambitions, which pose the most imminent challenge to the nonproliferation regime. Will diplomacy prevail, both in the six-party talks involving Pyongyang and in the dialogue that the "European Union 3" is conducting with Tehran? If not, will sterner measures such as UN Security Council sanctions be invoked? Or, under yet unforeseen circumstances, will military force be used? Or will these countries be allowed to pursue their nuclear ambitions, much like India and Pakistan did after their nuclear tests in 1998?

Amidst all this uncertainty, the role of the United States looms large over this nuclear future. Washington's leadership of the nonproliferation regime and its efforts to prevent the spread of nuclear weapons will be critical for success. This has been true since the dawn of the nuclear age and is unlikely to change anytime soon. Yet the challenges are many and formidable, the stakes are enormous, and success is far from assured. Failure will shape the contours of the international system for decades to come and undermine the security of countries around the world. If the United States cannot summon the wisdom, determination, and patience to prevent a nuclear tipping point, then we may once again face another age of anxiety, or worse.

Notes

1. There is a substantial literature on tipping points. See, for example, Thomas C. Schelling, *Micromotives and Macrobehavior* (W. W. Norton, 1978); Mark Granovetter, "Threshold Models of Collective Behavior," *American Journal of Sociology*, vol. 83, no. 6 (1978), pp. 1420–43; and Mark Granovetter and R.

Soong, "Threshold Models of Diffusion and Collective Behavior," *Journal of Mathematical Sociology,* vol. 9, no. 3 (1983), pp. 165–79. More recently, this concept has been popularized in Malcolm Gladwell, *The Tipping Point: How Little Things Can Make a Difference* (Little, Brown, 2000).

2. Senate Select Intelligence Committee, *Current and Projected National Security Threats to the United States: Hearing before the Committee on Intelligence,* S. Hrg. 108-161, 108 Cong. 1 sess., February 11, 2003.

3. Bernard Lown, "Does Humankind Have a Future?" Address to the 1st International Physicians for the Prevention of Nuclear War World Congress, Airlie House, Va., March 20, 1981, available at www.ippnw.org/NeverWhisper.html.

4. Statement before U.S. Senate confirmation hearing, February 2, 1993. As reported in Douglas Jehl, "CIA Nominee Wary of Budget Cuts," *New York Times,* February 3, 1993, p. A18.

5. Office of the Secretary of Defense, *Proliferation: Threat and Response,* January 2001, p. 1, located at www.ciaonet.org/cbr/cbr00/video/cbr_ctd/cbr_ctd_11a.pdf (March 2004).

6. Many studies have examined countries' motivations for acquiring nuclear weapons. For an excellent recent discussion, see Scott D. Sagan, "Rethinking the Causes of Nuclear Proliferation: Three Models in Search of a Bomb," in Victor A. Utgoff, ed., *The Coming Crisis: Nuclear Proliferation, U.S. Interests and World Order* (MIT Press, 2000), pp. 17–50.

7. Article 6 of the NPT stipulates, "Each of the Parties to the Treaty undertakes to pursue negotiations in good faith on effective measures relating to cessation of the nuclear arms race at an early date and to nuclear disarmament, and on a treaty on general and complete disarmament under strict and effective international control."

CHAPTER 2

Reconsidering a Nuclear Future: Why Countries Might Cross over to the Other Side

KURT M. CAMPBELL

For nearly half a century, a central aspect of U.S. diplomacy and national security strategy has been to prevent the spread of nuclear weapons. Over the last decade, this pursuit has focused primarily on stopping unsavory regimes such as North Korea, Iran, and Iraq from acquiring or developing a nuclear capability; and after September 11, there was new urgency to stop terrorists from getting their hands on such destructive power. Yet, for all the attention given these usual suspects, there has been remarkably little consideration of another class of future potential proliferators: those states that in the past chose to forgo the nuclear option but, for a variety of reasons, could now revisit that decision and pursue a nuclear capability.[1] Today there is a real risk that the concerted diplomatic efforts during and since the cold war aimed at slowing, halting, or reversing nuclear proliferation may be starting to unravel—this time involving so-called responsible states that decades ago decided against developing a nuclear capacity.

Countries such as Egypt, Germany, Japan, Saudi Arabia, South Korea, Syria, Taiwan, and Turkey have all been mainstays in the non-nuclear club even while some of them quietly flirted with nuclear weapons in the past. However, usually a combination of security guarantees, domestic politics, and international pressure was enough to dissuade them from pursuing the nuclear course—in the simplest terms, the potential costs outweighed the perceived benefits. But much has changed that could upset the delicate balance of incentives and disincentives that were so laboriously put in place during and after the cold war. There have been rapid changes in the international system, and there are now major new sources of global upheaval and uncertainty: the now-distant end of a bipolar, "stable" global environment in which security guarantees were a central part of the U.S.-Soviet standoff; emergence of the new nuclear states of India and Pakistan; the dominant preeminence of American power and concerns about the future strategic direction of the United States; weak and potentially failed states and havens of lawlessness and volatility throughout an arc of instability from South America to Africa, the Caucasus, and Southeast Asia; and new threats from terrorists with global reach.

Each of the states named above has experienced enormous domestic changes, and for many, the surrounding regional situation or larger international environment has become less stable and, in some cases, more ominous. For instance, talk of a nuclear option was virtually unthinkable in Japan a decade ago, but there has been, more recently, a rising chorus of commentators both in and out of government that publicly supports open debate around the highly contentious matter of Japan's potential nuclear future. It would be an exaggeration to suggest that a collection of comments and opinion pieces indicates a nuclear program on the horizon, but it would also be imprudent to rule out a future with more nuclear powers without more careful study and examination.

The potential for nuclear proliferation among states that had formerly forsworn the option deserves study and attention from U.S. policymakers; it is timely to consider what collection of incentives—or erosion of disincentives—might provoke a country now placed squarely in the non-nuclear camp to reconsider its nuclear options. Identifying the potential factors that could lead to a new round of proliferation among these countries should now be seen as a critical new component of American intelligence collection and analysis, preventative diplomacy, and U.S. decisionmaking on issues ranging from national strategy to public diplomacy.[2]

Five Factors to Consider for Future Nuclear Proliferation

What specific conditions would inspire a country to retreat from a well-established, non-nuclear national identity in favor of an arsenal that

includes atomic devices and the means for their delivery? The most likely case would probably involve several circumstances interacting and reinforcing each other in complex ways. Five key international and domestic factors that could lead to a reversal in a country's nuclear posture are
  —a change in the direction of U.S. foreign and security policy,
  —a breakdown of the global nuclear nonproliferation regime,
  —the erosion of regional or global security,
  —domestic imperatives, and
  —increasing availability of technology.

Of course, no one single feature of the new strategic landscape may give one great pause; instead, the various ways multiple factors might accumulate and reinforce one another will account for many of the new dangers. For example, there have always been terrorist groups, but there has never before been the simultaneous concentration of terrorist groups with global reach, the diffusion of bomb design information, and the possibility of unaccounted nuclear material from the former Soviet Union.[3] Another example is the increasing ease with which a country like Pakistan can miniaturize a nuclear device with assistance from China and place it on top of a ballistic missile purchased from North Korea. This type of transnational trade in weapons of mass destruction and related technologies is a growing development and one that can exponentially increase the threat of nuclear proliferation.[4] These technical and regional factors coincide with an unstable international period, in which there are concerns about the direction of U.S. foreign policy and anxieties about the sustainability of the global nonproliferation regime. (For example, the apparent international nonchalance in the matter of North Korea's brazen flouting of the International Atomic Energy Agency mandate could be viewed as a symptom of the regime unraveling.)

Direction of U.S. Foreign and Security Policy

Perhaps the most important ingredient in a new international calculation of the attractiveness—or perceived necessity—of acquiring nuclear weapons is the question of the future direction of U.S. foreign and security policy. For decades U.S. friends and allies—such as Japan, South Korea, Taiwan, Germany, Egypt, and others—have come to depend on several aspects of American policy when making calculations about their own security and the question of forswearing nuclear weapons. These aspects include the stability of the American nuclear deterrent and U.S. security guarantees; U.S. rhetorical commitment to, active pursuit of, and participation in global non-proliferation policies and regimes; American restraint in publicly contemplating the use of nuclear weapons, particularly against a state that does not possess weapons of mass destruction; and U.S. commitments not to decouple U.S. security from that of its allies through the development of defensive systems. A number of recent developments may suggest directional changes in some of these areas. And indeed, it is precisely the anxieties associated with such new directions in American security policy that potentially could spur some serious reconsideration of formerly forsworn nuclear options.

Many in the international community perceive that the United States has made a major change in its approach to deterrence, in favor of preemption and preventive war. They see evidence for this in the 2002 Nuclear Posture Review, the 2002 U.S. National Security Strategy, and U.S. policies toward Iraq.[5] Coupled with the U.S. desire (however justified in some cases) to jettison cold war–era agreements such as the Anti-Ballistic Missile (ABM) Treaty, this perception leads some to conclude that U.S. policy has become more unilateralist and focused on U.S.-only concerns, to the exclusion of its global commitments and responsibilities.[6] While the real impact of these relatively recent impressions is yet to be determined, a sense of U.S. drift away from its allies and an internationalist foreign policy (real or perceived) may cause some countries—mostly those who have traditionally relied on U.S. security commitments to provide an ultimate guarantee against attack—to question the stability of their own security situation. Current U.S. security commitments in Europe and Japan are still grounded in the viability and consistency of the U.S. nuclear umbrella. But questions about American commitment to security alliances and partners are sharply on the rise, and as a hedge against increasing U.S. unpredictability, it is possible that countries would develop nuclear arsenals to fulfill regional and international security goals.

U.S.-German relations, for example, suffered major—and potentially permanent—rifts over the recent war in Iraq, and there is a widespread perception in Germany that the United States has made major changes to its approach to foreign and security policy.[7] It is not inconceivable that an eventual distance between the two countries—no longer standing side-by-side in a life-or-death struggle against the Soviets—would have emerged in any case. But there is little doubt that recent events have created a great deal of bad feeling on both sides. Perhaps exacerbating a perception that the United States is drifting away from Germany is the removal of a substantial number of American troops from German soil. However sensible militarily, the timing could contribute to the impression that the United States is "leaving" Germany in a much larger and more purposeful sense.[8] In the near term, Germany is looking toward Europe for its security future to a much greater degree than in the past. Today, Germany's non-nuclear status is virtually ingrained in its political and foreign policy cultures, and most current commentators think it extremely unlikely that a serious movement could emerge in Germany to reconsider proudly held non-nuclear credentials. Yet it is reasonable to ask how sustainable is a situation in which Germany relies on a French or British nuclear deterrent as its ultimate security guarantee.

Relations between South Korea and the United States are also strained. Disagreements over how to handle North Korea, accidents involving U.S. troops and Korean civilians, anti-American demonstrations, and differences over the timing of moving U.S. forces away from the Demilitarized Zone have introduced a substantial irritant into the U.S.–South Korean alliance.[9] On the one hand, there is appreciation for the role that the United States has played in defending South Korea and the need for U.S. forces to continue deterring the North. On the other hand, there is a desire for greater autonomy and independence, as well as an abiding suspicion (fifty years of evidence notwithstanding) of eventual abandonment by the United States.[10] It is certainly conceivable that Korea could begin to feel so uncertain or resentful of the United States that it would seek a way to guarantee its security without the U.S. umbrella.

It is worth pointing out that perceived U.S. unilateralism could cut both ways. If U.S. actions are seen as necessary to cope with perceived international security threats, such efforts could allay concerns of friends and allies and demonstrate that the U.S. is willing to tackle tough security problems. Strong action against North Korea, for example, will reassure Asian friends, most notably Japan and South Korea. Still, predictability over time is key—you never know when the unilateralism will break for you or against you. So the United States must be careful to balance a tough stance with international norms; even subtle changes in nuclear doctrine and deployments can have dramatic unintended consequences among U.S. allies and friends.

U.S. rhetorical and policy commitment to the global nonproliferation regime also has a significant impact on international confidence in the regime and its ability to carry out its charter. Previous American administrations, both Republican and Democratic, have made the Nuclear Non-

Proliferation Treaty (NPT) a centerpiece of U.S. strategy to prevent the spread of nuclear weapons. More recently, however, there has been a perception that the Unites States is retreating from its historic emphasis on this international regime.[11]

Another key issue is the potential development by the United States of new nuclear weapons and renewed underground nuclear testing. The NPT provides that non-nuclear weapons states will not seek to develop nuclear weapons—but at the same time it also obligates the nuclear weapons states to work toward eventual disarmament. However impractical this may seem at the moment, this obligation is taken seriously by many of the states party to that treaty. Further development of nuclear weapons by the United States could be interpreted as a retreat from the path of disarmament and the obligations enshrined in the treaty (thereby potentially weakening interest and confidence in the global nonproliferation regime more generally).[12] In addition, countries that view the United States as a real or potential threat may treat greater U.S. nuclear capability as a spur to further develop their own deterrent.

Certainly, the United States is not the only factor in the calculations countries make about their own security, but it is a major one. The policies and actions of the most powerful and influential country in the world affect every nation and have an impact on everything from global and regional security to economic stability, international norms and practices, and the sustainability of whatever global consensus exists. Much like the brilliant (or simply martinet) professor whose students write down his every sneeze or cough lest they miss something that will be on the final exam, U.S. actions are closely observed, noted, and interpreted by states around the world. American policy can, sometimes inadvertently, increase or decrease confidence substantially—a key component in any country's evaluation of whether—or when—a nuclear capability is required.

Breakdown of the Global Nonproliferation Regime

Since the dropping of the atomic bomb on Nagasaki in August 1945, the world has not witnessed a nuclear device used in anger, and—contrary to expectations—for much of the cold war, nuclear proliferation was actually slowing down, with China becoming the last member of the so-called nuclear club in 1964. Events of the last decade, however, have seen a dramatic weakening of this trend. Although unacknowledged by the nonproliferation treaty, three new nuclear powers have emerged, and a number of "rogue" states are widely known to be pursuing nuclear programs and to be close to fielding a weapon—if they have not already succeeded in doing so.

India and Pakistan—each of which had active nuclear programs for decades—openly became nuclear weapons countries when both detonated nuclear devices in May 1998. They have been further developing their nuclear arsenals since then. It is an open secret that Israel possesses a nuclear deterrent. North Korea has been openly flouting the global nonproliferation regime for nearly a decade and is estimated to already possess at least a few nuclear devices. Iran is widely believed to be continuing a decades-long effort to develop nuclear weapons, and it may be only months away from a functional device.[13] Other states are further behind in the pursuit but no less ardent.

To be sure, the nonproliferation regime has been battered by the reality of newly emergent nuclear weapons states, but what is also critically important is the lack of real consequences for those countries that have defied the international community. The three known but unacknowledged nuclear powers have suffered little to no long-term diplomatic or economic penalties for their defiance, and Iran and North Korea continue their programs apace. Some critics see the current high standing in Washington of Israel, India, and Pakistan as actually encouraging other potential nuclear states on the brink to take that next fateful step.[14]

Eroding Regional or Global Security

Existing or historic tensions between neighboring nations could lead one or more states to reconsider the value of developing a nuclear capability. As general insecurities transform into systemic rivalries, a state could consider nuclear capabilities as a way of getting the strategic upper hand or balancing a larger, nuclear neighbor. For example, as India strengthened its nuclear program, and it became clear that nuclear weapons were within its grasp, Pakistan found it increasingly necessary to develop nuclear capabilities of its own. Japan, troubled by China's economic growth and military expansion as well as by reemergence of historic tensions in the region, has reacted with renewed debate on the nuclear issue, at least by some. China's unambiguous nuclear status, combined with Japan's traditional non-nuclear posture, underscores a high level of anxiety in Tokyo. In addition, tension between China and Taiwan is mounting, threatening to lead to an arms race with greater potential for conflagration over time.

A similar dynamic between certain eastern or central European states and Russia is also easily conceivable, should President Putin's ambitious opening to the West fail or conservative elements in Moscow reemerge and rekindle long-running tensions on the continent. According to this scenario, a bullying Russia might intimidate either an aspiring or a newly minted member of NATO, spurring the country in question to seek a nuclear card in the regional competition as the ultimate deterrent to Russia's misbehavior.

A nation's desire to achieve a balance of military power with it neighbors is another possible incentive for it to adopt a pro-nuclear stance. In South Korea, for instance, there has been considerable concern for a long time that an increasing conventional military capability in the North could present an overwhelming and destabilizing challenge to the government in the South. This concern was similar to the belief at the height of the cold war that the conventional might of Warsaw Pact member countries threatened the stability and security of Western Europe. Concerns over an enduring and widening gap in conventional forces on the Korean peninsula have eased somewhat with the chronic problems plaguing the North, but imbalances in conventional forces have catalyzed nuclear innovations elsewhere. For example, the imbalance in battlefield forces in Europe directly led to the development of tactical nuclear weapons for the European theater. In this context, the nuclear capability of NATO forces was seen as the great equalizer that would enable Western Europe to face off against the far superior conventional might of the Soviet Union and the Warsaw Pact (at least in theory and on paper).

Currently, the increasingly militarized relationship between China and Taiwan across the Taiwan Strait has sparked similar concerns. China's seemingly inexorable buildup of a conventional arsenal of fighter planes, medium-range ballistic missiles, naval assets, and expeditionary forces suggests a worrisome trend. Many fear that, at some point in the future, absent external assistance, Taiwan could become vulnerable to a conventional onslaught by the mainland.[15] For this reason, Taiwan has considered a nuclear alternative at points in the past, but it was dissuaded through quiet pressure from Washington. An increasing conventional military imbalance coupled with any sense of alienation or lack of support from Washington could cause Taiwan's leaders to reevaluate their non-nuclear stance.

Regional nuclear proliferation would also create a major incentive for neighboring states to acquire a similar capability. One of the primary reasons for seeking to block various states—such as Iran, Iraq, and North Korea—from achieving nuclear status has long been the concern about how such a capacity would affect neighboring states. A rogue state's successful acquisition of a nuclear weapon could trigger a range of potentially destabilizing regional responses, including the further proliferation of nuclear weapons beyond the rogue.[16] This central concern has been one of the driving forces behind U.S. diplomacy in the recent past, including the protracted negotiation of the Agreed Framework nuclear deal with North Korea in 1994. This issue is also arguably one of the animating features behind the "axis of evil" phrase in President Bush's 2002 State of the Union address and the harder U.S. line toward Iraq, Iran, and North Korea—all states that are seeking to develop or acquire nuclear weapons.

Policymakers realize that the regional impact of particular states acquiring nuclear weapons could be great, particularly in Asia and the Middle East, where nuclear and non-nuclear states barely maintain an uneasy coexistence. Further proliferation by rogues in these regions could have far-reaching consequences in terms of nuclear proliferation and heightened regional rivalries. For example, the development of a nuclear capability by North Korea might quickly lead to nuclear proliferation in Japan and South Korea, heighten tensions with an already nuclear-armed China, and destroy the tenuous balance of power in the region. The domino effect could reach farther, upsetting regional relations with the United States, Russia, and South Asia.

Finally, international stability is also an important factor, and global terrorism is one development that could contribute to a growing sense of unease. Much has been written about the national and global implications of the September 11, 2001, terrorist attacks against New York and Washington. While there is certainly heightened vigilance regarding new domestic threats inside the industrialized democracies and elsewhere, less attention has been focused on how an increase in domestic terrorism could lead to larger systemic insecurity. The logical response to greater homeland security challenges is to tighten borders, heighten intelligence and situational awareness, and increase cooperation with the U.S. and other leading states—not to seek to build nuclear weapons. Yet one cannot fully dismiss some potentially "illogical" responses to more widespread and frequent domestic attacks on a global scale. In such an environment, states might reconsider their nuclear position, viewing a nuclear capability as a psychological assurance domestically as well as a viable deterrent against external threats, particularly when nonstate actors have been supported by rogue regimes. The potential interaction between groups such as al Qaeda and rogue regimes with nuclear ambitions has not been lost on many American allies and friends abroad, and a nuclear capability could potentially be seen in this context as a deterrent to being targeted by the collusion of terrorists and rogues. While a manifest increase in homeland security threats globally is probably not enough on its own to trigger a nuclear recalculation, heightened anxiety over domestic vulnerability to external threats coupled with other troubling trends, either at home or abroad, could lead to a broader reassessment of nuclear options.

Domestic Imperatives

States in decline often suffer from a kind of societal insecurity over future economic and security shortfalls. Such anxiety could well provoke national consideration of nuclear options to forestall the heightened vulnerability that naturally accompanies decline. Just as failing or slipping states have sometimes sought to wage preventive war against rising and competitive states in the international system, declining states may well consider the nuclear option as a relatively cost-effective and technically achievable equalizer that could prevent the nation from sinking into oblivion or being tested by rising regional rivals. This complex societal dynamic of "regime pessimism" is currently in play among virtually all the states in the Middle East and, some might even argue, in Japan as well. Countries that once aspired to international greatness or at least to a level of prominence, but now fear irrelevance or worse, might regard nuclear weapons as a way to provide not only a psychological hedge but potentially a strategic one.

Countries that have previously chosen to renounce nuclear weapons have generally also implemented greater transparency throughout national security and scientific agencies as part of a nationwide move toward greater democratization. It is less clear, however, what kinds of domestic political developments might provoke the pursuit of nuclear weapons. India's populist political movements no doubt played a role in that government's decision to test a nuclear weapon in 1998, and the influence of Pakistan's military was similarly decisive in its internal deliberations about nuclear development over the course of the last decade. The important factor here is that not only regional and international developments drive potential proliferation; domestic political upheaval and bureaucratic politics can also have an overriding and potentially decisive influence on the fateful decision to move down the nuclear path. Secretive atomic power agencies or ministries, the national security apparatus, and military organizations are all key domestic variables in the complex decisionmaking surrounding nuclear choices.

The question of a country's previous experience with nuclear energy, politics, or weapons is an element that should not be overlooked when considering the potential for a nuclear breakout. For instance, the atomic bombing of Hiroshima and Nagasaki at the close of World War II still casts an enormous shadow over contemporary Japan when it comes to consideration of nuclear matters. The international circumstances would have to be extraordinarily worrisome to override the strong domestic opposition that would no doubt follow any Japanese decision to consider formal nuclear status. The depth of preconceived public attitudes surrounding nuclear capabilities is important in gauging how political choices are framed inside a country. These domestic circumstances are in some cases much more important than the strategic situation or regional challenges facing a particular country.

Increasing Availability of Technology

Another reason countries may revisit a decision not to pursue nuclear weapons is simply that the capability is now easier to acquire—and perhaps easier to acquire surreptitiously. Bomb design information has long been widely available, but the most difficult part of developing nuclear weapons—acquiring fissile materials—may have become easier. The main potential source for these materials is the former Soviet Union, where despite nearly a decade of heroic effort on the part of the United States, Russia, and others, large quantities of bomb-grade material are dispersed throughout a large area and are difficult to account for. The recent revelations concerning A. Q. Khan's surreptitious nuclear activities are also particularly worrisome in this regard. Although the potential availability of fissile material is unlikely to be the sole driver of a country's decision to go nuclear, a lowered bar for acquiring nuclear weapons, together with other rationales, may make proliferation more likely.[17]

Conclusion

None of these conditions necessarily indicates an impending breakout by any current non-nuclear country. Indeed, what is perhaps most notable about the international environment in this respect is how *few* countries have openly reconsidered earlier decisions to forgo nuclear development. Nevertheless, it is important to appreciate the particular influences that affect a given nation's calculations regarding its nuclear status. While the inhibitions that have stopped the nuclear club from growing have been preserved thus far, no one can be certain how long the systemic disincentives, the still powerful taboo associated in many quarters with things nuclear, the strong internal restraints, or simply the old patterns of thinking involving nuclear weapons will hold sway.

Misgivings and concerns about the long-term direction of U.S. policy on global strategy and nuclear policy are, and will continue to be, the single most decisive factor guiding the direction of would-be proliferators— both rogue and responsible. Washington has the power to shape the future of nuclear nonproliferation; whether this is a blessing or a burden is yet to be determined.

Notes

1. For an excellent treatment of why many advanced industrial countries chose not to seek nuclear weapons, see Mitchell Reiss, *Without the Bomb* (Columbia University Press, 1988).

2. Certainly, there are those who believe that nuclear proliferation can be stabilizing and that the developments described in this chapter are not cause for alarm, but rather for optimism. See, for example, Kenneth N. Waltz, "More May Be Better," in Scott D. Sagan and Kenneth N. Waltz, eds., *The Spread of Nuclear Weapons: A Debate* (W. W. Norton, 1995), p. 1. However, we assume that the United States desires to—and should—continue its long-standing policy of limiting nuclear proliferation.

3. For more on these new challenges resulting from the information revolution and technological change, and the manner in which they have enhanced the power of transnational issues and nonstate actors such as al Qaeda, see Joseph S. Nye Jr., "U.S. Power and Strategy after Iraq," *Foreign Affairs*, vol. 82, no. 4 (July-August 2003), pp. 60–73.

4. For an analysis of how this new form of transnational commerce in WMD among rogue states, terrorists, and international criminals is challenging the established nonproliferation regime, see James Sterngold, "Beyond North Korea: A New Nuclear Threat," *San Francisco Chronicle*, August 3, 2003. A graphic description of how this new network operates appeared in Joby Warrick, "On North Korean Freighter, A Hidden Missile Factory," *Washington Post*, August 14, 2003, p. A1.

5. See, for instance, Christine Kucia, "Counterproliferation at Core of New

Security Strategy," *Arms Control Today,* vol. 32, no. 8 (October 2002) (www.armscontrol.org/act/2002_10/secstrategyoct02.asp [March 2004]), and Jean du Preez, "The Impact of the Nuclear Posture Review on the International Nuclear Nonproliferation Regime," *Nonproliferation Review,* vol. 9, no. 3 (Fall-Winter 2002), pp. 67–81. For the administration's rejection of this interpretation, see Colin L. Powell, "A Strategy of Partnerships," *Foreign Affairs,* vol. 83, no. 1 (January-February 2004), pp. 22–34.

6. See, for example, Nicole Gnesotto, "Reacting to America," *Survival,* vol. 44, no. 4 (Winter 2002–03), pp. 99–106; Jean Yves Haine, "The Imperial Moment: A European View," *Cambridge Review of International Affairs,* vol. 16, no. 3 (October 2003), pp. 483–509; and Joanna Spear, "The Emergence of a European 'Strategic Personality,'" *Arms Control Today,* vol. 33, no. 9 (November 2003) (www.armscontrol.org/act/2003_11/Spear.asp [March 2004]).

7. Klaus Larres, "Mutual Incomprehension: U.S.-German Value Gaps beyond Iraq," *Washington Quarterly,* vol. 26, no. 2 (Spring 2003), pp. 23–42. See also Elizabeth Pond, "European Shock and Awe," *Washington Quarterly,* vol. 26, no. 3 (Summer 2003), pp. 191–203.

8. For more on the administration's plans to restructure the U.S. overseas military presence, and its possible effects, see Kurt M. Campbell and Celeste Johnson Ward, "New Battle Stations?" *Foreign Affairs,* vol. 82, no. 5 (September-October 2003), p. 95.

9. These problems are discussed in Seung-Hwan Kim, "Anti-Americanism in Korea," *Washington Quarterly,* vol. 26, no. 1 (Winter 2002–03), pp. 109–22.

10. See for example Norimitsu Onishi, "U.S. and South Korea Try to Redefine their Alliance," *New York Times,* December 26, 2003, p. A8.

11. George Perkovich, "Bush's Nuclear Revolution: A Regime Change in Nonproliferation," *Foreign Affairs,* vol. 82, no. 2 (March/April 2003), pp. 2–8.

12. See, for example, Sidney Drell and others, "A Strategic Choice: New Bunker Busters vs. Nonproliferation," *Arms Control Today,* vol. 33, no. 2 (March 2003), p. 3.

13. Anton La Guardia, "Iran's Nuclear Quest 'Irreversible in 18 Months,'" *London Daily Telegraph,* July 16, 2003, p. 15. For a review of the Iranian nuclear program, see Brenda Shaffer, "Iran at the Nuclear Threshold," *Arms Control Today,* vol. 33, no. 9 (November 2003) (www.armscontrol.org/act/2003_11/Shaffer.asp [March 2004]).

14. See, for example, Marvin Miller and Lawrence Scheinman, "Israel, India, and Pakistan: Engaging the Non-NPT States in the Nonproliferation Regime," *Arms Control Today,* vol. 33, no. 10 (December 2003) (www.armscontrol.org/act/2003_12/MillerandScheinman.asp [March 2004]).

15. On how the military balance is shifting in China's favor, see John Pomfret and Philip P. Pan, "U.S. Hits Obstacles in Helping Taiwan Guard against China," *Washington Post,* October 30, 2003, p. A1. The details of China's military modernization program are discussed in Department of Defense, "Annual Report on

the Military Power of the People's Republic of China" July 28, 2003 (www.defenselink.mil/pubs/20030730chinaex.pdf [February 2004]).

16. Indeed, a rogue state may deliberately threaten to promote proliferation further to deter or retaliate against American actions it opposes; see Francois Heisbourg, "A Work in Progress: The Bush Doctrine and Its Consequences," *Washington Quarterly*, vol. 26, no. 2 (Spring 2003), p. 85.

17. For an analysis of this dynamic, see Rensselaer Lee, "Nuclear Smuggling: Patterns and Response," *Parameters*, vol. 33 (Spring 2003), pp. 95–111. For a survey of possible illegal attempts to acquire nuclear material in the former Soviet Union, see William C. Potter and Elena Sokova, "Illicit Nuclear Trafficking in the NIS: What's New? What's True?" *Nonproliferation Review*, vol. 9, no. 2 (Summer 2002), pp. 112–20. For worried assessments about the risks of such nuclear leakage, see Graham Allison, "How to Stop Nuclear Terror," *Foreign Affairs*, vol. 83, no. 1 (January-February 2004), pp. 64–74, and Jon B. Wolfsthal and Tom Z. Collina, "Nuclear Terrorism and Warhead Control in Russia," *Survival*, vol. 44, no. 2 (Summer 2002), pp. 71–83.

CHAPTER 3

Will the Abstainers Reconsider?
Focusing on Individual Cases

ROBERT J. EINHORN

The preceding chapter identifies factors that, individually or in combination, might motivate countries to revisit their earlier decisions to forgo a nuclear weapons capability. Some of those factors (regional rivalries, conventional force imbalances) played critical roles in certain *past* decisions to acquire nuclear weapons (in the cases of Israel and Pakistan, for example). Another factor—the preeminent international role of the United States—exerts such a pervasive overall influence on international affairs today that it is reasonable to assume that it will also have a specific impact on national attitudes toward the nuclear option. Still other factors, such as the erosion of the international nonproliferation regime, have been cited by countries themselves as considerations that will weigh significantly in their national debates.

In theory, these and other possible factors could apply to a wide range of countries in different regions of the world. But nuclear proliferation does not occur in theory. It occurs in individual countries, in specific international and domestic circumstances, and with particular persons and organizations making discrete decisions.

Without reference to individual cases, it is impossible to make confident predictions about which trends or developments might bring the world to a proliferation "tipping point." Factors assumed in the abstract to be influential in future nuclear choices may turn out to have little or no impact in specific countries. In multilateral nonproliferation debates, for example, the assertion is frequently made that progress by Russia and the United States in reducing their nuclear arsenals—in accordance with their obligations under article 6 of the Nuclear Non-Proliferation Treaty (NPT)—will reduce the likelihood of non-nuclear weapons states deciding to obtain nuclear weapons of their own. But looking at the states that acquired nuclear weapons since the NPT was signed (India, Israel, Pakistan) or states that have actively sought them (Iraq, Iran, North Korea), it is hard to make the argument that any of them were influenced by the levels of U.S. or Soviet or Russian nuclear forces.

Advocates on opposing sides of some current security policy debates have argued that their preferred approach would reduce incentives for additional states to seek nuclear weapons or other weapons of mass destruction (WMD). Proponents of missile defenses, for example, claim that effective defenses would diminish the perceived utility of small, WMD-armed ballistic missile forces and would therefore discourage countries from pursuing such forces in the first place. Deployment of missile defenses, they contend, could also give U.S. friends and allies some protection against missile attacks from their neighbors and therefore reduce their incentives to acquire independent deterrent capabilities of their own. Opponents of missile defenses, however, argue that U.S. deployment of defenses would encourage countries that feel threatened by the United States not only to acquire WMD-armed ballistic missiles but also to expand that capability to the point where they were confident of being able to penetrate the defenses.

Similar arguments are put forward about the Bush administration's increased emphasis on preemptive military attacks in its national security strategy. Critics of the Bush security doctrine assert that it will give countries that see the United States as a potential enemy a much stronger incentive to acquire WMD—and to do so quickly and surreptitiously to avoid detection and preemption. Advocates of the new doctrine maintain that advertising a greater U.S. readiness to use force against emerging WMD programs will persuade would-be possessors of nonconventional military capabilities that going down the WMD path would be very risky.

Such arguments cannot be settled in the abstract. To understand whether missile defenses and the new security doctrine will encourage or discourage proliferation, it is necessary to examine how those factors affect the perceptions and behavior of specific states. It may turn out that they discourage (or encourage) proliferation in some states but not others. Or it may be that their impact is negligible.

So to evaluate the likelihood that states that had previously chosen to renounce nuclear weapons will reconsider their choices, it is not enough to speculate about the kinds of pressures or developments that could *theoretically* trigger such a reconsideration in a large and diverse group of countries. It is also essential to consider the extent to which such theoretical triggers, as well as other factors unique to those countries, are likely to have an impact in the specific circumstances surrounding individual countries. Therefore, before drawing conclusions about prospects for reaching a proliferation tipping point—and about the policies that could be adopted to slow or arrest movement toward such a tipping point—it is necessary to concentrate on specific countries in considerable detail. But which countries?

Since a key purpose of this study is to learn what might induce nuclear abstainers to reconsider their abstention, it makes little sense to look at non-NPT countries that have acquired nuclear weapons (India, Israel, and Pakistan) or at countries that joined the NPT cynically with the intention to seek nuclear weapons clandestinely (Iran, Iraq, North Korea, and, less notoriously, Libya).

In order to assess the durability—or fragility—of the nuclear non-proliferation regime, it is especially useful to focus on states that have refrained from pursuing nuclear weapons *for an extended period of time*. Therefore states that only made decisions to renounce nuclear weapons relatively recently—in the last ten to fifteen years—are not examined in this study. That includes South Africa (which built nuclear weapons but gave them up on the eve of majority rule when Cuban proxy forces for the Soviet Union no longer posed a threat), Argentina and Brazil (which had active nuclear weapons development programs but abandoned them with the transition from military to civilian governments), and Belarus, Kazakhstan, and Ukraine (which found themselves with nuclear weapons on their territory when the USSR collapsed but elected to send them to Russia and join the NPT as non-nuclear weapons states). Examining abstainers of longer standing is probably a better test of the tipping point phenomenon. In any event, the decisions of these recent renouncers have been thoroughly studied in the nonproliferation literature.

The cases that will be covered in the succeeding chapters are Egypt, Germany, Japan, Saudi Arabia, South Korea, Syria, Taiwan, and Turkey.[1]

All have formally forsworn nuclear weapons by adhering to the NPT and accepting comprehensive International Atomic Energy Agency safeguards on their nuclear facilities. Their selection for this study does not mean that none of them has ever given a thought to the nuclear option. South Korea and Taiwan, for example, long ago had an active interest in acquiring a nuclear capability, but they were pressured by the United States to abandon such plans and have been compliant with the NPT ever since. One or two others on this list may also have privately contemplated the idea of obtaining nuclear weapons. But there are no indications that any of these states have violated their NPT obligations, and their nuclear abstinence has lasted well over a quarter century.

It should be stressed that the inclusion in the study of the countries listed above does *not* reflect a judgment that they are likely to reconsider their earlier decisions and pursue nuclear weapons. Indeed, a number of them seem very unlikely to entertain any doubts about their non-nuclear status. Moreover, their selection does not mean that they are the only good examples of long-standing nuclear abstainers in the world today. A substantial number of other non-nuclear weapons states could also have been included but were not, largely for reasons of time and space.

The ones listed above were chosen because their particular cases can shed light on some of the critical factors likely to influence nuclear decisionmaking in the years ahead. Most of these countries (Japan, Saudi Arabia, South Korea, Syria, and Turkey) are neighbors of the so-called rogue states that have actively sought nuclear weapons. Several (Germany, Japan, South Korea, and Turkey) are formal treaty allies of the United States. In a substantial number of the countries (Egypt, Germany, Saudi Arabia, and South Korea), uncertainties and strains have recently emerged in their long-standing, close relationships with the United States. Some (Egypt, Syria, and Taiwan) are neighbors and rivals of existing nuclear weapons powers. In a few (Germany and Japan), historical considerations have made the acquisition of nuclear weapons a taboo. In a number of the countries (Egypt, Saudi Arabia, and Turkey), there could be political changes in coming years that might significantly alter the domestic environment in which important decisions about national security are taken. Several countries (Germany, Japan, and probably South Korea and Taiwan) have the technical and industrial capacity to produce nuclear weapons in a short period of time, while others either will lack the technical infrastructure to produce nuclear weapons indigenously for the foreseeable future (Saudi Arabia) or would be able to produce nuclear weapons indigenously only with substantial external assistance and over a prolonged period of time (Egypt, Syria, and Turkey).

While these countries differ in significant ways, including in the likelihood that they will reconsider their renunciation of nuclear weapons and in the factors that might motivate them to reconsider, they are alike in one ominous respect: if any one of these responsible citizens of the international nonproliferation regime chooses to rethink its nuclear future and to acquire nuclear weapons, the regime itself will be in serious trouble. They are like the canary in the mineshaft whose death signals unsafe conditions: if they go nuclear, the world will have taken a giant step toward the tipping point.

The starting point for each of the case studies is the country's original renunciation of nuclear weapons. All of the countries examined in the succeeding chapters adhered to the NPT. But that single, formal act of renunciation—that common denominator for the eight nuclear abstainers covered in this study—hardly conveys the wide diversity among them in the character and finality of their decisions to forswear nuclear weapons. Understanding the particular circumstances surrounding each of the renunciations is essential in order to evaluate prospects for rethinking and altering those national choices in the future. The authors of the case studies therefore look at a variety of questions:

—What were the main factors responsible for the formal renunciation of a nuclear weapons capability? How did the external security environment look to decisionmakers? Did the country have alliance relationships or other security ties that assured its security without resort to its own nuclear capability?

—What role did external political factors play? Did the country encounter pressures from foreign governments to renounce nuclear weapons? Did it anticipate negative consequences internationally if it pursued nuclear weapons?

—What role did domestic political factors play? Were there domestic pressures (either from within the government or from the public) pushing for or against acquiring nuclear weapons?

—Would it have been feasible for the country to achieve a nuclear weapons capability at the time? Did it have the technical capacity and economic resources to pursue an indigenous nuclear weapons program? Could it have obtained the necessary materials and technologies from foreign suppliers?

—What was the nature of the decisionmaking process? Was the question of whether to acquire nuclear weapons formally and explicitly addressed? Was a conscious national decision made or was the matter essentially deferred? Was adherence to the NPT the codification of a real decision to forswear nuclear weapons or an expedient and temporizing response to international pressures?

—Was the decisionmaking process public or did deliberations take place only privately within the government? Were the reasons for nuclear renunciation clearly articulated, publicly or in private?

—Did the country renounce nuclear weapons conditionally or unconditionally? Were any such conditions implicit or explicit? Did the country decide to hedge its renunciation by pursuing technical capabilities that would keep the nuclear option open and shorten the interval between a possible future decision to seek nuclear weapons and the realization of that goal? Was any such hedging strategy a conscious one, explicitly discussed and decided?

—Was the question of whether to acquire nuclear weapons seen within the country as "settled" at the time of formal renunciation or was it seen as subject to future review and reconsideration?

While reviewing the original renunciation establishes an important baseline for each of the countries, the heart of the case studies is the examination of factors *currently* affecting the likelihood that those countries will revisit their earlier choices. The authors address factors—such as those discussed in the preceding chapter—that may apply to a wide variety of countries. But they also look at conditions and developments unique to the specific countries. They focus on changes that have occurred since the original renunciations, both domestically and in the international environment, and consider whether such changes will lead decisionmakers to see the value of forswearing nuclear weapons in a new light. Among the questions they address in their analysis are

—What is the country's *current* technological and economic capacity to produce nuclear weapons indigenously? Is it easier now than previously for the country to acquire the needed materials and technology (and even nuclear weapons) from foreign suppliers?

—How has the country's international security environment changed? How does it assess the military capabilities and intentions of its neighbors? Does it look to the future with confidence or anxiety, and is an independent nuclear capability seen as relevant to its uncertainties and insecurities?

—Does the country believe it can count on the United States (or some other country or alliance relationship) to help ensure its security? Are bilateral relations with the United States changing, and how does that affect the country's calculations of its security requirements? What does it think about the more assertive U.S. national security strategy that is emerging, and what are the perceived implications of that strategy for its security?

—How do domestic political developments and trends affect the country's national security policies and choices? Who are the key deci-sionmakers and which are the key institutions, and what is their attitude toward acquiring nuclear weapons? Do old taboos and domestic support for country-specific, WMD-related legal restrictions persist?

—How does the acquisition of nuclear weapons by other countries (and the international response to such acquisition) affect the country's attitude toward having its own nuclear capability?

—How would a decision to reconsider the nuclear option be made: through a public debate or by the government in private?

—If the country decided to pursue a nuclear capability, would it pro-ceed openly or covertly? Is it able to make substantial headway toward such a capability without detection by the United States, the Interna-tional Atomic Energy Agency, or others? Would it decide to move as rap-idly as possible to a weaponized capability, or would it adopt a hedging strategy that kept its options open and shortened the lead time to a full capability?

—Are there signs that the country has already decided to rethink its nuclear abstinence or at least indications that some in the country favor that?

In seeking answers to these questions, the authors of the case studies face daunting methodological challenges. The most obvious one is finding information about a country's deliberations on the nuclear weapons issue. The subject of nuclear weapons is inherently sensitive, not just the technical aspects of building them but also the policy discussions sur-rounding them. When it comes to the matter of nuclear weapons, all gov-ernments—even democracies accustomed to sharing vast amounts of information with their publics—adopt highly restrictive procedures to prevent all but a small and tightly controlled circle of officials from attending meetings and having access to records.[2]

Related to the challenge of secrecy is the difficulty of obtaining infor-mation that reliably reflects a government's actual thinking and inten-tions. A government that is seriously thinking about pursuing a nuclear weapons capability will be extremely reluctant to share that information with anyone; it will almost always want to adhere to the public line that its policy has not changed and that it has no intention of acquiring nuclear weapons. Somewhat more candor might be expected from governments in talking about the factors that could, *in the future*, motivate them to rethink their non-nuclear status. But even in discussing such factors, governments may sometimes be inclined to use the opportunity to serve particular policy goals rather than to illuminate what may actually be driving them. For example, in the interest of discouraging a conventional arms buildup by a neighbor or of encouraging deeper nuclear reductions by the United States and Russia, a government may declare that it might be compelled to pursue its own nuclear capability if its neighbor does not stop acquiring arms or if the two leading nuclear powers do not accept further cuts in their nuclear arsenals. Of course, such factors may well have some bearing on the government's thinking about a nuclear weapons capability; but the purpose of making such statements is often less to reveal that thinking than to influence the policies of other governments.

While secrecy and misleading explanations may make it hard to find adequate, reliable information about a government's policy toward reconsidering its nuclear abstention, a more complicated challenge arises when a government does not have a policy toward nuclear reconsideration, secret or otherwise. In an area as sensitive and controversial as nuclear weapons, it is not surprising that governments will be hesitant to focus on their nuclear options, at least in a formal manner. Individual leaders or groups within a government may have given some thought to the problem but not seen any need to confide in others. Until a jarring development occurs that forces senior officials to react, attitudes toward revisiting the nuclear option may remain inchoate.

The authors of the succeeding chapters have done their best to address these challenges. They have exhaustively reviewed the available literature, sought the release from governments of previously unavailable information, and where feasible and promising, conducted extensive interviews. In pursuing interviews, the authors have cast their nets widely by talking not only to incumbent government officials but also to former officials, opposition leaders, scholars, journalists, and other knowledgeable sources. Where the promise of anonymity would facilitate franker discussions, the authors agreed to rules of nonattribution.

On the basis of their analysis, the authors attempt to draw a number of conclusions. First, they seek to identify the factors likely to be most influential in motivating the country they have studied to revisit its earlier decision to forgo nuclear weapons. An important consideration, in this regard, is whether the most influential factors are peculiar to that country (for example, the ascendancy of a particular domestic political group or the shedding of a national taboo) or potentially important in a significant number of countries (such as the acquisition of nuclear weapons by rogue states or the erosion of nonproliferation norms). If the former, the decision by a state to reconsider its nuclear renunciation is more likely to be an isolated phenomenon without wider implications for proliferation worldwide. If the latter, it is more likely to be an indication of what might become a broader and more dangerous trend, with countries marching toward the tipping point together.

Second, the authors assess the likelihood that the countries they have examined will decide to pursue a nuclear weapons capability, either as soon as possible or through a hedging strategy. Obviously, those assessments are highly speculative, not just because of the methodological difficulties noted above, but also because those decisions would depend on future conditions and events we cannot predict. But with all the obvious caveats, those assessments—by focusing on a critical category of states that has not received sufficient attention and that constitutes one of the last lines of defense of the international nonproliferation regime—can give us a much better appreciation of the dimensions of today's global proliferation challenge.

Third, drawing on their analysis of the factors most likely to kindle interest in acquiring nuclear weapons in the states they examined, the authors outline policies that the United States and other members of the international community could pursue to reduce the likelihood that those states will reverse their earlier decisions and seek nuclear weapons. With most policy analysis in the WMD field concentrating in recent years on stopping and containing the nuclear and other WMD ambitions of countries like Iran, Iraq, Libya, and North Korea, this focus on trying to prevent the nuclear abstainers from approaching the proliferation tipping point can fill a critical policy void.

Notes

1. Taiwan, as the "Republic of China," signed the NPT on July 1, 1968, and deposited an instrument of ratification on January 27, 1970. Since then, the United States and most other NPT parties have recognized the People's Republic of China as the sole legal government of China. Nonetheless, the authorities on Taiwan state that they will continue to abide by the provisions of the treaty, and the United States and other NPT parties regard them as bound by its obligations.

2. For a discussion of the difficulties of obtaining reliable information on nuclear decisionmaking, see Ariel E. Levite, "Never Say Never Again; Nuclear Reversal Revisited," *International Security*, vol. 27, no. 3 (Winter 2002–03), pp. 61–66.

PART 2

Case Studies

CHAPTER 4

Egypt: Frustrated but Still on a Non-Nuclear Course

ROBERT J. EINHORN

Considering the factors that have historically motivated countries to acquire nuclear weapons, one might assume that Egypt would be a likely candidate, sooner or later, to reconsider its decision to renounce a nuclear weapons option. It has fought several wars and enjoyed only a "cold peace" with a next-door neighbor that possesses both nuclear weapons and a significant edge in conventional military capability. It lives in a volatile region that is home to the world's greatest concentration of programs for weapons of mass destruction. It was one of the first third world countries to embark on a civil nuclear program, has trained a large number of capable nuclear scientists, and has talked frequently about pursuing an ambitious nuclear power program. Its military has played a powerful, even dominant, role in its political system. As heir to a great civilization, a founding member of the movement of non-aligned countries, and a natural leader of the contemporary Arab world, it has seen itself playing a central role in the affairs of the Middle East and on the world stage. It has regarded its nuclear asymmetry with Israel as intolerable and made elimination of that asymmetry a persistent, highly

The author is grateful to several staff members at the Center for Strategic and International Studies—Sarah Banner, Mary Beth Nikitin, Jane Vaynman, and Chen Zak—for their valuable contributions to this chapter.

publicized objective of its diplomacy. Its previous leaders have vowed publicly to match any Israeli nuclear weapons capability.[1] Its current leader, President Hosni Mubarak, has pledged that when Egypt needs nuclear weapons, it "would not hesitate" to acquire them.[2]

Yet, while Egypt seems to fit the profile of a country with a reasonably strong likelihood of pursuing nuclear weapons, there are few if any signs that it is headed in that direction. Indeed, available evidence suggests that Egypt's decision to renounce nuclear weapons may well be, in the words of Presidential Adviser Osama el-Baz, "final and irreversible."[3] Egyptian leaders seem to have reached the conclusion years ago that a nuclear weapons capability is not in their country's best interest and that seeking that capability would undermine higher national priorities, especially peace and stability in the region, economic development, and close ties with the United States. Moreover, by forgoing a substantial nuclear energy program and allowing Egypt's nuclear scientific expertise to atrophy, Egypt has left itself without reliable, near-term options to acquire the fissile materials needed to build a bomb, especially through indigenous production.

Some Egyptian politicians and strategic thinkers regret that their country has largely burned its bridges to a nuclear weapons capability. Egypt's energetic and capable diplomats are frustrated that they have been unable to close the regional nuclear gap by pressuring Israel to give up its nuclear capability. Egyptian proponents of nuclear power are discouraged that their plans have had so little support at the top. But while a substantial number of Egyptians are dissatisfied with the nuclear status quo, almost no one expects the situation to change.

Egyptian officials and nongovernmental experts can imagine a range of regional and international developments that could generate pressures—within the government, among the elites, and in the "street"—for rethinking the wisdom of Egypt's continued nuclear abstinence (for example, Israel openly declaring its nuclear capability or another state in the region acquiring nuclear weapons). Virtually all Egyptian observers agree that such developments would require some sort of strong Egyptian response. But most of them believe that as long as President Mubarak or a like-minded successor remains in charge, there is little prospect—short of such traumatic events as a military attack on Egyptian territory or the use of nuclear weapons somewhere in the Middle East—that Cairo's response would be to embark on a nuclear weapons program.

The Nasser Years: Egypt Explores the Nuclear Option

Egypt's formal entry into the nuclear field came in 1955 with the creation of the Egyptian Atomic Energy Authority (AEA). The motivation at the time was apparently peaceful—to enable Egypt to reap the economic and other benefits from this new and promising technology.[4] But the founders of the nuclear program were clearly aware of its military potential. Ibrahim Hilmy Abdel Rahman, secretary of Nasser's cabinet and secretary general of AEA's governing council, was reportedly told that, for the time being, the program should focus on peaceful applications but should be pursued in a way that would preserve the military option.[5]

Much of the AEA's activity in the late 1950s involved sending Egyptian scientists abroad for training. To help the Egyptian program build its human infrastructure, nuclear cooperation agreements were concluded with the Soviet Union and India.[6] An important step in creating the program's physical infrastructure was taken in 1956, when the Soviet Union agreed to construct Egypt's first nuclear reactor, a small, two-megawatt light-water research reactor located at Inshas. Completed in 1961, its small capacity meant that it could not produce enough plutonium to constitute a proliferation risk.[7]

The Egyptian nuclear program's early concentration on civilian applications shifted toward a more conscious interest in the military option in response to concerns about Israel's nuclear intentions. In December 1960, Israeli prime minister David Ben-Gurion publicly acknowledged that Israel was building a nuclear reactor at Dimona in the Negev Desert, a fact Israeli authorities had earlier tried to conceal. A few days later, Egyptian president Gamal Abdel Nasser said that if Israel acquired nuclear weapons, Egypt would have to acquire them at any price.[8]

The years that followed Ben-Gurion's revelation were the period of most active Egyptian interest in obtaining nuclear weapons. An indication of the program's enhanced military orientation was the appointment of Salah Hedayat—a leading proponent of an Egyptian nuclear weapons capability with close ties to the Egyptian military—as director general of the AEA, minister of scientific research, and director of the nuclear facility at Inshas.[9] During the early 1960s, the Egyptian government boosted its budget for nuclear programs, stepped up its efforts to recruit and train nuclear scientists, approached a wide range of countries for assistance, examined prospects for mining thorium and uranium in Egypt, and explored elements of the nuclear fuel cycle that could eventually enable it to produce fissile material for nuclear weapons. In this latter connection, Egypt made initial attempts to produce heavy water, conducted experiments in fabricating uranium fuels, and approached the United States and Soviet Union, both without success, to acquire a radiochemistry laboratory that would have helped Egypt learn how to extract plutonium from spent reactor fuel.[10]

Especially frustrating for the nuclear program was the failed effort to acquire a nuclear reactor large enough to produce plutonium for nuclear weapons. After years of discussions with potential reactor vendors, Egypt in 1964 solicited bids to build a 150- to 210-megawatt reactor near Alexandria that would be used for electricity generation and desalinization. An agreement was concluded with Siemens, a German company, which offered a natural uranium fueled, heavy-water moderated reactor—preferable from a nuclear weapons standpoint because it would avoid the hurdle of having to import enriched uranium fuel. However, due to a falling out between West Germany and Egypt, the agreement was canceled in 1965.[11] Egypt then turned to Westinghouse, and a letter of intent was signed in 1966. But by then the Egyptian economy was in bad shape, and the United States turned down Egypt's request for a $100 million loan to finance the sale. The deal was shelved and with it any Egyptian hopes of having in the near term the physical infrastructure needed to manufacture nuclear weapons.[12]

Recognizing the difficulties of producing nuclear weapons indigenously, especially with a nuclear program that had started from scratch just several years earlier, Egypt also tried to acquire already made nuclear bombs or bomb-making technology from abroad. Several attempts were apparently made between 1963 and 1967 to purchase nuclear weapons or weapons technology from the Soviet Union and China, but both of those nuclear powers rebuffed the Egyptians.[13]

Internal divisions between the nuclear scientists and military managers of the nuclear program—including the feud between former military officer Hedayat and chief scientist Abdel Maaboud El Guibaily—also played a key role in impeding the program. When bureaucratic pressures forced Hedayat to step down from his position as minister of scientific research in 1964 and a year later from his role as head of the AEA, proponents of a nuclear weapons capability lost a key vantage point for shaping the program.[14]

Egypt's crushing defeat in the Six Day War of June 1967 was a critical turning point in its efforts to acquire nuclear weapons. The loss of oil from the Sinai, the closure of the Suez Canal, and the decrease in foreign assistance in the aftermath of the war had a devastating impact on the Egyptian economy, and funding for the nuclear program was frozen. All AEA capital projects were canceled, and activities were limited to planning and paper studies.[15] More fundamentally, the war changed Egypt's strategic outlook. Regaining Egyptian territory occupied by Israel became the paramount national objective, and this meant devoting scarce resources to rebuilding and strengthening Egypt's conventional arms capabilities, not giving priority to the nuclear option.[16]

In retrospect, it is clear that the 1960s—and specifically the period between Ben-Gurion's admission about Dimona in 1960 and the Six Day War in 1967—was the crucial window of opportunity for Egypt's nuclear weapons program. A variety of useful steps were taken to build a cadre of trained specialists and to explore key weapons-related technologies. But the nuclear weapons program was stymied during a critical period due to a combination of factors: the reluctance of foreign governments to provide assistance in sensitive areas, economic constraints, lengthy delays in pursuing the reactor deal, bureaucratic frictions, U.S. high-level expressions of concern about Egypt's nuclear and missile programs, and a vigorous Israeli covert campaign against German scientists assisting Egypt's missile and nuclear programs.[17] Jim Walsh, the American analyst who has most thoroughly chronicled Egypt's nuclear program, sums up Egypt's efforts in the 1960s: "The historical record leaves little doubt that the government repeatedly sought the acquisition of nuclear weapons, and yet it never made the kind of national commitment that would have made the bomb a reality. There was no equivalent to the Manhattan Project or even to Egypt's own High Dam project. Instead, there was drift, delay, and missed opportunities."[18]

Some knowledgeable Egyptians have questioned whether Nasser ever truly decided to acquire nuclear weapons. Head of the Al-Ahram Strategic Studies Center, Abdel Moneim Said, believes that Nasser "looked at options" but doubts that he had decided to proceed.[19] Mostafa Elwi Saif, professor at Cairo University, says Nasser's public remarks about matching Israel were for public consumption and that the president had no real commitment to nuclear weapons. The efforts of the early 1960s, in his view, did not reflect a strong managerial focus or a clear strategic choice.[20] Mostafa al-Fiqi, chairman of the People's Assembly Foreign Relations Committee and a former senior diplomat, notes in connection with the early nuclear efforts: "We Egyptians are good beginners; but we're not so good at following through."[21]

The Sadat Years: Egypt Makes a Strategic Choice

The Six Day War had taken much of the wind out of the sails of Egypt's effort to acquire the bomb.[22] Egypt moved farther away from the nuclear option in September 1970, when Nasser died and Anwar Sadat took his place. Sadat, like his predecessor, stated that Egypt would obtain nuclear weapons if Israel did so.[23] However, such assertions by Sadat have been portrayed not as a true indicator of his intentions but as an attempt to reassure the Egyptian public and bureaucracy and to dissuade Israel from pursuing its nuclear program.[24] Regaining Egyptian land lost in June 1967 was Sadat's overriding priority, and he did not see nuclear weapons as important to achieving that goal.[25]

The October 1973 war did not recover Egypt's territory, but it helped restore Egyptian pride and self-confidence, and it paved the way for President Sadat's trip to Jerusalem in November 1977, the Camp David accords in September 1978, and the Egyptian-Israeli peace treaty in March 1979. The state of war with Israel, together with concerns about Israel's nuclear program, had been the principal motivation for Egypt considering the nuclear weapons option in the early 1960s. While the formality of a peace treaty did not eliminate the perception in Cairo that its neighbor to the east constituted a threat, it significantly undercut the rationale for an Egyptian nuclear weapons capability, especially for an Egyptian leadership that had never been strongly wedded to attaining such a capability.

Some Egyptians saw the peace negotiations as an opportunity to get Israel to renounce its nuclear capability and remove the nuclear asymmetry that they regarded as intolerable politically, if not also militarily. In particular, Foreign Minister Isma'il Fahmy asserted in 1976 that Israel's adherence to the Nuclear Non-Proliferation Treaty (NPT) should be a condition for concluding a peace treaty.[26] During the peace negotiations, Egypt apparently proposed that both nations renounce nuclear weapons.[27] But the peace arrangements were concluded in the absence of assurances by Israel to give up nuclear weapons or join the NPT.

While the 1979 peace treaty did not include an Israeli commitment to give up nuclear weapons, it did result in something of perhaps greater value to Egypt—a strong bilateral relationship with the United States.

For about a quarter century, U.S.-Egyptian relations had been strained by Egypt's close political ties and arms supply relationship with the Soviet Union, its belligerency toward Israel, and its prominent position in the Non-Aligned Movement (which often put Cairo and Washington on opposite sides of major international issues).[28] The 1978–79 peace negotiations—with the United States centrally involved in the process and a de facto guarantor of the result—dramatically changed the character of U.S.-Egyptian relations.

An important component of the "peace package" was a U.S. commitment to provide Egypt major foreign assistance, in part to compensate Cairo for the loss of aid from Arab governments it would suffer as punishment for making peace with Israel. Since 1979 that commitment has resulted in an average of over $2 billion annually in economic and military assistance for Egypt.[29] The United States also committed to organize a peacekeeping force in the Sinai—the Multinational Force and Observers—to monitor the agreed demilitarization arrangements and the Egyptian-Israeli border.[30] Over time, these treaty-related commitments led to much stronger bilateral ties.

In the area of defense cooperation, the United States became Egypt's main supplier of military equipment. In addition, the two countries have conducted large-scale, joint military exercises, engaged in military-industrial cooperation (for example, coproduction of the M1A1 tank), drawn up contingency plans for U.S. access to Egyptian military facilities in times of crisis, and fought together in Operation Desert Storm in 1991.[31]

Political ties have become just as close. Since 1979 the two governments have worked together closely on a growing range of issues and at all levels, including regular meetings at the presidential level. The United States has counted on Egypt to be a moderating influence in the Arab world and especially to play a constructive role in promoting peace between Israel and its neighbors.

The post-1979 connection with the United States has brought benefits to Egypt that go well beyond material support, both economic and military. Cairo's role as America's partner in the Arab-Israeli peace process and often as Washington's trusted agent in dealing with the Arab world has reinforced Egypt's standing in the Middle East and elsewhere. The relationship has also had important payoffs for Egyptian security. Cairo understands that strong U.S. ties with Israel preclude Washington's providing Egypt the kind of security guarantee that other close U.S. friends and allies have received (that is, to come to an ally's defense if it is threatened or attacked). However, Egyptians know that the United States has a very powerful stake in the Egyptian-Israeli peace and would go to great lengths to maintain it, including vigorous efforts to prevent any future conflict from erupting between its two key friends in the region.

Having negotiated peace with Israel and put relations with the United States on a promising course for the future, President Sadat decided in 1980 to tackle a third vital strategic question—whether to ratify the NPT. Egypt had signed the treaty in 1968 but not ratified it, hoping that its reluctance to be legally bound would provide leverage to press Israel to join it in renouncing nuclear weapons. Twelve years later, it had become increasingly clear that Israel was not about to join the NPT, and so the issue became whether Egypt should adhere on its own.

While Sadat and his ruling National Democratic Party favored ratification, Egyptian opinion was far from unanimous. Some officials in the Foreign Ministry reportedly felt that Egyptian adherence was unjustified in light of Israel's failure to budge on the nuclear issue, while some in the military objected on national security grounds.[32] In the People's Assembly, the Labor Party and its leader, Ibrahim Shokri, called for delay in ratification to allow time to pressure Israel to join the treaty so that Egypt would not have to fall down on its knees before its neighbor.[33]

An argument that carried considerable weight at the time was that NPT adherence would facilitate Egypt's access to foreign nuclear equipment and technology for its civil nuclear energy program.[34] From the early 1970s, Sadat had been interested in nuclear power and its implications for economic development. In the wake of the October 1973 war, Egyptian nuclear authorities discussed the purchase of nuclear reactors with several countries, especially the United States. But the consummation of the U.S.-Egyptian reactor deal proved elusive, with lengthy delays resulting from concerns in Congress about Egypt's nuclear intentions, U.S. requirements for tightened safeguards in nuclear cooperation agreements as a result of India's 1974 nuclear test, and Egyptian difficulties financing the sale. After the Carter administration refused in February 1980 to waive the regulation making only NPT parties eligible for U.S. power plant financing, Egypt drew the conclusion that it would have to join the treaty if it wanted to go forward with its nuclear energy plans.[35] In December 1980, Sadat announced that Egypt would ratify the NPT, and in February 1981, Foreign Minister Kamal Hassan Ali presented the treaty to the People's Assembly for its approval. He told the legislature that "Egypt found itself unable to develop its electric power through access to nuclear energy unless it ratified the Non-Proliferation Treaty" and that waiting for Israel to adhere would "allow others to veto the development and promotion of our powerful programmes needed to achieve prosperity and well-being of our people."[36] The argument was persuasive and the People's Assembly ratified the treaty.

Taken together, Sadat's decisions between 1977 and 1981 constituted a fundamental strategic choice for Egypt—in favor of peace with Israel, stability in the Middle East, economic development for Egypt, close relations with the United States, and renunciation of nuclear weapons. Although the period of most active Egyptian interest in nuclear weapons had ended by the time of the Six Day War in 1967, Sadat's strategic choice over a decade later codified Egypt's nuclear abstinence, reinforced it, and placed it in a coherent strategic context.

The Mubarak Years: Maintaining a Non-Nuclear Course

With Sadat having achieved Egypt's central foreign policy goal of recovering lost territory, Hosni Mubarak—who became Egypt's leader after Islamic militants gunned down Sadat in October 1981—could afford to give priority to the domestic goals of economic development and internal stability.[37] A key part of that domestic agenda was meeting Egypt's growing energy requirements. Egyptian supporters of nuclear energy, who had seen their hopes first elevated and then dashed during both the 1960s and 1970s, believed that accession to the NPT would finally enable them to realize their ambitious nuclear power plans.

Soon after NPT ratification, framework agreements were signed to purchase two nuclear power reactors from each of four countries—the United States, France, Germany, and Canada. The program called for an output of 8000 megawatts by 2000.[38] Bids were solicited in 1982, but the process soon bogged down as financing problems arose and the Egyptians announced a series of postponements.[39] Then came the Chernobyl nuclear accident in April 1986, and Minister of Electricity and Energy Maher Abaza announced that construction of reactors in Egypt would be suspended until all safety issues had been fully resolved.[40] Mubarak had never been an enthusiast for nuclear power. Chernobyl gave him an excuse to pull the plug on a program he was not keen on pursuing for a variety of reasons.

With Egypt burdened by heavy debts in the late 1980s, Mubarak did not think it could afford large investment projects such as power reactors.[41] "If we set up a network of three or four stations," Mubarak explained, "we would start with $2 billion, but this figure would reach $5–6 billion by the time it was finished; that is, the final figure would be between $18–20 billion. Frankly, I would be leaving a debt for the citizens, a burden on the people. I cannot do this."[42] More fundamentally, the early conviction that nuclear power was critical to meeting Egypt's energy needs became less and less convincing as large reserves of natural gas were discovered and projections of economic growth were scaled back. In the view of Energy Minister Maher Abaza, "We are in no hurry for reactors now because we have all the alternatives. We have oil and gas . . . water and wind. . . . Thus we do not need to rush to demand nuclear plants now. This situation is in contrast with the past when we feared that oil would be depleted in ten years and that we would have no alternatives."[43] Mubarak concurred: "Egypt does not have a need for a nuclear plant in a country that is full of natural gas reserves."[44]

In retrospect, Chernobyl marked the end of any serious Egyptian pursuit of nuclear power. For years thereafter, and even up until the present time, Egypt's nuclear professionals have tried to keep their hopes alive. They continued to speak about an eight-reactor program and held seemingly purposeful discussions with potential reactor vendors.[45] There were confident predictions about reactor construction schedules that no one took seriously. [46] In an effort to generate public support, they sometimes made the case that pursuing a nuclear power program would have the benefit of also giving Egypt a nuclear weapons option.[47]

Senior Egyptian officials have dismissed optimistic remarks about the future of Egypt's nuclear power program as bureaucratic posturing and morale building by nuclear bureaucrats who play no significant role in national decisionmaking.[48] They point out that while previous plans have not been formally rescinded or suspended, there has been no senior-level approval to proceed.[49]

Forty years after Egypt began discussing the purchase of a large nuclear reactor, the first power plant has yet to be built. Nonpower applications of nuclear energy have fared somewhat better. In 1997 Egypt completed the construction at the Inshas site of an Argentine-supplied, twenty-two-megawatt light-water research reactor that has produced radioisotopes for medical, agricultural, and industrial purposes. Also at Inshas are a pilot facility for manufacturing fuel elements for the research reactor, a waste management center, and a small, French-supplied hot cell complex for research in plutonium extraction.[50] More recently, nuclear cooperation agreements have been concluded with Russia (April 2001), South Korea (August 2001), and China (January 2002). The scope of activities to be carried out under these agreements is still unclear. Much of what is known is fairly modest (for example, assistance by Russia in the operation of a Russian-supplied electronic accelerator, production of radioisotopes under the Korean agreement, Chinese assistance in the location and mining of uranium deposits in the Sinai), although cooperation reportedly may extend to more sensitive fuel cycle areas (for example, Chinese cooperation in the production of uranium hexafluoride).[51]

Even with recent enhancements, Egypt's nuclear research program remains quite limited. While its infrastructure has expanded and its nuclear specialists are gaining useful experience in areas of relevance to a military program, the relatively small scale of the facilities and activities involved and the fact that International Atomic Energy Agency (IAEA) safeguards will apply in most cases significantly reduce opportunities to exploit Egypt's research program to acquire nuclear weapons. Moreover, while Egypt has trained a substantial number of nuclear specialists, many of them have left the country in search of work opportunities.[52]

With the demise of its ambitious civil nuclear energy program in the late 1980s, Egypt faced a growing dilemma. It had been clear at least as far back as the 1973 war that Israel had nuclear weapons. It had become equally clear—first with Egypt's adherence to the NPT and then with its failure to acquire a nuclear infrastructure capable of supporting a nuclear weapons option—that Egypt was not going to match Israel's capability, at least not in the foreseeable future. This asymmetry with Egypt's past enemy and possible future regional rival was very disturbing to the Egyptian elite and public alike. The 1979 peace treaty had reduced the perceived military threat from Israel but not eliminated it. Beyond whatever direct threat Israel's nuclear arsenal posed to Egypt, Cairo also feared that Israel's possession of nuclear weapons would make it very difficult to prevent others in the Middle East, most notably Iraq and Iran, from acquiring them, with destabilizing consequences for Egypt and the entire region. The asymmetry was also seen as having adverse political implications, especially for Egypt's desire to play an influential role in regional affairs.[53]

For Egypt's leadership, the preferred way to resolve the dilemma posed by the nuclear asymmetry was to get Israel to roll back its capability. According to Presidential Adviser el-Baz, the answer was "not to go nuclear, but to force the other side to denuclearize."[54] Efforts to do so dated back to the 1960s, when Nasser in 1966 called on Israel to join the IAEA's safeguards system.[55] Between its 1968 signature and 1981 ratification of the NPT, Egypt frequently demanded that Israel join the treaty, including Sadat's public appeal in 1977.[56] During the negotiations leading up to the 1979 peace treaty, Egypt sought unsuccessfully to make Israel's renunciation of nuclear weapons part of the agreement.[57] Multilaterally, Egypt (with cosponsor Iran) supported a United Nations General Assembly resolution in 1974 calling for the Middle East to be made a nuclear-weapons-free zone, and it has continued every year since then to sponsor comparable resolutions.[58] In April 1990, President Mubarak put a strong personal stamp on Egypt's regional arms control and disarmament initiatives by calling for a Middle East zone free of all weapons of mass destruction.[59]

The diplomatic campaign to put pressure on Israel's nuclear capability stepped up dramatically in the 1990s. In the working group on Arms Control and Regional Security (ACRS), one of the five multilateral bodies established in 1992 by the Madrid Middle East peace process, Egypt pressed relentlessly for focusing on the nuclear issue, while Israel favored an incremental approach that dealt initially with confidence-building measures and deferred the nuclear issue until a comprehensive peace in the region was achieved. The impasse eventually led to the end of ACRS in late 1995.[60] At the NPT Review and Extension Conference in April and May of 1995, Egypt took the position that it could not support making the NPT permanent unless Israel took concrete steps toward joining the treaty. In the end, although Israel was unwilling to commit to NPT membership, Egypt agreed not to block a consensus to make the NPT permanent in exchange for adoption of a resolution calling for efforts to make the Middle East a zone free of all weapons of mass destruction. A third opportunity to press Israel involved the Chemical Weapons Convention (CWC). When the CWC was opened for signature, Egypt urged other Arab states not to commit unless Israel adhered to the NPT. Some Arab governments followed Egypt's lead, but most broke ranks (including Algeria, Jordan, and Saudi Arabia) and became parties to the convention.[61]

These attempts to pressure Israel on the nuclear issue presumably had a variety of motivations. Even if Egypt did not have realistic hopes of getting Israel to give up its nuclear capability altogether, it might have calculated that these were good opportunities to get the United States and other supporters of ACRS, the NPT, and the CWC to exert pressure on Israel and get it at least to move incrementally in the desired direction. The highly publicized diplomatic campaigns also seemed designed to reassure the Egyptian people that their government was working hard to correct an imbalance that their leaders had often described as dangerous. In terms of regional foreign policy goals, the nuclear diplomacy was probably viewed as a means of reasserting Egyptian leadership on an issue sure to have strong emotional appeal in the Arab world.[62] In that connection, Israelis (and many American observers of Egypt's diplomatic campaign) believed Cairo was using the nuclear issue as a device to embarrass and isolate Israel and impede the normalization of relations between Israel and the Arab countries. Finally, it served to lay down a marker that, even if the nuclear asymmetry was tolerable in the short run, it should not go on indefinitely.

Whatever the mix of motivations, and whatever the value the Egyptians may have derived from their diplomatic initiatives, the campaign has not succeeded in closing the gap between Egyptian and Israeli nuclear capabilities and has not brought the Middle East closer to being a zone free of all weapons of mass destruction. Indeed, the failure of diplomacy to address the nuclear asymmetry has increased Egyptian frustration with the nuclear status quo and produced a backlash in Cairo against international arms control agreements. Since adhering to the NPT in 1981, Egypt has not joined a single agreement.

Egypt's Renunciation of Nuclear Weapons

In an area such as weapons proliferation—where governments have strong incentives to conceal their intentions as long as possible and where they go to great lengths to keep their programs secret—it is only prudent not to take official statements at face value and not to be too categorical in drawing conclusions about the activities and intentions of particular countries. In the case of Egypt, it is also useful to bear in mind that it has pursued a chemical weapons program that it has denied having, cooperated with Iraq regarding both chemical weapons and ballistic missiles, and pursued the purchase from North Korea of technology for medium-range missiles, even though it had said it was not interested in missiles of that range.[63] Moreover, General Abdel Halim Abu Ghazala, a powerful minister of defense in the 1980s, reportedly sought Mubarak's approval in 1984 to start a nuclear weapons program, was turned down, and then proceeded to pursue the idea on his own. He allegedly colluded with Iraq in the nuclear area and schemed to smuggle both nuclear- and missile-related equipment from the United States. He was later sacked by Mubarak, who apparently had no knowledge of his exploits, but the episode indicated that at least some in the military apparently had an interest in nuclear weapons after Egypt joined the NPT.[64]

Recalling these reports of past Egyptian behavior on weapons-related issues is meant only to suggest that it is wise to proceed with some caution and a watchful eye in an area that is often quite murky and full of surprises—not to suggest that there are grounds to suspect current Egyptian behavior or intentions on the nuclear issue. Indeed, all available evidence points to the conclusion that Egyptian leaders long ago decided to renounce nuclear weapons and have stuck to that decision.

No single event marked Egypt's "decision" to forgo nuclear weapons. Egypt's renunciation came in stages. In 1967 the effort to acquire an infrastructure to support nuclear weapons was suspended, as national security priorities focused on winning back lost territory via conventional forces. Between 1977 and 1979, peacemaking and the recovery of Egyptian land undercut the chief rationale for an Egyptian nuclear capability and shifted priorities toward domestic needs. NPT adherence in 1981 formalized Egypt's non-nuclear status, and in 1986 the end of realistic hopes for a nuclear power program eliminated prospects for a robust nuclear infrastructure that could readily be adapted to bomb making. Concentration during the 1990s on disarmament diplomacy, the Middle East peace process, and domestic goals consolidated Egypt's non-nuclear choice. Each step along the way further narrowed the political and technical opportunities for reversing course and pursuing a nuclear weapons capability.

Despite the narrowing of options, Egypt has not, of course, completely closed off all future paths to nuclear weapons. Even today, if Egypt made the political decision to acquire nuclear weapons, it might eventually succeed. It has the necessary scientific talent, and if it were prepared to make significant sacrifices in terms of other national priorities, it would be able to find the economic resources to support a nuclear weapons program. But it would not be easy, quick, cheap, or without high risks. Egypt currently lacks the facilities and expertise to produce fissile material (plutonium or highly enriched uranium) indigenously. It would have to import much of what it needed, and that would be extremely difficult. Members of multilateral export control groups (primarily the Nuclear Suppliers Group) would refuse to provide certain sensitive technologies, and so Egypt would have to turn to countries like North Korea or to the shadowy network of brokers of various nationalities who have assisted countries like Iran, Iraq, North Korea, and Libya to obtain the wherewithal for their clandestine nuclear programs. With the heightened vigilance that exists today among Western governments and intelligence agencies, it is unlikely that Egypt could procure the necessary equipment, materials, and technologies without being detected and raising red flags. Even if Egypt could acquire the ingredients to build a nuclear weapons infrastructure, it would be a long time (perhaps four to six years) before it could manufacture fissile material, and during much of that period, it could expect to be the target of very strong international pressures to abandon the effort.

Given the obstacles to making weapons-grade nuclear material indigenously, Egypt—if it decided to acquire the bomb—could try the shortcut of purchasing already produced fissile material, weapons components, or even assembled nuclear weapons. However, while much international attention has deservedly been given to the risks of "loose nukes," especially from the former Soviet Union, purchasing a bomb is much more difficult than is often assumed. Indeed, so far there are no known cases of the illicit transfer of nuclear weapons or of enough fissile material to produce a nuclear weapon. In June 1998, President Mubarak said, "It is easy to buy nuclear weapons. After the fall of the Soviet bloc, I could have bought a bomb. I was offered one, and I refused."[65] His statement was never explained or substantiated. Perhaps the offer Mubarak referred to was a hoax, or more likely, he was trying to reassure the Egyptian people that they had not been left in the lurch, with no practical options to acquire nuclear weapons if they needed them.

But the reality is that Egypt does not have good options today for acquiring nuclear weapons—certainly none that could be counted on to produce results soon, predictably, and without generating a powerful international reaction. Meanwhile, the nuclear imbalance in the Middle East, which Egyptians decry as a source of instability and insecurity, may be increasing. Not only has Israel maintained its nuclear capability, but concerns are growing about nuclear programs elsewhere in the Middle East, especially in Iran.

The nuclear status quo is troubling to a substantial number of Egyptians. Some scholars argue that giving up the nuclear option was short sighted and forfeited an important source of leverage to pursue objectives such as Arab-Israeli peace.[66] Columnists criticize the Egyptian government for "nonchalance" on the nuclear issue and for relying too heavily on diplomatic initiatives rather than on more "decisive and daring" approaches.[67] Retired military officers regret the lack of balance in the region.[68] Diplomats note that the failure of diplomacy to address the nuclear issue only reaffirms that double standards are being applied in the Middle East.[69] Nuclear scientists continue to make the case that nuclear power should be an important component of Egypt's energy mix and that it is not too late to revive the power program.[70]

It is striking, though, that while the current state of nuclear affairs is seen as unsatisfactory in many quarters, there appears to be little doubt in Egypt that the nuclear issue has been settled. Presidential Adviser Osama el-Baz argues that such weapons "are not in Egypt's interest, now or tomorrow."[71] Speaker of the People's Assembly Ahmad Fathi Srour concurs: "No one in Egypt is currently thinking about becoming a nuclear power."[72]

So for the time being, at least, no Egyptian in any position of authority seems inclined to change Egypt's non-nuclear status. But what about the future? Are there circumstances in which Egypt would reconsider its decision to forgo nuclear weapons and either launch a nuclear weapon program straightaway or hedge its bets by seeking nuclear technologies and capabilities that could support a weapons program at some future time? There are many factors—individually or, more likely, in combination—that could conceivably play a role in motivating Egypt to rethink its nuclear options, but the four that seem most salient are Israel's policies and actions, especially with respect to its nuclear capability; nuclear proliferation elsewhere in the Middle East and beyond; the U.S.-Egyptian relationship and U.S. policies toward the region; and the evolution of Egyptian domestic affairs.

Israeli Policies and Actions

Egypt has been prepared to tolerate the decades-old nuclear imbalance with Israel in part because of its calculation that with the 1979 peace treaty and return of the Sinai, the risk of military confrontation between the two countries had been significantly reduced. In addition, Egyptian leaders have not been convinced that nuclear weapons are a militarily effective or necessary answer to the Israeli nuclear capability. They question, for example, the value of nuclear weapons in a region where it would be nearly impossible to discriminate between friends and foes. "Bombing Tel Aviv with nuclear weapons," a retired military officer said, "would mean bombing Palestinians. . . . It makes little sense to dump resources into a capability that wouldn't be used." [73] Moreover, Egyptian defense officials have believed that chemical, biological, and missile capabilities could play a useful deterrent role against Israel's nuclear arsenal.[74]

Another reason the nuclear asymmetry has been tolerable is that Egyptian strategists have traditionally viewed Israel's nuclear arsenal as weapons of "last resort" that would be used only if Israel's existence was in jeopardy.[75] That view was brought into question in 1986 when Mordechai Vanunu, a disaffected former technician at Dimona, claimed publicly that Israel's nuclear arsenal was larger and more advanced than previously assumed and therefore might be intended for war-fighting scenarios short of "last resort."[76] However, while the Vanunu revelations stirred up a debate in Egypt about the role of Israel's nuclear weapons, they did not seem to alter the judgment that an offsetting Egyptian nuclear capability was not necessary.

With the breakdown of the Madrid peace process that had helped during much of the 1990s to keep Egyptian-Israeli relations on a steady—if not fully satisfactory—course and the eruption of Palestinian-Israeli violence in the fall of 2000, Egyptians began to portray Israeli actions and capabilities in a more threatening light. Some Egyptian analysts say that Israeli Prime Minister Sharon's "language of power" has increased instability in the region.[77] The growing qualitative gap between Egypt and Israel in certain conventional military areas (and the alleged U.S. role in widening that gap) also is seen as a disturbing trend.[78]

Still, despite the chill in Egyptian-Israeli relations in recent years and increased Egyptian wariness toward Israel, there are no indications that the bilateral peace is in danger. Mostafa al-Fiqi, chairman of the People's Assembly Foreign Relations Committee, continues to believe the Israelis will not provoke Egypt because the bilateral peace treaty is too valuable to them.[79] Similarly, Nabil Fahmy, Egyptian ambassador to the United States, says he does not see Israel invading Egypt because Israelis remain convinced that the peace treaty serves the interests of both sides.[80] Under current circumstances, therefore, Egypt is likely to be prepared, however uncomfortably, to continue tolerating the nuclear imbalance with Israel and refraining from pursuing a nuclear capability of its own.

What changes in current circumstances could make a difference? One change that might make a difference would be Israel's becoming an overt

nuclear power, either by conducting a nuclear test or by simply acknowledging publicly that it has nuclear weapons. Israel has long maintained a
policy of nuclear ambiguity, neither confirming nor denying that it possesses nuclear weapons. According to Avner Cohen, the scholar who has
most thoroughly and publicly documented the Israeli nuclear program,
President Richard M. Nixon and Prime Minister Golda Meir reached an
understanding in 1969 regarding the public profile of that program. In
accordance with that understanding, the United States, while continuing
to support the principle of universal membership for the NPT, would no
longer press Israel to adhere to the treaty. For its part, Israel would neither test nuclear weapons nor declare that it possesses them.[81] Another
leading analyst of Middle East nuclear issues, Ariel E. Levite, maintains
that the United States periodically conveyed assurances to Egypt that
Israel would not "introduce" nuclear weapons into the region (the
equivalent, according to Cohen, of saying Israel would not test or
declare) and that those U.S. assurances contributed significantly to
Egypt's willingness to forgo the development of a full-fledged nuclear
weapons program.[82]

The thin veneer of official ambiguity about whether Israel actually has
the bomb has tended to shield Egyptian leaders from the public outcry—
and the domestic pressures to acquire a matching Egyptian capability—
that would arise if Israel were to admit what virtually all well-informed
Egyptians believe to be true. In part to avoid such a reaction in the Arab
world, Israel has clung tenaciously to its strategic ambiguity, even as the
veneer has become thinner and thinner. But if another country in the
region acquired nuclear weapons (for example, Iran), Israel might feel
that in order to ensure deterrence, it had to declare its own capability.

It is worth recalling that in 1976 the Egyptian foreign minister
asserted "that if Israel explodes a nuclear weapon, Egypt will obtain or
manufacture the same weapon; there can be no question of this."[83] After
nearly a quarter century of formal peace, it is not clear whether this "red
line" still exists. Moreover, Egypt's reaction to an Israeli public declaration might be very different from its reaction to an Israeli explosion. Still,
Egyptians seem to agree that even after decades of peace and regardless of
how Israel revealed its possession of nuclear weapons, the explicit confirmation of Israel's nuclear capability would produce a very powerful reaction in Egypt.

Egyptians can get quite emotional when the prospect is raised. "Egypt
would have to take drastic action," according to Amre Moussa, former

Egyptian foreign minister. There would be "immeasurable pressure" on "certain Arab countries to go nuclear. It would change the entire equation in the region. Israel would be saying, 'I am the dominant power.' Membership in the NPT for Arabs would become humiliating."[84] Current Foreign Minister Ahmed Maher also reacted strongly: "An Israeli declaration would be seen as throwing down the gauntlet. It would have a profound psychological impact in Egypt. We would have to react."[85]

But when pressed on how Egypt would react—and specifically on whether Egypt would react by pursuing its own nuclear capability—Egyptian officials get more circumspect. Senior military officers maintain that there would be no military reason to react because a declaration would not change anything—the world already knows that Israel has nuclear weapons.[86] While noting that the Egyptian "street" would react strongly to an Israeli declaration, a senior Egyptian official said that "when you move from the plane of feelings to the plane of practicality, it becomes unlikely Egypt would decide to go down the path of nuclear weapons."[87] Al-Fiqi shares that assessment: "We would feel terrible, we would shout in the streets, but in the end we would not go for nuclear weapons."[88]

Egypt would react strongly to an Israeli declaration of its nuclear capability, but the reaction would almost surely fall far short of going for nuclear weapons—for example, seeking UN resolutions condemning Israel, encouraging other countries to impose a boycott on trade and other activities with Israel, urging the major powers to pressure Israel to accept limits on its nuclear capability, adopting a more hedged rhetorical posture toward a possible future Egyptian nuclear capability, and even withdrawing from the NPT and pressing others to do so. In the military realm, Egypt could react by augmenting its conventional capabilities. It might even take modest steps to augment its nuclear energy infrastructure, in part to lay a foundation for further steps toward a military option should that later appear desirable and in part to provide a source of leverage to get the United States to lean on Israel.

Are there any things that Israel could say or do that could prompt Egypt to pursue nuclear weapons or at least to reconsider seriously whether Egypt should have them? There are, but the threshold is high. Among the developments most likely to produce such a response would be an Israeli use of nuclear weapons anywhere in the region, an Israeli invasion and seizure of Egyptian territory, and the unraveling of the bilateral peace treaty and return to the state of war.[89]

Nuclear Proliferation Elsewhere in the Middle East and Beyond

Egyptian concerns about nuclear proliferation in the Middle East are not confined to Israel. Egypt believes that acquisition of nuclear weapons by any country in the region would adversely affect its interests—by potentially posing an additional direct threat to its security, reducing the likelihood that Israel would eventually give up its capability, diminishing its regional political influence, and generally increasing tensions and instability in its neighborhood. This is why, in addition to pressing Israel to join the NPT, Cairo has placed such importance on a complementary, regional approach to the proliferation problem—making the Middle East a zone free of all weapons of mass destruction. Ambassador Nabil Fahmy says that from an Egyptian perspective, it would not be enough for such a zone to include Israel; it would also have to include countries like Iran.[90]

Over the past decade, prospects for preventing several Middle East countries from acquiring nuclear weapons have not looked very good. Although UN inspectors had in the early 1990s documented and dismantled most of Iraq's pre-1991 nuclear weapons program, concerns persisted in much of the world—especially after the inspectors left Iraq in late 1998—that Saddam Hussein's regime was either planning to regenerate its nuclear program or, in the judgment of the Bush administration and others, had already begun to do so. In the summer of 2002, information disclosed by an Iranian dissident group about two Iranian clandestine nuclear fuel cycle facilities and later confirmed by the International Atomic Energy Agency demonstrated that Tehran had made more progress toward its goal of acquiring nuclear weapons than even the United States had suspected. Libya, whose bumbling efforts to obtain nuclear weapons had never been taken very seriously, finally began to gain traction in its nuclear and missile programs at the end of the 1990s, sounding alarm bells in Washington and elsewhere. These developments—together with the continuation of Israel's program and doubts in certain quarters about the nuclear intentions of such other regional states as Syria—must have increased pessimism in Cairo about the likelihood of living in a nuclear-weapons-free region.

That pessimism may have been alleviated to some degree by events in 2003. The toppling of Saddam Hussein's regime—whatever may eventually be learned about the state of Iraqi programs on the eve of the U.S.-led invasion—has clearly removed the threat of an Iraqi nuclear weapons capability for the foreseeable future. Forced to admit many violations of its nonproliferation commitments and confronted with the prospect of United Nations Security Council sanctions, Iran agreed in November 2003 to suspend enrichment and reprocessing activities, to adhere to the IAEA's Additional Protocol (which requires Iran to accept more intrusive verification), and to cooperate fully with the IAEA to demonstrate that it is prepared to comply with its obligations.[91] Then in December 2003, Libyan leader Muammar Gadhafi—probably motivated by a desire to end U.S. sanctions, complete Libya's reintegration into the international community, and avoid becoming a target for regime change by the Bush administration—surprised the world by agreeing to disclose and eliminate his weapons of mass destruction and long-range missile programs.

In terms of the future of weapons of mass destruction in the Middle East, these developments were presumably viewed in Cairo as hopeful signs. But it is very unlikely that Egypt has concluded that the threat of further nuclear proliferation in the region has been eliminated. This is especially true in the case of Iran. Realistic and well-informed Egyptians probably share the assessment of the United States and many other countries that while Tehran's recent bowing to the will of the IAEA Board of Governors was a positive step, continued efforts will be required to persuade Iran to abandon its quest for nuclear weapons.

But if those efforts do not succeed and Iran eventually acquires nuclear weapons, would Egypt feel compelled to rethink its own nuclear options? Egypt has been wary of Iran since the 1979 revolution, suspecting Tehran of supporting Islamic extremists throughout the region. In 1981 the Iranian regime named a street in Tehran after Khalid al-Islambouli, the man who assassinated Anwar Sadat. In 1993 President Mubarak said that "if Iran succeeds in acquiring the bomb, it will be a great danger for the world."[92] However, in recent years, as Iran has showed less interest in exporting revolution and more interest in reaching accommodations with its Arab neighbors, tensions between Cairo and Tehran have decreased. In December 2003, Presidents Hosni Mubarak and Mohammad Khatami met on the margins of an international conference in Geneva, the first meeting between Egyptian and Iranian leaders in twenty-four years. The two countries have now agreed to restore full diplomatic relations, and Tehran's street signs will no longer bear the name of Sadat's assassin.[93]

Still, Egyptian concerns persist about Iran acquiring nuclear weapons. The Islamic Republic continues to be seen in Cairo as a political and ideological rival in the Middle East and Muslim world and a potential security threat to the Gulf Arabs. After the 1991 Gulf war, Egypt and Syria and the states of the Gulf Cooperation Council (GCC) joined together in a loose security arrangement labeled "GCC plus two," which was intended to give the Gulf states protection against stronger neighbors (that is, Iraq and Iran). Egyptians might calculate that without their own nuclear weapons, they would be in a weak position to come to the aid of a GCC country threatened by a nuclear-armed Iran—for example, if tensions arose between Iran and the United Arab Emirates (UAE) over Iran's occupation of three small islands in the Gulf claimed by the UAE.[94]

At the same time, Egyptians minimize the likelihood that Iran will actually get nuclear weapons, saying either that they doubt Iran has made a final decision to pursue a military nuclear program or that they believe the United States and the international community "will not allow" Iran to obtain nuclear weapons. There is also a view among senior officials that even if Iran did get the bomb, it would act "rationally" and "not pose a threat to Egypt."[95] In any event, the Egyptian public is much more concerned about an Israeli nuclear capability than an Iranian one and would not put much pressure on the Egyptian government to respond in the latter case.[96] With respect to the idea that if Iran acquired nuclear weapons, Egypt might also need them to fulfill its regional security responsibilities, senior officials point out that "the Gulf states have now found an American shield" and that any future Egyptian military operations to assist the GCC countries would almost surely be carried out as a coalition partner of the United States and would therefore not require an independent Egyptian nuclear capability.[97] Thus, while Iran's acquisition of nuclear weapons would be a jarring development for Egyptians and might lead to a more hedged Egyptian posture toward a future nuclear capability, it would not be likely—at least by itself—to result in a decision by Egypt to go for nuclear weapons.

Much the same can be said about the probable impact in Egypt of an Arab country acquiring nuclear weapons. Notwithstanding U.S. intelligence concerns in recent years about nuclear programs in the Middle East, senior Egyptian officials tend to discount heavily the possibility that Arab countries like Libya, Syria, or Algeria will actually pursue and obtain the bomb. They concede, however, that were any of their Arab neighbors to succeed in becoming a nuclear-armed state, this would be a major problem for Egypt. Depending on the circumstances, it might pose a direct security threat. At a minimum, it would be seen as posing the indirect threat of encouraging Israel to maintain or enhance its capability.

From a political perspective, it would be an embarrassment that a country other than Egypt had been the first Arab country to get the bomb.[98] But especially if the country did not have a very antagonistic relationship with Egypt, it would not be likely, in isolation, to persuade Egypt to reconsider its non-nuclear course.

It is often assumed that a factor that might motivate Egypt to pursue nuclear weapons is its desire to play a leading role in the affairs of the region.[99] Commenting on Egypt's possible reaction to a Middle Eastern country other than Israel getting nuclear weapons, Arab League secretary general Amre Moussa said, "Egypt will never accept playing second fiddle. It will do whatever it takes to maintain its position in the Middle East and in the Arab world."[100] Would it take Egypt acquiring nuclear weapons to maintain its position? Mostafa Elwi Saif suggests that it would not. He maintains that Egypt has not traditionally felt the need to rely on military capabilities in order to exercise its influence but instead has counted on its "geo-strategic, demographic, cultural, and political advantages to make up for military imbalance."[101] His colleague at Cairo University, Nadia Mostafa, similarly believes that Egypt has assumed that it could be a regional leader without having nuclear weapons. Although she disagrees with that assumption, she argues that it contributed to Egypt's decision to join the NPT, and she doubts that it will change.[102] Ambassador Nabil Fahmy believes that political factors would be secondary considerations for Egypt. According to him, any decision regarding the nuclear weapons option would be made on the basis of specific regional threats to Egypt's security and would not be driven by questions of status or prestige.[103]

Nuclear proliferation outside the Middle East could also affect Egypt's future nuclear choices. In May 1998, nuclear tests by India and Pakistan—and declarations for the first time by the two countries that they were nuclear weapons states—stimulated a lively debate in Cairo on the nuclear issue. Egyptians were worried that the South Asian nuclear developments could indirectly threaten them—in particular, that the Pakistani tests could spur Iran's nuclear efforts and that the weak international reaction to the South Asian tests might lead Israel to believe that it also could openly become a nuclear power at minimal cost.[104] More generally, those developments were unnerving in Cairo because they signaled that the global nonproliferation system might be eroding. Egypt's leaders had placed their bet clearly in favor of the Middle East and the world moving away from nuclear weapons. But here was a disquieting indication that movement might be in the opposite direction, with Egypt not very well positioned to make an adjustment.

While some in Egypt began thinking out loud about whether it made sense to leave the NPT, President Mubarak's reaction to the challenge posed by the Indian and Pakistani tests was to stay on course. Noting that the tests could open the door to proliferation for states like Iran, he said Egypt's response must be to work harder for a Middle East zone free of all weapons of mass destruction.[105]

So Egyptians are wary of global proliferation trends and are presumably watching current developments in North Korea and Iran with great interest. But they have apparently not decided to jump on any nuclear bandwagon because, in addition to all the other reasons why Egypt long ago decided to renounce nuclear weapons, the warning signs that have surfaced to date do not add up to the kind of specific threats to their security that could persuade them that it is time to change course. Moreover, Egypt probably still believes that the United States and other members of the international community would be rough on countries that go nuclear, especially those that leave the NPT. At present, the countries most likely to pursue that course have been considered "rogues," and Egypt would be reluctant to follow their lead and be treated like them. In the future, however, if more countries go nuclear (including less roguish ones) and both the stigma and penalties associated with going nuclear are reduced, then Egypt (and other non-nuclear states) may feel less inhibited. By itself, this would not motivate Egypt to acquire nuclear weapons. But if accompanied by strong security motivations, it could increase the likelihood of Egypt deciding to opt for a nuclear capability.

U.S.-Egyptian Relations and U.S. Policies

Strong bilateral relations between Egypt and the United States are a critical factor in Egypt's continued renunciation of nuclear weapons. Although the relationship does not involve a formal U.S. guarantee to come to Egypt's defense, America's huge stake in maintaining peace between Israel and Egypt provides assurance to Egyptian leaders that the contingency that long ago drove Cairo's interest in nuclear weapons—a military confrontation with its nuclear-armed neighbor—will remain very remote. Close bilateral defense ties—with Egypt enjoying the status of a U.S. "major non-NATO ally" and receiving over 50 percent of its arms from the United States—enable Egypt to bolster, and have confidence in, its conventional forces, which Egypt's military leaders have regarded as much more relevant to their country's security requirements than nuclear weapons.[106] Egypt's role as America's partner, both in the peace process and in America's wider dealings with the Arab world, has reinforced Cairo's standing as a regional leader. And over $2 billion annually in economic and military aid have been vital to promoting Egypt's economic and defense goals.

These benefits of the bilateral relationship have helped give Egypt the confidence to forgo nuclear weapons. In addition, they create strong disincentives against reversing course because Egyptians know that the United States would strongly oppose an Egyptian decision to go nuclear and that such a decision would put those benefits in jeopardy.[107]

It is not just the bilateral relationship that will affect Egypt's future nuclear choices: U.S. policies toward the region will also be important. Egypt wants the United States to pursue policies that foster a more stable and peaceful regional environment—the kind of environment in which Egypt would be comfortable remaining non-nuclear. Therefore, it wants the United States to be actively and evenhandedly engaged in brokering peace between Israelis and Palestinians and between Israelis and other Arab countries. It looks to the United States to promote stability in the Gulf region. In this connection, it favors an American military presence in the Gulf and a sustained U.S. effort to rebuild Iraq, but it hopes the United States will carry out its force deployments and its Iraq reconstruction policies in a way that will not generate opposition in the Arab world and especially the Egyptian street. Moreover, Egypt welcomes vigorous U.S. efforts to prevent Iraq and Iran from acquiring nuclear weapons, although it also asks the United States not to ignore the Israeli nuclear issue and is concerned that the Bush administration's muscular counterproliferation strategy could have some negative implications for its region.[108]

The continuation of active U.S. engagement in the Middle East—in the peace process, Gulf security arrangements, Iraqi reconstruction, and regional nonproliferation—and the maintenance of a strong bilateral relationship would decrease Egypt's incentives for reconsidering the nuclear option. But what if bilateral ties deteriorated or the United States backed away from its regional engagement policies, or some combination of the two occurred?

Estrangement between Egypt and the United States appears unlikely today. The uneasy post–September 11 period in the relationship—prompted by American outrage that the al Qaeda terrorists had some Egyptian roots—is largely over. The likelihood of a falling out between the two countries is small while President Mubarak remains in power. Still, one can postulate circumstances in which relations could become severely strained: a terrorist attack in the United States in which Egyptians are implicated, a spike in Arab-Israeli violence that the United States is accused of failing to stop, a sharp disagreement between Cairo and Washington over the pace of Egyptian political reform, or a congressional backlash against virulent anti-Americanism in Egypt that the government is perceived to condone. One can also imagine circumstances in which U.S. regional engagement might be scaled back or reversed: a less active involvement in the peace process out of frustration with continued Palestinian-Israeli violence, a reluctance to sustain a major commitment to Iraqi reconstruction if U.S. casualties increase, or an inability to maintain an adequate military presence in the Gulf if host governments encounter strong domestic pressures against granting the necessary access.

However likely or unlikely such developments may be, they would have an impact on Egypt's perceptions of its security environment and therefore on its attitudes toward the nuclear option. A U.S.-Egyptian rift, for example, could mean substantially reduced military aid and U.S. refusal to transfer critical weapons systems, which in turn could adversely affect Egypt's conventional arms capabilities. A diminished U.S. role in Gulf security arrangements and a U.S. failure to stay the course in rebuilding Iraq could lead to greater insecurity throughout the region, especially if instability erupted within Iraq and if Iran continued its pursuit of nuclear weapons.

The weakening of U.S.-Egyptian bilateral relations, by itself, would not be expected to spur Egypt to pursue a nuclear weapons capability. But if combined with other developments—such as a decreased U.S. political and military role in the Middle East, continued efforts of others in the region to acquire nuclear weapons, a sharp increase in Arab-Israeli tensions, and dramatic changes in the domestic political scene (as discussed in the following section)—it could well lead to strong pressures to revise Egypt's non-nuclear stance.

Domestic Factors

When asked whether they foresee a change in Egypt's commitment to forgo nuclear weapons, virtually all knowledgeable Egyptians—whether they are content with the nuclear status quo or not—respond that they do not expect any change. Then they quickly qualify their answer: "as long as Mubarak is in power." The man who has been president of Egypt since 1981 is seen as a strong leader with strong convictions, including on the importance of renouncing nuclear arms and concentrating national energies on such domestic priorities as education, health care, and employment. Moreover, the Egyptian political system gives him the power and authority to enforce his will. Its constitution provides that the presidential candidate, selected by the parliament, runs unopposed in a public yes-or-no referendum. The People's Assembly is dominated by the president's National Democratic Party, which essentially rubber stamps the policies of the administration.[109] A 1981 emergency law gives the security services sweeping powers, which were used in the early and mid-1990s to defeat a campaign of terrorism and destabilization by Islamic radicals aimed at bringing down the regime.[110]

Today Mubarak is firmly in charge. As Middle East expert Jon B. Alterman writes, "The state's crackdown on those who advocate violence has been successful. Violence against the state has subsided. No challenger to state control appears on the horizon."[111] Opposition political parties are small and ineffective, and groups considered a potential threat to the regime, such as the Muslim Brotherhood, are not permitted to run candidates for the parliament (although members of the organization can run for office and participate in the People's Assembly as independents).[112] To help himself govern, Mubarak has built an effective coalition that includes the armed forces, security apparatus, political elites, and business community, all of whom have a stake in maintaining his policies and the stability of the regime.[113]

What happens after Mubarak? The seventy-five-year-old president's fourth six-year term will expire in 2005, and many Egyptians believe he will step down at that time. So far he has not chosen a vice president or designated a successor, although much speculation revolves around his son, Gamal, who heads the National Democratic Party's policy secretariat. Alterman believes that given Hosni Mubarak's success at building loyalties and institutional arrangements that bolster support for the regime, any political succession (whether or not Gamal is tapped as the successor) "would almost certainly be smooth and orderly and would preserve the status quo."[114]

A smooth transition to a like-minded successor would presumably mean the continuation of Egypt's nuclear abstinence. But a successor might not have Hosni Mubarak's strong views on the nuclear issue or his tight grip on power and might therefore be more susceptible to pressures for change. From within Egypt's establishment, those pressures would likely come from the nuclear lobby, which has continued to press for the revitalization of its programs, as well as from politicians, retired military officers, and other opinion leaders who have long been uncomfortable with the nuclear status quo.

Pressures also could come from the street. People's Assembly speaker Srour warns that depending on future Israeli policies, the "young generation" of Egyptians could become a strong force favoring an Egyptian bomb.[115] Religious figures could get involved, too. In 1999 Mohammed Sayyid al-Tantawi, Sheikh of al-Azhar and the highest-ranking cleric in Egypt, called on Arabs and Muslims "to acquire nuclear weapons as an answer to the Israeli threat."[116] In late 2002, al-Azhar's Religious Ruling Committee issued a *fatwa* suggesting that development of nuclear weapons was a religious duty for Muslims. Head of the Religious Ruling Committee Sheikh Ali Abu al-Hassan, explained: "What is happening to the Muslims in all countries of the world is the result of weakness; and if the Muslims obtain this weapon, no one will conspire against them."[117]

In the past, such statements had little effect on government policy and were dismissed as "individuals venting their frustrations."[118] But in post-Mubarak Egypt, such voices might have to be taken more seriously. Qadry Said explains that "Egypt is changing. Governments now must listen to the feelings of the street. And the people want nuclear weapons. You Americans speak of democracy in the Middle East. But do you know what you would get in Egypt if the people voted on the nuclear issue?"[119]

The nightmare for many in and outside of Egypt is that Islamic fundamentalists with a radical Islamist agenda would somehow take charge in Cairo, either through the ballot box or otherwise. Whether that agenda would include a call for an Egyptian nuclear weapons capability is a matter of conjecture because Islamist organizations such as the Muslim Brotherhood have not taken a stand on the nuclear issue. But given what some Egyptian clerics have said about the need to offset Israel's nuclear capability and the temptation to exploit an issue with emotional and nationalistic appeal to mobilize domestic support, it would not be surprising if an Islamist regime sought to overturn long-standing Egyptian nuclear policy.

Many Egyptians see little chance of a fundamentalist takeover. Mostafa al-Fiqi, for example, asserts that "the Islamists will never come to power in Egypt. The military is opposed to that. The situation is under tight control."[120] Still, even if prospects for a radical shift in Cairo are remote, we cannot be sure about the policy post-Mubarak governments will adopt toward an Egyptian nuclear weapons capability. Much will depend on external factors. Even a government very different from the present regime in Cairo might see little incentive for going nuclear if there is no external threat that would justify such a course and if U.S.-Egyptian relations remained intact. But a key source of uncertainty is that whoever succeeds President Mubarak is likely to be less committed to the principle of renunciation, less constrained by concerns about a negative U.S. reaction, and less skillful in managing domestic pressures in Egypt than the man who has kept a firm lid on Egypt's nuclear ambitions for over two decades.

Conclusions and Implications for U.S. Policy

Countries do not achieve a nuclear weapons capability casually. It takes a major commitment of national resources and energies over a sustained period of time. Egypt flirted with the nuclear weapons option in the 1960s but never pursued the goal with the "we will eat grass" tenacity that others have demonstrated.[121] Instead, strong leaders—first Sadat and then Mubarak—determined that there was no compelling security rationale for an Egyptian nuclear capability, that other national objectives deserved priority, and that Egyptian interests were better served by getting others to build down rather than by Egypt building up.

Having suspended an active interest in nuclear weapons close to forty years ago, Egypt would have to overcome a great deal of non-nuclear inertia, both technical and political, if it wanted to launch a weapons program now. Technically, it would have to undertake a significant expansion of its still-inadequate nuclear infrastructure—a process that would take years—if it wanted to produce fissile materials indigenously. Or it could seek to purchase material already produced, which is a very uncertain path to the bomb and, in any event, would cap Egypt's capability at a level determined by the amount of material it could buy. Politically, it would have to reverse a non-nuclear orientation that has been a hallmark of Egyptian policy for decades, and it would be pursuing the option in a post–September 11 environment in which the United States and others will be monitoring proliferation developments carefully and coming down hard on those seeking nuclear weapons.

The difficulty of overcoming this inertia is a source of frustration to many Egyptians who recognize that it will be hard to correct the growing nuclear imbalance in the region, either through diplomacy or offsetting

Egyptian capabilities. Some observers believe this frustration will lead Egypt to greater public ambiguity about its nuclear intentions. A more ambiguous posture would be designed to create the impression internationally that Cairo has a viable nuclear option that it may choose to exercise in the future.[122]

But adopting a more hedged public posture regarding a nuclear capability would be a far cry from launching a crash program to acquire nuclear weapons or even from taking the initial steps to give Egypt a technical option to produce nuclear weapons in the future. It would take much more than the continuation of an uncomfortable status quo to induce Egypt actually to reverse course and seek nuclear weapons. Even significant regional developments such as an Israeli public declaration of its nuclear weapons capability or the acquisition of nuclear weapons by Iran would be unlikely, by themselves, to trigger an Egyptian decision to go nuclear. Such events would probably lead to a major policy review within the government and a strong response, but the response would most likely stop short of a decision to begin an Egyptian nuclear program. It would take either a near-cataclysmic event (such as the use of nuclear weapons in the region or the reoccupation of Egyptian territory) or the accumulation of several highly threatening developments to tip the balance in favor of pursuing the nuclear option.

Indeed, the most plausible path to an Egyptian weapons program would be the combination of several elements: highly threatening regional security developments (for example, a nuclear-armed Iran, the unraveling of the Egyptian-Israeli peace), a weakening of factors that currently contribute to Egypt's sense of security (such as the fraying of U.S.-Egyptian ties), and a lowering of the perceived penalties associated with a country going nuclear (for example, if first North Korea or Iran and then other, less roguish countries acquire nuclear weapons without paying a high price). A key variable cutting across all these factors is the leadership in Cairo. With a government led by President Mubarak or a strong, like-minded successor, the threshold for any decision to go nuclear would be higher. With a weaker government, especially a more populist one, the threshold could be significantly lower.

Any future decisions on the nuclear question will naturally be made by Egypt on the basis of its own calculations of national self-interest. The United States, however, can have an impact on such decisions by helping shape the regional context in which those calculations will be made. Pursuing the following policies could encourage Egypt to continue on a nonnuclear path.

First, the United States should press for progress toward a comprehensive Middle East peace. While the 1979 Egyptian-Israeli peace treaty was a key factor enabling Egypt to renounce the nuclear option, the unraveling of that peace and increased Arab-Israeli tensions would be factors that might motivate Cairo to reconsider that choice. Reconciliation and peace between Israelis and Palestinians, peace between Israel and Syria and other Arabs countries, and deepening of existing ties between Israel and Egypt (and Jordan) would significantly strengthen Egyptian incentives to remain non-nuclear. Following a lengthy period of detachment after it assumed office, the Bush administration became heavily engaged in promoting the Israeli-Palestinian "road map" but then stepped back in mid-2003 as the parties failed to fulfill their commitments and violence once again escalated. If it wishes to reduce pressures for proliferation in the Middle East (as well as to serve a wide range of other U.S. objectives), the United States should remain actively involved in efforts to achieve an accommodation between Israelis and Palestinians as well as a broader peace in the region.

Second, Iran must be prevented from achieving a nuclear weapons capability. Iran's acquisition of nuclear weapons would be a serious blow to stability in the Middle East and to hopes of keeping Egypt and other regional states from rethinking their non-nuclear status. Iran's recent willingness to suspend enrichment and reprocessing activities and adhere to the IAEA's Additional Protocol was a positive development but hardly an indication that Tehran has made the fundamental decision not to have nuclear weapons. Working closely with the Europeans, Russians, the IAEA, and key countries of the Middle East (including Egypt), the U.S. administration should do everything it can to bring Iran's leaders to the conclusion that continuing their efforts to acquire nuclear weapons would be too risky, too subject to detection, and too damaging to Iran's reputation and broader national interests—in short, a losing proposition. Only if confronted with a stark choice between becoming a pariah with nuclear weapons or a law-abiding member of the international community without them is Iran likely to make the right decision.

Third, Washington should discourage Israel from doing anything provocative in the nuclear area. A continuation of the de facto nuclear asymmetry between Egypt and Israel is probably tolerable in Cairo for some time to come. But to avoid creating strong public pressures in Egypt to obtain a capability of its own, the United States should urge Israel not to acknowledge its nuclear capability, even if Iran gets the bomb, and to avoid saying or doing anything else that could be viewed as an implicit nuclear threat or otherwise generate public pressures in Egypt on the nuclear issue. In addition, if peace efforts in the region begin to bear fruit and an official regional security dialogue is eventually resumed, the United States should encourage Israel to find a constructive way to address the nuclear issue—a way that is consistent with Israeli security interests (including the interest in preserving ambiguity) but at the same time demonstrates restraint in the nuclear area and addresses the Egyptian concern that the subject cannot forever simply be off the table.[123]

Fourth, the United States should continue to give high priority to promoting stability and security in the Gulf. Security developments in the Gulf, especially the future of nuclear programs in Iraq and Iran, will have an important impact on Egyptian perceptions of threat. The United States can reduce incentives in Egypt and throughout the region for acquiring independent nuclear capabilities by maintaining a sizable but politically sustainable (both in the United States and in regional host countries) military presence in the Gulf region and by staying the course in Iraqi reconstruction efforts as long as necessary to ensure the transition to a stable, self-governing Iraq that poses no threat to its neighbors.

Fifth, it will be crucial to maintain a strong U.S.-Egyptian relationship. As the United States pursues various aspects of this complex relationship, it should bear in mind the importance of ensuring that Egyptian governments—present and future—do not alter Egypt's non-nuclear status. That will mean close defense cooperation, which includes helping Egypt meet its conventional force requirements and promoting strong military-to-military relations. It also means demonstrating, through the character and quality of bilateral ties and the role the U.S. asks Cairo to play, that Egypt does not need nuclear weapons to maintain its leadership position in regional affairs. And to reduce the likelihood of a fundamentalist government that might entertain the idea of acquiring nuclear weapons, it means that the United States should do whatever it can to assist the Egyptians in achieving economic development and political reform.

Finally, the United States should seek to bolster the nonproliferation regime. Egypt and other key non-nuclear states must not get the impression that continued nuclear proliferation is inevitable, even normal, and that a country can "go nuclear" without paying a substantial price. That would give states that had renounced nuclear weapons an incentive to move quickly to acquire them lest they leave themselves at a severe disadvantage in an increasingly nuclear-armed region and world. The best way to avoid the perception that proliferation is inevitable is to stop it where the threat is now most urgent: North Korea and Iran. Failing that, it would be essential for the international community to impose a heavy penalty on those that choose nuclear weapons so as to discourage others from following suit.

At present, the likelihood of Egypt reversing course and acquiring nuclear weapons is small. While there is discontent in Cairo about the nuclear status quo, there appears to be no active effort underway to change it. Moreover, it would take a major change in circumstances to get Egypt to alter its long-standing posture, including the combination of a serious external threat and a substantial change in the composition and orientation of Egypt's leadership.

But while Egypt does not appear likely to reverse its nuclear renunciation, the consequences of it doing so would be far reaching. Egypt has been one of the stalwarts of the NPT regime; many states of the region have followed its lead. Its defection would be devastating. The United States and other interested governments must therefore do whatever they can to help keep Egypt safely in the non-nuclear camp.

Notes

1. In *Al-Ahram,* December 24, 1960, Gamal Abdel Nasser stated that if Israel produced nuclear weapons, so would Egypt. Cited in Khalil Shikaki, "The Nuclearization Debates: The Cases of Israel and Egypt," *Journal of Palestine Studies,* vol. 4, no. 3 (Summer 1985), p. 85. Anwar Sadat in December 1974 said that if Israel acquired the bomb, "We shall also find a way of having atomic weapons." See "Middle East Ready to Explode, Sadat Says," *New York Times,* December 17, 1974, cited in Steven J. Rosen, "A Stable System of Mutual Nuclear Deterrence in the Arab-Israeli Conflict," *American Political Science Review,* vol. 71 (December 1977), p. 1368.

2. Mubarak interview in *Al-Hayat,* cited in Elizabeth Bryant, "Egypt Might Consider Nukes," *United Press International,* October 5, 1998.

3. Osama el-Baz, conversation with author, Cairo, March 13, 2003.

4. Mohammed Hassanein Heikal, a close associate of President Nasser, quotes Nasser saying that "we missed out in the steam age, and also in the electricity age, but we ought not allow ourselves under any circumstances to be left behind in the atomic age." Cited in Jim Walsh, "Bombs Unbuilt: Power, Ideas, and Institutions in International Politics," Ph.D dissertation, MIT, 2000, chap. 6, p. 6.

5. Ibid., p. 7.

6. Ibid., p. 9.

7. Barbara M. Gregory, "Egypt's Nuclear Program: Assessing Supplier-Based and Other Developmental Constraints," *Nonproliferation Review,* vol. 3, no. 1 (Fall 1995), p. 22.

8. See Mostafa Elwi Saif, "Egypt: A Non-Nuclear Proactivist in a Volatile Region," paper presented at the conference on "The Domestic Roots of Proactivist Non-Nuclear Policy: A New Approach to Non-Proliferation" (Peace Research Institute Frankfurt, Bellagio, Italy, September 29–October 3, 1997), pp. 33–34.

9. Gregory, "Egypt's Nuclear Program," p. 21.

10. Walsh, "Bombs Unbuilt," chap. 6, pp. 10, 20.

11. Egypt was upset with West Germany over the latter's establishment of diplomatic relations with Israel and over its sale of U.S.-made tanks to Israel. For its part, West Germany objected to Egypt's improvement in relations with East Germany. See Walsh, "Bombs Unbuilt," chap. 6, pp. 24–25.

12. Ibid., pp. 25–26.

13. Gregory, "Egypt's Nuclear Program," p. 21.

14. Walsh, "Bombs Unbuilt," chap. 6, pp. 23–25.

15. Ibid., chap. 7, pp. 2–3.

16. Abdel Moneim Said, director of Al-Ahram Strategic Studies Center, conversation with author, Cairo, March 16, 2003.

17. Concerned about the prospect of a nuclear and missile race between Egypt and Israel, President John F. Kennedy dispatched John McCloy to see President Nasser in June 1963. McCloy told Nasser that while the United States had no information that the Dimona reactor was being used to produce nuclear weapons, the Israelis might well use the reactor for that purpose if Egypt continued its missile program. He suggested that both Egypt and Israel accept restrictions on their programs and indicated that the United States could assist in inspecting key sites, including Dimona. Nasser denied Egypt was pursuing nuclear weapons and rejected the U.S. arms control initiative. However, the episode made clear to Nasser that the United States would strongly oppose an Egyptian nuclear weapons program. For an account of the McCloy mission, see Avner Cohen, *Israel and the Bomb* (Columbia University Press, 1998), pp. 246–51. For details on the covert campaign, see Ian Black and Benny Morris, *Israel's Secret Wars: A History of Israel's Intelligence Service* (New York: Grove Weidenfeld, 1991), pp. 192–201.

18. Walsh, "Bombs Unbuilt," chap. 6, p. 37.

19. Abdel Said, conversation, March 16, 2003.

20. Mostafa Elwi Saif, professor at Cairo University, conversation with author, Cairo, March 18, 2003.

21. Mostafa al-Fiqi, chairman of the People's Assembly Foreign Relations Committee, conversation with author, Cairo, March 15–18, 2003.

22. There is evidence, however, that at least some Egyptian interest in acquiring nuclear weapons survived the 1967 war. According to Mohamed Hassanein Heikal, a leading Egyptian journalist and a confidant of President Nasser, Nasser sent a delegation from Egypt's nuclear authority to China in late 1967 to seek help for Egypt's nuclear program. Chou En-lai reportedly received the delegation but told them that China would not provide assistance and that Egypt would have to

rely on itself in the nuclear field. See Mohamed I. Shaker, *The Nuclear Non-Proliferation Treaty, Origin and Implementation, 1959–1979,* vol. 2 (Dobbs Ferry, N.Y.: Oceana Publications, 1980), p. 804.

23. See Rosen, "A Stable System," p. 1368.

24. Saif, "Egypt: A Non-Nuclear Proactivist," p. 38.

25. Abdel Said, conversation, March 16, 2003.

26. *Al-Ra'i al'Amm* (Kuwait), June 6, 1976, cited in Shikaki, "The Nuclear-ization Debates," p. 87.

27. In presenting the NPT to the Egyptian People's Assembly for ratification in 1981, Foreign Minister Kamal Hassan Ali said, "During the Camp David talks and in the course of Egyptian-Israeli Peace Treaty negotiations . . . Egypt did not fail to draw the attention of Israel to the importance of accession to the Non-Proliferation Treaty." State Information Service, *Egypt and the Treaty on the Non-Proliferation of Nuclear Weapons* (Cairo: 1981), p. 88.

28. The close Soviet-Egyptian relationship ended when Egypt expelled Soviet advisers in July 1972. Clyde R. Mark, *Egypt-United States Relations,* Issue Brief for Congress (Congressional Research Service, Library of Congress, December 12, 2002), p. 1.

29. Ibid., p. 10.

30. Ibid., p. 2.

31. Ibid., pp. 10–12.

32. Walsh, "Bombs Unbuilt," chap. 7, p. 11.

33. Saif, "Egypt: A Non-Nuclear Proactivist," p. 17.

34. Ibid., p. 13.

35. Walsh, "Bombs Unbuilt," chap. 7, pp. 10–11.

36. State Information Service, *Egypt and the Treaty,* pp. 89–90.

37. Saif, "Egypt: A Non-Nuclear Proactivist," p. 51.

38. Statements by Maher Abaza, Egypt's minister of power and energy, *Middle East News Agency (MENA),* May 19, 1984 (*BBC,* May 29, 1984), cited in Shai Feldman, *Nuclear Weapons and Arms Control in the Middle East* (MIT Press, 1997), p. 59.

39. Walsh, "Bombs Unbuilt," chap. 7, p. 13.

40. *Ruz al-Yusuf* (Egypt), November 6, 1989, cited in Feldman, *Nuclear Weapons and Arms Control,* p. 61.

41. Ali al-Saiedi, former chairman of the Nuclear Power Plants Authority and current minister of industry, conversation with author, March 16, 2003.

42. Hosni Mubarak, interview on ESC Television (Cairo), July 19, 1992; cited in Gregory, "Egypt's Nuclear Program," p. 25.

43. "Minister of Energy on Nuclear Power," *Cairo Al-Musawwar,* September 20, 1996 (Foreign Broadcast Information Service–Near East and South Asia [FBIS-NES] 96-213). Similar thoughts were expressed by Maher Abaza in conversation with author, March 15, 2003.

44. "Egypt Vague on Mubarak's Nuclear Deal with Russia, Early Exit from Moscow," May 1, 2001 (www.worldtribune.com/worldtribune/Archive-2001/me-egypt-05-01.html [February 2004]).

45. Regarding the eight-reactor program, see "Egypt is Ready to Begin Nuclear Energy Program," *Agence France-Presse*, March 13, 1995 (FBIS-NES-95-049). Egypt reportedly approached China to purchase 300-megawatt reactors. "China Tells of Possible Nuclear Plant Sales," *Washington Times,* July 31, 1992, p. A9; cited in Gregory, "Egypt's Nuclear Program," p. 25.

46. In May 2002, Electricity and Energy Minister Hassan Ahmed Yunes told the Egyptian Parliamentary Industrial Committee that a first nuclear power reactor would be constructed by 2010. "U.S Worried by Egyptian Plan for Eight Nuclear Reactors," May 29, 2002, *World Tribune.com* (http://216.26.163.62/2002/ss_egypt_05_29.html [February 2004]).

47. Mounir Megahed, general manager of feasibility studies at the Nuclear Power Plants Authority, wrote that a political decision to proceed with nuclear power plans "will be similar to President Nasser's decision to nationalize the Suez Canal. It will revive the spirit and the feelings of national pride which would provide the basis of popular support for the development plans and the sacrifices that may be required. . . . Beside nuclear power's role in mobilization and modernization, its role in enhancing Egyptian national security should not be neglected. . . . A mastery of nuclear technologies . . . cannot be reversed or compartmentalized; under certain conditions, it could facilitate the production of nuclear weapons." Mounir Megahed, "A Nuclear Boost," *Al-Ahram Weekly On-line,* no. 380, June 4–10, 1998 (http://weekly.ahram.org.eg/1998/380/op4.htm [February 2004]).

48. Al-Saiedi, conversation, March 16, 2003.

49. Ibid., and Abaza, conversation, March 15, 2003.

50. Federation of American Scientists, "Nuclear Research Center (NRC) Hot Laboratory and Waste Management Center (HLWMC)," June 11, 2000 (www.fas.org/nuke/guide/egypt/facility/nrc.htm [July 2, 2003]).

51. Jacques Schuster, "Intelligence Service—Cairo Wants to Build Nuclear Bomb; Egypt Is Said to Be about to Enrich Uranium with Help from China and to Purchase Long-Range Missiles," *Die Welt*, June 22, 2002.

52. A 1986 report indicated that 1,000 nuclear engineers and technicians had been registered by Egyptian authorities but that about half of them were working abroad. Cited in Feldman, *Nuclear Weapons and Arms Control*, p. 60.

53. For a discussion of the dilemma posed by Egypt's nuclear asymmetry with Israel, see Emily Landau, "Egypt's Nuclear Dilemma," *Strategic Assessment*, vol. 5, no. 3, November 2002 (www.tau.ac.il/jcss/sa/v5n3p5Lan.html [February 2004]).

54. El-Baz, conversation, March 13, 2003.

55. Nasser interview with NBC, April 22, 1966; cited in Saif, "Egypt: A Non-Nuclear Proactivist," p. 40.

56. Interview, *ABC News*, February 27, 1977; cited in Shai Feldman, *Israeli Nuclear Deterrence* (Columbia University Press, 1982), p. 67.

57. Ibid., p. 67.

58. Ibid., p. 68.

59. Mostafa Elwi Saif, "Nuclear Weapons and Arms Control in the Middle East: An Egyptian View," *Unione Scienziati per il Disarmo* (www.uspid.dsi. unimi.it/proceed/cast97/elwisaif.html [July 2, 2003]).

60. Emily Landau, *Egypt and Israel in ACRS: Bilateral Concerns in a Regional Arms Control Process* (Tel Aviv: Jaffee Center for Strategic Studies, Tel Aviv University, 2001), pp. 19–20.

61. Department of State, Bureau of Arms Control, "Chemical Weapons Convention States Parties and Signatories," Fact Sheet, June 3, 2003 (www.state. gov/t/ac/rls/fs/2003/21336.htm [July 3, 2003]).

62. Landau, *Egypt and Israel in ACRS*, p. 24.

63. See Dany Shoham, "Chemical and Biological Weapons in Egypt," *Nonproliferation Review*, vol. 5, no. 3 (Spring-Summer 1998), p. 51. In the 1980s, Egypt worked secretly with Iraq and Argentina to develop a 1000-kilometer-range missile called the Condor II. The project was terminated under pressure from the United States and others. See "Egypt's Missile Efforts Succeed with Help from North Korea," *Risk Report*, vol. 2, no. 5, September-October 1996 (www. wisconsinproject.org.countries/egypt/miss.html [July 7, 2002]), and Richard Sale, "N. Korean, Egyptian Missile Worries Congress," *United Press International*, August 2, 2001.

64. Walsh, "Bombs Unbuilt," chap. 7, pp. 16–19.

65. "Mubarak Says He Turned Down Offer to Buy Nuclear Bomb," *Associated Press Worldstream*, June 19, 1998.

66. Nadia Mostafa and Mostafa Elwi Saif, Cairo University, conversations with author, March 18, 2003.

67. Salama Ahmed Salama, "A Time to Dare," *Al-Ahram Weekly*, no. 380, June 4-10, 1998.

68. General Mahmoud Muhammad Khalaf, former commander of the Third Army and currently at the National Center of Middle East Studies, conversation with author, Cairo, March 18, 2003.

69. Nabil Fahmy, Egyptian ambassador to the United States, conversation with author, Washington, D.C., February 28, 2003.

70. Fawzi Hamad, former head of the Atomic Energy Authority, conversation with author, Cairo, March 18, 2003.

71. El-Baz, conversation, March 13, 2003.

72. Ahmad Fathi Srour, conversation with author, Cairo, March 16, 2003.

73. Qadry Said, conversation with author, Cairo, March 13, 2003.

74. In 1975 Egyptian minister of war Abdel Ghany El-Gamasy said, "Weapons of mass destruction are not limited to nuclear weapons. Egypt has enough of the other types of weapons of mass extermination and it has the capability of

retaliating to an Israeli nuclear blow by making use of these weapons." Feldman, *Israeli Nuclear Deterrence*, p. 69.

75. According to Egypt's former defense minister Amin Howeidi, "The nuclear weapons in Israel's hands are not for use in normal circumstances, because they are deterrent weapons, not combat weapons. . . . But they will become weapons of nuclear warfare if Israel's existence is endangered." See "Egypt's Former Defense Minister: How to Counter the Israeli Nuclear Deterrent," *Mideast Mirror*, vol. 9, no. 21 (January 31, 1995).

76. Landau, *Egypt and Israeli in ACRS*, p. 23.

77. Khalaf, conversation, March 18, 2003.

78. Qadry Said, conversation, March 13, 2003.

79. Al-Fiqi, conversation, March 15, 2003.

80. Fahmy, conversation, February 28, 2003.

81. Avner Cohen argues that, as a result of the 1969 understanding, Israel's policy of nuclear ambiguity changed to one of "nuclear opacity." Cohen, *Israel and the Bomb*, p. 337.

82. Ariel E. Levite, "Never Say Never Again: Nuclear Reversal Revisited," *International Security*, vol. 27, no. 3 (Winter 2002–03), pp. 63–64.

83. Interview with Foreign Minister Ismail Fahmy in *Al-Ahram*, April 30, 1976. Published in "Documents and Source Material: Arab Documents on Palestine and the Arab-Israeli Conflict," *Journal of Palestine Studies*, vol. 5, no. 3/4 (Spring/Summer 1976), p. 261.

84. Amre Moussa, currently secretary general of the Arab League, conversation with author, Cairo, March 15, 2003.

85. Minister Ahmed Maher, conversation with author, Cairo, March 15, 2003.

86. Senior military officers, conversations with author, Cairo, March 17, 2003.

87. A senior official, conversation with author, Cairo, March 15, 2003.

88. Al-Fiqi, conversation, March 15, 2003.

89. These were the developments cited most frequently by Egyptian interlocutors during an intensive series of discussions with the author in Cairo, March 13–18, 2003.

90. Fahmy, conversation, February 28, 2003.

91. Board of Governors, *Implementation of the NPT Safeguards Agreement in the Islamic Republic of Iran,* resolution adopted by the Board on November 26, 2003, GOV/2003/81 (Vienna: IAEA).

92. Feldman, *Nuclear Weapons and Arms Control*, p. 133.

93. Guy Chazan and Hugh Pope, "Syria, Libya and Iran Look to Thaw Chill with Neighbors," *Wall Street Journal,* January 8, 2004.

94. Senior Egyptian official, conversation with author, Washington D.C., February 28, 2003.

95. Senior officials, conversation, March 13–15, 2003.

96. Qadry Said, conversation, March 13, 2003.

97. Senior official, conversation with author, March 15, 2003; senior military officers, conversation, March 17, 2003.

98. Qadry Said, conversation, March 13, 2003.

99. According to Emily B. Landau, "Egypt's leadership interests are such that it will find it increasingly difficult not to be on equal standing in the non-conventional realm with other regional powers." Landau, "Egypt's Nuclear Dilemma" (www.tau.ac.il/jcss/sa/v5n3p5Lan.html [March 2004]).

100. Moussa, conversation, March 15, 2003.

101. Saif, "Egypt: A Non-Nuclear Proactivist," p. 48.

102. Mostafa, conversation, March 18, 2003.

103. Fahmy, conversation, February 28, 2003.

104. Landau, "Egypt's Nuclear Dilemma," p. 5; Fahmy, conversation, February 28, 2003.

105. Landau, "Egypt's Nuclear Dilemma," p. 5.

106. Mostafa Elwi Saif says that "the elite of Egypt's military theorists" believe in the primacy of conventional forces in meeting Egypt's security requirements. Saif, conversation, March 18, 2003.

107. Ambassador Nabil Fahmy acknowledges that the bilateral relationship would weigh heavily against any Egyptian decision to pursue nuclear weapons but points out that, in the dire security circumstances in which Egypt might contemplate going nuclear, Cairo would not be deterred by the prospect of losing U.S. assistance. (Fahmy, conversation, February 28, 2003.) Foreign Minister Maher shares that view but adds that it is hard to foresee such a "desperate situation in which Egypt would throw its relations with the U.S. out the window." (Maher, conversation, March 15, 2003.)

108. Egyptians know that they are not the targets of the Bush administration's greater emphasis on preemption. But some experts believe that if the United States develops new nuclear weapons and talks about using them in a wider range of contingencies, this could increase the perceived value of nuclear weapons for states of the Middle East, especially Israel, and even increase the likelihood that nuclear weapons will be used in the region. Ambassador Ramzy Ezzeldin Ramzy, deputy assistant minister for foreign affairs for international political relations and disarmament and currently Egyptian ambassador to the IAEA, conversation with author, March 17, 2003.

109. Christopher Cooper, "Islamists Are Ready if Democracy Rises in Middle East after Iraq War," *Wall Street Journal*, May 1, 2003, p.1.

110. Jon B. Alterman, "Egypt: Stable but for How Long," *Washington Quarterly* (Autumn 2000), p. 110.

111. Jon B. Alterman, "Islam in Egyptian Politics; From Activism to Alienation," *Middle East Journal*, vol. 57, no. 2 (Spring 2003), p. 322.

112. Cooper, "Islamists are Ready."

113. Alterman, "Egypt: Stable but for How Long," p. 113.

114. Ibid., p. 107.

115. Srour, conversation, March 16, 2003.

116. "Highest Ranking Official Cleric in Egypt Calls for Arabs and Muslims to Acquire Nuclear Weapons to Counter Israel," *Special Dispatch Series*, no. 59, November 19, 1999, Middle East Media Research Institute (MEMRI) (http://memri.org/bin/articles.cgi?Page=archives&Area=sd&ID=SP5999 [February 2004]).

117. Quoted in Yotam Feldner, "Egypt Rethinks its Nuclear Program. Part III: The Nuclear Lobby (Continued)," *Inquiry and Analysis Series*, no. 120, January 22, 2003, MEMRI (http://memri.org/bin/articles.cgi?Page=archives&Area=ia& ID=IA12003 [February 2004])

118. El-Baz, conversation, March 13, 2003.

119. Qadry Said, conversation, March 13, 2003.

120. Al-Fiqi, conversation, March 15, 2003.

121. In 1965 Pakistani foreign minister Zulfikar Ali Bhutto was reported to have said: "If India builds the bomb, we will eat grass or leaves, even go hungry, but we will get one of our own." Mike Moore, "Eating Grass," *Bulletin of the Atomic Scientists*, June 1993. Available online at www.thebulletin.org/issues/ 1993/j93/j93Moore.html [July 2, 2003].

122. Emily Landau states that "even if Egypt does not make a clear decision to go nuclear, it will most likely take steps to convince others that the decision exists as a viable option, and that Egypt is indeed a credible contender for creating some kind of balance in the region if the nuclear race continues." Landau, "Egypt's Nuclear Dilemma" (www.tau.ac.il/jcss/sa/v5n3p5Lan.html [March 2004]).

123. The author knows how sensitive and difficult this issue can be, having spent several years as cochairman of the Middle East Arms Control and Regional Security Working Group trying, unsuccessfully, to bridge Egyptian-Israeli differences. While concrete steps limiting Israel's nuclear capability do not seem realistic at present, Israel's reaffirmation of its long-standing position—that in the context of a durable and comprehensive peace in the region, it supports the goal of a Middle East free of all weapons of mass destruction—could have value in addressing concerns about a permanent nuclear asymmetry in the region.

CHAPTER 5

Syria: Can the Myth Be Maintained without Nukes?

ELLEN LAIPSON

Syria is one of the core states of the Arab system. It was often the strategic ground over which the rival regional powers—Egypt and Iraq—would compete; indeed, its capital Damascus ranks with Cairo and Baghdad in historic and cultural significance. In recent decades, despite the mounting toll of military and political setbacks in the struggle between the Arab state system and Israel, Syria's leaders have projected a self-image of enduring greatness and leadership of the pan-Arab cause. Syria's steadfastness in the face of changing geopolitical realities has been a matter of high principle for the Ba'athi government of Hafez Asad and his son and successor, Bashar. But to western diplomats this has often appeared to be a sign of a rigid system that has little agility in adapting to change and in acknowledging an enduring imbalance of power that constrains Syria's options to protect its security.

Other threats and uncertainties also shape Syria's national security policies. With the USSR's collapse, Syria lost a superpower patron. Today, it is wary of the great powers' intentions and seeks correct but not close ties to external major powers with influence in the region—the United States, Russia, and key European states in particular. Syria borders Turkey, a large NATO country that has as recently as 1998 intimidated

The author wishes to thank Erin Carmody of the Stimson Center for her able research assistance.

Syria with a conventional buildup to achieve its goals vis-à-vis Kurdish separatists. It also has an important relationship with Iran, the non-Arab regional power and nuclear aspirant. For now, the two states enjoy a strategic partnership, of sorts, with respect to the Palestine question, but that relationship also has its ambiguities and cannot be seen as providing any lasting solution to Syria's strategic vulnerability.

The pursuit of weapons of mass destruction, nuclear weapons in particular, must be viewed in the context of these regional realities: the enduring struggle to find a just solution to the Arab-Israeli conflict and the need to balance Syria's pride and self-image with the fact that it is surrounded by a number of larger and more powerful states. Syria will always be sensitive to its position relative to other major states on its borders and just beyond, and any change in its calculation about the desirability or feasibility of acquiring nuclear weapons will be driven not only by security imperatives but also by its perception of its status in the region.

Assessing the likelihood of a Syrian effort to go nuclear requires certain understandings or assumptions about the mindset of Syria's leaders. Do they operate from a position of feeling weak and vulnerable to regional and global powers, or do they believe their own rhetoric about Syria's vaunted role in the region? How realistic is their sense of Syria's weight and influence in the region? Do they believe that they could achieve a major change in their strategic position—through nuclear weapons, for example—without provoking Israeli or U.S. intervention? How much will regime change in Baghdad and the ambitious American agenda in the region affect Syria's calculations?

This discussion examines Syria's nuclear story in all its dimensions. What is the national security context for a possible pursuit of nuclear weapons? What are the practical considerations? How might Syria's decisionmakers determine whether it is feasible? Affordable? Worth the risk? What are the regional drivers that most likely shape Syria's thinking about nuclear weapons? What is the most likely course Syria will take, and what options are available to the international community to prevent the spread of nuclear weapons to Syria?

Syria's Quest for National Security

The 1967 Arab-Israeli war is a useful baseline from which to evaluate Syria's national security position and perspective. The war demonstrated and reinforced a more confident and militarily competent Israeli state, and it marked a generation of Arab leaders who struggled to find explanations for Arab weakness and strategies that would reverse some of the perceived injustices. From Syria's perspective, as a poor country dependent on its security relationship with the Soviet Union, the fact that the Soviets did little to help Syria in the 1967 war and later worked openly with the United States to end the 1973 war in a stalemate, meant that Syrian leaders had no choice but to consider alternative security policies that relied less on the Soviet Union.

As Hafez el-Asad rose to and consolidated power in the 1960s, he sought to achieve a measure of independence from the Soviets. According to a Syrian expert, Asad did not want to "Leninize" the Syrian state and tried to keep Syria's options open. In his early years as president, Asad avoided a binding friendship treaty with the Soviets. In 1981, however, the Reagan administration's new articulation of the U.S.-Israeli strategic partnership made it seem a political necessity. Asad presumably understood that he would never be supported by Moscow as robustly as the United States was prepared to back Israel, but the perception of parity was extremely important.[1]

Despite Syria's formal dependence on Soviet military supplies and doctrine, the Syrian-Soviet relationship was disappointing to both parties. The October 1973 war, the first Arab-Israeli war for Asad as president, is a case in point. The Soviets, according to Russian experts, did not approve of Arab plans in 1973 and worked actively with U.S. secretary of state Henry Kissinger to stop the war and prevent the defeat of either Israel or its Arab clients. And while some observers interpreted the two superpowers' move to nuclear alert in the early days of the crisis as evidence of the strength of the patron-client relationships, historical assessments suggest instead that some early miscommunication led to alerts as a precautionary move, but neither side would have contemplated allowing a regional war to escalate. They also assert that the Soviets did not consider Syria or Egypt to be under a Soviet nuclear umbrella or guarantee.[2]

Syrian security also was affected by internal turmoil at home and in neighboring Lebanon, always considered part of Syria's strategic and economic space. Lebanon's fifteen-year civil war began in 1975 and involved Syria in an increasingly tragic and counterproductive entanglement in Lebanese politics. Meanwhile, Syria faced an Islamic insurgency at home that it addressed with singular brutality: an estimated 20,000 civilians in a single city, Hama, were killed in a period of two to three weeks in 1982.

Faced with the relentless rise of Israel's military and political strength, the Soviet Union's unreliability as a strategic patron, and the loss of

Egypt from the Arab camp as a result of the 1978 Camp David Accords, Syrian national security decisionmakers made some strategic choices in an effort to mitigate the imbalance of power. While the rhetoric of "strategic parity" lingered on through the end of the cold war, in fact, Syrian national security doctrine was transitioning to greater emphasis on asymmetric warfare.

First, Syria looked for nonconventional options that would provide a form of deterrent to Israel, since real parity was not achievable. At some time in the 1970s, Syria began to develop a serious chemical weapons program, which did not require total reliance on the Soviet Union or another external patron. U.S. officials publicly acknowledged information on production of chemical warfare agents and munitions in the 1980s.[3] And by the 1990s, Syria's capability was considered mature and extensive in scope, its stockpile reported to include sarin and at least research and development of the nerve agent VX.

Syria's refusal to accede to the Chemical Weapons Convention is linked to the issue of nuclear weapons: it has consistently argued that it will only address the issue of reducing the threats in the region from all weapons of mass destruction in a comprehensive way, and it will not consider forgoing its own undeclared capabilities unless its principal adversary, Israel, is also obliged to do so with respect to its nuclear weapons.[4] President Hafez Asad indirectly acknowledged his chemical weapons program in responding to a journalist during a summit meeting with Egyptian president Hosni Mubarak: "Those who have nuclear weapons do not have the right to criticize others regarding any weapon, which they possess. If they want disarmament, we should start with nuclear ones. We, the Arabs, are ready to get rid of other weapons."[5]

The second strategic choice was to change the tone and content of Syria's relationship with the United States. The most dramatic manifestation was the decision to join the U.S.-led coalition in the 1990–91 Gulf war. While the decision was also consistent with Asad's calculations regarding Arab world politics, since he judged that Iraq's invasion of Kuwait was harmful to the Arab cause and must be reversed, it was nonetheless a high-risk and important choice. It signaled more clearly that Syria no longer expected its foreign policy to gravitate around Russia and wanted to ingratiate itself with the victor of the cold war, the United States. With U.S. support, Syria's service in the coalition was rewarded with a flow of more than $2 billion from grateful Gulf states. Syria benefited from the experience in military terms as well.[6]

The relationship with Washington improved, often in awkward fits and starts, with some in the U.S. foreign policy establishment remaining highly skeptical of Syria's ability to change its core policies toward Israel and Palestine, in particular. Syria was not able to persuade Washington to remove it from the terrorism list, and it resented what it perceived as an unwillingness to accept Syria as a normal state. Israeli and American experts attribute this failure to fully normalize ties to Syrian attitudes; in one memorable phrase attributed to Shimon Peres, Asad divorced war but did not marry peace. He was a strategic bachelor.[7] So Syria also spent the early years of the post–cold war period hedging its bets, investing in advanced missile technology, for presumably both conventional and chemical warheads. Today it possesses and produces Scuds of varying ranges, reportedly capable of carrying chemical warheads.[8] This growing missile capability generated a strong reaction in Israel and led to some new security thinking about how a future Israel-Syria conflict might play out. For example, the Golan Heights lost some of its strategic value, since Syria seemed to have acquired a capability to attack Israeli cities and the vital coastal strip without the need for a ground offensive.[9]

A third strategic calculation was Syria's cultivation of several terrorist organizations: the Palestinian Islamic Jihad, the Popular Front for the Liberation of Palestine-General Command, and Hamas, as well as intermittent ties to non-Palestinian groups such as Kurds or Armenians. Included on the U.S. state sponsors of terrorism list since 1979, Syria has come to see these relationships as cards it can play in its interactions with Israel and the United States. It can ratchet up the pressure on Israel when it deems it desirable and scale it back when compelled to do so. It has, on a few dramatic occasions, expelled known terrorist leaders of either marginal Palestinian or non-Arab groups (for example, the Turkish Kurdish PKK) when those relationships were seen as liabilities and were directly threatening the interests of the state. Syria argues that it can control its terrorist clients and that it plays a constructive role in managing the problem of cross-border terrorism. It has also made it clear that it will retain these ties until it has received something of greater value in return. Some experts believe that Syria would more readily give up its sponsorship of terrorism than its weapons of mass destruction.

Changing Dynamics with Israel

The most critical measure of Syria's perception of its security has been its policy toward Israel. The last decade has witnessed some remarkable change in Syria's willingness to engage in a new and higher-risk interaction with Israel, yet a lasting breakthrough has not occurred. At several points in the 1990s, it was possible to imagine a new relationship between Israel and Syria that would have dramatically reduced Syria's incentives to acquire nuclear weapons. The literature on the peace process in the heady years following the Madrid conference of 1991— which launched formal negotiations between Israel and Syria, Jordan, and the Palestinians—conveys the careful and tentative way in which Syria's decisionmakers were working to conceptualize the hard security aspects of a possible settlement with Israel. A benign interpretation would suggest that Syrian policy was shaped by a need to maintain the facade of balance or military parity with Israel, and by the view that arms control was a bargaining chip to get to a fair settlement. In this context, Syria was sensitive to issues of reciprocity, equality, and gradualism, and envisioned a possible trade between its chemical weapons and Israeli nuclear weapons.[10] Others take a more cynical view and believe that Syria has postured on arms control with the express purpose of damaging Israel's international image and warning Arabs to avoid any easy concessions to Israel. Syria may have never believed that arms control would work or would serve Syria's interests.

The most far-reaching bilateral negotiations took place in the mid-1990s during the first Clinton administration and were briefly resumed in the final year of the second Clinton administration. According to American officials who facilitated the process, President Asad of Syria, in failing health, was preoccupied with securing his son's succession and did not respond agilely when Israeli prime minister Ehud Barak belatedly specified what Israel was willing to offer in terms of territorial withdrawal from most of the Golan Heights. President Asad, only weeks before his death, told President Clinton at a hastily arranged summit in Geneva in March 2000 that he would not accept an American-brokered deal that would have led to an Israeli-Syrian peace treaty. Bashar Asad has more recently told reporters that Geneva failed because the United States and Israel did not deliver on their promises. Both versions are credible. Firsthand accounts of participants in those high-level talks are now appearing but will probably not fully explain why Syria did not seize the opportunity to transform its security and its relations with Israel and the United States.

Here Comes the Son

Hafez el-Asad died in June 2000 after nearly thirty years in power. He left a legacy of strict adherence to the abstract principles of the pan-Arab cause, even as his fellow Arab leaders were willing to adapt to a changing geostrategic landscape in the region. Recognizing that Israel would retain a nearly permanent superiority over any of its Arab neighbors, Asad seemed to prefer to play for the history books than bring change and risk to his society. One sensed that he was threatened by the political consequences should Syrians experience how much freer and more successful economically Israel actually was.

His son Bashar, trained as an ophthalmologist, seemed a reluctant politician, but a myth quickly grew around his youth, his western education, and his apparent fascination with computers and modern technology. Many speculated that Bashar would be an advocate of change, would seek to open Syria up both socially and economically, and might be more comfortable than his father dealing with Israelis and Americans. But by his second year in office, the heroic myth was starting to fade.

It has been noted that Asad senior, despite his perceived provincialism, received a European education during the French mandate in Syria, whereas his son attended Ba'athi schools and did not leave for training in the UK until he was an adult, by which time his political values were probably already formed. Diplomats who have served in Damascus see the new president as either captive of his father's entourage or a true believer in the strong security state that he inherited. They also consider him more impulsive than his cautious, risk-averse father, and increasingly prone to the same insularity that characterized the senior Asad's rule. Bashar briefly flirted with more liberal politics but quickly clamped down when Syrian sophisticates actually expressed political opinions. Syria has new political prisoners.

Since Bashar Asad assumed power, other regional changes have reinforced Syria's perception that a negotiated settlement with Israel is neither possible nor desirable under current circumstances. The Israeli electorate is shifting to the right, Palestinian politics have not yet moved conclusively to a new political order, and the lack of progress toward statehood has provoked a second Palestinian intifada that has endured intermittently since 2000, with the new dimension of suicide bombings creating more casualties and great psychological trauma for both Israeli and Palestinian societies. Syrian decisionmakers probably see the conflict as far from resolution and may be planning for many more years of low-grade tension with Israel; they probably do not imagine war as likely, although proxy war through terrorism will continue. They are more likely focusing their energies on retaining some deterrent capability vis-à-vis Israel than on amassing sufficient military power to defeat Israel.

It is less clear whether the failure to resolve the Palestinian problem is viewed in Damascus as harmful to Syrian interests or a useful excuse that postpones any need for Syrian leaders to revisit what compromises they might be willing to make to reduce the threat from Israel. Syrian leaders are known to hold the Palestinian leadership in low esteem, and many Syrians believe that the Palestinian drama is a diversion from the greater Israeli-Arab struggle. But Palestine also provides a near-permanent justification for Syrians to view the geopolitical conditions in the region as not ripe for change.

It also is important to consider how success in the Israel-Palestine conflict would affect Syrian thinking. An accelerated peace process in which new Palestinian leaders were able to negotiate with Israel or international mediators without Syria would most likely generate a negative reaction in Syria. This reaction would manifest itself both as public disdain for what would be seen as a bad deal and as private anxiety about Syria's diminishing ability to control the timing of change. Early 2003 efforts by Syria to engage the United States in the peace process did not bear fruit, and as the security environment in the Israel-Palestine arena continued to deteriorate, Syria took a more critical stance, including sponsoring UN resolutions condemning U.S. and Israeli policies.

The U.S.-led ouster of the Ba'athi regime in Iraq in April 2003 has generated a new crisis for Syria's sense of national security. Saddam Hussein and the elder Asad had developed a mutual loathing, and Syria joined the U.S.-led coalition to oust Iraq from Kuwait in 1990, but relations between Iraq and Syria had improved in the new millennium. Syria was frequently accused of violating UN sanctions by permitting trade and dual-use items to be shipped into Iraq, and the government in Damascus was in the awkward position of holding a UN Security Council seat when the council voted on Iraqi noncompliance in November 2002.[11] It was able to join in the consensus after considerable lobbying by France and Russia; but five months later, it held to a firmly antiwar position when the United States tried to obtain new Security Council support for its forcible disarmament policy, and it was absent for the May 2003 resolution to lift sanctions against Iraq. That resolution, UN Security Council Resolution 1483, also endorsed U.S.-U.K. occupation of Iraq, established a development fund as the successor to the oil-for-food program, and pledged to revisit the mandates of the UN arms inspections under the auspices of the UN Monitoring, Verification and Inspection Commission and the International Atomic Energy Agency (IAEA).

Since mid-2003 Syria has found itself in a new and uncertain security situation. It has been accused by the United States of harboring fleeing

Iraqi officials from the Saddam Hussein regime, assisting illicit trade, and possibly sheltering illegal weapons or other assets of the defeated regime. It is still in the doghouse over its support for Palestinian terrorists, and Israel's October 2003 raid against alleged camps on Syrian soil could well trigger a new phase of regional tension. Its chemical and biological weapons programs have been cited as causes of serious concern; the nuclear issue has also been the focus of some controversy as the Bush administration spars with intelligence experts over how to characterize the status of Syrian programs.[12] The Syrian government now finds itself as the new Iraq—a target of harsh criticism and demands for change in many aspects of its national policies. The regime remains brittle and unable to respond with agility to the glare of international attention. Secretary of State Colin Powell visited Damascus in early May 2003 and told the traveling press corps that Syria had promised to consider the U.S. concerns about weapons of mass destruction, harboring fugitives from Saddam's regime, and border and trade issues. Powell also pointedly said it was not the time to consider a weapons-free zone in the Middle East, one of President Asad's solutions to the regional security problem. By year's end, the administration signed into law the Syria Accountability and Lebanese Sovereignty Restoration Act of 2003 (P.L. 108-175), which calls for at least two new sanctions against Syria for a series of concerns, including its weapons of mass destruction programs.[13]

The Quest for Nuclear Technology: Cause for Concern?

Absent its neuralgic regional context, the chronicle of Syria's pursuit of nuclear technology and its relationship with the IAEA might not attract much attention. Syria joined the nonproliferation regime early and over thirty years has taken advantage of many technical support services the IAEA provides non-nuclear states. IAEA records indicate more than sixty technical projects in Syria, ranging from agricultural, medical, and energy-related research, and training activities. But the precarious regional security environment has prompted experts to exercise extra scrutiny over Syria's efforts over many years to acquire nuclear training and technologies. It is still at the early stages of developing in-country reprocessing capacity, and from the public record, it seems unlikely that Syrians have reached an advanced level of nuclear expertise that could be applied to a weapons program.

Syria signed the Nuclear Non-Proliferation Treaty (NPT) in 1968 and ratified it a year later. Public documents indicate that for Syria, this was a political act rather than the outcome of a formal deliberative process involving military and security officials. Syria's participation in the NPT may have been shaped both by Syria's close relationship with the Soviet Union, an early sponsor and advocate of the NPT, and by its concerns about Israel's evolving nuclear status. It must also be said that Syria entirely lacked the financial resources and the technical know-how to launch a serious nuclear weapons effort. Press and academic analysis of Arab-Israeli issues in the 1970s contain virtually no speculation about a possible Syrian interest in nuclear weapons. It seemed nearly beyond the imagination of regional experts. As for Syria, it saw itself as a small, third world country that had to rely on the great power system for its security.

Syria's ambassador to the United Nations Conference on Disarmament spoke of Syria's non-nuclear status: "The more third-world countries can have faith in the nuclear powers, the more developed becomes their feeling of security, and therefore the chances of easing of tensions. . . . My small country is justified in attaching the greatest importance to these guarantees [referring to SC resolution on guarantees for non-nuclear states]. We see close to our borders an Israeli nuclear reactor being built.[14]

Syria did not take advantage of any of the early safeguards arrangements and did not sign the bilateral protocols with the IAEA. It was one of forty-eight countries that failed to make the eighteen-month deadline to sign bilateral agreements with the IAEA on their plans to pursue peaceful nuclear energy programs. There was, according to one expert, no prejudice against countries that did not sign the protocols, and those states were presumed to have no activities to report.[15]

In 1976 Syria established the Atomic Energy Commission in Damascus, which conducted studies relating to possible acquisition of nuclear power reactors. It also was the institution that led negotiations with France over the possible transfer of nuclear technology.[16] According to current information, there is an organic link between the Atomic Energy Commission and a larger organization, called the Scientific Studies and Research Center (SSRC), an ostensibly civilian agency that is widely assumed to be linked to the military establishment and to be the locus of most new research and development on nonconventional weaponry and of missile-related technology exchanges and imports. The SSRC was created in 1971 and shortly thereafter was authorized by the president to work with the army to coordinate, for instance, its research and development with the military. Its director-general acquired ministerial rank in 1983. According to one account, it was SSRC experts who determined that a chemical and biological program was more suitable to Syrian means and capabilities than a nuclear program.[17]

In the early years of its relationship with the IAEA, Syria manifested little ambition in the nuclear technology arena. In the 1970s, it had only six projects with the IAEA: five relating to radioisotopes in animal science and agriculture, and one in nuclear energy. This level of activity did not stimulate much outside interest in whether Syria was contemplating a nuclear weapons program; Syria's relationship with its superpower patron provided important conventional support to maintain a semblance of deterrence for Syria vis-à-vis Israel. The Soviet Union neither encouraged Syria to seek capabilities comparable to Israel's nor did it have an explicit or implicit nuclear umbrella over Syria.

According to press accounts, Syria in the 1980s attempted to engage a wide range of countries in deals to acquire nuclear power reactors, presumably for energy purposes, but there is little discussion of Syria's end goals. One report refers to a 1988 attempt to create a $3.6 billion reactor program with technical help from the Soviet Union, Belgium, and Switzerland.[18] Other reports refer to unrealized plans involving France, the Soviet Union, Argentina, and India. In each case, plans went awry, due to subtle political pressures exerted on prospective sellers and to Syria's inability to provide necessary financing. Syrian officials would complain about unfair treatment as compared to Israel, which enjoyed various kinds of technical cooperation despite mounting evidence of its nuclear status. But Syrian officials were unable to offer clear explanations of the purposes of proposed reactor programs that would assuage international concerns.

Syria's first success in acquiring a nuclear reactor was the 1991 purchase of a thirty-kilowatt neutron source minireactor from China. This class of reactor is understood to have no military application; both China and Syria went through the proper international procedures, and Syria signed a safeguards agreement with the IAEA. The IAEA has conducted inspections at the site in Dayr al Jajar and does not appear to consider this reactor a cause for concern.[19]

Syria's efforts to purchase a nuclear reactor from Argentina continued through the first half of the 1990s. Syria negotiated the purchase of a ten-megawatt reactor, which Argentina did not deliver, reportedly under pressure from the United States. By 1994 Syria was threatening to file suit against Argentina, and a year later, Argentina announced it was pulling out of the deal.

Since 1997 Syria's most active and publicly acknowledged nuclear relationship has been with Russia, which has prompted new questions about whether Syria might have a military purpose in mind in pursuing nuclear technology. In early 1998, the two states signed an agreement on the peaceful use of nuclear energy, and the next year, Russia publicly announced the decision to provide one light-water reactor to Syria, subject to IAEA safeguards. After Syrian vice president Abd al-Halim ibn Said Khaddam's visit to Moscow in January 2003, both sides reported that military technology cooperation was a central part of the bilateral relationship.

Russian experts believe that the senior leadership in the Soviet Union and the Russian Federation has never supported and does not currently support Syrian acquisition of nuclear weapons. Russia makes a clear distinction between its goal of preventing any proliferation of nuclear weapons in the Middle East and an economic interest in small reactor sales that would fall short of contributing directly to weapons know-how. Experts concede that the Russian individuals or entities pursuing economic opportunities are not focused on the security implications and that the Russian state has yet to develop strong mechanisms to enforce a restrictive policy towards nuclear-related sales. Russian policy in the Middle East region can be characterized as confused, with no comprehensive strategy and probably without sufficient attention to developing effective counterproliferation policies. President Putin understands the importance of preventing the spread of nuclear technology, but his bureaucracy may not.[20]

This relationship initially stimulated only a low-to-moderate level of bureaucratic attention in the U.S. government, with formal expressions of concern but no proactive policy efforts comparable to the Russia-Iran nuclear relationship. Policymakers did not think the situation warranted a more aggressive approach, in part because they assumed Syria would recognize all the practical constraints on its freedom of action in pursuit of anything beyond a research reactor. American officials reported not sensing a high level of alarm from Israel, and that also contributed to the relatively mild tone and quality of early American démarches.

Syria has continually disavowed any ambition to use a nuclear research program for eventual weapons application. It has retained the high-minded public posture that was present in its early statements when it joined the NPT, has consistently referred to the need to make the Middle East nuclear free as part of a comprehensive peace settlement, and has made it clear that it would only consider a ban on chemical weapons in the context of a ban on nuclear weapons as well.[21] Most experts also believe that Syria's acquisition of other nonconventional weapons is for defensive and deterrent purposes, not for offensive use.[22] Syria has found other international vehicles to underscore its antinuclear weapons stance, as part of what it sees as its moral high ground in relation to Israel. In the deliberations over the International Criminal Court (ICC), for example, Syria proposed that the use or threat of use of nuclear weapons be included as a war crime in the ICC statute.[23] In 2003, as its two-year rotation on the Security Council was winding down, Syria pressed for a new resolution calling for a Middle East nuclear-free zone. Several permanent members, including the United States, found the Syrian initiative ill timed and ill conceived. Nonetheless, at a year-end summit at Sharm el-Sheikh, President Asad and Egyptian president Mubarak tried to capitalize on Libya's surprise announcement that it would give up its weapons of mass destruction (WMD) by putting new pressure on Israel and by revalidating their long-held rhetorical position that all states in the region should forgo weapons of mass destruction.

But Syria's public discourse in favor of arms control has rarely been the determinant of American policy in this difficult and complicated relationship. U.S. policy toward Syria has been driven principally by concerns about the peace process and Syrian involvement with anti-Israel terrorist groups; its nuclear activities generally have drawn less attention. In 2002 Washington began to shift its approach, using harsher language with respect to Syrian-Russian nuclear cooperation and expressing concern that any enhancement of nuclear know-how would improve Syria's options to pursue a weapons program. In turn, Syria has complained about the treatment of declared non-nuclear states by the nuclear powers, and the way their access to technology is hampered while Israel continues to receive various forms of technology transfer despite its abnormal nuclear status. In the last two years, Syria has been named consistently in unclassified testimony by diverse administration officials when listing countries of concern regarding nuclear proliferation. Undersecretary of State John Bolton has referred to Syria as on a second tier of countries of concern, right after the "axis of evil" states Iraq, Iran, and North Korea.[24] Israeli officials have been sensitive to this change in tone in U.S. public pronouncements and appear to be concerned that there may have been a shift in Syrian nuclear activities that will demand a more proactive

Israeli approach and greater coordination between Washington and Tel Aviv. In September 2003, Undersecretary Bolton repeated his concerns about Syria's nuclear research and development program, its advanced chemical weapons capabilities, and its presumed efforts to develop an offensive biological weapons capability. Bolton also linked Syria's WMD status to its proven ties to terrorist organizations and hinted at possible new sanctions against Syria or "other measures."[25]

It is important to consider that the Russian relationship may not be the sole or most important element in the nuclear equation for Syria if the regime is in the early stages of hedging its bets on a nuclear weapons program. Syria has a steady relationship with North Korea for missile technology and ties to Iran and Pakistan that could have a secret nuclear dimension, although most experts are quite skeptical that the politics with Iran or Pakistan would permit any clear and unambiguous nuclear sharing. Thus there are risks to focusing too much on a scenario based primarily on the Russian connection, which is relatively transparent and under IAEA guidelines, while a more clandestine relationship might more directly help Syria develop weapons options.

According to Ze'ev Schiff, one of Israel's most respected security experts, it is possible "that a number of Arab countries would one day form a coalition aimed at obtaining nuclear weapons."[26] Schiff further speculates that multiple Middle Eastern states armed with nuclear weapons could well induce a change in Israel's nuclear policy, but not necessarily in the direction the Arabs may hope: Israel could decide to give up its nuclear ambiguity, test, and decide to produce tactical nukes.

What can be said about how a decision to seek a nuclear weapons capability would be made? The young President Asad is only now being tested on national security matters; the tension between Syria and the international community over the fall of the Iraqi regime will provide useful insight into President Asad's crisis management skills. On the one hand, he has inherited his father's capacity to defy the international community on grounds of principle, but whether he possesses the steely nerves and ability to decide by avoiding decisions that characterized his father's rule has yet to be proven. Some believe Bashar Asad is more impulsive than his father and could well miscalculate under stress.

President Asad has retained some of his father's close advisers, particularly in the national security realm. Key figures who are still in the inner circle include Vice President Abd al-Halim ibn Said Khaddam and Deputy Prime Ministers Lieutenant General Mustafa Talas and Farouk al-Shara. These three survivors are all Sunnis, deeply loyal to preserving the status quo, and not likely to be generators of new and bold thinking on security matters. Other early holdovers from his father's era include prominent members of the Alawi sect: Ali Aslan, elevated to chief of staff of the army in 1998 (now retired), and internal intelligence chief Brigadier General Bahjat Suleiman. Their role may be to preserve continuity in the system while the president also turns to his generational cohorts and family circle: key confidants include brother-in-law Major General Assef Shawkat (military intelligence) and younger brother Maher (Republican Guard). It is unknown whether any of these advisers, old and young, have strong views on nuclear weapons and on new directions for Syria's national security policy.[27]

Decisionmaking is not transparent in Syria, but power is heavily concentrated around the president. The various security services play an important role in quelling any internal dissent but do not appear to be important sources of new ideas or strategic planning. One would expect that only Bashar Asad could initiate the process to consider whether Syria should change its nuclear weapons policy. Asad himself has provided some insight into how he makes decisions:

> I believe the basis (for decision-making) is an accurate analysis of the reality, since when the analysis is correct, the decision is, necessarily, correct. Hence, all my attention is directed at analyzing the reality, which includes different and complicated variables, both in the domestic front and in the relations with Arab and foreign countries. . . . It is important to gain respect, rather than sympathy. It is important to go with firm opinions and decisions. . . . We look for partnership in interests that will be useful for both sides.[28]

Regional Catalysts

If Syria were to change its nuclear weapons policy, its decision would most likely be shaped principally by perceived changes in the regional environment that were considered harmful to Syria's interests and to regime survival. It is worth imagining how shifts in the fortunes of other regional players or problems might affect Syrian calculations.

Iraq: Consequences of Regime Change and Disarmament

Regime change and disarmament of Iraq can be expected to have a profound impact on Syria, on its leaders' sense of security and on the way they consider Syria's national security requirements and options. An

American logic would lead to the conclusion that Syrian leaders would now assume it was simply not in their interest to make any further investment in a nuclear program, given the willingness of the U.S. government to use all necessary means to disarm a hostile state. Would Syrians think the same way?

It is possible that a small circle around Bashar Asad would see this tumultuous moment as an opportunity for Syria to regain a prominent leadership position, with the new Iraqi leadership's presumed close ties to the West undermining Iraq's role as the firebrand, vanguard state. Such an impulse would appear anachronistic to the West, but for the isolated Syrian leadership, the lure of Arab glory may prove powerful. The rhetoric of defiance against America's occupation of Arab lands resonates well with some Arab publics and converges with Syria's long preoccupation with Israeli occupation of Palestinian land. Such a mindset might deepen leaders' conviction that a clandestine nuclear program was an appropriate investment in Syria's strategic arsenal. It would likely push Syria to seek an outside partner or patron that would support a clandestine program, but identifying such a partner would be increasingly difficult. North Korea might be the most promising candidate, in terms of willingness to withstand the costs of discovery.

The Syrian regime could take a more cautious course, hunkering down and trying to stay out of the limelight. In such a scenario, decisionmakers would suspend any nuclear activity and seek to assure and be reassured by the IAEA and the safeguards process. The leadership might be more proactive in publicizing its cooperation with the IAEA and encourage new visits to its nuclear-related facilities.

But the Syrian regime may not have such options. Were the Bush administration to pursue an aggressive strategy against Syria, the leadership would find it hard to maintain its careful balancing act. The regime in Damascus, while seemingly secure, may be more brittle than readily apparent. The demise of the Ba'ath in Iraq may be causing invisible fissures in the political system, and with considerable pressure, it is possible that the still-neophyte Asad could misplay his hand, alienate key groups, and find that his base of support is weak and fragmenting.

Regime change in Syria is not inconceivable, although it would occur with considerably less preparation among opposition forces inside and outside the country than was the case in Iraq. Should the Asad clique of Alawis fall from power or flee, a prolonged period of chaos and uncertainty would occur. For the sake of argument, let us posit that power would eventually shift to a Sunni leader of some standing, whether civilian or military, and that figure would pledge to cooperate with the West and build more open and transparent political institutions and processes.

Would such a Syria eschew nuclear weapons? It is conceivable that such a leader could come to power having privately or publicly pledged to the international community that weapons of mass destruction would be foresworn. But it is hard to imagine any Syrian government reversing course on all its advanced weapons programs as long as the Arab-Israeli conflict persisted and the Golan Heights had not been returned to Syrian sovereignty. Domestic pressures might also be a factor, with a new leadership anxious to consolidate power by playing a powerful patriotic theme. Here, assuming it is not too late, the international community and the United States in particular might succeed in getting Syria to revalidate its no-nukes pledge but leave its other WMD programs for negotiations, in the context of future arms control talks with all the parties in the region including Israel.

Iran: Crossing the Nuclear Threshold

Should Iran succeed in completing its nuclear project and declare a nuclear weapons capability, Syria would face a confusing and conflicting situation. On the one hand, its devotion to the Arab cause would compel it to share a sense of anxiety and encirclement that other Arab regimes would feel more sharply than Syria, the Arab state that has closest ties to Iran. The formal reaction would be muted in part because Iran would likely work to dampen any hostile Arab reaction and would probably conduct active diplomacy to reassure Arab states that this achievement was not directed at them.

On the other hand, some believe that Syria, more than other Arab states, would be untroubled by an Iranian nuclear capability due to the virtual strategic partnership the two states have enjoyed since the early 1980s, when Syria forged an "enemy of my enemy" alliance with Iran and developed a mutually beneficial relationship that has included cheap oil for Syria and transshipment routes for Iranian weapons to Hezbollah and other anti-Israel forces. They suggest Syria would see an Iranian bomb as a useful deterrent against Israel and a newly assertive Iraq and as an important constraint on U.S. freedom of action in the region. According to this analysis, Syria would simply "not care that much."[29]

But Syria's identity derives from its national myth, deeply rooted in the pan-Arab ideal.[30] Despite decades of setbacks, Syrian rhetoric clings to images of shared Arab power and greatness. A nuclear-powered Iran, in addition to a nuclear Israel, would constitute yet another blow to the Arab psyche. Even if Iran were successfully managing rapprochement with most Arab states, deep fear of Iranian hegemony would persist. In the absence of any countervailing Arab power, Iran could achieve a more dominant regional position and have considerable leverage over the foreign policies of nearby Arab states. The Shia empowerment taking place in Iraq has made this scenario more compelling; Iran may ultimately wield considerable influence over a new Iraq, which would have consequences for other Arab states.

Syria could thus see an Iranian nuclear program as a challenge to its long-term strategic interests and conclude that nuclear weapons were critical to creating a more level playing field between the Arabs collectively and their powerful non-Arab neighbors (Iran, Israel, and Turkey). This logic would not necessarily require that Syria seek a nuclear capability alone. Were it determined that Libya, for example, were the most advanced in its pursuit of a nuclear program, would Syria be able to lead a political effort to coordinate with Libya, Egypt, and others to convert a national program into a regional one? Here Syria would have to rely on its claim to political leadership, its credibility and standing in the Arab-Israeli dispute, rather than on any concrete leverage through resources or coercive powers over the other Arab states.

It is also interesting to speculate whether it would make a difference if Iran had a different government: Would a more democratic Iran with nuclear weapons be seen in Damascus as a greater or lesser threat than nuclear weapons in the hands of conservative clerics? At present, Syria's relationship with Iran is an alliance of nondemocratic forces. The Asad regime is able to work with hardline clerics more easily than with forces for reform, who, if they dominated Iranian politics, would likely insist on greater transparency and would be more successful in relations with the international community. Assuming continuity in Damascus, a more democratic government in Tehran would probably result in deterioration in the tacit Syrian-Iranian alliance. Iran crossing the nuclear threshold, therefore, would be seen as even more dangerous for Syria.[31] In the small circle of individuals who might participate in such a debate, this scenario would probably strengthen the argument of those advocating a nuclear program.

Were Iran to achieve nuclear status and then lose it, either through a peaceful negotiations process or by hostile acts (ranging from special operations to sabotage up to full-scale military action to dismantle facilities), it would send a powerful signal to Damascus. It would make it harder to sustain the argument for expending scarce resources on nuclear weapons and could tip the balance in favor of a more prudent, slow, hedging strategy or total avoidance of considering any nuclear weapons. Syria would likely take seriously the will of the international community to prevent nuclearization of the region and would make a practical calculation that any future investment in nuclear activities would be too vulnerable to loss. For both political and practical reasons, Syria would probably learn the intended lesson.

The Peace Process: Permanent Condition or Subject to Change?

The Arab-Israeli conflict is the single most important factor in shaping Syrian perceptions of its security. The failure to achieve an enduring peace between Israel and its neighbors has been the regime's rationalization for its shortcomings in other requirements of statehood, so much so that one could even posit that success in the peace process would be profoundly destabilizing for Damascus. Since failure in the peace process is never seen as failure for the individual Arab states, it has become a permanent feature of the landscape with no discernible consequences or costs for regime survival. More than any other Arab state, Syria has intellectualized the lack of progress in relations with Israel as a virtue, a reflection of the higher purpose of its society. In is therefore important to imagine how any changes in the peace process would affect the calculations of its decisionmakers.

It is a given that Damascus would justify any movement toward acquiring nuclear weapons as related to the Arab-Israeli conflict. One could easily imagine Syria's ruling circle analyzing the poor prospects for change on Syria's terms, the increasing hardness of Israel's position, the shift to the right of the Israeli electorate, and therefore, the need to prepare for many more years of Israeli occupation of the Golan Heights and other Arab territories. Syria's leaders also fear that the Palestinians could make a deal without them, thus severely reducing Syria's bargaining power and regional influence. This logic might lead Syrian decisionmakers to believe they would accrue more leverage in relation to Israel if they worked to acquire nuclear weapons. Some believe that Syria's motivation might be to bargain away such weapons, that is, to use a weapons program to stimulate new negotiations.

Arabs are increasingly sensitive about the perceived double standard in the international community's virtual acceptance of Israel's nuclear status and its strong opposition to any Arab state's acquisition. Throughout the 1990s, when a slow process of unofficial or quasi-official dialogue began under the auspices of the multilateral working groups set up after the Madrid conference of 1991, Syria was reluctant to participate and avoided the working group on arms control and confidence-building measures. Its rationale was that only after considerable political work had been done to establish parameters of discourse between the states could the sensitive issue of national security capabilities be addressed. It was a cart before the horse problem for Syria: What is the political context for even acknowledging the existence of weapons? What assurances would Syria have that such discussions would be used in a constructive way and not to undermine Syria's ability to protect those assets in the event of renewed hostility?

Would a positive change in the peace process—including new steps to establish a Palestinian state and to freeze or roll back Israeli settlement activity—affect Syria's strategic calculations with respect to nuclear weapons? The Syrian elite must harbor great worries about being left behind should the Israel-Palestine peace process gain momentum. A best-case scenario would be for success in the Palestinian arena to be accompanied or followed by movement on the Israeli-Syrian track and the Israeli-Lebanese track. This would involve resolving territorial disputes, including the status of the Golan Heights, in exchange for gradual normalization of political and economic ties. Such normalization would probably proceed on a slower track than the Israel-Jordan experience or even the Israel-Egypt case, where the mutual acceptance at the leadership level permitted a rapid establishment of social and economic relationships. In contrast, normalization in the Israel-Syria case would likely proceed more gradually, with small interest sections and little tourism or discussion of joint economic ventures for some time. This judgment would prevail even if a more open and liberal government emerged in Damascus, for it will take time to persuade even the most cosmopolitan of Syrians to trust Israelis and to imagine mutually beneficial relationships.

Willingness to address respective weapons of mass destruction programs would emerge even more slowly, although it could well be embraced by Syrian leaders as the ultimate goal of the peace process. At one level, Syrians do want to redress the structural imbalances between Israel and themselves and may sincerely expect one of the fruits of a successful peace process to be a mutual commitment to arms reduction or, at a minimum, greater transparency in discussing the threat environment and national security requirements. Syria would have difficulty accepting any confidence-building process that was seen as asymmetrical, although Israel could argue that it plans for multiple potential adversaries and that any one peace treaty does not eliminate its enduring security requirements. Were Syria to make a similar argument—that is, its need for weapons of mass destruction is not determined by Israel alone but is driven by diverse threats—it could mean that a successful Israeli-Syrian peace process would have little direct impact on WMD programs in the two states. While Israeli decisionmakers might want to seek political normalization for its own sake, Syrian leaders, even in a post-Asad Syria, would be less likely to think a peace deal that had no real impact on Israel's strategic military capabilities was worth the effort.

A more propitious outcome could be achieved if the United States, as the presumed outside facilitator, were to build into a peace process between Israel and Syria the expectation that there would be a final chapter: a regional negotiation with all the earlier peace beneficiaries to build a new regional defense and security pact. It would require all parties to engage in confidence building, greater transparency, and various risk reduction activities: in short, a rich menu of techniques designed to maximize the benefits of peace, to demonstrate an improved regional threat environment, and to create conditions for reduced defense spending and eventual arms control. This would require a prior understanding with Israel, which seems unlikely to agree to any early discussion of its nuclear status but might be willing to find topics of mutual interest to begin the process. A deeply skeptical Syria would need to be convinced that Israel's nuclear program would eventually be on the table, in order for Syria to proceed at all and for it to be forthcoming on its own programs, such as those for chemical weapons.

As of early 2004, it is difficult to imagine this favorable scenario taking hold. It assumes a greater flexibility on the part of Israeli decisionmakers and it requires a bolder and more risky approach for the government in Damascus than either is willing to display. It does raise the question of whether a Syria believed to be in the process of seeking nuclear weapons would be more likely to consider this path than a Syria that had chosen to avoid the nuclear weapons path.

What Might Change Syria's Policy?

There is no solid, publicly available evidence to suggest that Syria is currently embarked on a nuclear weapons program—recognizing, of course, that it is a closed and secretive regime that has not been transparent about other aspects of its national security capabilities, including its clandestine missile relationships with North Korea, Pakistan, and China and its indigenous work on chemical and biological weapons. It is possible that Syria has already begun a discreet exploration of what research and investment in manpower would be required for a future decision to acquire nuclear weapons.[32] However, its public discourse and rhetoric, as well as an outsider's assessment of the practical constraints on a nuclear program, suggest that there is, for now, no change in Syria's policy—that is, to remain a member in good standing of the Nuclear Non-Proliferation Treaty, to seek a regionwide ban on weapons of mass destruction, and to remain ambiguous about its non-nuclear programs until there is a regional process in which it might be willing to consider reciprocal arms reductions.

Syria today cannot be confident about its security future, given the intractability of the Arab-Israeli dispute, the enduring special ties between the United States and Israel, the change in regional dynamics as a result of the fall of Saddam Hussein, and the pressure it is under to distance itself from the regional forces opposing the U.S. agenda in the area. Syria will be pressed to decide whether its interests are served by working with forces seeking an alternative to U.S. hegemony, or by demonstrating its moderation on reform and regional security. Choosing the wrong path could lead to severe economic and possibly military penalties. This moment presents acute dilemmas and choices for a leadership that is still untested.

In addition to the real security challenges it faces, Syria is sensitive to its role compared to that of its neighbors. Thus its leaders are likely to give special weight to any developments in the region that might adversely affect Syria's standing as a "leading" country in the Arab world. Should any of its neighbors cross a threshold with respect to nuclear weapons, it would likely have a profound effect on Syrian deliberations over its own nuclear status.

The United States and its potential actions to thwart the ambitions of small states have surfaced in 2003 as another critical driver. Before the Bush administration's "preemptive war" doctrine and the successful toppling of Saddam Hussein's regime in Iraq, Syria believed it could manage its relations with Washington with a careful mix of constructive cooperation and continued intransigence on a small number of issues over which Damascus hoped we would "agree to disagree." Until 2003 it almost certainly believed that it could successfully avert any deep destruction in bilateral ties by careful choices, such as agreeing to counterterrorism cooperation against al Qaeda (not against favored Palestinian groups) and supporting UN action against Iraq (the November 2002 UN Security Council Resolution 1441, which was arguably not an endorsement of military action). But its relationship with Washington is more precarious now, and it must carefully weigh its actions according to the reaction they may provoke in the capital of the single superpower.

In sum, the drivers that would probably have the most influence in shaping Syrian decisionmaking with respect to nuclear weapons are

—national security requirements deriving from power imbalances in the region,

—prestige considerations that might make Syria perceive a loss of status in the region because of other countries' nuclear advances,

—and a new dynamic in relations with the United States that could change Syria's calculations about how much freedom to maneuver it enjoys and whether regime survival is at stake.

The current tumultuous international environment could convince Syrian leaders that their small, insecure state should consider new options to deter hostile powers. It is likely that decisionmakers would be influenced both by the recent history of India and Pakistan, which endured sanctions for less than a year after the 1998 testing and are now virtually acknowledged as nuclear powers, and by the critical case of North Korea, which may demonstrate that a country gains leverage internationally by beginning the nuclearization process. It seems plausible that Syrian leaders would conclude that they should at least explore their options, to keep up with regional and global trends. This would conform with a pattern observed in other states to at least "hedge" on the nuclear option, as permitted by membership in the NPT.[33] The *realization* of this possible ambition, however, seems less likely today than before 2003, given the demonstrated willingness and ability of the United States to impose disarmament on a Middle Eastern state and the greater scrutiny likely to be given to Syria in particular.

One can develop a low-probability narrative of how Syria under Bashar Asad might come to favor developing a nuclear option. It would be triggered by a perception that Syria's ability to sustain its regime was deteriorating because of regional trends including a more aggressive American policy that had Syria in its crosshairs. A Syrian loss of other strategic assets—such as giving up support for terrorism or a weakening of its chemical weapons deterrent due to technological changes or other countermeasures—might also feature in Asad's deliberations. But such a decision would need to be implemented with great care with respect to timing, the need to maintain secrecy in the development phase, and cost. Syrian leaders would perhaps work with a trusted external power capable of maintaining operational security; they would try to divert or find resources that might not elicit public scrutiny; and they would almost certainly not provide any hint to their own public of such activities until some early achievements had occurred.

U.S. Options

The United States and the international community have opportunities to shape Syria's incentives and motivations at an early stage, before any serious investment in resources, pride, and politics has occurred. The fluid regional environment and the need for Syria in particular to demonstrate its own intentions with respect to an agenda for reform also offer Damascus an opportunity to use its non-nuclear stance as an asset in engaging the international community and enhancing its own security.

Outside actors wishing to influence Syrian policy should think hard about Bashar Asad's own style and intellectual formation. He may be more responsive to concrete analytical and informational exchanges than his father was. In this sense, helping him bolster his own knowledge base and sophistication about the risks, dangers, and costs of nuclearization might be a useful initiative, not unlike the way in which the U.S. government helped new prime minister Benazir Bhutto come to terms with the realities of her own country's nuclear program.[34] Offering to share information with Asad has its risks, but it might provide for a more open relationship than the ritualistic rhetorical exchanges that took place between his father and U.S. officials.

At present, there are many issues on the U.S.-Syrian agenda. It appears that the George W. Bush administration will place greater emphasis on terrorism and on breaking any unsavory links between Syria and Iraq than on the more long-term issue of weapons of mass destruction. But an integrated approach may be warranted: it is possible that if Syria were to make concessions on other issues, it could have a subtle and adverse impact on Syria's commitment to its WMD programs. It may be important to engage the Syrians on all issues at once.

As is often discussed in the Iran case, it may also be useful to consider what economic incentives can be provided to keep Syria a non-nuclear state. The Syrian economy is not strong, and the international community should look for opportunities to give the Syrians incentives to avoid sanctions and to make clear the consequences of any hints of noncompliance with its NPT obligations. Positive economic carrots will be hard to find when pressure tactics on terrorism and other issues are being applied, but Syria has a mercantile culture and may be receptive to certain kinds of economic and trade arguments.[35]

Syria may be an important case where coercive measures short of war can be effective. Its political and practical ability to pursue a nuclear program in defiance of new rules in the region will be quite limited. The demise of the Ba'athi government in Baghdad increased Syria's political isolation; its defense of Iraq in the months before the war strained its relations with moderate Arab governments who wanted to demonstrate their ability to bridge both the international and the Arab point of view. Syria could choose to defy pressure on its weapons program from the United States and European powers, hoping to generate support as the sole Arab power left to resist new colonialism and defend the Arab cause. Such a stance might win some sympathy both among the Arab elite and on the Arab street, but a more likely reaction from Arab governments would be to urge Syria to comply. Arab incumbents most likely would fear another American military campaign against an Arab state and would not support a defiant Syria bent on a self-destructive path.

There also are practical constraints on Syrian freedom of action. Syria has only two major ports and land routes from Turkey and Iraq; Jordan and Lebanon cannot be considered secure routes for clandestine shipments, with a presumed U.S. military presence monitoring the region actively. Syria's economic dependence on Europe can also be exploited to generate pressure on the regime.

Should the United States find coercive measures short of war ineffective, it would move to military contingencies. As with Iraq, U.S. officials would need to decide whether the objective was limited to setting back a nascent nuclear program, or whether a more ambitious set of goals, from ending Syrian support for terrorism to regime change, was desirable. In military scenarios, the United States would have to weigh the risks of Syrian use of chemical weapons against U.S. forces and the risks of a violent reaction across the region to another U.S. attack on a Muslim and Arab state. It would also have to calculate whether Israel would enter the picture, which would motivate Syrian fighters and the civilian population but also would generate greater losses for Syria in the likely event of its defeat.

Syria will need to decide its priorities in defending its image, its honor, and its security. Can it persuade the United States and others that it is a moderate country, committed to peace and economic reform? Or are domestic and regional pressures pushing it in a more confrontational direction, to associate with those who resist the American agenda? Would Syrian leadership of the anti-imperialist Arab front affect its calculations with respect to nuclear weapons?

The United States also has to weigh where an as yet unproven nuclear contingency ranks in the long list of problems in U.S.-Syrian relations. A narrow approach that puts nuclear weapons back in the taboo box might have a greater chance of success than a more ambitious and comprehensive agenda, but some will argue that the change in Baghdad makes the bold approach worth trying.

Notes

1. This preference for independence is an example of the gap between self-image and reality that marks the Syrian experience: scholars point out that the Syrian military, more consistently than any other Arab army, molded itself after the Red Army, and this Soviet-style management may best explain Syria's battlefield defeats. Michael Eisenstadt and Kenneth M. Pollack, "Armies of Snow and Armies of Sand: The Impact of Soviet Military Doctrine on Arab Militaries," *Middle East Journal*, vol. 55, no. 4 (Autumn 2001), p. 571.

2. Dmitri Trenin, deputy director of the Moscow Office of the Carnegie Endowment for International Peace, interview by author, Carnegie Endowment, Washington, D.C., February 25, 2003.

3. See, for example, testimony by former CIA director William Webster in 1989, as cited in Federation of American Scientists, "Syria—Special Weapons" (www.fas.org/nuke/guide/syria/ [February 2004]).

4. M. Zuhair Diab, "Syria's Chemical and Biological Weapons: Assessing Capabilities and Motivations," *Nonproliferation Review*, vol. 4 (Fall 1997), p. 104.

5. Ibid., p. 105.

6. According to one account, the two insights gained were that advanced fighter aircraft can defeat some technologies and that surface-to-surface missiles provide both political and military advantages. Daniel Pipes, *Syria Beyond the Peace Process*, policy paper 41 (Washington Institute for Near East Policy, January 1996), p. 41.

7. Ibid., p. 79.

8. "Summary of Syria's Chemical and Biological Weapons Program," Carnegie Analysis, *Proliferation News and Resources*, April 15, 2003 (www.ceip.org/files/nonprolif/templates/article.asp?NewsID=4671 [February 2004]).

9. Nonetheless, Israelis make other arguments—the need for surveillance, water rights—in explaining the continued strategic value of the Golan Heights to Israel. See Ze'ev Schiff, *Peace with Security: Israel's Minimal Security Requirements in Negotiations with Syria*, policy paper 34 (Washington Institute for Near East Policy, April 1993).

10. M. Zuhair Diab, "Arms Control and an Arab-Israeli Settlement: A Syrian View," in Richard Eisendorf, ed., *Arms Control and Security in the Middle East* (Washington: Initiative for Peace and Cooperation in the Middle East, 1995), pp. 11–14.

11. UN Security Council Resolution 1441.

12. Douglas Jehl, "New Warning Was Put Off on Weapons Syria Plans," *New York Times*, July 18, 2003, p. A8.

13. For Syria to avoid such penalties, it would need to provide assurances that it has changed its policies and behavior regarding terrorism, Lebanon, and Iraq.

14. UN General Assembly, Document A/C.1/PV.1628 3, December 3, 1968, p. 68-71226/A.

15. Lawrence Scheinman, Center for Nonproliferation Studies, Monterey Institute, interview by author, March 18, 2003.

16. Shai Feldman, *Nuclear Weapons and Arms Control in the Middle East* (Cambridge, Mass.: Center for Science and International Affairs, Harvard University, 1997), p. 67.

17. Dany Shoham, "Guile, Gas and Germs: Syria's Ultimate Weapons," *Middle East Quarterly*, vol. 9, no. 3 (Summer 2002), pp. 53–61.

18. Michael Eisenstadt, "Syria's Strategic Weapons," *Jane's Intelligence Review*, April 2003, p. 168.

19. Feldman, *Nuclear Weapons and Arms Control*, p. 67.

20. Trenin, interview, February 25, 2003.

21. John P. Hannah, *At Arms Length: Soviet-Syrian Relations in the Gorbachev Era* (Washington Institute for Near East Policy, 1989), p. 46.

22. Sami G. Hajjar, "Regional Perspectives on the Causes of Proliferation of Weapons of Mass Destruction in the Middle East," *Comparative Strategy*, vol. 19, no. 1 (January–March 2000), pp. 35–36.

23. Lawyers Committee on Nuclear Policy (LNCP), a national nonprofit educational association that uses national and international law to promote peace and disarmament (www.prop1.org/2000/9711icc1.htm [March 2004]).

24. "Libya, Syria Closer to Weapons of Mass Destruction," Geostrategy-Direct Intelligence Update, *WorldNetDaily*, November 6, 2002 (www.wnd.com/news/article.asp?ARTICLE_ID=29569 [February 2004]).

25. House International Relations Committee, *Syria: Implications for U.S. Security and Regional Stability: Hearing before the Subcommittee on Middle East and Central Asia,* 108 Cong., 1 sess., September 16, 2003.

26. Ze'ev Schiff, "Weapons of Mass Destruction and the Middle East: The

View from Israel," working paper (Houston: James A. Baker III Institute for Public Policy, Rice University, March 2003).

27. Information on Syria's decisionmaking process and players is scant. Some recent references include Murhaf Jouejati, "Understanding Syria's New Cabinet," policy brief (Washington: Middle East Institute, December 18, 2001); Michael Eisenstadt, "Who Rules Syria? Bashar Asad and the 'Alawi Barons,'" *PolicyWatch* no. 472 (Washington Institute for Near East Policy, June 21, 2000); "Bashar's Challenges: The Establishment and Its Discontents," *Estimate*, June 16, 2000; Eyal Zisser, "Appearance and Reality: Syria's Decision Making Structure," *Middle East Review of International Affairs*, vol. 2, no. 2 (May 1998).

28. *Al-Safir* (Lebanon), July 16, 2001, as excerpted in "An Interview with Bashar Asad," *Special Dispatch Series* no. 244 (Washington: Middle East Media Research Institute, July 20, 2001).

29. Kori N. Schake and Judith S. Yaphe, *The Strategic Implications of a Nuclear-Armed Iran* (Washington: Institute for National Strategic Studies, National Defense University, 2001), p. 29.

30. For a fascinating discussion of national myths and how they might feed nuclear ambitions, see Caroline F. Ziemke, "The National Myth and Strategic Personality of Iran: A Counterproliferation Perspective," in Victor A. Utgoff, ed., *The Coming Crisis: Nuclear Proliferation, U.S. Interests and World Order* (MIT Press, 2000), pp. 87–121.

31. A more democratic Iran might also respond to incentives (if it is not too late) to go slow in pursuit of nuclear weapons because other domestic priorities would need resources and attention. In such an event, the impact on Syrian calculations would be reduced.

32. Press reports of debates within U.S. government circles in July 2003 suggest that the fragmentary data about Syria's nuclear activities have not led to clear consensus about its current status or its strategic direction. See, for example, Jehl, "New Warning Was Put Off," and Warren P. Strobel and Jonathan S. Landay, "Intelligence Data on Syria Now Disputed," *Philadelphia Inquirer*, July 17, 2003.

33. An important comparative analysis of the hedging option is found in Ariel Levite, "Never Say Never: Nuclear Reversal Revisited," *International Security* (Winter 2002–03), p. 59.

34. Ibid.

35. The Syria Accountability Act, voted into law in late 2003, will be a further impediment to an incentives-based approach. See *Syria Accountability and Lebanese Sovereignty Restoration Act of 2003*, 108 Cong., 1 sess., H.R. 1828.

CHAPTER 6

Saudi Arabia:
The Calculations of Uncertainty

THOMAS W. LIPPMAN

The Kingdom of Saudi Arabia, rich but vulnerable, forswore nuclear weapons when it acceded to the Nuclear Non-Proliferation Treaty (NPT) in 1988. Previous to that, the Kingdom, like many Arab countries, had declined to sign the NPT because Israel had not done so, but this refusal was a political tactic, not an indication that Saudi Arabia aspired to acquire nuclear weapons.

Accepting the strictures of the NPT is a major commitment on an issue of national importance; yet in Saudi Arabia, the decision to do so was reached within the very small circle of senior decisionmakers around the king, with no public discussion or political preparation. That was to be expected. The most momentous decisions in Saudi Arabia's modern history, including the awarding of the first oil concession in 1933 and the invitation to U.S. and other foreign troops to enter the country in 1990, have been taken by this small group of insiders—usually the king and two or three of his brothers, a handful of trusted senior officials, and perhaps a representative of the religious hierarchy. In an open society, a country saddled with Saudi Arabia's strategic liabilities—vast territory, long coastlines, small population, soft targets, weak armed forces, and dangerous neighbors—might anticipate vigorous public argument about whether to forgo the nuclear option. No such debate could have been expected in Saudi Arabia, where the policymaking process is opaque, the press is deferential to authority, and the public participates only indirectly, if at all.

A decade ago King Fahd ibn Abdul Aziz created a "Majlis al-Shoura," or Consultative Assembly, an appointed group of sixty prominent men (since expanded to 120), which evaluates important government decisions and proposes new laws and regulations. The Majlis reviews major foreign policy issues and has occasionally questioned the foreign minister, but it has no decisionmaking power and cannot compel testimony. In 1988 when the decision to adhere to the NPT was made, not even this toothless organization existed. In the absence of a legislature or any system of governmental checks and balances, the king and his advisers were under no obligation to ventilate their thinking on nuclear policy before a wider audience, and they did not do so. According to Robert Pelletreau, a former assistant secretary of state for Near East affairs who specialized in the Arab world during his State Department career, Saudi Arabia has "excluded even the most senior military officers from national security decisionmaking."[1] For all these reasons, there is no documentary record to shed light on why Saudi Arabia surrendered the possibility of acquiring nuclear weapons. Nevertheless, there is no secret as to the reason for Saudi Arabia's accession to the NPT: it was done to placate the United States. Disavowal of nuclear ambition was a political decision for Saudi Arabia, not a strategic one. It was penance for a transgression against an indispensable patron.

The Chinese Missile Deal

Although it was a longtime strategic partner of the United States and a cold war bulwark against communism, Saudi Arabia incurred the wrath of the administration of President Ronald Reagan by clandestinely acquiring at least thirty-six CSS-2 intermediate-range ballistic missiles from China. (Some estimates put the number as high as sixty.) The missiles, behemoths weighing nearly seventy tons with a range of about 1,900 miles, were stationed in remote areas of the Kingdom and maintained by Chinese crews. Washington was not informed and learned of the deployment only by accident. The Saudis declined to permit American officials to inspect the missiles.

The Saudis have never delivered a persuasive public explanation for their decision to buy the missiles, but from their perspective the acquisition made sense. Elsewhere in the Persian Gulf region, the ballistic missile era had already arrived. The Kingdom's neighbors, Saddam Hussein's secular, antimonarchical Iraq and Ayatollah Khomeini's anti-Saudi revolutionary Iran, were at the time hammering each other with missiles in their long war; Egypt, Syria, Yemen, and, of course, Israel also had surface-to-surface missiles. Saudi Arabia, always insecure and fearful of encirclement, had no comparable capability. "Saudi Arabia was particularly interested in acquiring systems that could hit Tehran, while being deployed outside the range of Iranian surface-to-surface missiles," the military analyst Anthony Cordesman wrote.[2] True to their pattern of equating acquisition with strategy, the Saudis went shopping.

There was no prospect of purchasing intermediate-range missiles from Saudi Arabia's preferred military supplier, the United States, because missiles that could strike Tehran could also reach Israel. The Saudis knew from the hostile reaction in Congress to their earlier efforts to acquire sophisticated weaponry that Congress would never approve a ballistic missile sale even if the Reagan administration endorsed it. China was under no such constraints as a vendor; and while the Chinese were communists and normally not welcome even to visit vigorously anticommunist Saudi Arabia, they had no record of armed invasion of a Muslim country, as did the Soviet Union. As usual in Saudi Arabia, strategic self-interest trumped taboo.

From the American perspective, the Chinese missile deal appeared dangerous and destabilizing in several ways, even apart from the potential menace to Israel. It accelerated the Middle East missile race, demonstrated a streak of independence and duplicity that Washington did not anticipate from Riyadh, and introduced China as an arms supplier to a country that had made opposition to communism a cornerstone of its long relationship with the United States. And most alarming of all, the CSS-2 in its other known deployments carried nuclear warheads. Because of the CSS-2's inaccuracy, it is of little use in striking specific targets and therefore has military value only as a delivery system for nuclear, chemical, or biological warheads, for which precision targeting is much less important than it is for conventional weapons. The arrival of such missiles in Saudi Arabia was seen in Washington as an indication that the Saudis might be secretly pursuing nuclear weapons—perhaps even planning to allow other Arab countries to use them to attack Israel, deploying the feared "Islamic bomb."

The Israelis warned that they might attack the missiles to preclude any possibility that they would face a nuclear-armed Arab foe—a serious concern for Washington, given that Israel had bombed a nuclear reactor in Iraq a few years earlier.[3] American diplomats scrambled to pursue a complicated agenda with several moving parts: persuading the Israelis not to attack, making clear their displeasure with Saudi Arabia without disrupting an important strategic and commercial relationship, and persuading Congress not to cut off arms sales to the Saudis. According to Hume Horan, who was U.S. ambassador in Riyadh at the time, "The Israelis told us, let it be known, that we better do something about those missiles or they would. We told the Saudis that there are nations in the area that are very concerned and threatening to take matters into their own hands."[4] Richard Armitage, then assistant secretary of defense for international security affairs and later deputy secretary of state in the administration of George W. Bush, recalled dressing down Prince Bandar bin Sultan, the Saudi ambassador to the United States who had negotiated the missile purchase, in intemperate language, accusing the Saudis of virtually inviting an Israeli strike.

"I want to congratulate you," Armitage said to Bandar. "This is the law of unintended consequences. You have put Saudi Arabia squarely in the targeting package of the Israelis. You are now number one on the Israeli hit parade. If the balloon goes up anywhere in the Middle East, you're going to get hit first."[5]

Discovery of the missiles ignited a predictable storm in Congress. Within a few weeks, bipartisan majorities in the House and the Senate had approved resolutions opposing the sale of ground support equipment for Airborne Warning and Control System (AWACS) planes the United States had sold to Saudi Arabia in 1981. The administration postponed formal notification to Congress of a new sale of $450 million worth of military equipment. Secretary of State George P. Shultz traveled to Riyadh to seek a gesture that would quell the anti-Saudi clamor.

The United States was "highly concerned" about Saudi deployment of the CSS-2, Assistant Secretary of State for Near East Affairs Richard Murphy told Congress at the time, because "we had known it only in its nuclear capable mode in China." According to Murphy, who had previously served as ambassador to Saudi Arabia, "The Saudis took what was available in deciding to join the group of missile-possessing states in the region that included Iran, Iraq, Syria, as well as North Yemen and Egypt, among others. Iran's repeated use of missiles against Kuwait and the firing of a Scud missile at Kuwait's oil facilities on April 20, 1988, as well as attacks upon Iraq and reports about possible attacks upon Saudi targets simply underscored the justification in Saudi eyes for their acquisition of a system to counter missiles in unfriendly hands."[6]

Murphy told the House Foreign Affairs Committee that the Saudis "have assured us, at the level of the king, that they do not have and they have no intention of acquiring either nuclear or chemical warheads." The assurances took the form of a letter from King Fahd to President Reagan, Murphy said. The decision to sign the NPT represented "a change in longstanding Saudi policy and a serious international commitment which should further assure neighboring countries of Saudi Arabia's ultimate interest in stability in the region," Murphy told the committee.[7]

The NPT decision was made specifically to assuage Washington's anger over the Chinese missile deal, Murphy said years later. "We were damned upset and very worried, and they were aware of our shock. They had pulled a remarkable fast one. Our satellites hadn't been watching. Who would look for Chinese missile sites in the Saudi desert?"[8]

Edward Walker, who was chargé d'affaires at the U.S. embassy at the time of these conversations, said Saudi accession to the NPT "was a direct quid pro quo. We said, 'We can forget this if you sign.'"[9] Prince Bandar "cut a deal," according to a U.S. diplomat who was involved in the negotiations. "The missiles could stay, but the king would promise never go to nuclear and would join the NPT."[10]

(Unfortunately for Ambassador Horan, word of this agreement reached his embassy only after he had delivered a strongly worded protest over the missiles directly to the king, demanding that they be removed. News of the arrangement brokered by Bandar made it appear that Horan—of whom the Saudis were suspicious anyway because his father was a senior Iranian diplomat—did not have Washington's backing. At the king's request, Horan was removed, an episode that is still talked about in the State Department's Middle East bureau.)

Sixteen years after the secret acquisition, it is still not clear exactly why Saudi Arabia wanted the CSS-2 missiles if it truly had no intention of putting nuclear warheads on them. The best explanation seems to be the most obvious one: they felt they had to have some surface-to-surface missile capacity to protect themselves against dangerous neighbors. During Operation Desert Storm in 1991, the Saudis planned to fire some of the missiles at Baghdad in retaliation for Iraqi Scud attacks on Riyadh. Whether the Chinese would have assented to this is not known because American officials talked the Saudis out of a retaliatory strike. The U.S. argument was that the inaccurate missiles would probably cause extensive casualties among Iraqi civilians and Saudi Arabia would forfeit the moral high ground. In any case, the plan to strike Baghdad with the missiles confirmed that they did not have nuclear warheads.[11]

The missiles, now obsolete and of dubious military value, remain in Saudi Arabia, still fueled and maintained by Chinese crews because the Saudis have never been trained to operate them. To this day, the Saudis have declined to allow Americans to inspect them, but they are widely regarded by military analysts as having little if any military value unless they have been secretly upgraded. One recent study said they are "basically junk. The Chinese in essence hoodwinked the Saudis into buying an antique missile system worthless without its nuclear warhead."[12] Another said the missiles are "largely an exercise in political symbolism and have limited war-fighting capability."[13] Nevertheless, those missiles are fundamental to any discussion of whether Saudi Arabia might reconsider its decision to forswear nuclear weapons because if Saudi Arabia did acquire nuclear warheads, the CSS-2s would be the most likely delivery system. In missile-proliferation negotiations with the Clinton administration in 2000, the Chinese agreed not to "assist any country in any way to acquire ballistic missiles capable of delivering nuclear weapons," but they insisted that their arrangement with Saudi Arabia was "grandfathered."

The Official Saudi Line: A Nuclear-Free Middle East

Unlike some other countries that decided not to acquire nuclear weapons, Saudi Arabia did not give up an active program when it adhered to the NPT. Arms control specialists who believe that states seeking nuclear weapons do so for one of two reasons—security or status—said that the Saudis did not have either motivation. The country was never considered a proliferation threat before the acquisition of the CSS-2s; it lacks the technological expertise, industrial base, and disciplined commitment required to develop an indigenous weapons capacity. All analyses of Saudi Arabia's military and technological capabilities assume that nuclear weapons could be acquired only by purchase from another country—probably Pakistan but, in light of recent developments, possibly North Korea, which can be expected to sell to anyone with enough money if its nuclear defiance of early 2003 results in actual warhead production.

Saudi Arabia's defense minister, Prince Sultan ibn Abdul Aziz, who is second in line to the throne and one of the most powerful men in the Kingdom, has declared that Saudi Arabia "has a well-known policy which is against nuclear weapons in principle."[14] Its official position on the subject is to refrain from acquiring nuclear weapons and from helping other countries to do so, and to promote a nuclear-free zone in the Middle East—a goal the Saudis say cannot be achieved because Israel refuses to cooperate. This line was articulated in a statement to the United Nations on May 14, 1999, by Fawzi Shobokshi, Saudi Arabia's ambassador:

"While many regions around the world are achieving success in establishing nuclear free zones as a result of the cooperation and recognition of the need for peaceful co-existence in those regions, we find that the international [and] regional efforts to make the Middle East a nuclear free zone are fruitless," he said. "This is the result of the refusal of one country, Israel, to co-operate with these efforts. . . . Israel continues to refuse to join the Nuclear Nonproliferation Treaty or to subject its nuclear facilities to inspection by the International Atomic Energy Agency."[15]

Prince Sultan told an interviewer in that same year that "Israel has to give up this [nuclear] force and destroy it and sign the treaty concerning the non-use of weapons of mass destruction to which the countries of the region adhere."[16]

During international negotiations leading to an indefinite extension of the NPT in 1995, which in effect made its nonproliferation commitments permanent, Saudi Arabia was one of several Arab states that complained about U.S. tolerance of Israel's position. In the end, the Saudis agreed to indefinite extension only after adoption of a resolution that called on the nuclear weapons states to exert "their utmost efforts" to achieve a Middle East free of weapons of mass destruction.[17]

In truth, Saudi Arabia's statements about Israel are rhetorical folderol, issued to burnish the Kingdom's Arab credentials without requiring any action. The Saudis understand perfectly well why Israel is not prepared to make such a commitment. If Saudi Arabia were to consider the nuclear option, Israel would not be the reason.

Saudi Arabia has never signed the safeguards agreement that the International Atomic Energy Agency requires of NPT states, nor has it acceded to the Comprehensive Test Ban Treaty. However, Saudi Arabia's refusal to embrace all chapters of the nonproliferation canon should probably not be interpreted as coy evasion aimed at masking equivocal policies. It is more likely a continuing protest against Israel's abstention from international nonproliferation regimes rather than any hedging on the part of the Kingdom. According to the IAEA, "As far as the agency is aware, Saudi Arabia does not have any significant amounts of nuclear material or material in a nuclear facility that would require inspection under the Agency's standard comprehensive safeguard agreements." Nevertheless, the IAEA "is actively encouraging States [including Saudi Arabia] to conclude NPT safeguards agreements and additional protocols, through correspondence, seminars, workshops and other contacts."[18]

To demonstrate the irrevocability of their disavowal of nuclear weapons, some countries have taken steps such as enacting legislation or writing a nuclear ban into their constitutions. Such a course is not available to Saudi Arabia, where there is no legislature and the constitution is the Koran. Other than the strictures written into the NPT, the only formal barrier to the pursuit of nuclear weapons is the commitment of the monarch. Nonetheless, no credible evidence has ever surfaced that Saudi Arabia has sought to develop or acquire nuclear weapons, or that it desires to do so. A 2001 study by the Carnegie Endowment for International Peace ranked potential proliferator states as "high risk" such as North Korea; "renunciations" such as South Africa and Ukraine; and "abstaining countries" that could develop nuclear capability but chose not to do so, such as Taiwan. Saudi Arabia was not included in any category.[19] "No one considers Saudi Arabia a serious, or even minor, proliferation risk," according to Joseph Cirincione, director of Carnegie's nonproliferation studies.[20]

Moreover, military experts with direct knowledge of Saudi Arabia's armed forces and defense policies agree that nuclear weapons are not on the Kingdom's strategic agenda. "The Saudis don't want nukes, they have other priorities," said Bernard Dunn, who as a U.S. Army colonel was defense attaché at the American embassy in Riyadh from 1999 to 2002. "They have no desire for them and there's no evidence of any change. The U.S. intelligence community is not even thinking about this."[21]

Another American, a strategic analyst and military consultant who has lived in Saudi Arabia for decades, said, "In all honesty, in many years here, I have not once heard a discussion about acquiring WMD [weapons of mass destruction]. The country is strictly in a defensive posture and procurements have been geared accordingly—to stop incoming and that's it."[22]

"They can't afford the nuclear option and there's no real strategic need for it," said another American who closely follows Saudi military and strategic affairs. "Their other needs are so great, it's hard to imagine. Crown Prince Abdullah [their apparent and de facto ruler because of the prolonged illness of King Fahd] has stated that his opposition to WMD is total, on principle, and we believe him."[23]

The credibility of Saudi disclaimers of interest in nuclear weapons has been reinforced by the fact that Saudi Arabia, unlike Iran, has never sought to acquire commercial nuclear power generating plants. While such plants are nominally restricted to civilian use and are permitted—even encouraged—by the Nuclear Non-Proliferation Treaty, they are often viewed with suspicion by opponents of proliferation because they introduce fissionable materials and nuclear engineering expertise into environments where they would otherwise not exist. Because energy, in the form of crude oil and natural gas, is the one natural resource Saudi Arabia possesses in abundance, no proposal for nuclear power would be credible.

The Kingdom has, however, created an Atomic Energy Research Institute. Little has been written about this institute in the mainstream press, but it is not clandestine. Its research projects and the names and telephone numbers of its scientists are published on the website of the King Abdul Aziz City for Science and Technology.[24] It was established in 1988, with this announced goal: "To adapt the nuclear sciences and technologies and utilize them in support of the economic, industrial and agricultural plans of the Kingdom."

The first objective listed is "drafting a national atomic energy plan and supervising the implementation of the plan." Some of the research projects deal with topics that would be directly relevant should the Kingdom decide to move toward nuclear development for either civilian or military use, such as radiation monitoring and the transportation of radioactive material. Over the past decade, Saudi scientists have published peer-reviewed papers on such topics in professional journals and presented papers at international nuclear energy conferences, often in collaboration with scientists from Taiwan, a far more technologically advanced society. There has been no indication that these studies are anything more than academic exercises. In addition, some hospitals in the Kingdom have nuclear medicine programs using radioisotopes purchased from European suppliers, but radiological tools of diagnosis have never been seen as an avenue to the kind of nuclear expertise required for a weapons program.

The Khilewi Affair

A cardinal rule of intelligence and threat assessment is that one does not know what one does not know; thus it is theoretically possible that Saudi

Arabia has a clandestine development or acquisition program that has eluded detection by the most rigorous analysts. As closely as Saudi Arabia has been linked to the United States for more than fifty years, there have been several episodes, in addition to the CSS-2 affair, in which the Saudis have been less than candid with the Americans and less than forthcoming with information. These include the investigation of the 1996 Khobar Towers bombing and the initial response to the September 11, 2001, terrorist attacks. No possibility should be ruled out on the basis that no American has ever come across it. Could not a reasonable case be made in the Saudis' minds for the development of an alternative security relationship with a major power should relations with the United States deteriorate? A possible candidate for such a role would, of course, be China, a nuclear power that has a close relationship with Saudi Arabia's ally Pakistan and a growing need for imported oil. Sufficiently remote from the Persian Gulf not to pose a direct threat to Saudi Arabia and no longer part of any international communist movement, China could theoretically be an attractive partner. This is not to say that Saudi Arabia is actually seeking such a relationship with any country other the United States, but to be unaware of any such outreach is not to exclude it from the realm of possibility.

The surreptitious acquisition of the CSS-2 missiles and the establishment of the nuclear research institute are just two of the tantalizing and curious episodes that from time to time have stirred suspicion and speculation about Saudi Arabia's true intentions. Another was the affair of the so-called Saudi defector, Muhammad al-Khilewi.

Khilewi was a Saudi diplomat posted to the United Nations, where his portfolio included nonproliferation issues. In 1994 he left his post and asked for political asylum in the United States. He stirred a brief sensation with media interviews in which he claimed to possess documents proving that Saudi Arabia had tried to buy research reactors from China as part of a clandestine program to acquire nuclear weapons. He showed a *New York Times* reporter a document purporting to be a 1989 letter from the China Nuclear Industry Corporation to a nephew of King Fahd that said it was willing to sell small research reactors, known as miniature neutron source reactors, to Saudi Arabia. It was not clear whether the Chinese were seeking a new market or whether the Saudis had initiated the contact—assuming the letter was genuine. The Saudis asserted at the time that Khilewi's documents were forgeries, created by Khilewi on government letterhead stationery he used for his own purposes.[25]

Khilewi also asserted in media interviews that Saudi Arabia had provided financial support to Iraq's nuclear program. This allegation has never been proved but neither has it been effectively refuted. Saudi Arabia had openly promised to pay for reconstruction of Iraq's Osirak reactor after Israeli warplanes destroyed it in 1981, and the Kingdom supported Iraq throughout its long war with Iran in the 1980s, a time when Iraq had an advanced program to develop nuclear weapons.

Despite the flurry of excitement at the time, nothing has happened since 1994 to confirm any of Khilewi's allegations about a Saudi Arabian weapons program. Few if any of the purported documents have been made public. Khilewi stopped talking, at least in public.[26] In fact, the skimpy record indicates that the source of Khilewi's unhappiness with his government's nuclear weapons policy was not its efforts to acquire them but its accession to the NPT.

Shortly after his "defection," Khilewi sent a letter to Saudi Arabia's grand mufti, Sheikh Abdul Aziz bin Baz, with copies to Crown Prince Abdullah, members of the country's Consultative Assembly, and a London-based opposition group, the Committee for the Defense of Legitimate Rights, in which he listed assorted demands and complaints about his homeland. One of the demands was "refraining from entering into any unlimited and permanent international agreements especially nuclear agreements and refusing to make our land a dumping or testing ground for nuclear and other weapons."[27]

In a 1998 interview with *Middle East Quarterly*, Khilewi said, "It was clear to me that the current system of nuclear proliferation is wrong. The NPT is based on selective proliferation. It has a double standard. I myself am against nuclear proliferation in Saudi Arabia, Pakistan, and Iraq as I am against it in America, Israel, and India."[28]

These comments are virtually indecipherable, but they cannot be read as credible allegations that Saudi Arabia has a clandestine nuclear program. Senior officials of the Clinton administration who were responsible for Mideast affairs at the time Khilewi sought asylum, including Robert Pelletreau of the State Department and Bruce Riedel of the National Security Council, said they found nothing in Khilewi's debriefings to back up the media reports about a Saudi nuclear program. "There was no there there," Pelletreau said.[29]

There was another flurry of speculation in 1999 when Saudi Arabia's defense minister, Prince Sultan, became the first prominent foreigner to visit Pakistan's missile factory and its nuclear weapons facilities at

Kahuta. Neither country has ever revealed full details of that visit, but Pakistan denied that it had anything to do with nuclear weapons. The issue arose again in the late summer of 2003 when a British newspaper, the *Guardian*, reported that the Saudis had embarked upon a "strategic review" that included a reassessment of the Kingdom's non-nuclear posture. According to the newspaper, Saudi officials "at the highest levels" were studying options that included acquisition of a nuclear deterrent, development of a protective alliance with an existing nuclear power, and a new attempt to create a nuclear-free Middle East.[30] The credibility of this article was dubious: none of the reported "options" represented new ideas, it cited no sources for its information, and no other major publication confirmed the report. Uncharacteristically, the Saudis issued an immediate and unequivocal denial, in the form of a letter to the newspaper from Turki al-Faisal, the Saudi Arabian ambassador to Britain. "Although, like all governments, we constantly reconsider our policies in the light of events, we do not have and are not considering acquiring nuclear weapons," the letter said. "Saudi Arabia is a signatory to the non-proliferation treaties and would like these adopted by all. There is no atomic energy programme in any part of the Kingdom."[31]

A similar episode occurred a few months later, after a visit to Pakistan by Crown Prince Abdullah. A few politically conservative newspapers in this country and Britain reported that Abdullah and the Pakistanis had reached a secret pact in which the Saudis would send free oil to Pakistan in exchange for nuclear weapons technology. Given that Pakistan was already receiving Saudi oil at a deep discount without such technology transfers, such an agreement seemed unlikely, which may explain why the supposed pact was never confirmed by any mainstream news publication, as it would have been if it existed. State Department officials brushed off the reports.

Saudi Arabia's Strategic Vulnerability

Despite the official disclaimers, episodes such as the Khilewi affair and Prince Sultan's visit to Kahuta aroused media speculation about possible nuclear ambitions because there is a certain plausibility to the idea that Saudi Arabia might aspire to have at least a small nuclear capacity as a deterrent to aggression. There appears to be no possibility that Saudi Arabia—as long as it is ruled by the al-Saud family—would ever consider nuclear weapons for aggressive purposes because the Kingdom has not threatened any of its neighbors since the last border issues were settled decades ago; but deterrence is another matter. While the 2003 ouster of Saddam Hussein eliminated a hostile government in neighboring Iraq, the Kingdom's strategic weaknesses have not been ameliorated since the Chinese missiles were deployed in 1988, and its capacity to defend itself against the most powerful of its potentially hostile neighbors, Iran, has diminished.

With territory of more than 800,000 square miles (reference works differ as to the exact size), Saudi Arabia is a vast country, four times the size of France. Its capital, Riyadh, is in the center of the country, but otherwise its population centers and economic assets are concentrated along the Persian Gulf and Red Sea coasts. The oil installations that provide most of the country's revenue and the desalination plants that produce 70 percent of its drinking water are visible, vulnerable targets that could be devastated in short order by air assault or seaborne attack. Despite Saudi Arabia's large territory, it would be difficult for the population and the armed forces to retreat from the coasts and regroup in the interior because the interior is virtually uninhabitable; cut off from the coasts, the Saudis would be without food or water. Military supply lines would be severed.

Unlike Israel or Taiwan, Saudi Arabia does not face any external threat to its existence as a country. To the extent that the country is coterminous with the House of Saud, however, the existential threat could be perceived as real. If a transformation were engineered by a theocratic Iran or a fully democratic Iraq, or by domestic insurgents, the country of Saudi Arabia would remain but the government would change—in fact, the entire organizing principle of the Saudi state could change. Any discussion of the acquisition of nuclear weapons under the current Saudi leadership must recognize that the purpose would not be to preserve the existence of Saudi Arabia but to perpetuate the rule of the House of Saud.

For decades the Saudis have confronted real threats to their security, none of them involving the Arab conflict with Israel. Repeated conflicts with their neighbors and threats from external forces—Egypt and Yemen in the 1960s, the Soviet Union during the cold war, Iran in the 1980s, Iraq in 1990—have reinforced the sense of vulnerability inherent in a country of enviable assets and relatively small population.

In 1979, when Afghanistan was controlled by a pro-Moscow left-wing government but had not yet been invaded by Soviet troops, Secretary of State Cyrus Vance distributed to regional diplomatic posts a secret cable summarizing U.S. intelligence assessments of Saudi Arabia's strategic position: "The Saudis interpreted the Marxist takeover of Afghanistan last year as part of a Soviet-oriented campaign to encircle the Persian Gulf and the Arabian peninsula with radical regimes in preparation for the subversion of the conservative, oil-rich monarchies in the area. The Ethiopian revolution and the Marxist coup in South Yemen are seen in Riyadh as other parts of the Soviet effort to seize the oil wealth of the Middle East."[32]

The Iranian revolution of 1979 brought to power a regime even more threatening than communism, a menace to Saudi Arabia from the right rather than the left, challenging the very legitimacy of the House of Saud and its claims to primacy in Islam as custodian of Islam's sacred sites in Mecca and Medina. The Saudis watched in bafflement as the United States stood aside and let the Pahlavi regime, a virtual creation of Washington, be swept away—a development that seems to have permanently undermined Saudi confidence in American assurances. With the overthrow of the pro-Western Shah of Iran and his replacement by a rigorously anti-Western theocratic regime led by the charismatic Ayatollah Khomeini, Saudi Arabia faced across the narrow Persian Gulf a powerful, cohesive, well-armed, and similarly rich antagonist with more than four times the population. The outbreak of war between Iran and Iraq diverted this threat, but only temporarily. Today the menace of communism has evaporated, but the threat of encirclement by aggressive, anti-Western Islamic militancy that would target the House of Saud as a tool of the United States has replaced it. This threat would be exacerbated if a militant Shiite Islamic state emerged from the political confusion of postwar Iraq.

In an evaluation of Saudi Arabia's security position for the Congressional Research Service more than two decades ago, Richard M. Preece wrote, "Saudi perceptions are strongly influenced by a pronounced feeling of weakness, insecurity, a sense of encirclement by hostile forces, and an awareness that the armed forces would likely meet with severe difficulties in hostilities with neighbors such as Iraq, Iran, Israel, or even [South] Yemen."[33]

Knowing that their armed forces could never match the manpower of their larger neighbors, Preece observed, the Saudis sought to address their vulnerability by acquisition of large numbers of sophisticated, mobile weapons: "The premise underlying modernization of the armed forces—particularly the air force—was that they must achieve superior technology and a sophisticated air defense system with maximum mobility and firepower to compensate for limited manpower."[34]

The result of these concerns was a military buying spree of staggering proportions. Preece noted that an annual military budget of about $1 billion at the time of the 1973 Middle East war had leaped to $10 billion in the second half of the 1970s and peaked at $20 billion in 1981, after the fall of the Shah and the Soviet invasion of Afghanistan. And yet, "despite the size of these expenditures, Saudi defense forces are constrained by shortages of manpower, a lack of training and technological background, and illiteracy. There is a need for training in the operations, maintenance and managerial fields, for development of communications and the infrastructure, for new equipment to replace old existing equipment, and for incentives in the recruitment and retention of personnel."[35]

Most of what Preece wrote in 1981 is true in 2004, except that today Sudan would probably replace Yemen as a source of Saudi anxiety. By the end of the twentieth century, according to the State Department, Saudi Arabia was spending 13 percent of GDP on defense (compared to 8.9 percent in Israel and 4.5 percent in Pakistan).[36] Yet two decades of acquisition and training since Preece's analysis have not overcome Saudi Arabia's strategic weaknesses—especially because much of the investment in equipment and training has gone to the Saudi Arabian National Guard, an internal security force, rather than to the regular army and air force, and more than half of all defense spending for the past twenty years has been for facilities, such as ports, barracks, and hospitals, rather than for armaments. "No other country in the developing world has received so few actual arms per dollar," according to Anthony Cordesman.[37]

Saudi Arabia spent some $290 billion on defense from the mid-1980s through the mid-1990s.[38] Yet as 2003 began, it was the virtually unanimous assessment of military specialists in Riyadh and Washington that Saudi Arabia—despite its F-15 fighters and Abrams tanks and Bradley fighting vehicles—could not defend itself against a serious assault by Iran or Iraq, with armed forces more than twice as large.[39] Weaknesses in training, operations, logistics and maintenance, as well as fuzzy and undisciplined strategic thinking, have undermined whatever advantage the Saudis' massive purchases might have represented. "The military is a shambles, a hollow force not capable of defending the country, and in their heart of hearts they know it," said a senior American analyst in Saudi Arabia. "They have acquired expensive toys they can't maintain, but their thinking on strategic issues is shallow."[40] The regular armed forces "are in worse shape now than when they didn't show up at Khafji," in the first battle of Operation Desert Storm in 1991, an American officer said.[41]

Furthermore, Saudi Arabia no longer has an abundance of cash to throw at its defense problems—the $55 billion cost of Desert Storm and relatively low oil prices since the mid-1980s have resulted in chronic budget deficits—and the Saudis are cutting corners. American defense contractors interviewed in Riyadh in the fall of 2002 said the Saudis are transferring maintenance contracts away from original equipment suppliers, such as Boeing and Raytheon, to lower-cost local concerns that are not up to the task.

"With the chronic deficits and their need to keep the royals supplied with cash, they prefer to give contracts to lower bidders—local firms—who can't possibly do the work for that amount of money," said the Saudi Arabia representative of a major U.S. defense supplier. "But so what? The military is not operationally sound and deployable anyway, so what do they lose by giving the contract to somebody who comes in at $300 million under a projected budget amount?"[42]

Such comments could be dismissed as special pleading by a losing bidder, except that nobody disputes his assessment. As well equipped as they might be on paper, the Saudi armed forces could not defend their country against an all-out assault by Iran or Iraq; they would require and expect help from the country that has guaranteed their security for six decades—the United States. But if the Saudis doubted that the United States would come to their rescue in extremis, might they not wish to acquire a weapon that would deter their potential enemies?

States of Uncertainty

In the late spring of 2004, Saudi Arabia faces multiple, overlapping uncertainties involving several countries that could affect the ruling family's security decisions. It is certainly possible to envision a combination of events that would lead the country's decisionmakers to seek the putative security of at least a nominal nuclear deterrent.

These uncertainties begin with Saudi Arabia itself. The king, crippled by a stroke, has for several years ruled in name only. The de facto ruler and designated successor, Crown Prince Abdullah, turns eighty-one in 2004, and the next in line, Prince Sultan, the defense minister, is only a year younger. There is no clear line of succession beyond them. A House of Saud riven by an internal power struggle might offer a tempting target of opportunity for a hostile neighbor. If such a split led to the overthrow of the House of Saud by Islamic extremists taking their cue from Osama bin Laden or some like-minded fanatic, the country would almost certainly attempt to go nuclear. Bin Laden has said as much: "It is the duty of Muslims to possess these weapons."[43]

The country's economic problems could also enter into the calculations. Saudi Arabia's population growth is rapidly outpacing growth in GDP. Unemployment is widespread among the young. Two decades of efforts to diversify the economy away from petroleum have produced only modest results; absent a sustained oil price boom beyond the 2004 runup, the country has no way to generate substantial increases in revenue. In that environment, the era of multi-billion-dollar purchases of weapons systems has slipped into the past. According to the State Department, Saudi Arabia's military spending declined by almost 22 percent from 1998 to 2000; Saudi Arabia's purchases of American equipment under the Foreign Military Sales program declined from more than $25 billion in 1992 to less than $2 billion in 2000.[44] The biggest purchase of aircraft in the 1990s consisted of Boeing passenger jets for the national airline, not military planes.

In an analysis of Saudi Arabia's military force structure published by the U.S. Army's Foreign Military Studies Office at Fort Leavenworth, Kansas, C. A. Woodson wrote that the Saudis "emerged from Desert Storm sobered by the realization that their force structure development goals were not commensurate with the regional threats that they confronted. Accordingly, they candidly identified shortcomings, and carefully planned for their elimination. Witnessing first hand the technological advantages of modern warfare, particularly those possessed by the United States, they aspired to the deterrent capabilities that they afforded." However, according to Woodson, these aspirations were thwarted by a lack of money: "Today, fiscal shortcomings, precipitated by the dramatic mid-1980s decline in global oil prices and exacerbated by the costs of Desert Storm, together with normal problems of inadequate absorptive capacity for manning new technology, have hamstrung ongoing Saudi efforts to build effective deterrent capabilities against both secular enemies such as Iraq and Iran and the rise of political Islam."[45] That being the case, might not the clandestine purchase of a few nuclear warheads represent a relatively economical insurance policy against the country's multiple hobgoblins? After all, as Michael Eisenstadt has written, Pakistan's 1998 nuclear tests proved that "the atom bomb *is* 'the poor man's atom bomb.'"[46]

The second country of uncertainty is Iran. As the zeal and aspirations of the 1979 revolution fade into memory and a new, post-revolution generation seeks greater personal freedom, Iran is in ferment. Relations between Iran and Saudi Arabia have improved markedly since the 1980s, when Iran's anti-American, anti-Saudi agitation and Saudi Arabia's support for Iraq in the Iran-Iraq war poisoned relations to the point that even the pilgrimage to Mecca was disrupted. Relations reached their nadir during the 1987 pilgrimage to Mecca, when 402 people, mostly Iranians, were killed in clashes with Saudi police after the Iranians staged a political rally.

The two countries now cooperate civilly, if not always in full agreement, on matters of mutual interest, such as the pilgrimage, oil price management through OPEC, and the stabilization of Afghanistan, but inherent tension between Shia Iran and Sunni Saudi Arabia is never far beneath the surface. Regardless of what new leadership emerges in Iran over the coming decade, the country's overt development of nuclear power and nuclear technology will be source of anxiety across the Gulf in Riyadh, as well as in Washington and Jerusalem.

Russia is assisting Iran with the development of a commercial nuclear power plant at Bushehr. The United States objected strenuously to this arrangement, arguing that even if a nuclear plant was legitimately required for Iran's domestic electricity needs, it was ill advised because it would give the Iranians technology and expertise they need to develop a suspected clandestine nuclear weapons program. The inherent weakness in the U.S. position was that the Russia-Iran deal was legal under the terms of the NPT, which provides for parties to the treaty to share civilian nuclear technology with non-nuclear signatory states in exchange for their commitment not to seek nuclear weapons. In theory, countries that forswore nuclear weapons would still have access to the benefits of civilian nuclear technology, including nuclear power, because the declared nuclear states would help them acquire it. This is precisely what is happening in the Bushehr project.

It may be, as arms-control skeptics have argued, that the entire international network of nuclear proliferation controls was bound to unravel eventually anyway because it runs contrary to history: every weapon since the slingshot has been copied or acquired by those who felt threatened or diminished by its existence. Nevertheless, until now the NPT has restrained all signatory countries except North Korea. Russia's nuclear assistance to Iran has been depicted by Washington as a virtual invitation to Iran to circumvent the treaty.

The Russians, looking for hard-currency export markets, were not dissuaded by Washington's protests. Russia and Iran insisted that the Bushehr project was strictly for the production of nuclear power, no different from plants in other NPT signatory states in Europe and Asia. Moreover, the contract between Russia and Iran calls for the spent nuclear fuel from Bushehr to be sent back to Russia, which would ensure that Iran could not reprocess it to extract plutonium. Without the spent fuel, Iran would have no source of fissionable material for plutonium-based weapons.

Whatever assurance this arrangement may have provided, however, was shattered by revelations in early 2003 that Iran is much closer to an indigenous fissionable material capability than had been thought. Inspectors from the International Atomic Energy Agency discovered that Iran is well along on construction of a gas centrifuge uranium enrichment facility that could produce weapons-grade, highly enriched uranium by 2005. Iran then announced that it would produce uranium from its own mines and confirmed its enrichment program. Development of such an enrichment capability would place Iran within fairly short reach of the ability to produce a uranium-based weapon. Moreover, if Iran pursues plutonium-based weapons, the development of an indigenous nuclear fuel cycle—not dependent on Russian supplies—would presumably leave Iran free to do as it wished with the spent fuel, including reprocessing to extract plutonium.

According to Chas M. Freeman, a former U.S. ambassador to Saudi Arabia, senior Saudi officials have said privately that if and when Iran acknowledges having, or is discovered to have, actual nuclear warheads, Saudi Arabia would feel compelled to acquire a deterrent stockpile.[47] As George Tenet, the director of Central Intelligence, told Congress in early 2003, "Demand creates the market. The desire for nuclear weapons is on the upsurge. Additional countries may decide to seek nuclear weapons as it becomes clear their neighbors and regional rivals are already doing so."[48] Saudi Arabia could become one of those countries if it felt sufficiently intimidated. Iran's agreement at the end of 2003 to allow surprise international inspections of its nuclear facilities could assuage the fears of its neighbors, but it is too soon to tell whether Iran truly intends to back away from nuclear weapons.

The third country of uncertainty is Iraq, the once-friendly Arab neighbor that invaded Kuwait in 1990 and threatened to keep going into Saudi Arabia. Like everyone else, the Saudis are in the dark about what kind of Iraq will emerge from the ashes of Saddam Hussein's regime. The principle of "better the devil you know than the devil you don't know," along with the mandatory ritual obeisance to Arab solidarity, underlay Saudi Arabia's strenuous efforts to avert a U.S.-led war to overthrow the Iraqi dictator. As was predictable, the Saudis announced that they would not permit U.S. military operations against Iraq from facilities in Saudi Arabia, then quietly assented to virtually all American requests for operations from those same facilities. Now that Saddam Hussein is in U.S. custody and Iraq is groping its way toward some new form of government, the risks perceived by Saudi Arabia from Iraq could increase rather than diminish.

An Iraq fragmented along ethnic lines—Sunni Muslims, Shia Muslims, and independence-minded Kurds in the north—could engender the same kind of conflict that devastated Lebanon in the 1970s and 1980s and provoke just the sort of regional instability that the Saudis dread. An Iraq held together by some powerful and charismatic new strongman—an outcome that cannot be ruled out, despite President Bush's insistence that it will not happen—could be driven to seek vengeance against Saudi Arabia for its military ties to the United States. An Iraq dominated by an anti-American Shiite religious hierarchy allied with Tehran, which is a distinct possibility, would be a direct threat to the House of Saud—and potentially a nuclear-armed one.

Even the most benign of all possible Iraq outcomes projected by Washington—the rise of a truly democratic, representative secular government in Baghdad, receptive to new ideas and encouraging free expression—could be perceived by Riyadh as threatening because radical ideas, more dangerous than troops, might infiltrate across the Iraqi-Saudi border. Nuclear warheads provide no defense against domestic unrest, but the House of Saud could regard their acquisition as a prestige-building exercise that could head off some criticism. This would be a bread-and-circuses approach, in which the leadership could reinforce its legitimacy and burnish its Arab nationalist and Islamic credentials by acquiring superweapons.

The final country of uncertainty is the United States. For more than fifty years, Saudi Arabia understood that it could rely on Washington to protect it from external threats, even though the two countries have never had a formal mutual defense agreement. Every president from Franklin Roosevelt to Bill Clinton stated a commitment to Saudi Arabia's security, and the United States has long been the principal trainer and supplier of the Saudi Arabian armed forces. For decades the basic bargain of the relationship—the United States received Saudi oil and Saudi support in the struggle against communism in exchange for U.S. protection and American technology and investment—survived every strain, including the Arab oil embargo of 1973–74, irreconcilable differences over Israel, and the Chinese missile deal. Whether that bargain can survive the events of September 11, 2001, and their aftermath is an open question.

Saudi Arabia is in the uncomfortable position of being dependent for its security upon a country whose citizens fear and mistrust the Kingdom because of the participation of Saudis in the September 11 terror attacks and the Saudi record of financing Muslim extremists worldwide, while at the same time that very dependence upon the United States is the primary reason Osama bin Laden and his grim legions wish to overthrow the House of Saud. Dependence on the United States for security has been at once the House of Saud's greatest bulwark against external threats and its greatest political liability domestically and in the larger Arab world.

As horrified as Americans were by the September 11 attacks and the possibility of Saudi complicity, the Saudis have been shocked by the American response. In their view, the Americans they believed were their friends were all too eager to assume collective guilt, imposing visa restrictions and other security requirements even on Saudis with long histories of peaceful travel to the United States. Every American visitor to Saudi Arabia in the past two years has endured pained conversations with Saudis who reported that they have moved their investments, their corporate purchases, their vacation plans, or their children's education outside the United States.

Saudi Arabia cannot afford an open break with Washington, yet it has strong motivations to put some distance between itself and its patron. That is one reason why Saudi Arabia was reluctant to align itself publicly with the U.S. military campaign against Iraq and why the Saudis endorsed with alacrity the withdrawal of most U.S. military forces from the Kingdom after Iraq was defeated. The fewer American troops, the less provocation to militants and the less vulnerable the ruling family is to the accusation that it has squandered billions on defense without reducing its dependence on the Americans.

With the departure of American military units whose mission was to enforce flight restrictions in Iraq, the U.S. military presence in Saudi Arabia has reverted to the status quo ante 1990: the long-understood U.S. commitment to Saudi Arabia's security remains, but the only actual uniformed American presence are the small advisory units of the U.S.

Military Training Mission and the Saudi Arabian National Guard support team. Paradoxically, this should strengthen rather than weaken the political security of the House of Saud because it will no longer have to defend itself against accusations that it is allowing infidel troops to defile holy soil. Moreover, the Saudis can claim, with justification, that the American withdrawal was prompted not by the demands of Osama bin Laden but by the fact that the need for the troops ended with the downfall of Saddam Hussein.

No longer will be it true, as the analyst Joseph McMillan put it, that "the Saudi royal family is under steadily growing pressure to explain how it can claim to defend the Holy Places if it cannot even defend itself without the aid of unbelievers."[49]

From the American perspective, the potential downside of this change could be a loss of access to information about Saudi strategic thinking and of regular contact with Saudi military officers. From the perspective of the Saudis, they could regard the American pullout—along with the Bush administration's professed commitment to a democratic Middle East—as a sign of flagging American support for the House of Saud. Even before the Iraq war, in a paper arguing the case for Saudi acquisition of nuclear capability, Richard L. Russell observed that "it would be imprudent, to say the least, for Riyadh to make the cornerstone of [its] national-security posture out of an assumption that the United States would come to the kingdom's defense under any and all circumstances."[50] It might be even more imprudent now.

The so-called War on Terrorism—which over time will vary in intensity, commitment, tactics, and location—may not be a sufficiently strong bond to hold the United States and Saudi Arabia together, especially because it has inspired as much suspicion and resentment in both countries as it has mutual action. American and Saudi officials say that the terrorist attacks of May and November 2003 on housing compounds for foreigners in Riyadh have broken through the wall of denial and circumvention that characterized previous episodes in which Saudi-U.S. cooperation was called for. Security sweeps and even gun battles with suspected terrorists are now common in Saudi cities. A feckless Saudi response, like those that followed earlier attacks, would have further alienated Americans; if that had happened, an Iraq responsive to American ideals and willing to work with Washington on both security and oil issues might be a more attractive partner for the United States.

If, then, the Saudis can no longer assume that the armed forces of the

United States are their ultimate weapon against external threats, might they not wish to acquire a different ultimate weapon? The Saudi Arabian armed forces have never developed a coherent national security doctrine that could provide a serious basis for acquisition and deployment planning, let alone for a decision to acquire nuclear weapons. However, recall that there are cogent reasons why Saudi Arabia might pursue such a course: it is a rich but weak country with armed forces of suspect competence, out-manned by combat-hardened, truculent, and potentially nuclear-armed neighbors, and no longer confident that it can count on its American pro-tector. "From Riyadh's perspective," wrote Russell, "the acquisition of nuclear weapons and secure delivery systems would appear logical and even necessary." Those "secure delivery systems," Russell argued, would not be aircraft, which are vulnerable to ground defenses, but "ballistic-missile delivery systems that would stand a near-invulnerable chance of penetrating enemy airspace"—namely, the CSS-2s.[51]

Military experts say it is theoretically possible that the missiles could be made operational, modernized, and retrofitted with nuclear warheads acquired from China, Pakistan, or perhaps, within a few years, North Korea. Any attempt to do so, however, would present immense technical and political difficulties—so much so that Saudi Arabia might emerge less secure rather than more.

Even aside from the fact that such a nuclear program would place Saudi Arabia in the category of global nuclear outlaw along with North Korea and, by then, probably Iran, the acquisition of warheads would encounter strenuous opposition from the United States and Israel. Having watched Washington's reaction to Pakistan's nuclear tests in 1998, the Saudis are well aware that U.S. law requires economic and military sanc-tions against nuclear proliferators. And whereas Pakistan and India had friends in Congress, willing to help them escape the network of manda-tory sanctions, Saudi Arabia does not. If an angry Congress cuts off Saudi Arabia from future purchases of U.S. military equipment and forces the withdrawal of U.S. military trainers, and if Israel threatened a preemptive strike, the Kingdom's position would be precarious to the point of untenability.

Moreover, confrontation and defiance are not Saudi Arabia's style; the Saudis' weapons of choice are cash and diplomacy. It is difficult to imagine the princes of the House of Saud deliberately positioning themselves as global outliers and inviting reprisals from countries capable of inflicting serious political and economic damage on them. With hundreds of billions of dollars of private Saudi capital and government funds invested in the United States, the Saudis would be ill advised to risk an asset freeze.

To avoid such consequences, the Saudis could seek to acquire weapons secretly, as they did with the Chinese missiles. In the unlikely event that they could accomplish such a feat, the exercise could be self-defeating because nuclear weapons lose their deterrent value if their existence is unknown.

Either way, covert or overt, acquiring nuclear warheads and installing them on modernized, retrofitted CSS-2 missiles capable of delivering them would require Chinese cooperation, which is unlikely to be forthcoming. Once a problem proliferator and the probable source of technology and material for Pakistan's nuclear weapons program, China now has a higher interest in maintaining the nuclear cooperation agreement with the United States that went into effect in 1998, making possible U.S. commercial sales to China's civilian nuclear power program. Having joined the NPT system in 1992, China is obliged "not in any way to assist, encourage or induce any non-nuclear weapon State to manufacture or otherwise acquire nuclear weapons or other explosive devices, or control over such weapons or explosive devices."[52] Under the Nuclear Proliferation Prevention Act of 1994, China would face revocation of the U.S. nuclear cooperation agreement it worked so hard to secure, as well as economic sanctions, if it were deemed to have "aided or abetted" the acquisition of nuclear weapons.[53]

With India as a strategic rival, the Chinese had some reason to help Pakistan acquire nuclear capability, and they continued to assist Pakistan's program even after adhering to the NPT. No such consideration prevails in the Middle East. "The Chinese are not so stupid as to proliferate nukes, especially to the Arab world," according to Bernard Dunn. "If they had such an inclination, they could have armed half a dozen Arab states already. China is interested in expanding commercial ties, not adding to the balance of terror."[54]

The Pakistan Factor

Assuming that the Saudis would seek to acquire nuclear weapons despite all the potential negative consequences and that the Chinese would not cooperate, Riyadh would have to acquire a new fleet of missiles for delivery in addition to the warheads. This would greatly increase the cost, as well as the risk of detection, but it is theoretically possible. North Korea, a prolific retailer of missiles, would presumably be willing to sell warheads or at least fissionable material now that production is apparently going to resume. Yet doing nuclear weapons business with North Korea would put the Saudis so far outside the comfort zone of their relations with the United States, Europe, and Japan that it is difficult to imagine Riyadh taking such a step as long as the House of Saud reigns, regardless of the perceived threat. The other possible source would be Pakistan, with which Saudi Arabia has had a long and close relationship that survived Pakistan's multiple shifts from civilian to military rule and back.

Washington was alerted to the possibility of a Saudi turn to Pakistan for missiles and perhaps even nuclear warheads by Prince Sultan's 1999 visit to Pakistan's defense and nuclear facilities. It was believed to be the first time any outsider had been permitted to visit the Pakistani sites.[55] By that time, Pakistan was openly in possession of nuclear warheads, having tested six the year before in response to tests by India, and was nearing production of a new generation of ballistic missiles with a range of 1,500 miles—a possible replacement for the CSS-2s in Saudi Arabia.

As conservative, Sunni Muslim nations with overlapping interests and complementary strengths, Pakistan and Saudi Arabia had been considering formal security agreements since the 1950s. The appeal of such an arrangement was obvious: Pakistan had military know-how, trained manpower, and experienced forces but no money; the Saudis lacked military and industrial capability but had plenty of cash. According to the United Nations' global compilation of treaties, Saudi Arabia and Pakistan have a friendship pact dating to that era but no formal mutual defense agreement—indeed, Saudi Arabia has no formal defense agreement with any country and would be unlikely to enter such an arrangement with Pakistan out of fear of being dragged into the Kashmir conflict. But the security relationship between the two countries has been close since the late 1970s. After the tumultuous year of 1979—the most stressful in modern Saudi history because of Egypt's peace treaty with Israel, the Iranian revolution, and the armed takeover by radical dissidents of the Great Mosque in Mecca, followed by the Soviet invasion of Afghanistan—a small contingent of Pakistani troops was deployed to Saudi Arabia. One unit was stationed at Khamis Mushayt, in the far south, and the other in Tabuk, near the Jordanian border, far enough from the capital not to pose any threat to the ruling family. The Saudis, of course, footed the bill.[56] These troops remained until 1987, when oil prices hit historic lows and the Saudis could no longer afford them.

In cooperation with the CIA, the two countries worked closely throughout the 1980s to recruit, train, equip, and pay for the guerrilla war of Islamic resistance against the Soviet troops occupying Afghanistan. (Among the many Saudi individuals who participated in that conflict was Osama bin Laden.) The Saudis congratulated Pakistan after its 1998 nuclear tests, and a few months later Crown Prince Abdullah was received effusively on a visit to Lahore. In their joint statement about the visit, the two countries said that "views were exchanged in an atmosphere of brotherhood and understanding in which prevailed mutual trust and compatibility of points of view which characterizes the Saudi-Pakistani relations." The statement said the visit symbolized the "permanent bond between Saudi Arabia and Pakistan."

Given that history, it was perhaps not surprising that Defense Minister Sultan's visit the following year to the nuclear and missile facilities stirred speculation about its purpose. Neither Saudi Arabia nor Pakistan announced the visit at the time—in fact, the Pakistanis denied it had occurred—and only after speculative press reports began to appear some time afterward did they comment on it. On August 6, 1999, the spokesman of Pakistan's foreign office issued this statement:

> When his attention was drawn to news reports in the Western media about the visit of [the] Saudi Defense Minister to some of Pakistan's defense facilities, the Foreign Office Spokesman described the speculative comments in the reports as entirely unwarranted and baseless. The Spokesman said that the Saudi authorities have already denied the speculation about any possible cooperation between Pakistan and Saudi Arabia in the nuclear field. Pakistan has repeatedly affirmed its commitment to not transfer nuclear and sensitive technologies to any country. Pakistan has been abiding by this immutable and unilateral commitment in the past and will continue to do so in the future.

In his recent book about Pakistan, the experienced journalist Owen Bennett Jones wrote, "It is still far from clear what the Saudi defense minister was doing. He might have been interested in some of the weapons (nuclear or conventional) produced at Kahuta, but more likely than not he was just indulging in a piece of political tourism."[57] What is clear is that Pakistan chafed for years under the U.S. sanctions imposed for its previous nuclear weapons activities, including the loss of U.S. warplanes that Pakistan paid for but was never able to gain possession of because of restrictions imposed under U.S. antiproliferation laws, and would be reluctant to incur new sanctions by assisting a nuclear program in Saudi Arabia.

There is little doubt that Pakistan is pressing ahead with the development of additional nuclear weapons and the missiles by which to deliver them. In May 2002, Pakistan tested a new liquid-fueled missile known as the Haft-V, apparently based on North Korean technology, with a range of about 800 miles. That is less than half the range of the CSS-2s but still easily enough to reach critical targets in Iran, Iraq, and Israel from Saudi Arabia.[58] Later that year, the Bush administration revealed its concern that Pakistan was paying North Korea for its missile technology not in cash but in assistance to Pyongyang's nuclear program.[59] The CIA reported in January 2003 that Pakistan has "continued to acquire nuclear-related equipment, some of it dual use, and materials from various sources—principally in Western Europe."[60] Moreover, the discovery in early 2004 that Pakistan was the probable source for designs and materials used in Libya's clandestine nuclear weapons program undermined Pakistan's insistence that it has never been a nuclear proliferator. The government of Pakistan said that the sales to Libya were unauthorized transactions by rogue scientists, not government-to-government deals. But even if that is true, there is no obvious reason why such sales could not also have been made to other Arab countries.

Some U.S. government officials believe that Pakistan and Saudi Arabia have an understanding by which Pakistan's nuclear capabilities would be made available on demand to Saudi Arabia if the Saudis found themselves in extremis—a guarantee purchased, in effect, by Saudi funding of Pakistan's nuclear program. No known evidence supports this theory, and some experts openly discount it. Among these is Gary Samore, a longtime student of Saudi Arabian security policy who was a senior arms control and nonproliferation specialist at the National Security Council in the Clinton administration.

"I don't believe there's a deal that the Saudis already paid and could take delivery on demand, and if I were the Saudis I wouldn't trust the Pakistanis to deliver on such a deal," Samore said. "There's no doubt the Saudis have delivered a lot of money to Pakistan, and some went to support the nuclear weapons program, but I don't believe any such quid pro quo exists. What would be more likely would be that Pakistan would [again] station troops on Saudi soil, and those could include nuclear-armed forces."[61] These could be attack aircraft carrying bombs, missile squadrons deploying nuclear-tipped warheads, or ground troops, such as

Pakistan previously sent to Saudi Arabia, now equipped with tactical—as opposed to strategic—nuclear weapons. But against which potential foe of Saudi Arabia would Pakistan jeopardize its own interests by deploying nuclear weapons?

Policy Considerations for the United States

Taken together, the weight of the evidence and the experience of Saudi behavior over five decades indicate that Saudi Arabia does not seek to acquire nuclear weapons, could not develop an indigenous nuclear weapons program, and would encounter daunting, perhaps insuperable, difficulties if it sought to purchase such a capability from outside. Nevertheless, as we have seen, the Saudis have dangerous neighbors in a volatile neighborhood, and it is possible to envision circumstances under which the acquisition of nuclear weapons might seem a valuable and relatively economical option, bestowing an element of security and deterrence that could justify the political, economic, and strategic risks. The only country that can provide the Saudis with sufficient confidence of their security that no such undertaking would even be considered is the United States.

Before September 11, it probably was not necessary for the United States to take any specific steps or offer any new commitments in order to maintain Saudi Arabia's security confidence at a sufficiently high level that acquiring nuclear weapons would not cross the Saudis' minds. In the past, whenever the chips were down—the Yemen conflict of the 1960s, the "tanker war" of the 1980s, Desert Storm—the Americans had come through for Saudi Arabia. The American military presence and the vast, intricate network of economic ties between the two countries provided sufficient assurance of American protection. Now the game board looks much different.

The Saudis no longer have full confidence in American backing, and the current U.S. administration has little if any political reason to offer the Saudis any new commitments, especially if they require congressional assent. Moreover, long-term U.S. interests in the Middle East would best be served by avoiding any commitment to the preservation of the House of Saud specifically. The United States has strategic and economic interests in Saudi Arabia, but preservation of al-Saud rule is not necessarily one of them; a democratic government that maintained good relations with the West would be preferable.

If the Bush administration is serious about promoting democracy in the Middle East, fashioning an effective policy toward Saudi Arabia could pose a significant challenge. As the current Saudi leadership frequently points out, a change to an elective system in which the country's leader is chosen by popular vote would probably produce a militant Islamic regime hostile to the United States. On the other hand, even lip service to the democratic idea seems to require that Washington put some distance between itself and the al-Saud family. The issue is how to do that without provoking the Saudis into putting the nuclear option on the table.

One possibility, of course, is that the ouster of Saddam Hussein as ruler of Iraq will indeed pave the way to a new era of peace and stability throughout the Middle East, in which case the only conceivable threat to Saudi Arabia's rulers would be internal and the question of nuclear deterrent would become moot. Despite President Bush's optimism, such a development is improbable, given the region's history since the Treaty of Versailles, the apparent commitment of Iran to nuclearize, and the intractability of the Israeli-Palestinian question.

Some analysts advocate putting Saudi Arabia under the U.S. nuclear umbrella, perhaps through a Persian Gulf version of NATO. Assuming that Congress would ever approve such a guarantee, the advantage of this proposal is that it could be done without reference to any particular government in Riyadh. This solution might suffice if the threat to Saudi security is thought to be a frontal attack by Iran or some other external force. And if Iran becomes fully nuclear capable, such a guarantee might also serve U.S. interests through deterrence of Tehran. But if the threat to Saudi Arabia is non-nuclear and indirect, through insurgency, guerrilla strikes, and infiltration and sabotage of soft targets such as water desalination plants, a U.S. nuclear guarantee would not suffice because in such a case, even if Washington intervened militarily to prop up the ruling family, it would certainly not use nuclear weapons. The Saudis might well feel the need to develop a nuclear response capability that they would control themselves, NPT obligations or not. Short of a formal "nuclear umbrella" commitment, however, there are confidence-building steps the United States could take.

In a paper for the National Defense University, Joseph McMillan identified several relatively painless moves Washington could make to restore the bilateral relationship to its former comfort level. One was to "undertake a genuine strategic dialogue." According to McMillan,

> There is no shared understanding with the Saudi leadership on the strategic underpinnings of the bilateral relationship and the future of the region. American and Saudi officials have conflicting rationales

for the presence of U.S. forces in the Kingdom, conflicting under-standings of the threat, and undoubtedly conflicting perceptions over how to move forward. These consultations need to be frank, strictly private, regular and inclusive of all aspects of the U.S.-Saudi relationship, from security and oil to agriculture and education.[62]

McMillan also recommended that American officials stop issuing pub-lic characterizations of what Saudi Arabia has agreed or refused to do. Such comments "often have unpredictable and unproductive conse-quences," he wrote—that is, Saudi leaders, for domestic reasons, often find it necessary to take public positions contrary to Washington's lest they appear to be doing U.S. bidding.[63]

Another useful step would be to tell the Saudis directly—in confi-dence, but with absolute clarity—that any dalliance with the lure of nuclear weapons would be counterproductive. A respected senior offi-cial, speaking for the president, should be dispatched to deliver this mes-sage and spell out the consequences. This official should carry a private letter from a few senior members of Congress of both parties letting the Saudis know that—unlike Pakistan—they would have no support in Congress if they were to venture down the nuclear road. The Saudis do not appreciate being threatened and resent any communication that sounds like a command or an ultimatum; for those reasons, any such U.S. démarche should be undertaken only if there is reason to believe that Riyadh is contemplating a nuclear option.

Finally, the administration should select an appropriate moment, per-haps after Iraq has stabilized, to issue a new formulation of the so-called Carter Doctrine. In January 1980, in his State of the Union address a few weeks after Soviet troops marched into Afghanistan, President Jimmy Carter declared, "An attempt by any outside force to gain control of the Persian Gulf region will be regarded as an assault on the vital interests of the United States. It will be repelled by any means necessary, including mil-itary force." In October 1982, President Ronald Reagan made this com-mitment specific to Saudi Arabia: "An attack on Saudi Arabia would be considered an attack on the United States."

An unequivocal statement that the United States has vital interests in Saudi Arabia and will prevent disruption of the flow of oil, without regard to the differences of the moment or the identity of the ruler, could restore a measure of Saudi confidence that U.S. protection is all the deter-rent they need. It could also have the beneficial effect of putting any rival aspirants to power in Riyadh on notice that the United States would tolerate their regime only so long as American interests were not threatened. They should understand that the United States, in its new mood after September 11, will not accept any repetition of the 1979 humiliation in Iran or the emergence of Taliban-style rule. The statement should make clear that there are three outcomes the United States will not tolerate from any government in Saudi Arabia: disruption of oil flow, confiscation of U.S. assets, and acquisition of nuclear weapons. Having watched the downfall of Saddam Hussein, the powers in Riyadh will have every reason to take Washington seriously.

Notes

1. Robert Pelletreau, personal communication to the author, November 8, 2002.

2. Anthony Cordesman, *Saudi Arabia: Guarding the Desert Kingdom* (Boulder, Colo.: Westview, 1997), p. 48.

3. This contretemps was reported extensively in news accounts at the time. See, for example, David B. Ottaway, "Talk of Israeli Raid on Saudi Missiles Concerns U.S.," *Washington Post*, March 23, 1988, p. A23.

4. Hume Horan, interview by author, Washington, D.C., June 2, 2002.

5. James B. Mann, *About Face: A History of America's Curious Relationship with China, from Nixon to Clinton* (Alfred A. Knopf, 1999), pp. 169–70.

6. Richard Murphy, testimony to House Foreign Affairs Committee, 100 Cong., 2 sess., May 10, 1988.

7. Ibid.

8. Richard Murphy, interview with author, New York, July 9, 2002.

9. Edward Walker, interview with author, Washington, D.C., January 8, 2003.

10. Confidential communication to author, September 15, 2002.

11. Charles Freeman Jr., personal recollections, in *Frontline Diplomacy: The U.S. Foreign Affairs Oral History Collection*, CD-ROM (Arlington, Va.: Association for Diplomatic Studies and Training, 2001).

12. Thomas Woodrow, "The Sino-Saudi Connection," *China Brief*, vol. 2, no. 21 (October 24, 2002), p. 2.

13. Cordesman, *Saudi Arabia* , p. 47.

14. His statement can be found on Ain-al-Yaqeen, the website used by the Saudi ruling family for official pronouncements (www.ain-al-yaqeen.com/issues/19980701/feat3en.htm [February 2004]).

15. Ibid.

16. Prince Sultan ibn Abdul Aziz, interview with the newspaper *al-Hawadeth*,

September 10, 1999 (www.ain-al-yaqeen.com/issues/19990910/feat4en.htm [March 2004]).

17. "Assessing Arab Anger," *Proliferation Brief*, vol. 3, no. 15 (May 16, 2000).

18. Jan Alexander Lodding, IAEA verification officer, personal communication to the author by e-mail, January 31, 2003.

19. "A 'Nuclear Status' Map," maintained by the Carnegie Endowment for International Peace on its website (www.ceip.org/files/nonprolif/map/default. asp). It ranks potential proliferation states and is updated regularly.

20. Joseph Cirincione, personal communication to author by e-mail, February 3, 2003.

21. Bernard Dunn, interview with author, McLean, Va., October 2, 2002.

22. Confidential e-mail communication to author, October 31, 2002.

23. Confidential interview by the author, Riyadh, October 2002.

24. See www.kacst.edu.sa/en/institutes/aeri/index.asp [February 2004].

25. Paul Lewis, "Defector Says Saudis Sought Nuclear Arms," *New York Times*, August 7, 1994, p. 20.

26. He did not respond to a message, sent through his New York lawyer, requesting an interview.

27. Letter printed in Anders Jerichow, *The Saudi File: People, Power, Poltics* (St. Martin's Press, 1998), p. 54.

28. "Saudi Arabia Is Trying to Kill Me," *Middle East Quarterly*, vol. 5, no. 3, September 1998 (www.meforum.org/article/409/ [February 2004]).

29. Robert Pelletreau, personal communication, November 8, 2002.

30. Ewen MacAskill and Ian Traynor, "Saudis Consider Nuclear Bomb," *Guardian*, September 18, 2003.

31. Turki al-Faisal, "No Nukes," letters, *Guardian*, September 22, 2003.

32. Declassified State Department cable, "Intsum 914," October 11, 1979, copy in National Security Archive (George Washington University), file AF00694.

33. Richard M. Preece, *Saudi Arabia and the United States: The New Context in an Evolving "Special Relationship"* (Congressional Research Service, 1981) p. 6.

34. Ibid.

35. Ibid., p. 44.

36. U.S. Department of State, 1999 annual report on military spending to House and Senate Appropriations Committees.

37. Cordesman, *Saudi Arabia*, p. 107.

38. Ibid., p. 4.

39. At the beginning of 2003, Iraq's armed forces had about 400,000 troops. Iran had about the same number in its regular units and another 120,000 in the Republican Guard. Saudi Arabia had 191,500 men in uniform, but that total included 65,000 members of the national guard, whose mission is internal security, and 15,500 in the navy, a lightly equipped force that would have little value

against an invasion by armored units. Iraq's military strength was, of course, virtually obliterated by "Operation Iraqi Freedom." Iran is only now recovering from the losses of its eight-year war with Iraq, but it could still probably overwhelm Saudi Arabia.

40. Confidential e-mail communication to author, February 3, 2003.

41. Bernard Dunn, interview with author, October 2, 2002.

42. Confidential interview by author, Riyadh, October 2002.

43. See Jane Corbin, *Al-Qaeda* (New York: Nation Books, 2002), p. 58.

44. Department of State, 1999 annual report on military spending to House and Senate Appropriations Committees.

45. C. A. Woodson, *Saudi Arabian Force Structure Development in a Post Gulf War World* (Ft. Leavenworth, Kan.: Foreign Military Studies Office, 1998), p. 2 (http://fmso.leavenworth.army.mil/fmsopubs/issues/saudi/saudi.htm [February 2004]).

46. Michael Eisenstadt, "Dual Bomb Blasts in South Asia: Implications for the Middle East," *PolicyWatch* no. 318 (Washington Institute for Near East Policy, May 29, 1998).

47. Chas Freeman, interview with author, Washington, D.C., May 6, 2002.

48. George Tenet, *The Worldwide Threat in 2003: Evolving Dangers in a Complex World*, report to Senate Select Committee on Intelligence, 108 Cong., 1 sess., February 11, 2003.

49. Joseph McMillan, "U.S.-Saudi Relations: Rebuilding the Strategic Consensus," *Strategic Forum*, no. 186 (November 2001), p. 4.

50. Richard L. Russell, "A Saudi Nuclear Option?" *Survival*, vol. 43, no. 2 (Summer 2001), p. 70.

51. Ibid., p. 73.

52. Rodney W. Jones and others, *Tracking Nuclear Proliferation, 1998: A Guide to Maps and Charts* (Carnegie Endowment for International Peace, June 1998).

53. Public Law 103-236, 103 Cong., 2 sess. (April 30, 1994).

54. Bernard Dunn, e-mail communication to author, November 1, 2002.

55. Jane Perlez, "Saudi's Visit to Arms Site in Pakistan Worries U.S.," *New York Times*, July 10, 1999, p. A7.

56. Nadav Safran, *Saudi Arabia: The Ceaseless Quest for Security* (Harvard University Press, 1985), p. 363.

57. Owen Bennett Jones, *Pakistan: Eye of the Storm* (Yale University Press, 2002), p. 219.

58. Alex Wagner, "Pakistan Tests Three Nuclear-Capable Ballistic Missiles," *Arms Control Today* (June 2002) (www.armscontrol.org/act/2002_06/pak-testjune02.asp [March 2004]).

59. Glen Kessler, "Pakistan's N. Korea Deals Stir Scrutiny," *Washington Post*, November 13, 2002, A1.

60. Central Intelligence Agency, *Unclassified Report to Congress on the Acquisition of Technology Relating to Weapons of Mass Destruction and Advanced Conventional Munitions, July–December 2001* (January 2003).

61. Gary Samore, interview with author by telephone, November 28, 2002.

62. McMillan, "U.S.-Saudi Relations," p. 11.

63. Ibid.

CHAPTER 7

Turkey: Nuclear Choices amongst Dangerous Neighbors

LEON FUERTH

Turkey has been accustomed to the presence of large numbers of nuclear weapons on its territory for protracted periods of time, in exchange for membership in NATO under conditions of particularly close relations with the United States. In the belief that this relationship would provide protection against extreme threat, Turkey was prepared to support all the elements of the nonproliferation regime.

Despite this, there have been times when Turkey was actively interested in developing nuclear energy, including a complete nuclear fuel cycle. What makes these episodes interesting from the point of view of this study is that in connection with them, Turkey developed contacts with the nuclear energy programs of such countries as Argentina and Pakistan, during periods when both of them were working on nuclear weapons programs under cover of projects for developing nuclear energy. Not surprisingly, Turkish interest in acquiring a nuclear energy industry was resisted by the United States and other nuclear weapons states for fear of the proliferation potential. These suspicions were not baseless.

The collapse of the Soviet Union and the Warsaw Pact eliminated—seemingly, forever—what might have been Turkey's sole motivation for

Austin Carson of the Center for Strategic and International Studies (CSIS) provided research assistance for this chapter. Bulent Aliriza of CSIS provided valuable feedback on early versions of the draft.

believing that security lay in the possession of nuclear weapons, whether those of the United States deployed on Turkish territory or, in theory, those of Turkish origin. And there are major inhibitions against a Turkish reappraisal of its renunciation of nuclear weapons. However, even though Turkey is not likely to reconsider its non-nuclear status at the present time, it is possible to imagine circumstances where that might occur. It would require a chain of events whose cumulative impact would convince Turkish elites that the survival of the nation could no longer be ensured by its security relationship with the United States, and that Turkey must therefore take on all the risks and costs of a nuclear weapons program.

A number of factors could contribute to such a change of view:

—Doubts regarding the NATO guarantee of effective collective security, which could be caused by the alliance's political weakening as a consequence of its expansion; serious deterioration of the alliance as the result of internal frictions, such as occurred in connection with Iraq; or by evidence of the loss of political will by the United States to honor its nuclear guarantee for an ally.

—The collapse of the nonproliferation regime and ensuing regional nuclear acquisitions. This could result from the failure of American efforts to block North Korean and Iranian attempts to acquire nuclear weapons. Evidence of an unchecked Syrian nuclear weapons program would have a similar impact.

—A strong shift in Turkish public opinion toward a more Islamic or nationalist orientation, which could happen if the present government fails to revive the economy—especially in conjunction with the loss of any reasonable hope that Turkey will ever be accepted by the European Union.

—A revival of Russian expansionism directed toward the reestablishment of dominance in the Caucasus and Caspian regions.

—The creation of a power vacuum in the Middle East as the result of multiple failures of American policy for the post-war reconstruction of Iraq or the failure of the United States to make progress toward resolving the Israeli-Palestinian conflict.

—Permanent damage to U.S.-Turkish relations because of American anger at Turkey's failure to substantially assist during the war with Iraq or as the result of serious subsequent disputes, such as might develop from the rise of a Kurdish neostate in northern Iraq.

Circumstances such as these are not implausible, given recent events. A combination of them could have the impact of a "perfect storm" on even so basic an element of Turkish policy as the renunciation of nuclear weapons. Even though Turkey is not known to harbor ambitions to develop a nuclear weapons capability, the chance of a profound change of mind cannot be set at zero. It would be wise not to take either Turkey's general policy or its nuclear policy for granted.

The Cold War Years: Turkey under the U.S. Umbrella

From the earliest days of the cold war, U.S. planners understood that Turkey was vital for the defense of the West, although there were substantial shifts in precisely how that role was conceptualized. During the days of greatest peril, from 1946 until the creation of NATO in 1949, Washington believed that Western Europe could be easily overrun by the Soviets and that a war of liberation would have to begin with air bombardment of Russian targets from bases as far away as Egypt, with Turkey serving to block Soviet advance toward that final strategic redoubt. This was the basis for American decisions in 1947 to provide military aid to Turkey, with special emphasis on the construction of bases for American longer-range aircraft capable of reaching Soviet oil resources in Romania and the Caucasus.

With the creation of NATO, however, American planning shifted toward the defense of Western Europe proper, with the objective of creating a military force capable of defending the continental core from its own soil. American interest in Turkey declined accordingly, as it was reassigned from the role of prospective main front to secondary flank. With the outbreak of war in Korea in 1950, the Joint Chiefs came to see further strengthening of U.S. military ties to Turkey as a potential distraction, and therefore opposed the intensified defense relationship the Turks themselves hoped to build.[1] In the end, however, U.S. planners realized that the Turks might respond to perceived American indifference by adopting a policy of neutrality, which would have been disastrous for the defense of Western Europe. These concerns ultimately trumped the more conservative approach, leading the United States to support full membership in NATO for Turkey and Greece in 1951.

In 1952 a U.S. review of the role of nuclear weapons in the defense of Western Europe concluded that in a war with the Soviet Union, NATO could prevail if two conditions were met: more ground forces to compensate for losses, and "if SACEUR [Supreme Allied Commander

Europe] was given predelegated authority which allowed him to use nuclear weapons immediately on D-Day."² This study ultimately became part of the so-called NATO New Look strategy, formally adopted by the alliance in 1957. With this approach, American nuclear weapons became a central pillar of the alliance's strategy for deterring and responding to Soviet aggression.³

The flight of Sputnik in October 1957 showed that Soviet rockets had advanced to the point of being able to threaten the United States and called into question the deterrent and war fighting credibility of short-range nuclear weapons deployed in Europe. Would the United States carry out a strategy for the defense of Europe that might immediately result in the nuclear destruction of American cities? The American interim response to this challenge was to deploy intermediate-range ballistic missiles in Europe, for the purpose of bringing targets deep inside the Soviet Union within range of nuclear bombardment.

U.S. deployment of such missiles within striking distance of the Soviet Union would contribute, in due course, to Soviet deployment of missiles in Cuba, placing them within range of much of the eastern seaboard of the United States. According to one scholar, "the Cuban missile crisis of October 1962 and the Kennedy Administration's abandonment of the strategy of massive retaliation for one of flexible response together constituted a watershed in the cold war. In Turkey, however, these developments contributed to a concern that, in the event of Soviet aggression, Turkish territory might be traded for time. . . . The announcement in January 1963 that Jupiter missiles would be removed from Turkey followed too closely not to have a significant effect on the Turks."⁴

The United States would soon begin deploying ballistic missiles with intercontinental range, thereby mooting the value of the intermediate-range missiles withdrawn from Europe. But the problem of the credibility of the nuclear deterrent in relation to the defense of Europe would never be fully resolved. Any use of nuclear weapons, including tactical weapons deployed in Europe, could rapidly escalate out of control and result in a general nuclear exchange between the United States and the Soviet Union. The Eisenhower approach appeared to lock the United States into a strategy for defending Europe that could be self-immolating. Yet the value of nuclear weapons as a deterrent lay precisely in the credibility of the threat that they would be employed.

Declassified documents show that the Eisenhower administration tried to parse the issue by predelegating authority for the use of nuclear weapons in a variety of scenarios, including first and foremost a Soviet attack on the United States. It is important to know, however, that Eisenhower does not seem to have predelegated authority for the use of nuclear weapons in the event of an attack on Western Europe; instead, for that contingency, there were instructions to reserve, if at all possible, a nuclear decision for the president alone.

The Kennedy administration adhered to this approach.[5] However, the administration found it an extremely uncomfortable arrangement and searched for a revised approach, ultimately known as "Flexible Response."[6] Flexible Response applied primarily to strategic nuclear forces and aimed to give a president much more control over the onset of nuclear war and its scope at any given stage. But what looked better to the United States looked bad to Europeans for precisely the same reason: to Europeans flexibility for a U.S. president meant that the deterrent effect of the U.S. nuclear guarantee would be diminished by the possibility that, at the moment of truth, the United States would pull back, thus increasing European exposure to Soviet blackmail.

Securing European support for this new approach required extended missionary work, including the development of new consultative institutions to facilitate a greater two-way flow of information and discourse about nuclear weapons. One of the first and most fundamental steps in this direction was the establishment in 1965 of the ad hoc Working Group on Nuclear Planning. Turkey was a member of this group from the beginning: not as a matter of established precedence but as the result of selection by lot.[7] The issue of predelegation turns up repeatedly in the records of NATO discussions, continuing on into the Johnson administration. Turkish interest in the subject showed up early, beginning in 1965, when a Turkish representative is known to have proposed that "advance authority be given to NATO commanders to use tactical [nuclear] weapons bypassing political consultation in an emergency."[8]

During the same period of time, the United States was also turning to arms control in hope of containing and minimizing the threat of a global nuclear catastrophe. By the fall of 1966, the United States and the Soviet Union reached basic understandings about the core provisions of what would become known as the Non-Proliferation Treaty (NPT). [9] A declassified U.S. document of February 1967 reports on attitudes among NATO allies relating to the NPT. Turkey declared itself to be in basic agreement with the treaty, but it raised the question of security guarantees for non-nuclear states and specifically asked whether predelegation of authority to fire nuclear weapons would be permissible under the treaty.[10] These repeated Turkish questions went straight to the heart of the nuclear issue from their perspective. Turkey had embraced the idea that its security required linkage to that of Western Europe; that the fate of Western Europe depended on the United States' nuclear guarantee and deterrence; and that Turkey had an important role in upholding this entire structure. But Turkey had already experienced fluctuations in the level of U.S. readiness to accept nuclear risk for the sake of defending Western Europe, not to mention Turkey. Now, in the NPT, Turkey saw something at once desirable and worrisome: a step toward containing the spread of nuclear weapons, including at its heart an apparently clear pledge by the United States and the Soviet Union to eliminate their own arsenals; and just as clearly, a step that could further weaken nuclear deterrence over the long term.

Turkey signed the NPT on January 28, 1969, but actual ratification did not occur until April 17, 1980.[11] The delay might well have been caused by the very great turbulence in Turkish political life during this time, when the nation was brought to the edge of civil war and the Turkish military stepped in to exert overt control.[12] But it is also possible that the delay was evidence of reservations or even of a desire to keep the nuclear option open.[13]

Turkish Post–Cold War Policy: Uncertain Trajectory

The end of the cold war brought an odd mixture of relief and disquiet to Turkish planners. On the one hand, the Soviet Union ceased to exist. Turkey no longer shared a long border with an empire governed from Moscow—the first time that could be said in over three centuries.[14] On the other hand, Turkish planners worried that the end of the Soviet threat could also result in a decline in the value of NATO as a safeguard for Turkish security against new threats not shared by states comprising the alliance's geographic core.

At the top of that list, of course, was Greece. It is true that Turkish-Greek relations entered a relatively clement period around this time. But this improvement followed years of periodic crisis and depended upon a number of factors that could prove evanescent—from goodwill that followed the Greek people's response to the August 1999 earthquake to negotiations with the EU for the admission of Cyprus that were resulting in constructive diplomacy aimed at a resolution of the Cypriot-Turkish issue. But if these efforts were to fail, Turkey and Greece might be pitched back into political crisis and even military confrontation. In the post–cold war period, it could not be ruled out that Europe would side with Greece or would lose the sense of urgency that had galvanized its efforts to mediate earlier crises and work for a long-term solution.[15]

The greater Turkish concern, however, related to the United States. With the Soviet Union gone and the Warsaw Pact dissolved, would the United States continue to attach the same strategic importance to the security of Turkey as it had for decades past? There would be no truly convincing answer to that question until the transformation of U.S. world-strategy following September 11, 2001.

It took almost a decade for Turkey to work through a comprehensive statement of post-Soviet policy in the form of a Defense White Paper, issued in August 2000. The White Paper begins by asserting that the most important task for international work in general is "to make peace and security permanent."[16] The paper makes it immediately clear that to accomplish this objective, Turkey intends to rely upon the effectiveness of a web of organizations, including NATO, the Organization for Security and Cooperation in Europe, the Western European Union, and the European Atlantic Partnership Council. In this respect, Turkish security policy for the twenty-first century is presented as an updated version of the general policy that guided Turkey through the last half of the twentieth century. Turkey would base its security on the assumption that Western institutions that had developed during the cold war would continue to function effectively in new circumstances, and that they would therefore view Turkey as an important part of their general schema for the collective defense of mutually shared basic interests.

On the other hand, the White Paper also shows clearly that the focus of Turkish concerns had shifted south and east, to the regional and ethnic issues of the Middle East, the Caspian, the Balkans, and the Caucasus. In addition to these, the White Paper addressed crosscutting new issues such as the proliferation of weapons of mass destruction, religious fundamentalism, smuggling of drugs and weapons of all kinds, and international terrorism. In all these matters, the Turkish White Paper reflected the sensibilities of a country feeling uniquely exposed to new risks at a time when its old allies were luxuriating in a sense that their own future was secure:

Turkey is located at the center of the triangle formed by the
Balkans, Caucasus and the Middle East, where the new threats and
risks are concentrated. Turkey is in a region where the interests of
the global powers and formations intersect. This situation, stemming from Turkey's geostrategic location, has not changed until the
present and will not change in the twenty-first century. It is evaluated
that the importance and place of Turkey in the new world order
will become even more strengthened.[17]

The meaning of "strengthened" is not left in doubt. It is clear that
Turkey aims, in the twenty-first century, "to become a country producing
strategy and security that could influence all the strategies aimed at her
region and beyond" and "to become an element of power and balance in
her region."[18]

Turkish security policy therefore rested on two fundamental assumptions: first, that Turkey will have an enhanced role to play in her region;
second, that Turkey's security ultimately depends on confidence that it will
not operate alone but rather with the full backing of friends and allies.
These overall assumptions also apply to Turkish thinking about the role
of arms control as an active element of international security. Turkey is a
full member of the Antarctic Treaty, the Partial Test Ban Treaty, the NPT,
the Seabed Treaty, and the Comprehensive Test Ban Treaty (CTBT) along
with the Missile Technology Control Regime, the Zangger Committee on
nuclear exports, and International Atomic Energy Agency safeguards
agreements.[19] Most Americans would have to be reminded what these
agreements are all about. For the Turks, however, these agreements represent real, structural elements of national security policy and an integral
part of the strategy whereby Turkey grounds its security on faith in the
value of Turkish solidarity with the international community.[20]

The Erosion of Basic Policy

The logic of the White Paper suggests that it will be possible for Turkey to
smoothly adapt its old strategy to new circumstances by adhering to well-
established general principles dating back all the way to Ataturk's dictum,
"Peace at home and peace abroad." In fact, Turkey faces problems that
may not respond well at all to old formulations, and Turkish elites know it.

To begin with, the collapse of the Soviet Union did not—from the
Turkish perspective—forever remove the possibility of having to confront

Moscow with military force. For almost a decade after the fall of communism, Turks worried that the weakness and chaotic condition of the Russian Federation might result in a return to dictatorship—perhaps communist, perhaps ultranationalist.[21]

It is very likely that Turkish concerns about chaos in Moscow have faded in view of President Putin's success in restoring a modicum of respect throughout Russia for the authority of the Federation government. Of course, that is not a finished story. Putin's accomplishments look solid enough, but for Turkey the flip side of the restoration of order in Russia is the possibility of a revived Russian state, intent upon recovering lost ground, politically and militarily.[22] Turkish statesmen have had to deal with Russian expansionism since the time of the tsars. Today's leaders know this history, and for them Turkey's relatively calm relationship with Russia seems likely to be a mere interlude before a resumption of the old struggle.[23] Turkish leaders see the region separating their country from the Russian Federation—Georgia, Azerbaijan, Armenia, Kazakhstan, and Turkmenistan—as a zone of instability and perhaps of crisis.[24]

There are cultural ties that Turks feel with peoples in this region and a sense of calling to keep watch over the "Turkic near-abroad." Turkish elites see their country, in the aftermath of the Soviet Union, as "the emerging great power in the region," with responsibilities for proactive engagement in the Caucasus, Central Asia, and the Middle East.[25] For Turks the war in Nagorno-Karabakh amounted to a challenge to Turkey's sense of enhanced responsibilities.[26] Sentiments of this kind are reflected in the thinking of military leaders, who noted in the White Paper that Turkey "needs to be able to preempt threats to Turkish interests before they cross onto Turkish territory."[27] Nor are these simply rhetorical concerns. Steps have been taken to increase Turkish influence among the Turkic-speaking states of Central Asia, including military cooperation agreements with Uzbekistan and Kyrgyzstan.[28]

In short, Turkey sees its region much as Moscow sees it: an area whose power structure is as unstable as its geology—a region whose strategic importance always calls out for organization under the leadership of a dominant power. The question is, which power fills the vacuum?

Turks cannot rule out the possibility that old rivalries will be rekindled; indeed, many Turks believe this is inevitable. It is equally clear to some that any such rivalries could result in Turkey having to deal with a resurgent, nuclear-armed Russia. What worries them most is their belief in the persistence of a Russian instinct for dominance and the idea "that the threat of the use of nuclear weapons could remain a dangerous possibility in order to support the foreign policy drive toward empire."[29] In fact, the radical decline of conventional military forces available to the Russian Federation led its military leaders to explicitly outline, in the 2000 Military Doctrine of the Russian Federation, circumstances in which Russia might use nuclear weapons first.[30] This represented a reversal of the Soviet Union's decades-long declaratory policy against first use of nuclear weapons. Weak or not, Russia remains a country that still has thousands of operational strategic nuclear warheads and tens of thousands of tactical nuclear weapons.

It is unlikely that Turkish military leaders ever doubted that the Soviet Union would make first use of weapons of mass destruction in a war with NATO. But the new Russian doctrine makes it explicit and official. Turks see the shift in Russia's declaratory nuclear policy not as an attribute of Russian weakness but as a policy in aid of Russian assertiveness.[31] President Putin's comments about the role of nuclear weapons in Russian strategy, and his report that development of new strategic weapons is under way, can only reinforce Turkish apprehension.[32]

To calibrate the depth of Turkish anxieties about regional instabilities and threats, one need only reflect upon Turkey's remarkable alliance with Israel—a country with no friends anywhere else in the Islamic world and one whose security, it is important to note, rests heavily on the universal assumption that it possesses nuclear weapons and the means to deliver them.[33] Even the destruction of Saddam Hussein's regime will not entirely relieve concerns, for Iran will still be there and will still be working steadily on its weapons programs. The recent disclosure that Iran is developing a uranium enrichment capability and blunt assertions by some Iranian leaders of Iran's right to acquire a nuclear weapon must remove any doubt on this score.[34] And if Iran succeeds, it would "be in a position to claim leadership of the Islamic world, and to exercise increased influence on Turkish domestic politics to the detriment of Turkey's Western-type secular democratic regime and Western-oriented foreign policy."[35]

Moreover, if Turkish politics were to continue to shift in the direction of a more Islamic-centered consciousness, as they might well do, then the foundations of Turkish thinking about national security might undergo profound change. "According to the Islamists, Turkey must fear not only the Russian nuclear arsenal but equally that of the United States, whose very military presence in Turkey is intended to cut the latter off from closer bonding with the Moslem world. Thus they argue that Turkish security thinking and planning need to be restructured on the basis of decoupling from the United States and NATO."[36] Such thinking is bound to be reinforced powerfully by the United States' invasion and occupation of Iraq.

In the crisis over Iraq, the new government of Turkey, led by majority-party leader Recep Tayyip Erdogan, responded to the United States less as an ally and more as a vendor of services to be sold at the highest price. Perhaps it was simple inexperience that led the government to allow members of its party to vote their conscience, but that is the point: the vote in Turkey's parliament rejecting the government's motion to allow U.S. troop access for an invasion across Iraq's northern border was a major signal of profound attitudinal changes that are well advanced in Turkish society as a whole.

The government evidently thought that a huge financial package from the United States would make a compelling case for going along with the U.S. request, especially in combination with other, less public assurances it might well have received about U.S. support in the future. The representatives of the Turkish people, however, accurately reflected deep popular sentiment by rejecting the same proposition—albeit by a narrow margin. They did so in full knowledge that Turkey would lose billions of dollars in American financial assistance and that they had foregone an opportunity to reaffirm the Turkish security relationship with the United States at a time when a positive decision would have mattered immensely.

Not even a warning from the Turkish General Staff sufficed to reverse the parliament's decision.[37] It is important to note that the General Staff might have acted before the vote but chose to lay low, notwithstanding the importance of the issue. Moreover, the near confrontation between Turkey and the United States over Turkey's desire to place its own troops in northern Iraq only demonstrated the potential for a major breach in relations at the level of military security.

In the end, of course, Turkey heeded U.S. warnings and did not send its forces into northern Iraq, and relations may yet mend if only because both sides realize how important it is that this occur. But there is little doubt that the United States paid in time, money, and perhaps in casualties because Turkey effectively prevented the timely opening of a northern front. A once-sturdy relationship has been shaken. The language of alliance and partnership has been replaced by reports in the Turkish press providing verbatim quotes, attributed directly to President Bush, amounting to direct threats against the Turkish economy.[38]

Something fundamental may have changed in Turkey's view of what constitutes its greatest source of security and what constitutes its greatest source of risk. In most respects, especially during the last two years leading up to war with Iraq, Turks have their reasons for seeing the U.S. relationship less as a source of security and more as a source of risk. First, there is a risk of blow-back from a U.S. attack on Iraq, underscored by the bitter controversy within NATO on the question of reinforcing Turkish defenses against possible Iraqi military reprisals. Another risk is that as a consequence of the revival of Kurdish separatism nourished by a quasi-autonomous Kurdish government in northern Iraq, there would be a rekindling of the kind of violence that led to the deaths of nearly 40,000 people during Turkey's fifteen-year struggle against the PKK (Kurdistan Workers Party).[39] Third, there is the possibility that even limited Turkish military cooperation with the United States would further dim Turkey's prospects for joining a European Union dominated by antiwar France and Germany. And of course, there is the domestic political risk arising from a deep reluctance among the Turkish people to militarily engage against Iraq on the side of the United States.

The end of Saddam Hussein's rule over Iraq closes the book on a threat that Turkey had more or less learned to live with—and opens another full of new and troubling unknowns. Foremost among these questions is whether the United States will have the staying power to remain in Iraq for as long as it takes to reconstruct that country physically and politically. Notwithstanding the Bush administration's assurances, such a commitment far exceeds anything the president or his supporters have ever been willing to countenance before, notably in Afghanistan.[40] The huge costs of occupation and reconstruction, and the prospect that scores of thousands of American troops will need to stay in Iraq for years, may prove more than the American public will tolerate, even if the Bush administration tries to honor its commitment.[41] Future events in the battle with international terror could have a profound impact on the will of the American people to sustain a lengthy postwar commitment—and it is certain that the aim of international terror will be to strike a blow precisely at domestic American support for continuing occupation of Iraq. It is also possible that the attention and resources of the United States will be quickly drawn away from the reconstruction of Iraq because of the need to deal with a crisis on the Korean peninsula.

The end of Saddam Hussein's regime could lead to profoundly improved circumstances throughout the Middle East, as President Bush has predicted—from a dramatic reduction in terrorism to peace and democracy breaking out across the region.[42] But it is equally plausible that the "law of unintended consequences" will operate as usual. Terrorism will not decline because Iraq was not the main source of organization or funding for the terrorist network. Efforts to push Israel to agree to an accelerated timetable for the establishment of a Palestinian state may fail in view of deep Israeli disillusionment with efforts to negotiate a swap of land for peace. Pressures from the United States for the full democratization of key moderate Arab governments may result in political destabilization by empowering radical groups. Interest in weapons of mass destruction may deepen between Iran and Syria. Weakened U.S. relations with the governments of Saudi Arabia and Egypt will diminish our ability to dissuade them from buying new long-range missiles from North Korea, which will have every reason to push such sales aggressively.

If the United States creates a power vacuum in Iraq, Turkey's security will be severely compromised. The failure of American post–Iraq war policy in the Middle East would leave Syria free to aggrandize itself. Syria is a state sponsor of terrorism, with programs for the development of weapons of mass destruction; it has reasons to look for leverage against Turkey, particularly in connection with access to water resources that Turkey controls. Iran—in the absence of the Iraqi threat—may finally join the community of nations. But a better bet is that Iran's conservative clerical masters will only see in Saddam Hussein's fate even greater reason to pursue nuclear weapons in the hope of fending off the United States. And Russia, seeing the United States emerge as hegemon over the Middle East, may find reason to tolerate an increased flow of technology for weapons of mass destruction into Iran. That would be especially likely in the event that the United States does not use its decisive influence as the occupying power to make sure that huge contracts for participation in the development of Iraq's energy resources are awarded to the Russians.

But the greatest threat of all for Turkey would be for the Kurds of northern Iraq to move toward independent statehood and to develop an overtly irredentist philosophy appealing to the Kurds of neighboring regions, particularly in Turkey itself. Such a development is far from anything the United States intends and, in fairness, is beyond anything leaders of the Iraqi Kurds have espoused. On the contrary, they are careful to speak meticulously in terms of Kurdish autonomy within an intact Iraqi state. But there is no guaranteeing the future. Should Turkey find itself at odds with a reformed Iraq that is an American protectorate, a major break in U.S.-Turkish relations would become possible.

Meanwhile, from the Turkish perspective, NATO will be seen as seriously damaged by residual transatlantic bitterness over continuing disagreements about the future of postwar Iraq. The Security Council's authority may be further diminished for similar reasons. And arms control may seem to be a spent process, given U.S. disinterest in formal negotiations and distaste for treaties—and particularly if the United States cannot find a way to stop North Korea's nuclear weapons program.

Moreover, changes in United States nuclear policy during the present administration stand to make a very strong impact on Turkey. Turkey's decision to abjure nuclear weapons rests on the NPT's basic trade-off: non-nuclear weapons states promise not to seek nuclear weapons; nuclear weapons states promise to seek their complete elimination. The CTBT represented a logical end point for the fundamental premise of the NPT, that nuclear weapons should be delegitimized over time and that the goal should be their abolition, however long that might take.

The administration of George W. Bush has effectively rejected these concepts. The United States has rejected the CTBT and is showing an interest in the development of new types of nuclear warheads.[43] The central bargain of the NPT has been repudiated—not just implicitly, but explicitly by many key officials of the present administration. According to one nonproliferation expert, "these officials seek not to create an equitable global regime that actively devalues nuclear weapons and creates conditions for their eventual elimination, but rather to eradicate bad guys or their weapons while leaving the 'good guys' free of nuclear constraints."[44]

When considering how these changes in U.S. nuclear policy will affect Turkey, it is important to evaluate their impact on other avowedly nonnuclear states in the Middle East. Not only has the current U.S. stance eroded a basic international inhibition, but it should also be clear to countries such as Egypt that for political reasons, the United States has no intention of pressuring Israel into negotiations aimed at creating a nuclear free zone. Therefore, from Egypt's perspective, a second inhibition is gone, with the disappearance of any hope—however thin—that negotiations could eliminate Israel's nuclear forces. Combine this with the possibility of continued proliferation of weapons of mass destruction in other parts of the world, such as North Korea or Iran, and Egypt's nuclear restraint could become a source of political vulnerability for President Mubarak. Egyptian newspapers have lauded North Korea's success in getting the United States' attention, and they have demanded that their country not accept a second-best position if it comes to the presence of nuclear weapons in the Middle East. There may or may not be a link between that kind of thinking and the announcement that Egypt plans to have a nuclear power station of its own by 2010.

Furthermore, in March 2003, Syria, another supposedly non-nuclear state in the Middle East, signed an agreement with Russia to build a large nuclear desalinization plant on the Syrian coast. The arrangement contains many parallels with the deal cut between Russia and Iran a decade ago, which the Iranians have since used to create a nuclear infrastructure far in excess of that required for maintenance of nuclear power reactors. These examples constitute a sort of spreading "nuclear measles" that can put pressure on Turkey to reconsider its non-nuclear status.[45]

The days when the United States could think of Turkey as a reflexive ally seem to be gone. To the extent the United States might have had Turkish support for war in Iraq, it would only have been because the United States agreed to pay a steep price for that help, up front. If things do not go well for U.S.-Turkish relations because of the policies of the new Turkish government, then the relative importance of Turkish self-reliance will grow. As for the hope of eventual membership in the European Union, it may soon be clear to Turkey whether European public opinion, always critical, regards Turkey permanently as both unqualified and culturally alien to the very idea of Europe. The former attitude is a temporary, if prolonged, problem; the latter one is irredeemable.

It is fair to say that from Turkey's perspective, the security landscape is changing for the worse. If this process continues and accelerates, old, well-accepted concepts about Turkish security may lose their credibility and perhaps be left behind as Turkey tries to adjust to its new role and its new circumstances. Under these pressures, Turkish attitudes toward nuclear weapons should not be regarded as utterly beyond challenge or change. In fact, a minister in the previous government has already suggested this course in a public statement. Referring to the growing threat of nuclear weapons in the region, the transport minister noted that "our possession of the nuclear bomb will strengthen our security and enhance our deterrence amid this nuclear environment."[46] One can apply a high discount to that statement, but it is still remarkable and may one day be regarded as the earliest hint of an upheaval yet to come. An even bigger hint, however, may lie in Turkey's renewed interest in nuclear energy.

How Turkey Might Acquire Nuclear Weapons—or Hedge Its Bets

The now-classic path to a nuclear weapons capability is to hide it behind a large-scale civilian nuclear energy program. Periodically, Turkish authorities have declared their interest in civilian nuclear energy, based on their projections of the country's needs for electricity. Turkey's energy requirements are estimated to grow between 5 to 8 percent through 2010, and there have been times when Turkey appeared to be in a race to keep its energy supply from becoming the limiting factor in its economic growth.[47] Turkey's installed electric power capacity must be doubled by 2010 to meet this growing demand.[48] The country imports a substantial amount of its unmet energy needs: 82 percent of its oil consumption in 2000 was met through imports.[49] There is limited additional hydroelectric capacity, and most of that is in the eastern part of the country. Turkish vulnerability due to its dependence upon imported hydrocarbons is accentuated by the political volatility of some of its main sources: the Middle East; the Caspian region, with pipeline links still under development; Russia, which may or may not be a reliable partner for the longer term; and Iran, which is still off limits unless Turkey wants to dare serious consequences from the United States.[50]

Nuclear energy has been of considerable interest to Turkey for a very long time, and there have been five independent attempts to foster a civilian nuclear capacity since 1970. Negotiations for nuclear power plants have been conducted with Swedish, German, French, Canadian, American, Korean, and Argentine firms. All such efforts ultimately failed because of political interruptions, economic limitations, and Western nonproliferation pressure.[51]

There was a particularly tenacious nuclear supply relationship between Turkey and Pakistan, extending from the late 1970s through the 1990s, which persisted despite pressure from the United States to stop and contrary to assurances from the Turkish government, at the highest levels, that the relationship had in fact been terminated. There were fears that the basis of the relationship was the export of dual-purpose technology useful for uranium enrichment from sources in Turkey or transshipped by Turkish middlemen to Pakistan.[52] Starting in 1980 and continuing until 1989, the United States sent over 100 diplomatic démarches to Turkey regarding this relationship.[53]

The Pakistan-Turkey nuclear partnership began sometime in the mid-1970s with the signing of a nuclear cooperation agreement to pursue equipment and expertise.[54] In 1980 the relationship took on a new level of significance when the United States secretly warned Turkey that a shipment of inverters aboard a ship flying Turkish flags was assisting in Pakistan's nuclear weapons program. The Turkish foreign ministry replied that Turkey was legally powerless to stop a private firm's exports.[55]

The U.S. State Department responded to this declaration of powerlessness by stepping up the diplomatic pressure. In mid-June 1981, Washington sent a cable to the American embassy in Ankara directing it to threaten Turkey's economic aid if the government was not able to control the export of sensitive material to Pakistan.[56] U.S. ambassador Robert Strausz-Hupe confronted Foreign Minister Ilter Turkmen and high-level military officials on the matter.[57] This diplomatic intervention was accompanied by a quiet decision by the United States to allow the bilateral nuclear cooperation agreement with Turkey to expire, thereby imposing a de facto nuclear fuel embargo on Turkey's research reactors.[58]

The results of this pressure were disappointing from the American perspective: Turkey continued to claim a bottom-line inability to effectively stop the exports of a private firm. Moreover, the uranium embargo was circumvented through establishing a French supply chain.[59] Meanwhile, the Turkey-Pakistan link continued to operate very effectively. In fact, according to testimony by Senator Alan Cranston (D-Calif.) during a closed session of the Senate Foreign Relations Committee, as of 1984, "the majority of materials smuggled from the West to Pakistan continue to move through Turkey, principally from West German and French companies."[60]

In July 1987, the State Department again broached the subject with high-level Turkish officials. Then undersecretary for political affairs Michael Armacost traveled to Ankara to join Ambassador Strausz-Hupe in confronting the Turkish government about its ineffective ban on inverter exports. The results were the same: three months later the Turkish foreign ministry announced that Turkey fulfilled its nonproliferation commitments with great care and denied selling any nuclear arms materials to Pakistan.[61]

By 1988 the United States decided to confront the Turkish government at the highest level possible: President Reagan was to receive President Evren on June 27, 1988, and would raise the issue of Turkey-Pakistan nuclear cooperation. In papers prepared to support President Reagan (by then national security adviser Colin Powell), the problem was described as serious enough to "severely damage" the U.S.-Turkey relationship.[62]

Transcripts of the meeting in a recently declassified White House memo show that the issue was in fact raised at the very top of the meeting. President Reagan noted that it was "very important" that the Turkish government successfully block exports of sensitive nuclear material to Pakistan because Pakistan possessed the technology for nuclear weapons. Evren responded that "there had been nuclear enrichment exports from Turkey to Pakistan" but that these had been banned by the Council of Ministers. The remaining discussion of the issue is excised in the transcript, leaving twenty-one lines of discussion unknown.[63] Secondary sources hint that this portion of the conversation included an explicit threat that assistance would be cut off by Congress without effective action, a discussion of the uranium embargo, and possibly U.S. aid to help enforce the export ban.[64]

Reagan followed up their discussion by mentioning the Turkey-Pakistan nuclear cooperation at a meeting with Turkish prime minister Ozal five months later. As Powell's background notes indicate, President Reagan thanked Prime Minister Ozal for cooperating with an interagency team of U.S. experts sent to Turkey to assist in export controls. Reagan then stressed the importance of continued cooperation.[65]

The cumulative effect of these interventions was successful; while no definitive evidence from U.S. government documents is yet available, experts with knowledge of the politics of the episode graded Reagan's bid a success.[66] After almost a decade of nonproliferation intransigence, the Turks finally ended their exports of uranium enrichment technology.

But was this supply relationship the only facet of nuclear cooperation between Turkey and Pakistan? A definitive answer to the question of whether this relationship included transfers of weapons-related knowledge from Pakistan to Turkey must be suspended until the documents from this period complete declassification review. However, there were allegations by the Greek and Indian press to the effect that the Turks were getting more than money from the deal; that Turkish scientists were on-site at Pakistani nuclear facilities receiving advanced training. One analyst of Turkish nuclear history argues that such allegations were baseless and politically motivated, but that is far from certain.[67] Expert comment and press reports from non-Greek and Indian sources support the possibility of direct Turkish training in advanced nuclear weapons technique. In a November 1986 interview with the Turkish newspaper *Cumhuriyet*,

American arms control analyst Charles Van Doren mentioned that in addition to the export of uranium enrichment technology, there were "clues that there was technical cooperation between the two countries in 1982."[68] Perhaps the best evidence for this came in a 1989 interview of Pakistani minister of state for defense Cheema in the Istanbul-based *Hurriyet* newspaper. Noting that

> The accumulated knowledge in one country should be shared by the other between Turkey and Pakistan, Cheema said: 'I am afraid that everyone knows what the other does in this world. . . . The Western countries have tried to prevent us from moving together and they will continue to do so in the future. . . . Regardless of the strenuous effort made by the Christian world, fraternal relations between Turkey and Pakistan have increased. It is as if we have integrated to become a single whole.'[69]

The history of the Turkey-Pakistan relationship has contemporary significance because of what it illustrates about the nature of relations between Turkey and the West. During the late 1970s, when Turkey signed the nuclear cooperation agreement and had most likely begun exports of enrichment technology, U.S.-Turkish relations were at the lowest point in the post–World War II era. The U.S. arms embargo against Turkey in 1975, in response to Turkish intervention in Cyprus the previous year, soured relations and created a climate of hostility. Even more important, Turkey's foreign policy at the time was moving toward a more "balanced" orientation—that is, less dependent upon the United States. General Evren, the head of state from 1980 to 1989, strongly advocated shifting Turkey's regional strategy away from total dependence on the West and toward more balanced relations with the East. In May 1983, for example, Evren responded to Western criticism on human rights, economic reforms, and democratization by claiming that Turkey could do without the West if the West continued to make things difficult. His goal was to create a more "multidimensional, balanced foreign policy," and consequently he developed closer ties to neighbors in the Middle East, North Africa, and, most significant, Pakistan.[70] Only intervention at the presidential level, eight years after the first diplomatic activity, was able to convince Evren and the Turkish military elite that relations with the West were more important than continued nuclear supply to Pakistan.

Turkey's 1988–1991 negotiations with Argentina also illustrate the intersection of civilian nuclear ambitions and nonproliferation concerns.

In 1988—the same year the United States confronted Turkey with its ultimatum over Pakistan—the Turkish government tried to partner with Argentina for the development of nuclear energy by signing a fifteen-year nuclear cooperation agreement. The scope of the agreement was expansive, looking to front-end fuel cycle technologies as well as reactor construction. In October 1990, the two countries agreed to jointly develop and build a modular low-power reactor of Argentine design; most important, the reactors were to be built with the intention of exporting the technology to other countries. The United States made repeated inquiries through the embassy in Ankara about the possible effect the Argentine-Turkish nuclear relationship would have on other countries in the region, particularly Pakistan.[71] However, in 1991 Turkey canceled the deal after pressure by the United States, Germany, and the Soviets, who agreed that "Turkey's acquisition of nuclear technology would be disadvantageous."[72]

As recently as the summer of 2000, Turkey was still actively seeking financing for the construction of nuclear power plants. However, in July of that year, the Turkish government was forced to freeze this program because of the state of the country's finances.[73] For two years after the cancellation, it appeared government interest in nuclear power might finally have ended. In November 2002, however, the trade and industry minister of the new Islamist Justice and Development Party (AKP) government announced its intention to revive the program, though without mentioning when.[74] Further evidence of Turkey's continued interest in nuclear power came at the International Atomic Energy Agency's Forty-Sixth General Conference, where the Turkish delegation reaffirmed its commitment to the development of innovative nuclear power sources for commercial usage.[75]

Finances are a major problem, given the state of the Turkish economy and the fact that the financial community probably will be uncertain about the economic prospects of Turkey under the new Erdogan government. But Turkey is one of the few potential growth markets for nuclear power anywhere in the world, and Western vendors of nuclear power equipment must regard it as a possible lifeline for an industry that is otherwise stagnant. They may well be prepared to press lenders to be more forthcoming. Ordinarily, the United States could be expected to resist Turkish interest in nuclear energy because of concerns about proliferation. However, Turkey's importance to the United States as a bulwark against Islamic extremism may override that concern. It would in any event be hard for the present administration to take a hard line against Turkish nuclear energy plans if the United States ultimately takes no effective action to block the nuclear ambitions of North Korea and Iran, or potentially Syria.

Even if the United States and other potential suppliers were to exercise all due diligence concerning nuclear exports to Turkey, there are other exporters who might not. Enough technology and equipment is now available for lateral trade between Pakistan and North Korea and potential customers for nuclear weapons technology to permit such programs to flourish. Israel, in theory, is also a possible source for such technology for the Turks—but the chance of a technology or material transfer as a matter of formal policy is slight, given repercussions for Israel's relations with the United States. On the other hand, unauthorized transfers of Israeli technology cannot be ruled out. Finally, there is the possibility that individuals with knowledge of nuclear weapons design have found their way into Turkey already. There have been reports that scientists have found their way from the Newly Independent States into Turkey over time.[76]

Deciding to Go Nuclear

The standard model of national security decisionmaking in the Turkish government is that real power is exercised behind the scenes by the Turkish military. The reality is probably more intricate, with civilian political leadership important to national security decisionmaking, if not the dominant partner. Certainly, the apparatus for a partnership exists through the machinery of the Turkish National Security Council. The National Security Council (NSC) has functioned, since the coup in 1980, as the primary national security policymaking organ. It is a small body composed half of civilian and half of military top officials; however, the military elite sets the agenda of the NSC and empirically controls the direction and scope of its decisions.[77]

A decision to move Turkey toward a nuclear weapons capability would demand the participation of both military and civilian leadership. The question is what would bring both groups of leaders into alignment on the issue, especially given the weight of the argument against reopening the nuclear issue. It is important to present that argument at full strength, as it might appear to Turkish officials, were it ever to be inscribed on the agenda of the NSC.

First, even the suggestion that Turkey might be thinking of reversing itself on nuclear weapons would precipitate a severe crisis in relations with the United States. The United States would be virtually certain to confront Turkey as it has done repeatedly in the past. In this confrontation, the United States would employ the full weight of its economic influence, bearing on the critical needs of the Turkish government for credit and especially for relative leniency from the International Monetary Fund. The Turkish government would find it especially ill advised to initiate such a confrontation in the midst of a period of extended economic weakness.[78]

To get past these objections, and to overcome the reluctance of the Turkish military to see relations with the United States so severely damaged, it would be necessary to imagine a consensus somehow developing that Turkish national security was likely to become much more challenged in the future by forces—such as regional proliferation—that require a nuclear deterrent. It is easier perhaps to imagine this kind of conclusion developing among the civilian leadership than the military. Presumably, the leaders of the armed forces are already concerned by the fact that Turkey is now under the leadership of an Islamist government. The military cannot be at all confident that the current government will succeed in creating a stable middle ground, one that permits Turkey to remain a reliable partner in security relationships with Europe and the United States.

In the event of a political shift in the direction of anything even remotely like Islamic radicalism, the Turkish military might well intervene to correct the drift. But any such action also carries great risks, including the possibility of widespread civil disturbance. Still, the military might choose to fall in behind a more Islamic, more nationalist political leadership if it concluded that for whatever reasons, Turkey could no longer depend upon its old security relationships, especially with the United States, and that other developments were turning Turkey's renunciation of nuclear weapons from a security asset to a major security deficiency.

Such a combination of developments may be improbable but far from impossible. Europe may yet reject Turkey as a member of the EU. Relations with the United States have been damaged by events surrounding the war with Iraq. There are major uncertainties for Turkey in the aftermath of the war, which may place Turkish policy at ever-deeper cross-purposes with the objectives of the United States. Proliferation of nuclear weapons in Iraq will no longer be an issue, but Turkish concerns may be intensified by failures of American nonproliferation policy elsewhere—especially in Iran, where matters pertaining to Turkey's self-image as well as security are involved.

Keeping Turkey on the Non-Nuclear Road

Any measures designed to enhance the credibility of NATO, the United States, and the European Union as reliable underwriters of Turkish national security will work to diminish the risk of a Turkish decision to acquire nuclear weapons. One side effect of the establishment of the EU defense system is that it may diminish Turkey's confidence since it is not a member of the EU system as it takes form and it is worried about declining NATO vitality—not just because of EU actions but also because of diminished American regard for the institution.

The gradual spread of ballistic missile systems into the Middle East is another problem to keep in mind. Progressively longer-range Iranian missiles will have their psychological effect. So, too, would the appearance of longer-range systems in Saudi Arabia. It would not simply be a question of whether states such as these might ever be a threat to Turkey but rather an issue of appearances and parity. The development of a ballistic missile defense system in which Turkey could participate, with costs largely written off, would be a potential help.[79] Strong and successful efforts to block the spread of nuclear weapons or other weapons of mass destruction in the region would also be key. Recent news that Iran will allow intensified international inspection of its nuclear facilities is positive.[80] But that is against the backdrop of Iranian acknowledgment (when confronted) of a previously covert uranium enrichment facility. We are a long way from resolving this problem, and there is no guarantee that in the end we shall. But if Iran were to acquire a nuclear weapons capability, the impact on Turkey would be powerful.

Strong financial support for non-nuclear energy alternatives is important. Some experts have questioned whether Turkey truly needs nuclear energy as a backup to gas and oil. But Turkish concern about dependence on energy from politically unstable sources is real. The law of unintended consequences may also apply to the Bush administration's doctrinal support for democratic transition in the Middle East. An unsuccessful transition in Saudi Arabia, for example, would be profoundly destabilizing, not just for the region but potentially for the world because of its ripple effects on the politics of oil. One may also question what effect a democratic transition would have on countries such as Azerbaijan and Kazakhstan, which represent Turkey's major alternative hopes for energy supplies on the scale needed to sustain vigorous economic growth. It is important also that the United States resist Russian efforts to drive American influence out of the Caspian region. We need to be present and to act as a stabilizer.

The recent reappearance of terrorism in the streets of Istanbul shows the fragility of that country's peace.[81] Few Americans are aware of the terrible costs of Turkey's long struggle with Kurdish terrorism, and Europeans have tended to be unresponsive and, in fact, to place blame exclusively on Turkish policies. Now, after the apparent resolution of that conflict, terrorism reappears—this time as a metastasis of al Qaeda. These attacks are not just against symbolic targets that happen to be located in Turkey: they represent the hatred of Islamic terrorists for the kind of modernizing secularism that the modern Turkish state embodies. Our assistance should be constant and vigorous—not just because it is needed to help an old ally protect itself but because it can help restore a sense of confidence in Turkey's relationship with the United States. That confidence, in turn, is one of the psychological defenses we need to safeguard against the appearance of a demand for security that ultimately might include reconsideration of the nuclear option.

In particular, overall U.S. foreign policy needs to be reformulated based on recognition that the so-called arc of crisis—loosely corresponding to much of the Islamic world, with its demographic 'youth bulge,' economic shortfalls, and deepening environmental problems—will occupy the attention of the major international players over the next generation. In this process, Turkey will be a participant of major strategic value to the United States. Acknowledging this will help create a more long-range and consistent American approach than we now have. It would instill in Turkey a sense that the American link is destined to remain strong and reliable. It would also help if the United States reengaged in the establishment of formal and binding agreements to limit the spread of nuclear weapons—but that is outside the political range of the present administration. Perhaps, however, the administration will take into account the impression that will be formed in countries such as Turkey if the United States were to pursue the development and testing of new nuclear weapons.

There are good reasons why all these things should come to pass. There are other reasons why they may not. From the Turkish perspective, the future is no longer nearly as predictable as in the past. It follows that fundamental aspects of Turkish thinking about national security—including the decision to abjure nuclear weapons—may not continue to be sacrosanct.

Postscript

In the period after submission of this chapter, the government of Turkey has moved to reduce the formal influence of the Turkish General Staff as a driver in the processes of the Turkish National Security Council. These changes, enacted by vote of the Turkish parliament in the first week of August 2003, are in response to requirements laid down by the European Union as one of its conditions for Turkish membership.[82] It remains to be seen whether this change will more than superficially alter what has been the reality of a strong behind-the-scenes influence exercised by the military.

Notes

1. Bruce Kuniholm, "The Evolving Strategic Significance of Turkey's Relationship with NATO," in Gustav Schmidt, ed., *A History of NATO: The First Fifty Years*, vol. 3 (New York: Palgrave, 2000), p. 346.

2. Michael O. Wheeler, "NATO Nuclear Strategy, 1949–90," in Gustav Schmidt, ed., *A History of NATO: The First Fifty Years*, vol. 3 (New York: Palgrave, 2000), p. 127.

3. The transformation was profound, whether measured in material or doctrinal terms. "When Eisenhower left office in January 1961, the nuclear stockpile consisted of over 18,000 weapons with yields ranging from a kiloton to several megatons. . . . The authority to use nuclear weapons under certain conditions had been predelegated by Eisenhower to the unified and specified commanders." Indeed, "in a little over seven years, Eisenhower's 'New Look' transformed the size and composition of the nuclear stockpile, custody arrangements, and . . . employment policies." Peter J. Roman, "Ike's Hair-Trigger: U.S. Nuclear Predelegation, 1953–1960," *Security Studies*, vol. 7, no. 4 (Summer 1998), pp. 121–23. Roman is citing declassified instructions from the Joint Chiefs of Staff issued in 1959. Department of Defense, "Memorandum for the U.S. Commander in Chief, Europe, Regarding Instructions for Expenditure of Nuclear Weapons in Emergency Conditions for Retaliation in the Event of a Nuclear Attack upon the U.S.," memo, top secret (issued December 3, 1959; declassified August 8, 1997), 5 pages.

4. Bruce R. Kuniholm, "Turkey and NATO: Past, Present and Future," *Orbis*, vol. 27, no. 2 (Summer 1983), p. 424.

5. White House, "Memo for President Johnson from McGeorge Bundy Regarding Existing Plans for U.S. Military Authorization to Use Nuclear Weapons for Retaliation When There Is Not Time to Contact the President," memo, top secret (issued September 23, 1964; declassified September 10, 1998), p. 1.

6. Leon V. Sigal, *Nuclear Forces in Europe* (Brookings, 1984), pp. 14–15.

7. Department of State, "Circular Telegram from the Department of State to the Posts in the NATO Capitals," central files, NATO 7, confidential. Approved by Assistant Secretary John M. Leddy. See Department of State, Office of the Historian, *Foreign Relations of the United States: 1964–1968*, vol. 13: *Western Europe Region* (Government Printing Office, 1995), entry no. 217, November 18, 1966.

8. Department of State, "Telegram from the Mission to the North Atlantic Treaty Organization and European Regional Organizations to the Department of State," central files, DEF 4 NATO, secret, priority. See Department of State, *Foreign Relations*, entry no. 113, November 28, 1965.

9. Arms Control and Disarmament Agency, *Arms Control and Disarmament Agreements: Texts and Histories of Negotiations* (1982).

10. Department of State, "Status Report on the Views of Various Countries Consulted about the Proposed Nonproliferation Treaty. These Countries Include: Belgium; Canada; Denmark; West Germany; France; Greece; Iceland; Italy; Japan; Luxembourg; the Netherlands; Norway; Portugal; Turkey; the United Kingdom," memo, secret (issued February 12, 1967; declassified April 14, 1999) p. 9.

11. Mustafa Kibaroglu, "Turkey," in Harald Muller, ed., *Europe and Nuclear Disarmament* (Brussels: European Interuniversity Press, 1998), p. 179.

12. Ibid.

13. "The traditional weight and hence the undisputed influence of the military on the decision making process on matters relating to national security was probably a factor that delayed ratification for some time. During the 1970s, when interest in nuclear as well as other weapons of mass destruction and their delivery means was growing in neighboring countries like Iran, Iraq, and Syria, the Turkish military elites might not have wanted to give an impression by means of a hasty ratification that Turkey would definitely forego the nuclear option." Ibid.

14. Catherine the Great's victory against the Turks in 1774 brought the Russian empire to the shores of the Black Sea for the first time. Douglas A. Howard, *The History of Turkey* (Westport, Conn.: Greenwood Press, 2001) p. 55.

15. "Turkey: External Affairs," *Jane's Sentinel Security Assessment (Eastern Mediterranean)*, vol. 13 (November 6, 2002), pp. 5–6.

16. Ministry of National Defense (Turkey), "Defense White Paper 2000" (www.msb.gov.tr/Birimler/GnPPD/GnPPDBeyazKitap.htm [January 21, 2003]).

17. Ibid.

18. Ibid.

19. Christer Berggren, "Annex A. Arms Control and Disarmament Agreements," in *SIPRI Yearbook 2002* (Oxford University Press, 2002), pp. 764–77.

20. "Defense White Paper 2000."

21. Duygu Bazoglu Sezer, "Turkey's New Security Environment, Nuclear Weapons and Proliferation," *Comparative Strategy*, vol. 14 (1995), p. 150.

22. One prominent Russia scholar argues that Vladimir Putin himself embodies this imperialist Russian revival. See Stephen J. Blank, "Putin's Twelve Step Program," *Washington Quarterly*, vol. 25, no. 1 (Winter 2002), pp. 147–60.

23. Sezer, "Turkey's New Security Environment," p. 151.

24. Ibid., p. 153.

25. Cengiz Candar and Graham E. Fuller, "Grand Geopolitics for a New Turkey," *Mediterranean Quarterly*, vol. 12, no. 1 (Winter 2001), p. 22.

26. "Turkey: External Affairs," p. 9.

27. H. Sonmez Atesoglu, "Turkish National Security Strategy and Military Modernization," *Strategic Review*, vol. 30, no. 1 (Winter 2001), p. 29.

28. Ibid.

29. Sezer, "Turkey's New Security Environment," p. 155.

30. "The Russian Federation keeps the right to use nuclear weapons in response to the use of nuclear weapons or other WMD against Russia or its allies, as well as in response to the large-scale conventional aggression in critical situations for the Russian national security." From the "Military Doctrine of the Russian Federation," *Nezavisimaya Gazeta* (Russia), April 22, 2000, p. 5. Cited in Yuri Fedorov, "Russia's Doctrine on the Use of Nuclear Weapons," paper prepared for Pugwash meeting no. 279, London, November 15–17, 2002 (www.pugwash.org/reports/nw/federov.htm. [February 2004]).

31. "From a broader perspective, the position of the new military doctrine sanctioning first-use of nuclear weapons is seen as an instrument at the service of Russia's larger foreign policy objective of deterring other regional states from competing with Russia for influence and control in the former Soviet Union." See Sezer, "Turkey's New Security Environment," p. 155.

32. "Putin Tells the Nation Russia Can Be Rich and Strong Again" (in Russian), RTR Russia TV, May 16, 2003, in BBC Monitoring, May 16, 2003 (Westlaw).

33. On the motivation for the Israeli-Turkish alliance, see "Turkey: External Affairs," p. 17.

34. Massimo Calabresi, "Iran's Nuclear Threat," *Time*, online edition, March 8, 2003 (www.time.com/time/world/article/0,8599,430649,00.html [February 2004]).

35. Sezer, "Turkey's New Security Environment," p. 165.

36. Ibid., p. 168.

37. Karl Vick, "After Calls on Turkey, U.S. Put on Hold," *Washington Post*, January 8, 2003, p. A14.

38. "Intimidation from Bush," *Cumhuriyet* (Istanbul), February 25, 2003, pp. 1, 8.

39. "Turkey: External Affairs," p. 6.

40. Office of the Press Secretary, "President Discusses the Future of Iraq," February 26, 2003 (www.whitehouse.gov/news/releases/2003/02/20030226-11.html [February 2003]).

41. Eric Schmitt, "Army Chief Raises Estimate of G.I.'s Needed in Postwar Iraq," *New York Times*, February 25, 2003.

42. Press Secretary, "Future of Iraq."

43. Thomas Graham Jr. and Damien J. LaVera, "Our Dangerous New Nuclear Posture Review," March 2002 (www.nyu.edu/globalbeat/syndicate/graham031102.html [February 2004]).

44. George Perkovich, "Bush's Nuclear Revolution," *Foreign Affairs*, vol. 82, no. 2 (2003), p. 2.

45. Henry Sokolski, "Two, Three, Many North Koreas," *Weekly Standard*, vol. 8, no. 20, February 3, 2003 (www.weeklystandard.com/Content/Public/Articles/000/000/002/168zucpu.asp [February 2004]).

46. "Minister Reportedly Calls for Possession of Nuclear Bomb," *Al-Hayat* (in Arabic), March 14, 2000, p. 7 in *BBC Summary of World Broadcasts*, March 16, 2000 (Nexis).

47. Ayhan Demirbas, "Energy Facilities and Nuclear Power Program by 2020 in Turkey," *Energy Sources*, vol. 23, no. 5 (2001), p. 401.

48. Department of Commerce, "Turkey—Energy," Trade Information Center, 1999 (www.export.gov/comm_svc [March 2004]).

49. "Turkey—Energy," *Market Briefs*, Publication of the Showcase Europe Program by the U.S. Department of Commerce, 2002; see also Demirbas, "Nuclear Power Program," p. 414.

50. Statistics on Turkish energy needs originate with the state-run pipeline and transport company (BOTAS). These figures have been challenged as being overstated for the purpose of promoting projects important to BOTAS, such as the purchase of Russian natural gas. Bulent Aliriza, "Turkey's Caspian Energy Quandary," *Caspian Energy Update*, August 13, 2002 (www.csis.org/turkey/ceu020813.pdf [February 2004]).

51. The most comprehensive overview of the history of these deals is in David H. Martin, "Nuclear Threat in the Eastern Mediterranean: The Case against Turkey's Akkuyu Nuclear Plant," Nuclear Awareness Project, Uxbridge, Canada, June 2000 (www.cnp.ca/issues/nuc-threat-mediterranean.pdf [February 2004]).

52. There is also troubling evidence of a flip side to this relationship, whereby Turkish scientists were allowed direct access to Pakistani nuclear facilities. This will be discussed later in the chapter.

53. "US Report Confirms Bomb," *Asian Recorder*, August 12–18, 1992, p. 22505. This publication is a weekly digest of Asian events compiled in New Delhi, India.

54. Rodney W. Jones, "Pakistan: Emerging Nuclear Supplier Issues," in William Potter, ed., *International Nuclear Trade and Nonproliferation* (Lexington, Mass.: Lexington Books, 1990), p. 224.

55. David K. Willis, "On the Trail of the A-Bomb Makers," *Christian Science Monitor*, December 1, 1981, p. 1; and "Turkey's Role in Pakistan's Nuclear Programs," *Cumhuriyet* (Istanbul), November 10, 1986, p. 7, in Joint Publications Research Service (JPRS), *Worldwide Report: Nuclear Development and Proliferation*, JPRS-TND-87-006, March 20, 1987, p. 1.

56. Willis, "On the Trail of the A-Bomb Makers," p. 1.

57. "Turkey's Role in Pakistan's Nuclear Programs," in *Worldwide Report*, p. 2.

58. "'Secret' U.S. Nuclear Fuel Embargo Reported," *Hurriyet* (Istanbul), April 12, 1989, p. 13, in JPRS, *Nuclear Developments*, JPRS-TND-89-009, May 5, 1989, p. 40.

59. Ibid., p. 39.

60. Rick Atkinson, "Use in Arms Feared; Nuclear Parts Sought by Pakistanis," *Washington Post*, July 21, 1984, p. A1.

61. "Spokesman Denies Nuclear Sales to Pakistan," *Anatolia* (Ankara), October 28, 1987, in JPRS, *Nuclear Developments,* JPRS-TND-88-001, 1988, p. 95.

62. Colin Powell, "Meeting with Turkish Prime Minister Turgut Ozal," memo, White House, secret (issued December 15, 1988; declassified November 2, 1999 [sanitized]), p. 2. The memo is a background paper for President Ronald Reagan's meeting with Ozal regarding U.S.-Turkish relations; Turkish economic situation; and U.S. military assistance to Turkey.

63. White House, "Memorandum of Conversation with President Evren of Turkey," memo, secret (issued June 27, 1988; declassified October 28, 1999 [sanitized]), pp. 1–2.

64. "Nuclear Fuel Embargo," in *Nuclear Developments*, p. 39. This article indicates that the issue of the uranium embargo "was taken up by Turkish officials, including President Kenan Evren and Prime Minister Turgut Ozal, during their contacts in the United States." Powell's background paper for the Ozal meeting says, "When Turkish President Evren visited you in June, you told him that, by law, you would have no choice but to cut off all assistance to countries engaged in such exports" and also refers to an "interagency team of experts" assisting Turkey in export controls. Powell, background paper, memo, December 15, 1988, p. 2.

65. Powell, background paper, memo, December 15, 1988, p. 2.

66. "U.S. Expert Interviewed in South Asian Arming," *Times of India*, July 11, 1988, p. 18, in JPRS, *Nuclear Developments*, September 2, 1988, pp. 17–19 (www.nti.org/db/nuclear/1988/n8802824.htm [March 2004]).

67. Kibaroglu, "Turkey," p. 191.

68. "Turkey's Role in Pakistan's Nuclear Programs," in *Worldwide Report*, p. 2.

69. "Minister Discusses Nuclear Cooperation with Turkey," *Hurriyet* (Istanbul), May 4, 1989, p. 17, in JPRS, *Nuclear Developments*, JPRS-TND-89-010, May 23, 1989, pp. 23–24.

70. Kuniholm, "Turkey and NATO," p. 434. On Evren's relationship with Pakistan, see Mustafa Kibaroglu, "Turkey's Quest for Peaceful Nuclear Power," *Nonproliferation Review*, vol. 4 (Spring-Summer 1997), p. 35.

71. "'Secret Talks' with Argentina on Nuclear Plant," *Hurriyet* (Istanbul), September 14, 1989, p. 10, in JPRS, *Nuclear Developments*, JPRS-TND-89-019, October 6, 1989, p. 31.

72. "Argentina to Help Acquire 'Nuclear Technology,'" *Hurriyet* (Istanbul), May 25, 1988, pp. 3, 15, in JPRS, *Nuclear Developments*, June 21, 1988, p. 39 (www.nti.org/db/nuclear/1988/n8804185.htm [February 2004]).

73. Mike Buckthought, "Pulling the Nuclear Plug," *Briarpatch*, vol. 28, no. 7 (September 2000), pp. 17–19.

74. "Turkish Minister Says Nuclear Energy Plan Revived," *Reuters News*, November 27, 2002.

75. "Statement by Ambassador H. Aydin Sahinbas of Turkey to the 46th General Conference of the International Atomic Energy Agency, Vienna, 16 September 2002" (www.iaea.org/About/Policy/GC/GC46/Statements/turkey.pdf [February 2004]).

76. Berrak Kurtulus, "Cooperation in the Fields of Education and Science between Turkey and the Turkish Republics," *Eurasian Studies*, no. 17 (Spring-Summer 2000), pp. 45–46.

77. Bulent Aliriza, Turkey Program, Center for Strategic and International Studies, interview with author, Washington, D.C., March 12, 2003.

78. Ibid.

79. On Turkish interest in ballistic missile defense, see "Turkey: External Affairs," p. 6; and "Missile Defense System Sought," *Turkish Daily News* (Ankara), May 15, 1993, p. 3, in JPRS, *Proliferation Issues*, JPRS-TND-93-015, May 24, 1993, p. 29.

80. "Iran Signs Up to Nuclear Checks," *BBC News*, December 18, 2003 (http://news.bbc.co.uk/1/hi/world/middle_east/3327065.stm [February 2004]).

81. "Turkey Blasts 'Threat to Peace,'" *BBC News*, November 15, 2003 (http://news.bbc.co.uk/1/hi/world/europe/3272815.stm)

82. Amberin Zaman, "Army Loses Political Authority in Turkey," *Daily Telegraph*, July 31, 2003, p. 14.

CHAPTER 8

Germany: The Model Case, A Historical Imperative

JENIFER MACKBY

WALTER B. SLOCOMBE

Germany was, in an important sense, the birthplace of nuclear physics, and concern about potential Nazi development of nuclear arms was a major driver behind American and British nuclear programs during World War II. For a generation, the question of whether—and if so, how—Germany would have a nuclear military role was a major issue in German politics, in internal NATO debates, in relations between West Germany and the Soviet Union, and, indeed, in the general nonproliferation process.[1]

Three times Germany has legally committed itself to non-nuclear weapons status. First, in 1954 the Paris Protocols to the Treaty of Brussels conditioned membership of the Federal Republic of Germany (FRG) in NATO and the Western European Union (WEU) on it renouncing the right to produce nuclear weapons on its territory, while the European Atomic Energy Community safeguards system ensured the observance of this non-nuclear status. Then, in its 1975 accession to the Nuclear Non-Proliferation Treaty (NPT), West Germany pledged not to possess nuclear weapons of its own (while protecting the option of sharing in the delivery of the weapons of others). Finally, in the Two-plus-Four Treaty of 1990, which ended the four-power control of Germany, a newly reunified Germany renounced all weapons of mass destruction.[2] In addition, Foreign Minister Hans Dietrich Genscher confirmed Germany's renunciation of

175

atomic, biological, and chemical weapons at the NPT Review Conference in August 1990.

In recent years, both the strategic situation and internal German conditions and opinions have reinforced Germany's abjuration of nuclear weapons. For the foreseeable future, there seems little, if any, prospect of that decision being called into question, much less changed. Today, Germany is arguably the most resolutely non-nuclear major nation in the world and is in some respects the quintessential example of a nation that accepted non-nuclear weapons status only with considerable reluctance but whose decision to do so has only been reinforced by time and changed circumstances.

However remote the prospect of Germany acquiring nuclear weapons seems today, that possibility was fundamentally important to the initial decision by the United States and Britain to develop nuclear weapons during the Second World War, and the nuclear status of Germany remained an open question for many years thereafter. To assess the success of Germany in its efforts to remain non-nuclear entails an analysis of the cold war and the fear of Germany that survived World War II.

Accordingly, this chapter traces the history of the imposition of non-nuclear-weapons status on Germany in the context of German rearmament and German assumption of a central place in NATO military preparations. It outlines the compromises that led to a limited potential for West Germany to deliver United States–controlled nuclear weapons and to a strong German role in developing NATO nuclear doctrine and policy. And it traces the process by which Germany, under heavy external pressure, finally and permanently abandoned any possibility of an independent nuclear weapons status. Finally, it examines the changes in Germany's strategic position and its political culture that have led to today's situation in which there is no discernable possibility of that non-nuclear commitment being challenged, much less changed.

From Unconditional Surrender to Rearmament

When the United States suspected that Hitler might be developing atomic weapons, it launched the Manhattan Project in an all-out effort to beat Nazi Germany to the bomb. In fact, the Allies discovered at the end of the war that although Germany had commenced an atomic weapons program in 1939 at the Uran Verein (Uranium Society) in Berlin, by 1944 Germany had progressed only about as far as the Americans and British in 1941. It had not succeeded in separating U-235 or in constructing a chain-reacting uranium pile.[3]

The end of the war brought with it a complete dismantling of the German military establishment, and, a fortiori, of any military nuclear program. Immediately after the Nazi surrender, the Allies prohibited all goods and installations in Germany of "possible value for war purposes," including specifically those suitable for the development of nuclear energy. A special 1946 scientific decree permitted basic research in nuclear physics only subject to rigorous accounting and inspection procedures. Strict control continued over the manufacture, sale, and possession of war materiel, including weapons for police and for hunting. In the nuclear area, the Allied High Commission regulated "the production, import, export, transport, storage, use and possession of radioactive materials." A German could not produce deuterium gas, metallic beryllium, thorium, or uranium or construct facilities capable of separating isotopes of uranium with a yield potential in excess of 1 milligram of U-235 per twenty-four hours.[4]

But that initial disarmament did not end the story of a potential German nuclear weapons capability. Within a decade after 1945, the issue of German acquisition of nuclear weapons arose as an aspect of German rearmament and remained an issue until the mid-1970s, when Germany ratified the Non-Proliferation Treaty. At each stage, West Germany's relationship to nuclear weapons was a subject of controversy, both inside the Bonn republic and in its international relations—with its allies as well as with its Soviet adversary.

The early postwar years were marked by concern about a revived German military power, which was understandable in the context of prior history but was also in serious conflict with Western—and especially American—interest in fostering a revived German military as a contribution to defense against the much-feared prospect of a Soviet attack. For many European countries that had been invaded by Germany in the twentieth century, German rearmament was reluctantly acceptable only if accompanied by renunciation of nuclear weapons. For the Soviet Union, concern that West Germany, once it had its own military forces, would move to acquire nuclear weapons was both a genuine issue and a highly useful propaganda theme, conjuring up visions of revived German militarism, threats to the balance of power in Europe, and even a unilateral West German effort to achieve reunification by force. Conversely, although many West Germans rejected any notion of nuclear weapons for their country, for many others, imposed non-nuclear status was both a troubling symbol of discrimination against a reformed and irreversibly democratic nation and potentially a source of military weakness, or at least of worrisome dependence on other nations being prepared to take enormous risks for Germany's defense.

In the 1950s, West Germany and its allies shared an interest in stronger Western defense, but they differed sharply on the details of Bonn's contribution. The United States—and to a lesser degree Britain—were unwilling to bear the burden of defending Germany without German assistance and wanted Bonn to contribute significantly to its own and the collective defense, preferably concentrating on ground troops. France desired only a controlled German rearmament within a European framework but eventually rejected the European Defense Community proposals that it had originally backed as a means of ensuring that new German forces would be "European" in character. As France had not yet developed its own nuclear military capabilities, it did not wish Germany to be the first to do so—and strongly preferred that it never do so.

As for West Germany's government, it wanted rearmament only if its troops were treated on "a fully equal status . . . with respect to weapons and command."[5] Chancellor Konrad Adenauer viewed rearmament as a way to become a sovereign Western partner. In a context where rearmament was seen as a confirmation of the Federal Republic's sovereignty and nuclear weapons were increasingly being talked about as "just another form of artillery" (and the principal strength of the West on the battlefield), it was not surprising that Adenauer, like many West Germans, found it hard to accept that West Germany should be expected permanently—and unilaterally—to forgo nuclear weapons.

As a practical matter, the rearmament and resumed sovereignty of West Germany and its entry into the Western alliance system depended upon the country not possessing nuclear weapons. The London-Paris accords of 1954 provided for the accession of Germany to NATO and contained the pledge "not to manufacture in its territory any atomic weapons . . . defined as any weapon which contains . . . nuclear fuel . . . and which, by . . . uncontrolled nuclear transformation of the nuclear fuel . . . is capable of mass destruction . . . [or] any part, device, assembly or material especially designed for . . . any [such] weapon."[6] When the Paris accords became effective on May 5, 1955, the Federal Republic of Germany became the first Western nation to voluntarily renounce the production of nuclear weapons.

The pressures of the cold war were such that less than a decade after the Nazi capitulation, the Federal Republic agreed to participate—and its allies agreed to allow it to participate—in both NATO and the WEU. Under the agreement of 1954, Germany was not allowed to have more than twelve divisions in its army or more than 500,000 men in its forces. Chancellor Adenauer pledged not to use force to implement boundary changes or reunification and not to manufacture on the territory of the Federal Republic atomic weapons or certain other types of major offensive armaments. In his memoirs, Adenauer stated that he made the nonproduction pledge without prior consultations and that it was one of his "few personal decisions."[7] In return, the Federal Republic received "the full authority of a sovereign State" as well as guarantees regarding its military security and political status. Adenauer agreed to these restrictions "voluntarily" as long as the Allies recognized the general principle of equality. For their part, the Allies stated that their goal was to bring about the reunification of Germany. Indeed, the protocols to the Paris accords provided for the end of the occupation regime.

Because the accords were quickly ratified, lawmakers did not focus on Adenauer's pledge not to produce nuclear weapons in Germany. Instead, they saw it as yet more evidence that Germany was turning away from militarism and no longer coveting power, thus proving its shared aims with Western countries. Although Adenauer knew little about weapons of mass destruction, "no question was raised as to the wisdom of the chancellor's declaration."[8] Some years later, however, during the 1965 federal election campaign, Adenauer claimed that the pledge was understood to be subject to a decision by the Federal Republic that conditions could change.[9] Though few agreed with this interpretation, Adenauer gained what was crucial at the time: sovereignty for Germany and acceptance into NATO. Other NATO countries saw that the division of Germany after the war had made it vulnerable to expansion by the Soviet Union, and thus the acceptance into NATO served both to reassure as well as to constrain Germany.[10]

Keeping the Option Open: Bonn and Tactical Nuclear Weapons

The 1954 pledge not to produce nuclear weapons was extremely important, but it was not absolute. It did not prevent Germany from importing nuclear weapons or from controlling nuclear weapons through bilateral or multilateral arrangements; nor did it keep it from developing nuclear weapons outside of its territory. Nuclear fuel, equipment, and material were not restricted for civilian purposes or for medical and industrial research in the scientific field. Germany had the right to develop atomic energy for peaceful purposes.

Many experts believe that the renunciation was not genuinely voluntary but rather the result of insistence by Bonn's allies, in particular France. While many—including many in West Germany—believed that a voluntary renunciation served German national interests, others thought that, on the contrary, the actions in 1954, and even those later on, were more in the nature of temporary—and dangerous—expedients. Germany might have preferred to renounce nuclear renunciation. As late as 1995, one scholar characterized these German attitudes by saying, "Bonn's rejection of atomic weapons was never the result of a policy that turned on self-imposed moderation, but always the consequence of external conditions and power relations. . . . The Republic wanted to have a maximum of military options as well as freedom of nuclear trade . . . the treaty was accepted, but only at the price of containing major loopholes—loopholes that would allow tons of plutonium to pass through them. . . . The Federal Republic has always kept open the door that would lead to having its own nuclear weapons."[11]

Some high-level West German politicians viewed Germany's renunciation of nuclear weapons, as specified in the Paris protocol to the 1954 Treaty of Brussels, as a temporary measure. Adenauer thought that the Federal Republic would have nuclear weapons after it recovered from the war. This was not just a passing opinion of the immediate postwar period. During the debate over the NPT in the late 1960s, Adenauer called the proposal for Bonn's accession a "death sentence" for the Federal Republic.[12]

To understand his view, it is critical to recognize that Adenauer doubted the wisdom of West Germany accepting permanent non-nuclear status not out of any atavistic militarism but because of concern over the centrality of nuclear weapons in the defense of Germany and about German access to decisions by Washington regarding nuclear weapons. He considered these issues important not just for defense against a Soviet attack, but also for the future of Germany's sovereignty and eventual unity.

Following the formal entry of Germany as the fifteenth member of NATO on May 9, 1955, Bonn began to worry about its dependence on the nuclear weapons of others, as well as about the durability of the American guarantee for German security. Western strategy in the 1950s increasingly emphasized both the doctrine of massive retaliation and the role of tactical nuclear weapons to make up for the lack of conventional force levels in Europe. Even the opposition Social Democratic Party (SPD)—strongly antinuclear in principle—claimed that neither the American strategic nuclear capability nor NATO forces would protect Germany.

The original concept for West German rearmament within NATO had been that by 1959 Bonn would raise a force of 500,000 soldiers—at least implicitly to provide the bulk of NATO's manpower—while the United States, to a lesser degree Britain, and eventually France would provide the nuclear punch. However, soon after the NATO-WEU accession agreements took effect, West Germany's defense minister, Franz Josef Strauss, informed the alliance that for economic and demographic reasons, the Federal Republic would not in fact be able to field the 500,000-man force that had been projected. A few days later, he declared that Germany would continue to renounce the production of nuclear weapons but proposed that NATO should make atomic weapons available to German forces. Thus, West Germany would use "modern technology" to make a smaller Bundeswehr equal in combat strength to the originally promised 500,000-man force.

German reluctance to be permanently denied nuclear weapons and Strauss's argument that tactical nuclear weapons could offset the military effects of deploying a smaller force were wholly consistent with U.S. and British military policy in the mid-50s, which held that in a future war, nuclear weapons would inevitably play an integral, even dominant role, not only as instruments of ultimate deterrence but as decisive battlefield weapons. In 1953 the Eisenhower administration became concerned over the budgetary implications of planning for a long military competition with the Soviet bloc. Eisenhower and his advisers feared that greater manpower on the communist side—or at least a greater capacity to compel manpower into military service—would give Moscow a permanent advantage. Given the prospect of limited conventional force contributions from European members of NATO, the United States thought that it would be impossible to mount a conventional NATO defense that could credibly counter the Soviet threat. Moreover, Europe was very wary of the prospect of a renewed conventional war fought on European soil, leaving both Russia and America in de facto sanctuary.

The United States and its European allies could therefore agree to adopt a strategy to use the tactical nuclear weapons being developed as the principal instruments not just of deterrence but also of military defense.

Tactical nuclear weapons would not only extend and reinforce deterrence by giving greater flexibility to U.S. and NATO commanders; they would also provide a means to offset the supposedly inherently superior Soviet conventional capabilities on the battlefield. This "New Look" nuclear doctrine, by making nuclear weapons central to deterrence as well as to operational combat, inevitably raised the issue of whether West Germany should have such weapons.

Some officers of the new Bundeswehr had been trained in the United States about nuclear doctrine and use of tactical nuclear weapons and concluded that what was sound military policy for the United States was sound for the Federal Republic as well. When German defense leaders argued that Germany should have access to or at least the means to deliver—if not produce—nuclear weapons, they were also implicitly rejecting what they perceived as a discriminatory imbalance in the alliance. West Germany, they argued, should not just provide a NATO "infantry." If West Germany had arms inferior to the Americans (much less the British and French), in the event of war, a Soviet attack could be aimed mostly at the German divisions in the NATO "shield," entailing huge casualties and leaving West German defense at the mercy of allied decisions on the use of nuclear weapons.

To some degree, American leaders accepted these concerns of West Germany and other allies as valid and reasonable. President Eisenhower hinted that U.S. restrictions regarding nuclear sharing might be relaxed, stating, "We should not deny our allies what . . . your potential enemy already has. We do want our allies to be treated as partners and allies, and not as junior members of a firm who are to be seen but not heard. So I think that it would be better, for the United States, to make our law more liberal as long as . . . we are confident . . . they'd stand by us in time of trouble."[13] In 1958 U.S. law was changed to permit some increased nuclear sharing. In practice, however, the new flexibility was limited to Britain. The administration backed off broader changes that would have allowed sharing with Bonn as well as other allies, including France, when Congress—or at any rate its powerful atomic energy committee—expressed its disapproval, and little progress was made on relaxing limits on direct sharing of nuclear technology with allies.

West German political and military leaders also feared that without control over nuclear weapons, they would lack influence over decisions regarding their own security. They were concerned that their allies would hesitate to use nuclear weapons in defense of Germany, and they realized the consequences of such use. German leaders began to appreciate the implications for Germany—both East and West—of the prospect that a war in Central Europe would be immediately and deliberately escalated by NATO into a massive use of short-range nuclear weapons. Even if only NATO used tactical nuclear weapons, the effects on the two Germanys and their populations would be devastating—and it was clear that the USSR, as well as NATO, could use nuclear weapons on the battlefield.

A 1955 NATO exercise codenamed "Carte Blanche," which involved a notional Red Army invasion across the inner German border that was met with NATO tactical nuclear weapons, projected casualties of 1.7 million dead and 3.5 million wounded—almost all Germans—even without a Soviet nuclear counterblow.[14] When the results leaked, West Germany was confronted with the depth of its nuclear and defense dilemma—a dilemma that was not fully resolved until the collapse of the Soviet Union.

The problem was complex: neither Germany nor its allies were really prepared to pay (either in money or other sacrifices) for a conventional defense that could confidently stop a Soviet attack; but even if they had been, a conventional war on German soil would be a catastrophe. However, resort to nuclear weapons had its own drawbacks. If the Soviets attacked and nuclear weapons were not used defensively by NATO, Germany would be overrun (and substantially destroyed); if they attacked and nuclear weapons were used, Germany risked decimation. Immediate massive escalation to general nuclear war between the United States and the USSR might be a good deterrent, but there were doubts as to the willingness of the United States to risk—indeed to ensure—its own destruction if only European states had been attacked.

This multifaceted dilemma never had a satisfactory solution, but it did produce a continuing German insistence that nuclear weapons were central to its defense and that Bonn had a right to a strong, perhaps even decisive, voice in NATO's nuclear policies and wartime decisions. In the face of domestic opposition to any West German reliance on nuclear forces, Adenauer and Strauss both responded that Germany had to accept the risks of nuclear deterrence as a requirement of NATO membership. And for some West Germans, at least in the early years, those risks also produced a desire to have—or at least not permanently renounce—their own nuclear forces, to be used or withheld on terms they would decide.

To the debate in the late 1950s and early 1960s over NATO nuclear policy, posture, and doctrine was added the realization that the Soviet

Union's missile developments—for both theater and longer-range ballistic missiles—meant that it would soon acquire the ability not just to devastate Western Europe and particularly West Germany with nuclear weapons, but also to strike with massive effect against the territory of the United States. Even an American all-out strike at Soviet long-range nuclear forces could not eliminate that potential. To some degree West Germans (and other Europeans) had found comfort during the 1950s by the thought that if there were a Soviet attack on Europe, the United States could respond with nuclear strikes at the USSR without much risk to the American homeland and that this prospect would deter such a Soviet attack. However, once the Soviet Union achieved strategic parity with the United States, Germany questioned whether American strategic nuclear forces could be relied on to deter an attack and guarantee the security of Germany.[15]

During the period from 1957 to 1960, the Federal Republic increased its participation in NATO, particularly in Supreme Headquarters Allied Powers in Europe, through which it nurtured its bilateral relations with the United States as well as with the alliance as a whole. The grim history of the previous years began to fade. In seeking equality and integration, Germany became involved as a partner in planning, decisionmaking, and armament. As the Bundeswehr developed, West Germany also began to succeed France as the power with the largest conventional arms in continental Europe. West Germany remained underdeveloped in military technology, however, and trusted in the policy of American-provided nuclear deterrence while it devoted its attention more to domestic economic priorities.

Inside the Bonn republic there was, from the beginning, a strong opposition to any consideration of acquiring nuclear weapons. In the national elections of 1957, the opposition SPD had called for Germany to renounce nuclear weapons and for all atomic weapons to be withdrawn from the country in order to assist in both the nonproliferation and reunification efforts. Also in 1957 a group of eighteen prominent German scientists, many of whom had conducted nuclear research under the Nazi regime, signed the Göttingen Appeal stating that the Federal Republic would advance world peace most by rejecting the possession of atomic weapons. In their appeal, the scientists added that none of them "would be prepared to take any part in the production, testing or use of atomic weapons."[16] Each German decision on nuclear policy was marked by bitter debates in the Bundestag and often by massive demonstrations and protests.

Even Adenauer's government recognized the problems that a German nuclear capability could cause. In the late 1950s, when the United States offered to deploy in NATO countries its Thor and Jupiter missiles capable of striking targets in the USSR, Adenauer declined, on the ground that such a deployment in West Germany would arouse too much opposition from the USSR as well as from Bonn's NATO allies.[17]

At the same time, however, the West German military sought to share in the use of battlefield nuclear weapons. "The Germans must adapt themselves to the new circumstances," Adenauer said. "Tactical atomic weapons are in practical terms a further development of modern artillery."[18] After bitter debate and in the midst of massive public demonstrations, the Bundestag, in March 1958, voted to approve the acquisition by the Bundeswehr of capabilities to use "the most modern weapons"— universally understood to mean nuclear arms.[19] The eventual—and, on a limited scale, continuing—resolution of the question of a Bundeswehr role in NATO's tactical nuclear forces—without it producing or acquiring its own weapons—came through the development of a system whereby the West German (and other European) military had the capability to deliver tactical nuclear weapons owned and controlled by the United States. By 1960, as part of a seven-year buildup to 350,000 men in the armed forces, Bonn was committed to acquiring—mostly from the United States—a range of dual-capable strike aircraft, artillery, and short-range missiles that was to become the second-largest western capability for delivering nuclear warheads.

These dual nuclear-conventional delivery capabilities were to be controlled under a "dual-key" system: U.S. consent would be required to release the weapons to West Germany (or another ally participating in the system), and the consent of West Germany (or the other ally) would be required for their delivery. Although many other NATO allies were also purchasing the same nuclear delivery system to support such sharing arrangements, concerns were often expressed with special force about West Germany somehow manipulating these arrangements to enable it to use nuclear weapons unilaterally in a crisis. For example, the Joint Committee on Atomic Energy expressed shock when it found during an inspection tour only a small number of American soldiers guarding American nuclear weapons loaded on German aircraft.[20]

The U.S. (and German) response was that not only were such concerns unfounded as a matter of principle, but technical obstacles were in place that would prevent anyone—including the allies at whose bases the weapons were stored—from using the weapons without U.S. approval.

Specifically, by 1961 permissive action links or other electronic locks were installed on all nuclear weapons in Europe, even those on NATO high-alert status.[21] Only the American president could order that they be fired and release the necessary codes.

These assurances and arrangements did not, however, put wholly to rest the fears of some and the hopes of others that Bonn would eventually acquire nuclear weapons under its own absolute control. For example, the European Atomic Energy Community (Euratom), established in 1957 to improve the supply of nuclear energy, was still suspected by some to be linked to the development of a European, and particularly a German, atomic bomb. Further, Adenauer had stated in 1956 that he wanted "to achieve through Euratom, as quickly as possible, the chance of producing our own nuclear weapons." [22]

A German Role in Strategic Deterrence? The MLF and Beyond

Dual-capable, dual-key systems, despite their formidable military potential, did not entirely address Bonn's concerns about indefinite reliance on U.S. nuclear forces. West Germany had long considered supporting the creation of an "atomic NATO." Initially, this force was seen as being entirely separate from and independent of the United States. In 1957 Strauss had even decided to cooperate with France and Italy on joint development and production of nuclear weapons, supposedly without the United States knowing of the effort.[23] The weapons were to be produced in France, so that the Paris protocol would not technically be violated. The United Kingdom and the United States discovered the scheme and denounced these efforts for joint production, seeing them as a threat to the ban on production of nuclear weapons and a highly divisive force in the alliance. Nothing came of the project.

Contemporaneous shifts in French policy on nuclear weapons and on its relationship to NATO and the United States more generally sharpened German concerns during this period. At a meeting with Adenauer in July 1960, de Gaulle stated categorically that France would resume national responsibility for its defense with its own military and would not submit its forces to others' orders. Further, he said that the alliance could not remain an integrated transatlantic organization. Adenauer recognized that de Gaulle's decision had potentially profound implications for Germany's security, going far beyond implicit withdrawal of automatic French commitment to the military defense of West Germany. He returned to Bonn convinced that France would cause the United States to withdraw from NATO and that the organization would cease to exist, fatally undermining the premises of West German security policy.

With these new nuclear problems, NATO began more than a decade of seeking a way to give the European members of the alliance—and particularly the Federal Republic—a hand, or at least a voice, in the use of NATO's nuclear force.[24] From 1957 to 1960, the options debated within Germany, as well as within the alliance and the United States, included the transfer of warheads from producer states; indirect participation by non-nuclear allies, through the Supreme Allied Commander Europe (SACEUR), in decisions about nuclear weapons; and creation of some sort of European or joint U.S.-European nuclear force.

General Lauris B. Norstad, SACEUR from 1956 to 1963, was sympathetic to European concerns about broader sharing in the control of nuclear weapons and the defense of Europe. He proposed that NATO should become almost a fourth nuclear power or, in any case, a first step toward giving the allies a nuclear capacity on a NATO basis.[25] Norstad believed that this would allow the European members appropriately greater influence over the use of NATO's nuclear weapons and that, in any event, greater understanding about what kinds and qualities of weapons were in the stockpiles would ease German (and other allies') fears.[26] To some degree, doubts about the reliability of the U.S. deterrent were the product of secrecy. Political and military leaders complained that they still did not know how many and what types of weapons were stored on German soil or how or when they would be used. As Strauss frequently repeated, the European allies "did not know whether they had potatoes or warheads stored on their territory." Norstad also thought it might address some of Germany's desire to develop its own capacity.

In September 1960, Norstad introduced a proposal for an atomic NATO, based on cooperation between the United States and its European allies. Those initial proposals contained many of the features of the ultimate resolution that was to be reached after years of arcane debate. SACEUR was to have direct control over a NATO nuclear stockpile comprising land, sea, and air missiles committed by the United States (and the United Kingdom) for European defense. Warheads would be used according to the guidelines agreed to unanimously by the North Atlantic Council.

Strauss expressed official German public support for NATO as a fourth nuclear power, but others were less enthusiastic. Chancellor Adenauer met with Prime Minister Michel Debre to solicit acceptance of this idea from France but was without success. The Soviet Union opposed all aspects of West German rearmament, reserving special scorn for anything resembling a nuclear role for the Federal Republic. It made clear its concerns— no doubt partly sincere—about revived German militarism and claimed that Bonn was strengthening its military in order to negotiate reunification from strength.

The Soviet Union presented the Gromyko plan in 1956, and Poland advanced the Rapacki proposals at the United Nations in 1957 and in Warsaw in 1958. All these plans had the common element of banning nuclear weapons sharing. The Rapacki plan proposed nuclear weapon exclusion zones covering the territory of Poland, Czechoslovakia, and the two Germanys, where nations would "undertake the obligation not to manufacture, maintain or import for their own use and not to permit the location on their territories of nuclear weapons of any type, as well as not to install on or to admit to their territories installations and equipment designed for servicing nuclear weapons including missile-launching equipment."[27]

These Soviet-sponsored plans effectively barred NATO nuclear weapons in continental Europe while leaving unlimited Soviet deployments only a few hundred miles from the inner German border. Nonetheless, they appealed to the fears of many that the military—and especially the nuclear—confrontation in the center of Europe was highly dangerous.

Bonn replied to these and other denuclearization ideas by arguing that if the territory of West Germany were denuclearized it would have a very different political and military status than the other allies, and that this discrimination was incompatible with an alliance of equals. Reflecting the then current enthusiasm for tactical nuclear weapons, Bonn also argued that if tactical nuclear weapons were withdrawn, the American troops would retreat from the front line, leaving West Germany stripped of conventional defense (and a link to the American deterrent) as well as nuclear defenses.

The nuclear debate occurred in a broader context, both of controversy over the British application to join the European Common Market and also the crisis over the future of Germany. Bonn had insisted, and the NATO allies at least nominally agreed, that German reunification was a key NATO goal. In 1958 Khrushchev proposed East-West talks on a united Germany and demanded an end to Western presence in Berlin. The allies, in response, presented the "Herter Plan" in 1959, which would lead to free elections after a two-and-a-half-year period, during which time the German Democratic Republic and other Eastern European states would pledge not to produce nuclear (and also chemical and biological) weapons. The Federal Republic supported this plan through the 1960s.

Meanwhile, doubts were growing in the United States about the wisdom and credibility of making nuclear weapons in Germany the centerpiece of NATO strategy. Increasing awareness that tactical nuclear weapons were not a cheap, simple, high-confidence strategy resulted in a review of this policy. When John F. Kennedy assumed the presidency in 1961, he stated that NATO should strengthen its conventional forces, though he also reaffirmed that the United States would use any necessary military means, including nuclear weapons, to defend Western Europe.[28] Improved conventional forces, in the new administration's view, would provide more credibility and flexibility and might postpone or even avert escalation to a nuclear conflict.

Tactical nuclear weapons, far from being abandoned, were deployed in unprecedented numbers, and nuclear retaliation remained at the core of NATO (and U.S.) doctrine. When the Berlin Wall was constructed, the United States quickened the pace of delivery of dual-capable equipment and the stockpiling of U.S.-controlled warheads in Europe dedicated to NATO defense. Nonetheless, U.S. doctrinal preferences had changed fundamentally. Instead of instant resort to nuclear weapons, a strategy of escalation was formulated whereby a Soviet action would be countered first with conventional forces to allow Moscow time to consider and negotiate. In the case of continued Soviet action, the West would employ a graduated use of nuclear weapons, beginning with tactical and only later moving on to strategic weapons. [29]

Although Germany publicly supported this U.S. strategy, privately it questioned the need for, and even the conceptual wisdom of, strengthened conventional capabilities and the American retreat from a promise of virtually automatic massive nuclear response to conventional attack. Quite apart from reluctance to make the investments needed to mount a fully credible conventional defense, Bonn feared that the new policy opened the door to the prospect of a conventional conflict on German soil that would be immensely destructive, even if NATO somehow succeeded in halting the Soviet advance. To the Federal Republic, the suggestion of an increased conventional capacity and a nuclear doctrine of gradual escalation meant that the United States was not committed to the use of nuclear weapons and that deterrence would be gravely undermined.[30]

Strauss noted that "an atomic bomb is worth as much as a brigade and costs much less."[31]

Concomitantly with advocacy of a more nuanced role for nuclear weapons in NATO defense, Washington stressed its willingness for European allies to become more involved with decisions involving nuclear weapons. However, the United States had not decided exactly how this greater involvement was to be implemented, and sharply different schools of thought evolved regarding nuclear sharing.

An influential group of second-tier officials in the State Department believed that the answer was a Multilateral Force (MLF) that would entail joint U.S.-allied hardware and manning, joint control, and common strategic nuclear forces. Ultimately, the United States would give up the power to block an allied decision to use the force.

Secretary of Defense Robert McNamara, in contrast, argued that actual joint operation and control of a nuclear force was both impractical operationally and dangerous conceptually. Instead, the European allies should have an increasing role in nuclear decisionmaking while the president of the United States would retain centralized control of nuclear weapons. McNamara opposed joint nuclear forces because, as he said in June 1962, "There must not be competing and conflicting strategies to meet the contingency of nuclear war. . . . Our best hope lies in conducting a centrally controlled campaign against all of the enemy's vital nuclear capabilities."[32] As another strategic analyst more bluntly put it, "Giving NATO an artificial strategic capability would make no sense."[33]

During the early 1960s, West Germany continued to believe that its size, position as the storehouse for the nuclear weapons of the alliance, and exposure to the initial force of any Soviet attack should confer upon it special status. The ongoing Berlin crisis heightened Bonn's desire to share in NATO nuclear control, but Bonn also came to believe that common European nuclear forces could provide a theater-based counter to the large numbers of Soviet missiles targeted on European cities during the 1950s and 1960s. If the decision on the use of these European nuclear forces could be made by Europeans independently of the United States, Moscow would be disabused of any notion that it could attack Europe (and West Germany in particular) and be immune from nuclear response because the United States would be unwilling to use U.S.-based strategic forces—and risk retaliation against the United States itself—as long as only Europe was under attack.

Adenauer cast these concerns in terms of the need for an instant response. He believed that a situation could arise in which an immediate decision would have to be made when the fate of all could be decided in one hour and the president of the United States could not be reached. "We must arrange within NATO so that a decision can be taken to use atomic weapons even before the President is heard from."[34] It seems likely he was worried less that a U.S. response would come late than that it would not come at all.

Germany suggested establishing a mechanism among the allies for making a quick decision—a guarantee of approval of firing by the president of the United States—and for ensuring that Germany be consulted and given access to decisionmaking. It also considered privately ideas such as creating a five-member executive group (United States, United Kingdom, France, Germany, and a rotating member from the Mediterranean), or creating regional decisionmaking bodies, or a system of weighted voting.[35] Strauss suggested that for the sake of a nuclear alliance, even the United States should give up some national rights over nuclear weapons.

Some Americans were enthusiastic supporters of a system whereby the United States and its allies would share not only in prewar doctrinal decisions but also in managing and manning a nuclear force over which they would share operational control. In 1962 Under Secretary of State George Ball discussed the establishment of a "sea-based NATO MRBM force under truly multilateral ownership and control."[36] Strauss and Foreign Minister Gerhard Schröder were told that the United States would share information from feasibility studies regarding a common force as soon as they were completed.[37] George Ball reassured Adenauer that Germany would have an equal role in the MLF, perhaps as a member of an "executive control committee" composed of five members, that the MLF would not lead to the denuclearization of Europe, and that it would be placed under the supposedly more "European" SACEUR instead of the "Anglo-Saxon" SACLANT (Supreme Allied Commander Atlantic). After talks between the United States and the United Kingdom in December 1963 in Nassau, the United States discussed with Germany the creation of a multilateral nuclear force and held out the possibility that, eventually, the United States would cede its veto right over the use of such a force.

German support for the MLF was not absolute. Bonn was concerned about the complex formula for mixed manning and operation, the possibility of a retained American veto, and the cost and other implications of a future increase from the originally proposed 200 missiles in the MLF in order to counter Russia's 700–800 medium-range ballistic missiles. German military and political leaders feared that the Europeans would have to pay dearly for MLF and still not share adequately in decisionmaking.

Nonetheless, although this force would not meet all the yearnings of Germans for increased participation in decisions regarding NATO and the possible use of tactical nuclear weapons, West Germany supported the MLF and dedicated its efforts in this direction. It realized that an MLF would involve Bonn in U.S. and NATO nuclear planning, would make it practically impossible for nuclear weapons to be removed from its territory without its consent, and would necessitate more regular nuclear consultation by the United States with other members of NATO. In the view of Washington, the MLF would provide greater integration within NATO, a base for French and British nuclear forces, and above all, keep Germany from feeling that it had to develop its own nuclear capability. Because West Germany would participate in decisions on NATO's use of nuclear weapons, it might relieve the United States of the continuous demands from Bonn for assurances of American resolution and willingness to risk nuclear war for European defense.

As Robert Bowie, a strong MLF advocate, stated:

> The German leaders have repeatedly stated that the Federal Republic cannot indefinitely accept a second class status or discrimination. . . . Over the long pull, the 1954 WEU limitation can hardly keep Germany from demanding equal nuclear status with the United Kingdom and France. If Germany is not treated as an equal, the discrimination will produce friction and discord. Aversion to a German national nuclear force would create tensions and cleavages within the alliance that the Soviets would certainly exploit. In either case the unity of the alliance would be seriously impaired."[38]

Bowie maintained that the MLF would satisfy the concerns of both Bonn and its allies.

President Kennedy had never been a fully committed MLF advocate.[39] However, a year after the initial Ball proposals, a new American president, Lyndon Johnson, and a new German chancellor, Ludwig Erhard, agreed that "the proposed multilateral force would make a significant addition to this [Atlantic] military and political strength and efforts should be continued to ready an agreement for signature by the end of the year."[40] It appeared that support had increased in both countries.

Erhard stated in the Bundestag in November 1965 that the Federal Republic was discussing with the allies the possibility of a joint nuclear organization:

We have repeatedly made known that we do not desire national control of nuclear weapons. We should, however, not be kept out of any nuclear participation simply because we are a divided country. The partition of Germany is an injustice. It must not be augmented by another injustice, by making it more difficult for us—who are rendering substantial contributions to the Western alliance—to defend ourselves against the open threat from the East. Such views weaken the alliance and simultaneously encourage the Soviets to insist on the partition of our continent."[41]

Many in Washington, especially in the Pentagon, remained skeptical. They argued that the MLF was impractical operationally; that, in any event, the nuclear weapons of the MLF would not add much militarily; and that multinational control was inconsistent in principle with the emerging insistence on strong centralized control from Washington over any use of nuclear weapons. However, MLF was attractive to policymakers who were increasingly focused on achieving a broad international nonproliferation agreement, the key to which was preventing Germany from developing nuclear weapons.

With time the practical and operational problems of a nuclear force manned by a multinational crew and under multinational control became clearer—as did the lack of united American support for the concept and especially for any renunciation of an ultimate U.S. veto over its use. No doubt these problems were not altogether unwelcome to those American critics of MLF who had never been keen on an arrangement whereby, in theory, European allies could force the use of American-supplied nuclear weapons without U.S. consent—and who recognized more clearly than some MLF advocates that unless "common control" made such use possible, it would not be meaningful to the allies.

The MLF concept staggered on for a while, the progenitor of endless transatlantic discussions and study groups, but serious American efforts were redirected toward a different goal: finding ways to give the allies, including West Germany, an alternative to a separate force. The U.S. proposed to shift control over submarine-launched ballistic missiles—usually considered part of the U.S. strategic force—to SACEUR (still subject to U.S. presidential authorization). In addition, the U.S. would allow

European participation in nuclear planning for these weapons assigned to SACEUR. It was hoped that such arrangements would forestall schemes for a truly independent European nuclear capability.

In 1965 Adenauer—and temporarily Strauss—left the active political scene, and power in Bonn shifted to leaders more open to this American approach. New federal chancellor Ludwig Erhard, Foreign Minister Gerhard Schröder, and Defense Minister Kai-Uwe von Hassel wished above all to have smooth relations with Washington. Accepting the basic concept of a "flexible," that is, less than automatically nuclear, response to a Soviet attack, Bonn agreed to a draft NATO nuclear doctrine (MC 100/1, drafted in 1963) that provided for a "pause" before using nuclear weapons in case of a conventional attack.

In parallel with this support for MLF, von Hassel presented to Washington in November 1964 a set of ideas whereby a ladder of force intervals, dependent on military and political requirements, would be employed instead of what was referred to as the "firebreak" between using conventional or nuclear weapons.[42] Conventional weapons would be used to meet a conventional attack at the border, and limited nuclear weapons would be employed selectively at an early stage. These would include "atomic demolition mines, nuclear air defense weapons, and, if need be, nuclear battlefield weapons."[43] If this last warning did not work, nuclear escalation would commence in hours or days.

As an alternative to the MLF, the United States offered West Germany a role in the Nuclear Committee and its working group on nuclear planning, with permanent participation in the NATO Nuclear Planning Group to come later. Secretary of Defense McNamara saw a limited role for Europe and control sharing. West Germany stressed that participation in NATO nuclear groups was complementary to developing an integrated force, and consideration of such a force continued among officials on both sides of the Atlantic. But, in essence, pursuing the approach of offering allied participation in planning meant dropping any idea of a mixed-manned, jointly controlled force, while retaining the concept of greater allied participation in policymaking; greater access to information about nuclear forces, including the size and condition of stockpiles of nuclear warheads in each NATO country; and American commitment of nuclear forces operationally distinct from the U.S. strategic force. Advocates of this approach were convinced that greater access to information about U.S. nuclear capabilities and plans in the NATO context would make the Germans more confident in the credibility of the U.S. deterrent, more conscious of the dilemmas of deterrence, and less inclined to seek technological solutions to what was essentially a political and psychological problem that could never be wholly resolved.[44]

While the MLF debate was going on in NATO, Adenauer and de Gaulle concluded the Franco-German Treaty of Friendship and Cooperation on January 22, 1963. It provided for military cooperation and consultation, including quarterly meetings of defense ministers, exchanges of military personnel and defense units, and increased efforts at joint conventional arms production. Cooperation with France was attractive to some in Bonn—quite apart from the broader issues of advancing German-French reconciliation and unity on European integration—because France supported deterrence by massive nuclear retaliation.[45] Accordingly, German "Gaullists" opposed German participation in the MLF and believed that France's force de frappe could provide a basis for a European force. One of them, former minister of defense Franz Josef Strauss, said in June 1963, "We Europeans should not place blind confidence in the reliability and trustworthiness of the Americans, who do not wish without more ado to let themselves be drawn into atomic war. . . . The only solution is to pool the British and French weapons . . . supported by the full transfer of American know-how. Thus in the long run a European atomic force would come into existence under the precondition, of course, of political union."[46]

France initially accepted the idea of German participation in the MLF. However, with time de Gaulle opposed German participation in an integrated nuclear force. In the second half of 1964, France insisted on Bonn making a choice between European integration on the one hand and German involvement in the MLF on the other. President de Gaulle and German Gaullists criticized the shortcomings of the Franco-German treaty. Erhard then suggested the idea of joint control over the development and use of French nuclear weapons.[47] De Gaulle repeated the pledge of protection for Germany but did not address the subject of common planning or control over French weapons. Subsequently, de Gaulle's growing resistance to an integrated nuclear force that included Germany manifested itself in his remarks about conditions for the reunification of Germany. He stated that Germany "must recognize that any settlement of its frontiers and its armament will be in agreement with all its neighbors, those on the East and those on the West."[48] De Gaulle also told Gromyko in 1965 that France and Russia had similar interests, as nuclear powers, in a non-nuclear Germany.

Erhard's Christian Democratic Union (CDU) government gave way in 1966 to a Grand Coalition of CDU and SPD. For the first time in the post-1945 period, the traditionally antinuclear SPD shared executive power in Bonn. West Germany ceased support for the MLF proposal, and by mid-1968 the concept quietly passed from the scene, the product, as its putative targets might have said, of its internal contradictions.[49] The United States had seen it as a second-strike force, whereas Germany had viewed it as a European theater force for early, first-use response to invasion.

Significantly, neither the prolonged debate over MLF nor its eventual demise gave rise to any serious rethinking of the basic German acquiescence to renunciation of a truly independent, national nuclear capability. During this decade (1954–66) of innumerable deliberations—the theme of which was the need for a distinctively European nuclear potential—Germany did not make either official or unofficial efforts to acquire a national production capability.

The Non-Proliferation Treaty

As the MLF debate faded, West German nuclear policy became enmeshed in the debate over the establishment of a broad—in principle, universal—agreement by nations without nuclear weapons to abjure them permanently. Simultaneously, with the crises over Berlin and Cuba and the debates over European nuclear capability, both the United States and the USSR began to press proposals for a broad agreement restricting the acquisition by other nations of nuclear weapons.[50] In 1961 the United Nations General Assembly approved unanimously an Irish resolution calling on all states, especially the nuclear weapons states, to conclude an international agreement to refrain from transfer or acquisition of nuclear weapons. The Soviet Union and the United States also presented plans during the period from 1960 to 1962 to ban the transfer and acquisition of nuclear weapons.

The Germans, who had seen Bonn's earlier renunciation as a badge of discrimination against their country, were strongly opposed to embodying that renunciation in an agreement to which the USSR was a party. When the United States presented its first draft of a nuclear nonproliferation treaty, Strauss thought it would be a nightmare to have Germany endure a "military Versailles" and, as the third greatest economic power in the world, then be discriminated against, between East and West. It would be easy to "calculate from historical experience alone when a new Fuhrer type would promise and probably also require nuclear weapons, or even worse for a Germany treated in this way."[51]

In August 1965 the United States presented a draft treaty on the non-proliferation of nuclear weapons that provided for the possibility of an MLF and a European force, though there was to be no transfer of nuclear weapons to the national control of a non-nuclear state. Further, it did not mention progress on the German problem as a condition for expecting West German acceptance of permanent non-nuclear weapon status. The German Gaullists, joined by Adenauer, stated that "the American plans are so horrible that in the long run Europe will be delivered over to the Russians. . . . If this treaty comes into being NATO is finished. England is then in the atomic club for good, despite its many debts, which will be paid for with our money."[52]

Others cast their objections in commercial rather than strategic terms. In January 1967 two prominent West German security analysts, Rudolph Botzian and Uwe Nerlich, stated that International Atomic Energy Agency (IAEA) controls were "particularly unacceptable for the Federal Republic of Germany—apart from political and other reasons such as insufficient patent coverage—especially when, and as long as, there are still substantial differences between the East and the West in their interpretation of the NPT which would become a burden to it in an even more severe form."[53]

Also in 1967, there was support for a just-under-the-threshold nuclear development program similar to that being attempted by India and, to a lesser degree, by Japan. This would anticipate an acceleration and expansion of the present efforts, to the point where a shift to extensive plutonium production for military purposes was possible within a period perhaps as short as a month or even a week. By the end of 1966, Germany had invested about DM 4.3 billion ($1.1 billion) in atomic energy research and development, and 8,000 scientists worked at the state-owned atomic research centers. Some of these research projects could be used for military purposes.[54]

Whatever their views on the practicality of the MLF, West German leaders were unwilling to accept permanent legal constraints against their nation joining in some form of multinational nuclear force. When it came to the negotiations in Geneva on the NPT, Schröder said that Germany would accede to the treaty only when German security against Soviet MRBMs was ensured through an MLF—at least unless Moscow was prepared to compromise on reunification. The MLF provided an obstacle in the negotiations on the NPT for some three years because the Soviet Union—for whom the prospect of permanently blocking a nuclear capability for Germany was a primary objective in the whole NPT process—strongly opposed allowing any MLF-type option for the Federal Republic. The Soviet Union stated that agreement could not be reached on nonproliferation if the United States and its allies insisted on retaining the option of nuclear-sharing arrangements within NATO that would, it maintained, give the Federal Republic of Germany access to or control of nuclear weapons.

German willingness to make the MLF a bar to successful negotiation of an NPT met with strong opposition in the United States. Senator Robert Kennedy and the chief negotiator of the United States in Geneva, William C. Foster, spoke for many Americans when they emphasized that nonproliferation was more important than the MLF. Many Germans—and other Europeans—shared this perspective and, indeed, concluded that permanent, internationally binding renunciation was the right choice for Germany. The liberal Free Democratic Party said in January 1967 that the German government should "come out with a clear and final renunciation of atomic weapons . . . [that is] the abandonment of every German claim for a share in the nuclear potential of the West and . . . limitation of the right to veto in the event of the employment of atomic weapons, as well as participation in special working groups for general planning and target planning."[55]

By 1969 the Soviet Union was ready to improve relations with the Federal Republic if Bonn met the NPT requirements. However, the Brandt government, for all its commitment to the Ostpolitik reconciliation with the East, remained suspicious of the NPT. Germany fought to minimize the impact of safeguards on its nuclear industry, to adopt liberal language regarding constraints on nuclear exports, and to insist on an earlier termination date for the NPT than the twenty-five years contained in article 10.

The influence of the Federal Republic on the NPT negotiations was particularly strong in article 4, which safeguards nuclear energy. Willy Brandt was concerned that the non-nuclear weapons states should be able to use atomic energy to "prevent the existing technological gap between nuclear weapons states and non-nuclear weapons states from getting even bigger."[56] Germany's signing of the NPT was predicated on the fact that freedom of nuclear research and development would not be limited and that only the production of complete explosive devices would be prohibited by the treaty.[57] Bonn linked its 1969 signature to some nineteen restrictive interpretations, including reservations intended to preserve West Germany's civilian nuclear industry and hence its technological base for a military nuclear program.

It appears that the main impetus for these reservations was a genuine concern—not limited to West Germany—that the NPT could be manipulated to restrict not just weapons proliferation but commercial competition in civilian nuclear fields. The West German business and scientific communities wanted to maintain access to nuclear fuel supplies for domestic and export purposes, as well as to continue research, including on breeder reactors, without being limited by strict definitions regarding nuclear weapons. Furthermore, Germany wanted to prevent possible industrial espionage by IAEA multinational teams of inspectors. Ironically, more than three decades later, the German government decided to phase out nuclear energy. "Most Germans want to do away with nuclear energy, which the government will phase out over the next twenty to twenty-five years," according to an official at the Ministry of Defense.[58]

However, in signing the NPT, the Brandt government also emphasized its security concerns. It declared that the security of the Federal Republic of Germany would continue to be ensured by NATO or an equivalent security system—and hence, implicitly, by nuclear deterrence. Germany would continue to be free to participate in and have access to nuclear arrangements, such as the Nuclear Planning Group of NATO; to host the deployment of nuclear weapons of its allies on its territory; and to participate in joint civil nuclear projects. Moreover, NATO interpreted the NPT as consistent with dual-key arrangements, which potentially would allow the Federal Republic status as a nuclear weapons power in the event of war.[59]

Upon signing the NPT, the Federal Republic attached a number of concerns in a declaration. To begin with, it stated that the treaty could never be applied to hamper research or development in the peaceful uses of nuclear energy. In this connection, it drew attention to the statement made by the U.S. Permanent Representative to the United Nations on May 15, 1968; in particular,

There is no basis for any concern that this Treaty would impose inhibitions or restrictions on the opportunity for non-nuclear weapon states to develop their capabilities in nuclear science and technology. . . . The whole field of nuclear science associated with electric power production . . . will become more accessible under the Treaty, to all who seek to exploit it. This includes not only the present generation of nuclear power reactors but also that advanced technology, which is still developing, of fast breeder power reactors which, in producing energy, also produce more fissionable material than they consume." [60]

Furthermore, reflecting the domestic debate on the treaty regarding paragraph 3 of article 3 and article 4 of the treaty, Germany declared that the transfer of information, materials, and equipment could not be denied to non-nuclear weapons states merely on the basis of allegations that such activities could be used for the manufacture of nuclear weapons or other nuclear explosive devices. Germany also expressed concern that there not be incompatibility between the aims of the Non-Proliferation Treaty and those of the treaty establishing Euratom, stating that it would postpone ratification of the NPT until negotiations were concluded to that end between the Commission of the European Communities and the IAEA.

Germany insisted that the safeguards would only be applied to source and special fissionable material and in conformity with the principle of safeguarding effectively the flow of source and special fissionable materials at certain strategic points. It said it understood that each party to the treaty would decide for itself which equipment or material should fall under the export provisions of paragraph 2 of article 3.

Even with all the protections and conditions, it took the Federal Republic of Germany—still deeply split over Ostpolitik as well as specifically nuclear issues—seven years to ratify the NPT. Opponents argued that the NPT safeguards would interfere with the civilian use of nuclear power and denounced the treaty as a "nuclear Versailles."

The ratification of the NPT had been so debated that the Federal Republic felt compelled in 1975 to include a declaration that summarized the Note and Statement it had submitted upon signature in 1969. In the declaration of 1975, the FRG

—reaffirmed its expectation that the treaty would be a milestone on the way toward disarmament and international détente and that the nuclear weapons states would intensify their efforts to comply with article 6 of the treaty (on nuclear disarmament);

—underlined that the security of the FRG continued to be ensured by NATO;

—stated that the treaty could not hamper further development of European unification, especially the creation of a European Union, "with appropriate competence";

—understood that the application of the treaty's safeguards would not lead to discrimination against the FRG's nuclear industry in international competition;

—and stressed in this connection the importance of the application of safeguards to Germany's peaceful nuclear facilities.

The German statute for implementing the verification agreement came into effect ten years after accession to the NPT. While the German export law and regulations were adapted to NPT obligations, a liberal export policy and lenient implementation made the FRG a real challenge for the non-proliferation regime. Nevertheless, Germany supported the acceptance of full-scope safeguards at the fourth NPT review conference, and it has reformed its Foreign Trade Law and the War Weapons Control Law.[61] However, much tighter export controls were established in Germany following a number of scandals in the 1980s and early 1990s.

Scientific and Technical Capabilities

There is no question that Germany today has the technical capacity to develop nuclear weapons quickly, if it chose to do so. Indeed, Germany and Japan have been called "virtual nuclear weapon states" because of their large civilian nuclear industry, civilian nuclear power complex, and large stocks of plutonium. In 1966 a fast breeder pilot facility in Karlsruhe began operation; in 1967 public spending on the atomic industry in West Germany almost doubled, and construction started on a reprocessing plant with an annual capacity of thirty tons of nuclear material. According to the IAEA, in 2002 Germany had twenty-seven nuclear power reactors and eighteen research reactors with critical assemblies. It has two fuel fabrication plants, one reprocessing plant, one enrichment facility, one research and development facility associated with enrichment technology, eleven separate storage facilities, and six "other" facilities. Some nineteen reactors supply about a third of the country's electricity (160 billion kilowatt-hours in 1999), according to the World Nuclear Association. On the eve of the NPT Review and Extension Conference in 1995, Germany held the largest stock of plutonium among the non-nuclear weapons states. More than 2,000 kilograms of plutonium were stored at Hanau in Hesse, and another 6,600 kilograms of German plutonium were stored in France. [62]

Germany's civilian nuclear programs have not escaped proliferation concerns. When Germany began to consider using weapons-grade uranium in an FRM-II research reactor in Garching, the United States protested that it would jeopardize efforts to end the use of weapons-grade uranium in civilian programs and would increase the risk of theft or loss of highly enriched uranium (HEU). At the NPT Review and Extension Conference in 1995, Germany prevented consensus on text recommending that "no new civilian reactors requiring high-enriched uranium be constructed."[63] Instead the conference adopted this text: "The Conference recommends that States planning new civilian reactors avoid or minimize use of highly enriched uranium to the extent that this is feasible, taking into account technical, scientific and economic factors."[64] The German FRM-II research reactor, which just started up on March 2, 2004, is the first reactor fueled with HEU to begin operating in over ten years.[65] The reactor is to use high-density fuel initially developed to convert reactors to less highly enriched uranium.

Notwithstanding this example, Germany is generally seen to value nonproliferation over economic interests. Germany was initially reluctant to support the 93+2 addition to the IAEA safeguards system because it was concerned that the reformed safeguards might impinge on its civilian use of nuclear energy.[66] However, it has accepted them now and encouraged others to do the same.

Germany has supported nuclear projects in Pakistan and South Africa that were ostensibly for civilian purposes but formed part of the technological base for those nations' nuclear weapons programs.[67] In 1990 Germany decided that before delivering nuclear-related items to another country, the recipient would have to accept full IAEA safeguards. This principle was adopted by all major suppliers in April 1992.[68] More recently, Colonel Muammar Gadhafi announced he would dismantle his nuclear weapons program following the seizure of a German-owned freighter that was carrying uranium enrichment equipment bound for Libya. In September 2003, British and American intelligence authorities had notified Germany that the boat's cargo included illegal equipment. The German company that owned the ship ordered the freighter to be diverted to an Italian port, where British and American authorities found the centrifuge parts.[69]

With German accession to the NPT, the question of a distinctly national nuclear capability was formally laid to rest. Bonn continued to be deeply concerned about maintaining the effectiveness of NATO's nuclear guarantee. When the Soviet Union, in the late 1970s, started deploying SS-20s to modernize its missile force targeted on Western Europe, Chancellor Schmidt demanded that NATO respond to eliminate the threat, both by arms control and by a force deployment of its own. Despite widespread opposition from European—and particularly German—public opinion, NATO eventually agreed to deploy in Europe an additional American nuclear strike force composed of Pershing II ballistic missiles and ground-launched cruise missiles capable of reaching targets in the Soviet Union. Concurrently, NATO sought—ultimately successfully—to reach arms control agreements with Moscow that would eliminate the SS-20 threat.

West Germany took the lead in this controversy. It was Bonn's fixation on the SS-20 that converted what could have been seen as a routine modernization into a major strategic challenge, and it was Bonn's threat to undermine the U.S.-Soviet bilateral strategic arms control process that forced Washington and the other NATO allies to agree on a deployment response. And, paradoxically, it was German public opposition to that response that forced Washington to pursue a separate arms control agreement on the intermediate-range nuclear forces of both sides. Significantly, however, in all the immensely divisive debate and all the multiple potential courses of action advocated by the various players and observers, there was scarcely any discussion of a distinctly national German nuclear force as a response to the strategic challenges presented by the Soviet deployments or to West German doubts about the continuing viability of the U.S. nuclear guarantee. How far German policy had shifted is indicated by Bonn's decision, in 1979, to decline the U.S. offer of dual-key control for the Pershing II missiles it proposed to deploy to West German bases.[70]

Unification

The debates over the deployment and limitations of intermediate-range nuclear forces were scarcely over when profound changes in the Soviet Union and its satellites produced fundamental shifts in the political and strategic position of Germany. One effect of these shifts was to permanently put to rest any question of Germany acquiring a national nuclear weapons capability by fundamentally transforming Germany's security situation. The fall of the Berlin Wall, the reunification of Germany, the collapse of the Soviet Union, and the dissolution of the Warsaw Pact from

1989 to 1991 fundamentally altered Germany's strategic situation. On the one hand, these dramatic developments ended the East-West confrontation and the division of Germany and of Central Europe, thereby simultaneously eliminating the principal military threat to the Federal Republic—a Soviet-led invasion—and achieving its principal international policy ambition—reunification of Germany. At the same time, these developments opened the way for the definitive end—in the 2+4 agreements—of all special restrictions on Germany arising from its Nazi past.

However, even though those agreements committed the unified Germany to adhere to all the international obligations of both former German states—including the NPT—the lifting of the de jure and de facto limits on German sovereignty was expected, in some quarters, to reopen the issue of German possession of nuclear weapons. As SPD politician Peter Glotz wrote in *Die Zeit* on April 19, 1992, a conservative politician will eventually appear "who will spill the beans by speaking out openly and saying that it would be absurd that Brazilians, Indians and even Libyans will get atomic weapons but not Germans." In March 1992 the *New York Times* wrote about a Pentagon planning document that warned that Germany and Japan might become nuclear states. "Nuclear proliferation, if unchecked by superpower action, could tempt Germany, Japan and other industrial powers to acquire nuclear weapons to deter attack from regional foes."[71]

In recent times, a few Germans have indeed called for a German atomic force or at least for a discussion of the issues. Arnulf Baring of the Free University of Berlin publicly called for a national debate on the subject. "Regardless of what was agreed upon in 1954 and later, and regardless of what the NPT has said since 1968, this is one of the problems which we have to tackle in the future."[72]

For the most part, however, such calls have found no response. German development of a separate nuclear weapons capability "is a nonissue that is not discussed or written about. What purpose could it possibly serve?" said Walter Stützle, recent deputy secretary of defense. "Once the EU becomes a real union, with decisionmaking power and sovereignty, then French and British nuclear weapons would become an issue. No new arguments have been advanced ever since the discussion about Germany's accession to the NPT."[73] As former foreign minister Klaus Kinkel said, "Germany is the best proof that the renunciation of nuclear weapons is not a disadvantage. We have no privileges to defend in this regard and rejected weapons of mass destruction a long time ago. There can be no doubt that this decision is final."[74]

With the fall of the wall, the perceived superiority of Warsaw Pact forces fading into history, and Russia occupied with its economic problems, Germany feels no immediate security threat. The countries neighboring Germany, including France, a nuclear weapons state, are friends and allies. Disputes over territory, religious clashes, or ethnic quarrels have faded away. Even with Russia, serious areas of security-related dispute have all but vanished. There are increasing exchanges in economic, cultural, and other relations. "We see no threat, so development of nuclear weapons would not be possible," said one analyst. "The Russian Federation is unlikely to become a threat. For us, we are a non-nuclear weapon state, and that is our identity."[75]

Moreover, whatever else changed with the collapse of the Soviet empire, German reliance on allies—whether in Europe or across the Atlantic—endured. Germany is a member of important alliance structures, including NATO, the Western European Union, and the European Union. The EU is not a security alliance, but it has established common interests among the members, has bound the relationship between Germany and its former adversary, France, and is in the process of developing a common defense capability. For all the disputes, NATO still draws the United States and Europe together on most security matters. Germany has been integrated within NATO and has participated in decisions about nuclear doctrine, target setting, and procurement in the Nuclear Planning Group, established in 1967. In addition, the Organization for Security and Cooperation in Europe, the North Atlantic Cooperation Council, and the NATO-Russian Council provide the opportunity to resolve complaints and future conflicts.

As part of this alliance structure, Germany must rely on the nuclear weapons of the United States and, in principle, its European nuclear allies, Britain and France. So far, neither popular opposition to nuclear weapons nor Germany's improved security position has led Germany to directly challenge NATO or U.S. nuclear doctrine. Although the new SPD-Green coalition in 1999 proposed a new review of NATO nuclear policy, it backed off under pressure from the United States and other allies, and the German government has maintained its support for NATO nuclear posture and for nuclear weapons to be deployed on its territory as a way of coupling the strategic arsenal of the United States with European security interests.[76]

This alliance structure retains strong German public support as a reason to forego acquisition of nuclear weapons. In a study conducted in May 1995, when Germans from East and West were asked how they would feel if there was no alliance structure and there was some nuclear threat to Germany, almost 78 percent of the respondents said that nuclear weapons would enhance Germany's prestige and sovereignty.[77] If, however, there were a strong NATO, WEU, and American presence in Europe, only 4 percent saw such a necessity. In short, American commitment to protect Germany and German participation in European security and alliance structures still mitigate any perceived need for German nuclear weapons.

Moreover, a growing number of Germans support the elimination of nuclear weapons altogether. A poll in 1998 showed that 87 percent of Germans believed that the nuclear weapons states should "start getting rid of their nuclear weapons as quickly as possible" and that the German government should immediately eliminate the nuclear weapons based on German soil.[78]

For a country that was synonymous with military power in the first half of the twentieth century and started two world wars, Germany is now the least military oriented of any major nation. Its defense budget has decreased and its military equipment is aging. While the United States spends 3.3 percent of its gross domestic product on armed forces, Germany spent 1.5 percent last year, compared to the United Kingdom and France, where such spending hovered around 2.5 percent. [79] Germany is downsizing its army and decommissioning from one-third to a half of even its most modern tanks.

The discussion in Germany over military policy now focuses on how to achieve a truly integrated European security and defense policy. With the enlargement of the EU and the development of a rapid reaction force, Germany and France may play a central role. "Germany is working for mobility, projecting military forces to real security risks," said an official at the Ministry of Defense. "This is only possible because we do not expect Russia to be a threat any more. Now there is a need for military options to deal with terrorism and rogue states." [80] Germany has become a major contributor to international peacekeeping efforts, reaching beyond NATO territory to the Balkans and even to Afghanistan. Reflecting this new priority, a foreign ministry official said,

> For security in Europe we count on NATO. There is not a realistic scenario where Germany would reverse its decision regarding nuclear weapons. Our policy is to strengthen NPT and get as many other countries as possible to sign it. The threats of the future are nationalism, religious fanaticism, terrorism, and the lack of

democracy. These are reasons to strengthen the NPT. Nuclear deterrence and asymmetric threats do not function against terrorists."[81]

To be sure, some observers have speculated that Germany would reconsider its nuclear renunciation if the U.S. nuclear umbrella were to be withdrawn. Germany still shelters under U.S. and NATO nuclear guarantees—whatever the real significance of those guarantees under current conditions. In theory, were U.S.-German policy divisions to increase greatly or the United States to withdraw wholly from NATO and its commitments to the security of its European allies, there could be pressure on Germany to reconsider its non-nuclear position, particularly if Russia were somehow to reemerge as a threat in such a context. Some observers have indeed argued that in the highly unlikely event that the United States were to withdraw from the continent and Germany was no longer able to depend on the American nuclear umbrella, it would seek nuclear guarantees from the European nuclear allies or might even seek its own nuclear weapons if it felt threatened. [82]

Even laying aside the extreme unlikelihood of such a profound breach in transatlantic relations, it is by no means clear that such developments would induce Germany to develop nuclear weapons of its own. Although some politicians on the conservative end of the spectrum might prefer a national nuclear force, public opinion is so opposed to even civilian uses of nuclear energy—much less nuclear weapons— that it would "be suicidal for any serious politician to make a political platform out of this subject."[83] As one analyst put it,

> There is no scenario in which Germany would acquire nuclear weapons. If the U.S. withdraws from NATO, if Europe breaks apart, if a new general takes over in the Russian Federation, threatening Germany, and if tensions increase drastically, *even then* Germany would not try to develop nuclear weapons. This would be for Hollywood. Germany would try to engage in discussions; we are trying to keep other states from getting nuclear weapons. We had U.S. nuclear weapons and troops in Germany to contain the Soviet Union. They had a function. Now it would be more a burden than anything else for Germany to have nuclear weapons."[84]

Indeed, far from reconsidering its decisions, Germany has pressed for far-reaching arms control measures, in forums such as the European

Union, the United Nations, and the Geneva Conference on Disarmament. Within these bodies Germany has supported nuclear disarmament and in 1997 proposed specific measures toward this end. These included the verification of the abolition of nuclear weapons; elimination of nuclear weapons-capable material; and guaranteed security against nuclear, biological, and chemical weapons. Germany also supported more conventional arms control projects such as START II, the inclusion of tactical nuclear weapons in bilateral U.S.-Soviet limitations, and a ban on the production of fissile material for weapons purposes.

Germany is party not only to the Non-Proliferation Treaty but also to the Chemical Weapons Convention, the Biological Weapons Convention, the Comprehensive Nuclear Test Ban Treaty, the Conventional Forces in Europe Treaty, the Vienna documents on confidence building, and the Open Skies Treaty. It has been active in the efforts to apply IAEA safeguards in nuclear weapons states and to increase transparency in military and civilian nuclear establishments. It also supports the Nuclear Suppliers Group, the Missile Technology Control Regime, and the Australia Group.

In 1992 Germany and Italy, which years earlier had considered cooperating in developing nuclear weapons, joined the consensus of the G-7 to make the NPT permanent and thus also their "inferior" nuclear status. Germany promoted enhancing IAEA safeguards, and it supported the nuclear suppliers' agreement on full-scope safeguards as a condition of supply, which had been agreed upon in Warsaw in April 1992.[85]

In 1994 the Bundestag adopted a resolution to extend the NPT indefinitely. Not one deputy voted against the treaty, and there was broad support for Germany to maintain its non-nuclear status. Germany strongly supported the efforts of the European Union to convince non-nuclear weapon states that were undecided or opposed to an indefinite extension of the NPT to support indefinite extension. "Germany has become one of the strongest supporters of the NPT, and Germany's decision to be a non-nuclear weapon state can be considered permanent."[86]

Rather than choosing to keep the nuclear option open, Germany has based its defense on preventing proliferation by others. It encouraged Ukraine, Belarus, and Kazakhstan to accede to the NPT and established a program to keep nuclear weapon specialists from emigrating. Germany thus sees itself as a guardian and champion of the nonproliferation regime, at least as far as those nations whose possession of nuclear weapons could potentially affect its own security. As one official put it, "A fundamental conviction of German society is that weapons of mass destruction must be banned. No government would weaponize, even if technically it would be possible. Germany has been working very hard to strengthen the NPT regime and NPT safeguards. This government has decided to step out of nuclear power completely and pursue alternative energy sources."[87]

Conclusions: Non-Nuclear and Proud

The German experience presents perhaps the clearest case of nuclear weapons renunciation becoming a permanent policy.[88] In some respects, this is a remarkable nonproliferation achievement. For the whole period starting a few years after 1945, Germany has certainly had the technological capability to develop and produce nuclear weapons, had it decided to do so. At least until the Berlin Wall fell in 1989, Germany was in the exceedingly unattractive position of being highly vulnerable to attack by a nuclear power, the USSR, and yet totally dependent on allies, chiefly the United States, for a nuclear response.

The same logic that led Britain and France to develop national nuclear forces—as insurance against whatever uncertainties they (or the Soviets) felt about the credibility of the U.S. nuclear guarantee—applied with equal vigor to West Germany. Moreover, Bonn's initial renunciations were the product less of internal decision than of external pressure—and not just from Moscow. For many Germans, abjuration of nuclear weapons was not a choice freely made but rather a badge of discrimination—the product of what they saw as an increasingly anachronistic suspicion of Germany's democratic and peaceful bona fides.

Nonetheless, even before the end of the cold war, West Germany came increasingly to accept that going without a national nuclear capability served its national interest. Perhaps most important, Bonn—like Seoul and Taipei—recognized that its ultimate guarantee of security rested on its alliances, not just with the United States but with its other NATO allies as well. Even at a purely technical military level, joint defense—including nuclear deterrence—through NATO afforded West Germany greater security than any unilateral approach could have done. Bonn also consistently recognized that, politically, any deviation from its non-nuclear stance would mean a massive crisis with the Soviet Union and diplomatic as well as political isolation from its allies. Apart from whatever response the USSR might have made to a cold war decision by the Federal

Republic to achieve nuclear weapons independence, any such move would have shaken NATO to the core. Increasingly, Bonn came to understand that its choice was between nuclear weapons or a strong set of alliance relationships, and it recognized that the right choice was the latter.

Germans, during the cold war and afterward, have been conscious of the argument that nuclear weapons are a badge of status, of membership in the club of nations that, if not superpowers, are nonetheless major international players. However, Germany, first as the Federal Republic and then as a unified nation since 1990, has been able to attain and maintain unquestioned status as a major power without nuclear weapons.

Moreover, for the most part, West German debates on nuclear weapons policy were conducted with a high degree of participation by the public, the media, and the political classes. German public opinion—and the opinion of key political elites—turned increasingly against any proposal to revisit the renunciation decision. From the beginning, the West German left opposed any flirtation with nuclear arms as both morally wrong and strategically disastrous. Increasingly, the mass of public opinion in West Germany rejected Germany having nuclear weapons and only accepted reliance on NATO's deterrent with great reluctance.

Undoubtedly some countries have pursued nuclear weapons more for status than for security. However, Germany, like its erstwhile Axis ally Japan, has become powerful because of its economic might rather than its military might, and its renunciation of nuclear weapons may even have reinforced its prestige.[89] It has even managed to achieve its principal international objective—reunification—without becoming a nuclear state.

The process of unification itself posed unique challenges to Germany's security. Differences between East and West in the education, culture, and training of new personnel had to be bridged on the road to integrating the military and defending a greatly enlarged territory. Contrary to its situation after World War I, when Germany was considered a recluse, it is now surrounded by friends, and without declared enemies. "Germany has no revanchist-aggressive schemes for which nuclear weapons could be put to use. . . . Germany has realized all its primary goals of the early 1950s—it has become rich, influential, secure, and now united. All this was achieved without nuclear weapons and, it is submitted, only because it did not have them."[90]

Events since 1989 have only reinforced those supporting a united Germany's non-nuclear position. Public opinion has shifted even further in an antinuclear direction, to the point of eliciting a government commitment to close down all Germany's civilian nuclear power plants. Far from call-ing for a greater, more independent defense capability, mainstream opin-ion has moved in a direction that tends to reject any prospect of German use of military force for anything less crucial than territorial defense or more demanding than peacekeeping. With the important exception of the Balkans, the end of the cold war did not produce renewed intra-European military conflicts, as some had expected, that would have forced Germany to rely more on its own resources for its defense. The strategic situation of Germany today is such that any nuclear threat that it would face would be at least as immediate and threatening to its allies as well.

Moreover, despite all the recent conflicts over the 2003 Iraq war, Ger-many is still a leading member of NATO and a powerful force for defense integration in Europe. Discussion of a possible U.S. drawdown of forces now based in Germany is unlikely to change its very close links to the United States and its European allies. Far from standing alone against a dangerous nuclear-armed adversary, Germany finds itself in the enviable position of facing no serious immediate threat and knowing that whatever threat might emerge in the future can be confronted side-by-side with powerful friends.[91] If, somehow, confidence in NATO should falter, Germany would have the option of relying on common European defenses—likely, EU based— that would include the nuclear forces of Britain and France.

It is not, of course, inconceivable that there would ever again be a seri-ous—and potentially special and unique—external military threat to German security. In particular, the future course of Russia—still armed with a nuclear arsenal second only to that of the United States—is suffi-ciently uncertain that this contingency cannot be entirely discounted. But even with such a catastrophic scenario, it is not clear that Germany would regard nuclear arms as the way to solve the problem. Even if Ger-man public opinion were to change and Germany were no longer to honor its commitments, both political and economic constraints would pose severe obstacles. The German economy, industry, and monetary sys-tem are linked to the economies of the rest of Europe, and Germany is committed to the European political union. Germany is also aware that any unacceptable demonstrations of power on its part would likely be met with damaging unified European economic or political sanctions.[92]

One thing is certain: any debate on a future nuclear weapons role for Germany would be prolonged and highly public—as were the earlier debates on the subject going back to the 1950s. The memory can be short—even in the German Ministry of Defense (which is housed in the building where Hitler's opponents were killed on July 20, 1944)—but not that short. "After World War II, Strauss and Adenauer thought about nuclear weapons, but now it is totally forgotten," said an official recently in the Ministry of Defense. "The security of Europe depended entirely on nuclear weapons, but Germany decided not to pursue them. We don't need them; we have NATO. I can't see any reason or international situation in which this would change. Germany is involved in the Nuclear Planning Group of NATO and the dual-capable discussions, as we have dual-capable aircraft and could carry nuclear weapons, but this is only done within the alliance. In the new security environment of today, nuclear weapons play a less and less important role."[93]

Notes

1. This chapter deals with the Federal Republic of Germany; the German Democratic Republic ratified the Non-Proliferation Treaty on October 31, 1969.

2. "Treaty on the Final Settlement with Respect to Germany September 12, 1990," article 3.I.1 (www.usembassy.de/usa/etexts/2plusfour8994e.htm [July 8, 2003]).

3. Catherine M. Kelleher, *Germany and the Politics of Nuclear Weapons* (Columbia University Press, 1975), p. 12.

4. Department of State, "U.S.-U.K.-French Agreement on Prohibited and Limited Industries," in *Germany, 1947–1949: The Story in Documents* (Government Printing Office, 1950), p. 367.

5. Konrad Adenauer, *Erinnerungen, 1945–1953* (Stuttgart: Deutsche Verlags-Anstalt, 1965), p. 395.

6. Protocol III on the Control of Armaments, annex I (incorporating the provisions of annex II, paragraph 103), reprinted together with the other protocols modifying the Brussels and North Atlantic treaties in Senate Committee on Foreign Relations, *Protocol on the Termination of the Occupation Regime in the Federal Republic of Germany and Protocol to the North Atlantic Treaty on the Accession of the Federal Republic of Germany*, Executives L and M, 83 Cong., 2 sess. (1954).

7. Adenauer, *Erinnerungen*, p. 347.

8. Kelleher, *Germany and the Politics of Nuclear Weapons*, p. 28

9. Later the Vienna Convention on the Law of Treaties (1969), article 62, provided for the possibility of withdrawal from a treaty, in some instances, if a fundamental change of circumstances has occurred with regard to those existing at the time of the conclusion of the treaty.

10. Robert S. Litwak, "Non-Proliferation and the Dilemmas of Regime Change," *Survival*, vol. 45, no. 4 (Winter 2003–04), p. 9.

11. Matthias Küntzel, *Bonn and the Bomb: German Politics and the Nuclear Option* (London: Pluto Press, and Amsterdam: Transnational Institute, 1995), pp. xvi and 167.

12. *Der Spiegel*, 1967, no. 10. Cited in Matthias Küntzel, "Germany and the Origin and History of the NPT," in Huub Jaspers and others, eds., *Beyond the Bomb: The Extension of the Non-Proliferation Treaty and the Future of Nuclear Weapons* (Amsterdam: Transnational Institute, 1995). See also www.antenna.nl/wise/beyondbomb/1-2.html#3 (July 2003).

13. "Transcript of Eisenhower's News Conference on Domestic and Foreign Matters," *New York Times*, February 4, 1960, p. L12.

14. David N. Schwartz, *NATO's Nuclear Dilemma* (Brookings, 1983), p. 42.

15. These questions came especially from France, where analysts, led by General Galois, argued that a nation vulnerable to nuclear attack could not be expected to risk its national survival in the defense of even the best of allies. Ibid., p. 38. For a discussion of the implications of strategic nuclear parity between the United States and the USSR, see Walter Slocombe, "The Political Implications of Strategic Parity," International Institute for Strategic Studies, Adelphi paper no. 77 (Oxford University Press, 1971).

16. "Das Göttinger Manifest der 18 Atomwissenschaftler vom 12. April 1957" (www.dhm.de/lemo/html/dokumente/JahreDesAufbausInOstUndWest_erklaerung GoettingerErklaerung/index.html [March 2004]). Signers included Max Born, Walther Gerlach, Otto Hahn, Werner Heisenberg, Fritz Strassmann, and Karl Friedrich von Weizsäcker.

17. Schwartz, *NATO's Nuclear Dilemma*, p. 71.

18. "Adenauer Calls Atom Arms Vital," *New York Times*, April 6, 1957, p. L3.

19. Schwartz, *NATO's Nuclear Dilemma*, p. 73.

20. John Steinbruner, *The Mind and the Milieu of Policy-Makers: A Case Study of the MLF* (Princeton University Press, 1968), p. 71.

21. Kelleher, *Germany and the Politics of Nuclear Weapons*, p. 140.

22. Schwartz, Hans-Peter, *Adenauer. Der Staatsmann: 1952–1967* (Stuttgart: Deutsche Verlags-Anstalt, 1991), p. 299, cited in Küntzel, "Germany and the Origin and History of the NPT."

23. Küntzel, "Germany and the Origin and History of the NPT."

24. For a considerable period, the United States clung to the hope that these nuclear sharing arrangements would induce de Gaulle to reconsider his decision to withdraw France from participation in NATO military activities and perhaps even to abandon his programs for an independent French nuclear capability.

25. Steinbruner, *The Mind and the Milieu of Policy-Makers: A Case Study of the MLF*, p. 74.

26. See Kelleher, *Germany and the Politics of Nuclear Weapons*, p. 187. Norstad, like many others since, believed that if the allies, particularly Germany, understood nuclear issues better, they would have more realistic expectations and fewer worries.

27. "The Polish Government Memorandum Concerning the Creation of an Atom-Free Zone in Central Europe, Warsaw, February 14, 1958," in *The Rapacki Plan: Documents* (Warsaw: Department of Information for Abroad of the Polish Press Agency [PAP], 1961), p. 4.

28. "U.S. Weighs Shift in NATO Program," *New York Times*, April 16, 1961, p. L1.

29. See William W. Kaufmann, *The McNamara Strategy* (Harper and Row, 1964), pp. 66–67.

30. Kelleher, *Germany and the Politics of Nuclear Weapons,* p. 165.

31. *Der Spiegel*, October 10, 1962, p. 50, cited in Küntzel, "Germany and the Origin and History of the NPT."

32. Steinbruner, *The Mind and the Milieu of Policy-Makers: A Case Study of the MLF,* p. 395, quoting McNamara's Ann Arbor speech in the *Department of State Bulletin,* July 9, 1962, p. 68.

33. Albert Wohlstetter, "Nuclear Sharing: NATO and the N+1 Country," *Foreign Affairs*, vol. 39, no. 3 (1961), p. 383.

34. "Adenauer Wants U.S. to Eliminate NATO Atom Curb," *New York Times*, November 17, 1961, p. L1.

35. "NATO Nuclear Arm is Pressed by Bonn," *New York Times,* December 13, 1961, p. L1; Charles Murphy, "NATO at a Nuclear Crossroads," *Fortune,* December 1962, p. 220.

36. "The Developing Atlantic Partnership," *Department of State Bulletin,* April 23, 1962, p. 668.

37. Kelleher, *Germany and the Politics of Nuclear Weapons*, p. 189.

38. Steinbruner, *The Mind and the Milieu of Policy-Makers: A Case Study of the MLF,* p. 384.

39. See Schwartz, *NATO's Nuclear Dilemma,* pp. 111–13, for a discussion of the internal U.S. bureaucratic discord over the MLF effort and evidence of the limited endorsement the scheme had at senior levels.

40. *Bulletin* (official daily publication of the Press and Information Office of the Federal Government [of Germany]), June 16, 1964.

41. *Bulletin* (official daily publication of the Press and Information Office of the Federal Government [of Germany]), November 16, 1965.

42. Uwe Nerlich, "The Nuclear Dilemmas of the Federal Republic of Germany," *Europa Archiv*, no. 17 (1965), p. 11.

43. Kai-Uwe von Hassel, "Organizing Western Defense," *Foreign Affairs*, vol. 43, no. 2 (January 1965), pp. 210–11.

44. John MacNaughton, a senior aide to Secretary MacNamara, quoted his boss, the leading advocate of this view, as telling him, "We are going to insist that the Germans stop talking about a finger on the trigger without a plan to use it. . . . We are going to make them resolve the question of whose finger, and when it is to push." Schwartz, *NATO's Nuclear Dilemma,* p. 183.

45. See "Flexible Response, a French View," *Revue de defense nationale*, August–September 1964.

46. *Die Welt*, January 22, 1963, in Kelleher, *Germany and the Politics of Nuclear Weapons*, p. 240.

47. Wilfred L. Kohl, *French Nuclear Diplomacy* (Princeton University Press, 1971), chap. 7.

48. President de Gaulle, press conference, February 4, 1965, in *Speeches*, no. 216 (New York: Ambassade de France, Service de Presse et d'Information, 1965).

49. Schwartz, *NATO's Nuclear Dilemma*, p. 122.

50. Kelleher, *Germany and the Politics of Nuclear Weapons*, pp. 257, 278–80.

51. *Rheinischer Merkur*, August 27, 1965, and *Die Welt*, August 23, 1965, cited in Kelleher, *Germany and the Politics of Nuclear Weapons*, p. 258.

52. *Der Spiegel*, September 1, 1965, pp. 19, 21.

53. Rudolf Botzian and Uwe Nerlich, "Auswirkungen eines Vertrages uber die Nichtverbreitung von Atomwaffen auf den zivilen Sektor technisch-industrieller Entwicklungen," Stiftung Wissenschaft und Politik (SWP), January 23, 1967, Ebenhausen, p. 12.

54. *Der Spiegel*, cited in Küntzel, *Bonn and the Bomb*, p. 66.

55. Government document, cited in Küntzel, *Bonn and the Bomb*, p. 80.

56. Government document, cited in Küntzel, *Bonn and the Bomb*, p. 160.

57. Küntzel, *Bonn and the Bomb*, p. 163.

58. Interview with Ministry of Defense official, Berlin, April 3, 2003.

59. Küntzel, *Bonn and the Bomb*, p. 157.

60. *Status of Multilateral Arms Regulation and Disarmament Agreements*, 4th ed., vol. 1 (United Nations, 1993), p. 136.

61. Wolfgang Kötter, "German Non-Proliferation Policy," in *Germany, Europe and Nuclear Non-Proliferation* (Southhampton: Mountbatten Centre for International Studies, University of Southampton, September 1991), pp. 11, 15.

62. Küntzel, *Bonn and the Bomb*, p. xvii

63. "Article III—Physical Protection." Working paper of the 1995 Review and Extension Conference of the Parties to the Treaty on the Non-Proliferation of Nuclear Weapons, document NPT/CONF.1995/MCII/WP.8, para 3.

64. "Report of Main Committee II," document NPT/CONF.1995/MC.II/1, para 36.

65. Technische Universität München, "TUM Research Reactor Produces the First Neutrons," press release (www.frm2.tu-muenchen.de/index_en.shtml [April 2004]). See also Alexander Glaser, "Weapons Uranium: Bavaria Bucks Ban," *Bulletin of the Atomic Scientists*, vol. 58, no. 2 (March 1, 2002), p. 20 (www.the-bulletin.org/issues/2002/ma02/ma02glaser.html [February 2004]).

66. Oliver Meier, "A Civilian Power Caught between the Lines: Germany and Nuclear Non-proliferation," paper presented at the conference Germany as a

Civilian Power—Results of Recent Research, Trier University, December 11–12, 1998 (Berlin: Berliner Informationszentrum für Transatlantische Sicherheit [BITS], 1998), p. 17.

67. See Lally Weymouth, "Third World Nukes: The German Connection," *Washington Post*, December 13, 1991, p. A29.

68. Harold Muller, "Europe's Leaky Borders," *Bulletin of the Atomic Scientists*, June 1993 (www.thebulletin.org/issues/1993/j93/j93Muller.html [July 10, 2003]).

69. "U.S. Seized Shipload of Nuclear Equipment Bound for Libya in October," *New York Times*, January 1, 2004.

70. Schwartz, *NATO's Nuclear Dilemma*, p. 232.

71. Patrick E. Tyler, "U.S. Strategy Plan Calls for Ensuring No Rivals Develop," *New York Times*, March 8, 1992.

72. Arnulf Baring, *Deutschland, was nun?* (Berlin: Siedler, 1991), p. 209.

73. Interview with Walter Stützle, Berlin, April 3, 2003.

74. Andreas Zumach and Niklaus Hablutzel, "Kinkel spielt mit Atombomben," *Die Tageszeitung*, May 11, 1995, cited in Meier, "A Civilian Power Caught between the Lines," p. 11.

75. Interview with Joachim Schmidt, Peace Research Institute of Frankfurt, Berlin, April 1, 2003.

76. German Ministry of Defense, *1994: Weissbuch zur Sicherheit der Bundesrepublik Deutschland und zur Lage und Zukunft der Bundeswehr*, white paper (Bonn: 1994), p. 52.

77. Mark N. Gose, "The New Germany and Nuclear Weapons: Options for the Future," *Air Power Journal: Special Edition 1996* (USAF Institute for National Security Studies [INSS], 1996), p. 11.

78. Poll commissioned by the International Physicians for the Prevention of Nuclear War (IPPNW) Germany on June 2, 1998. See Meier, "A Civilian Power Caught between the Lines," p. 8.

79. Craig S. Smith, "German Military Ranks as NATO Laggard," *International Herald Tribune*, March 19, 2003, p. 2.

80. Interview with Ministry of Defense official, Berlin, April 2, 2003.

81. Interview with Michael Klor-Berchtold, deputy director, North America Division, Ministry of Foreign Affairs, Berlin, April 2, 2003.

82. In the 1970s, because neighboring countries feared a resurgent Germany, François Mitterand, among others, advocated keeping Germany divided in order to preserve security in Europe.

83. Harald Müller, "A View from Germany," in Harold A. Feiveson, ed., *The Nuclear Turning Point: A Blueprint for Deep Cuts and De-Alerting of Nuclear Weapons* (Brookings, 1999), pp. 341 and 347.

84. Interview with Henning Riecke, senior research fellow, Research Institute of the German Council on Foreign Relations, Berlin, April 4, 2003.

85. Harald Müller, "The Non-Proliferation Treaty and the German Choice

Not to Proliferate," in David Carlton and others, ed., *Controlling the International Transfer of Weaponry and Related Technology* (Brookfield, Vt.: Dartmouth Publishing, 1995), p. 181.

86. Meier, "A Civilian Power Caught between the Lines," p. 2.

87. Interview with Rüdiger Lüdeking, director, Nuclear Arms Control and Non-Proliferation, Ministry of Foreign Affairs, Berlin, June 16, 2003.

88. To be sure, dual-key arrangements for U.S. nuclear weapons to be delivered by German planes gave—and indeed still give—Germany a limited nuclear role. But since these arrangements (aside from being marginal in scale) depend on prior U.S. consent for the weapons to be released, they fall far short of a German finger on the trigger; rather they mean that there must be a separate German decision to release the safety catch before certain U.S.-controlled weapons could be delivered.

89. As long ago as 1963, Harvard professor Thomas Schelling remarked that "Germany is the only country in the world that could prove that a state can be big, prosperous and powerful without the atomic bomb, the only country that could take away the status of wielding the sceptre of power from the atomic weapons by voluntarily renouncing such weapons—the only country that could take over the initiative of disarmament from the United States and the Soviet Union." See Thomas C. Schelling, "Kontinuität und Neubeginn in der NATO," in *Europa-Archiv*, no. 13 (1966), p. 471.

90. Müller, "Non-Proliferation Treaty," p. 183.

91. In fact, the customary accusation from Americans and others that supported the Iraq war is that Germany is too ready to dismiss the threat of weapons of mass destruction from geographically distant "rogue states" and ignores the danger they pose to European and German security.

92. Catherine McArdle Kelleher, "The New Germany: An Overview," in Paul B. Stares, ed., *The New Germany and the New Europe* (Brookings, 1992), p. 45.

93. Interview with Ministry of Defense military official, Berlin, April 3, 2003.

CHAPTER 9

Japan: Thinking the Unthinkable

KURT M. CAMPBELL

TSUYOSHI SUNOHARA

In the twilight of the 1980s, at the height of Japanese economic power, a Japanese comic book—or *manga*—called *Silent Service* appeared. The storyline unfolds with the United States and a secret Japanese government cell conspiring to build Japan's first nuclear-powered and -armed submarine. On its maiden voyage, the submarine's crew, led by Commander Shiro Kaieda, mutinies and dives into the dark depths of the Pacific. Kaieda christens the sub *Yamato*, a twin reference to the name of ancient Japan and also the namesake of Japan's most famous but ultimately doomed battleship of World War II. The *Yamato* uses brilliant operational tactics to outmaneuver the combined fleets of the United States and the Soviet Union and launches nuclear strikes to humiliate and defeat both superpowers. In the end, despite the radioactive carnage that he has unleashed, Captain Kaieda is revealed to be a fervent pacifist, working for global nuclear disarmament and the establishment of a transnational military organization to enforce world peace. Enormously popular and scrutinized closely for clues about Japan's innermost attitudes about achieving nuclear weapons status, *Silent Service* provides a glimpse into the complexities of Japanese sentiments regarding nuclear weapons.

Japan represents the ultimate contradiction among the potential nuclear aspirants explored in this volume. Its standing as a non-nuclear

218

nation is a virtual bedrock of the nonproliferation regime, the inspiration and example of the early era of the Non-Proliferation Treaty (NPT). Having experienced the horrors of Hiroshima and Nagasaki, Japan's political structures and national psyche have engendered a deeply enshrined cultural taboo (until very recently) against even public discussion of the nuclear option. In addition, Japanese leaders have repeatedly expressed their confidence in the U.S. nuclear umbrella provided by the Japanese-American defense treaty and reinforced by the deployment of substantial U.S. military forces on Japanese territory. Indeed, the Japanese case is often seen as the model of how extended deterrence guarantees serve to curb incentives for nuclear proliferation.

At the same time, suspicion and speculation have persisted that, given the right set (really the wrong set) of international and domestic conditions, Japan might seriously consider the nuclear option. Recently, prominent Japanese have openly broached the issue of Japan's acquiring a nuclear arsenal to help manage what many in Japan see as severely untoward developments in the regional and international security environment. Japan is one of the most technologically advanced countries, relies heavily on nuclear power for its domestic energy consumption, and has vast stores of plutonium that could be used in nuclear weapons. If it ever did cross the Rubicon into the realm of the atomically armed, there is near-universal recognition that the potential consequences would be enormous and unpredictable—and quite possibly extremely dangerous.

This chapter first discusses the factors that led Japan to refrain from acquiring nuclear weapons during the cold war. In particular, it explains why Japanese leaders confidently entrusted their ultimate security to Washington and its robust nuclear arsenal. Next is an analysis of the factors that have arisen since the cold war's end that have induced some Japanese to call for a reassessment of Japan's nuclear abstention.[1] The chapter then concludes with an examination of what U.S. policies could best avert the advent of a nuclear-armed Japan—a development that would be potentially catastrophic for both East Asia and the larger global international security environment.

Japan's Nuclear Weapons Debate during the Cold War

Unlike some of the other countries in this study, the Japanese government never made a formal decision on whether or not to pursue a nuclear option. During World War II, while Germany and the United States were racing to become the first county to develop nuclear weapons, Japan clandestinely developed two separate plans for atomic weapons development. Discovered and dismantled by the allied powers at the end of the war, the two programs, known as the "Ni" and "F" projects, were hampered by material shortages and were never a major priority for the country's leaders.[2] (The Japanese military proved more successful at developing biological and chemical weapons, some of which were used against military targets and civilian areas in China during the war.)

While occupying the country after World War II, U.S. authorities drafted a new constitution for Japan that limited the number and kind of security forces the new government could maintain. Chapter 2 of article 9 of the so-called Peace Constitution explicitly states that "the Japanese people forever renounce war as a sovereign right of the nation" and that "land, sea, and air forces, as well as other war potential, will never be maintained." While nuclear weapons are not specifically mentioned in the constitution, they are usually considered to be offensive weapons and would therefore be forbidden. However, the ambiguity of the constitution on the question of nuclear weapons has left room for successive Japanese elites to debate the possibility (mostly in private) of developing this capability.

During the cold war, senior Japanese officials, including a succession of prime ministers, periodically indicated in unguarded moments their support for Japan's acquiring an independent nuclear weapons capacity. But pressure both from their domestic constituencies and from Japan's most important security ally, the United States, kept them from acting on their desires. Instead, they made many public statements affirming their commitment to a non-nuclear Japan and focused their energy on rebuilding the war-torn country and revitalizing its faltering economy. In particular, Prime Minister Shigeru Yoshida in the 1950s took advantage of the language of the Peace Constitution to deflect pressures, primarily from the United States, to undertake even a substantial buildup of the country's conventional military forces.

Furthermore, on December 19, 1955, Japan's national legislature, the Diet, adopted the Atomic Energy Basic Law, which clearly states: "The research, development, and utilization of atomic energy shall be limited to peaceful purposes."[3] Japan joined the International Atomic Energy Agency (IAEA) in 1957. The policy of assigning priority to domestic reconstruction succeeded so well that by the late 1960s Japan had the second-largest economy in the free world.[4]

Japanese elites felt comfortable focusing on economic reconstruction because they had strong confidence that the United States would defend Japan against any external military threats—even if such a defense required Washington to threaten the use of nuclear weapons. This concept and context of extended deterrence was enshrined in the language of the U.S.-Japan Defense Treaty. Article 5 states: "Each party recognizes that an armed attack against either Party in the territories under the administration of Japan would be dangerous to its own peace and safety and declares that it would act to meet the common danger in accordance with its constitutional provisions and processes."

In 1957 Prime Minister Nobusuke Kishi, a strong nationalist from the long-ruling Liberal Democratic Party (LDP), attempted to reinforce the American security guarantee. When Prime Minister Kishi brought a revised defense treaty to the Japanese legislature for ratification, however, massive public protests forced him and his cabinet to resign. Besides opposing the revised treaty itself, many Japanese had reacted negatively to Kishi's statement to the Diet that while Japan had thus far chosen not to develop nuclear weapons, it was not unconstitutional for it to do so.[5] This was one of the earliest public statements by a Japanese official discussing the possibility of Japan's acquiring a nuclear capability. (In 1960 the Treaty of Mutual Cooperation and Security between Japan and the United States replaced the 1951 Security Treaty between the two countries, but the American security guarantee remained unchanged.)

The next prime minister, Hayato Ikeda, focused primarily on economic matters and shied away from controversial security issues. His successor, however, was perhaps the most ardent advocate of developing an independent Japanese nuclear capability. Eisaku Sato, the younger brother of Prime Minister Kishi, took office in November 1964 during a period of deep security anxiety in Japan. Just one month earlier, China had tested its first nuclear device, which revived concerns among Japanese that they could be drawn into a Sino-American nuclear conflict. The successful Chinese atomic bomb test also prompted several senior Japanese leaders, including Yasuhiro Nakasone and Shintaro Ishihara, to call for a reexamination of Japan's policy of nuclear abstention.[6]

In addition, the United States was on the brink of a full-scale war in Vietnam, and the Chinese Cultural Revolution was beginning to take shape. These developments led many Japanese to see the prospect of a dramatically deteriorating Sino-American relationship. Most important, influential Japanese began to fear that with its new nuclear capability,

China could make Japan a "nuclear hostage" in the event of a crisis on the Korean Peninsula, a military conflict in the Taiwan Strait, or an escalation in the Vietnam War.[7]

When newly elected prime minister Sato met with President Lyndon Johnson privately in January 1965, one of his first comments was that "if Chicoms [Chinese Communists] had nuclear weapons, the Japanese also should have them."[8] This statement shocked the Johnson administration, especially when Prime Minister Sato followed it by saying that "Japanese public opinion will not permit this at present, but I believe that the public, especially the younger generation, can be 'educated.'"[9] Never before had a Japanese leader expressed so openly the desire to develop nuclear weapons, even if it these sentiments were only private ruminations.

Throughout the Sato administration, political elites, including Sato himself, discussed and made statements supporting Japan's ultimate pursuit of the nuclear option. Advocates suggested that tactical nuclear weapons, as opposed to the larger strategic weapons, could be defined as defensive, and therefore were permitted under the constitution. A Japanese defense agency White Paper, commissioned by its pro-nuclear director (and future prime minister) Yasuhiro Nakasone, stated that "as for defensive nuclear weapons, it would be possible in a legal sense to possess small-yield, tactical, purely defensive nuclear weapons without violating the Constitution. In view of the danger of inviting adverse foreign reactions and large-scale war, we will follow the policy of not acquiring nuclear weapons at present."[10]

The Johnson administration became increasingly anxious about Sato's intentions and made one of its top priorities securing Japan's signature to the NPT, which the UN Security Council had endorsed in 1968. At the same time, Sato was trying to convince the United States to turn the island of Okinawa, which was then still fully administered by the United States, back to Japan. Sato made this one of his campaign pledges in 1964 and was desperately trying to develop a feasible strategy to obtain this goal. He knew that the issue of greatest contention surrounding Okinawa was that U.S. nuclear weapons stored on the island could be quickly used against China, North Korea, or Vietnam in an emergency. The Japanese public, with its severe "nuclear allergy," would never countenance nuclear weapons remaining on the island after it reverted back to Japanese control. In order to counter this difficult domestic situation, Sato began heavily courting the Johnson administration. He made a number of statements in favor of U.S. policies during the Vietnam War and allowed U.S. nuclear-powered aircraft carriers to dock at Japanese ports.[11]

To reassure the anxious Japanese public, Prime Minister Sato announced to the National Diet in December 1967 the adoption of the "Three Non-Nuclear Principles." These held that Japan would not manufacture, possess, or permit the introduction of nuclear weapons onto Japanese soil. These principles, which were subsequently adopted by the Diet but are not considered a law, have remained the foundation of Japanese nuclear policy to the present day.[12]

According to Kei Wakaizumi, a senior policy adviser to Sato, soon after the declaration of the non-nuclear principles, Sato realized that the principles, as originally formulated, might be too constraining.[13] Therefore, in a February 1968 address to the Diet, Sato clarified the non-nuclear principles by declaring the "Four Nuclear Policies." These were 1) promotion of the peaceful use of nuclear energy; 2) efforts toward global nuclear disarmament; 3) reliance and dependence on U.S. extended deterrence, based on the 1960 U.S.-Japan Security Treaty; and 4) support for "the Three Non-Nuclear Principles under the circumstances where Japan's national security is guaranteed by the other three policies."[14]

Sato and the other leaders of his Liberal Democratic Party wanted to emphasize that the Three Non-Nuclear Principles could only be sustained in conjunction with the other policies, thus leaving the door open for Japan to develop nuclear weapons if the situation so mandated (that is, if there was significant regional proliferation or a "malfunction" of the U.S. nuclear umbrella). Despite the fact that Sato articulated and stood by these principles, he was less supportive in private, going so far as to tell then U.S. ambassador to Japan U. Alexis Johnson that they were "nonsense."[15]

Shortly after these declarations, in the spring of 1968, Sato commissioned a secret, nongovernmental study on Japan's nuclearization, rather misleadingly entitled "The Study Group on Democracy." The study's findings were summarized in the *1968/1970 Internal Report*, which became one of the most controversial documents in modern Japanese history when it was leaked to the public in 1994.[16] The report was conducted by four Japanese university academics with broad training in regional affairs and nuclear technology, and they consulted widely with government officials and industry representatives in developing their recommendations. The purpose of the effort was to "explore the costs and benefits of Japan's nuclearization in a comprehensive way."[17]

In the wake of the announcement of the Non-Nuclear Principles, Sato's government needed concrete reasons justifying Japan's abstention from the nuclear club. The *1968/1970 Report* provided just that. It mitigated Sato's natural hawkishness, especially toward China, by demonstrating the technical, political, and strategic problems associated with a nuclear path, and thereby confirmed in a very persuasive fashion that Japan's best interest lay in maintaining its non-nuclear status.

Although the technical and economic barriers to the development of a Japanese nuclear capability (which were examined in the 1968 portion of the document) have been largely overcome with time and technological advancements, it is the political and security concerns that have had the greatest impact on Japanese leaders. First, in assessing the threat from China, the report basically concluded that the U.S. nuclear umbrella would be sufficient to protect both Japan and South Korea from Chinese aggression in East Asia, even if Beijing possessed intercontinental missiles capable of hitting the United States. Second, it explained how Japan would remain extremely vulnerable even if it acquired a small nuclear arsenal. Most telling, the report noted that even the detonation of a single hydrogen bomb could have devastating effects given that over 50 percent of Japan's population was located in just 20 percent of its territory. Third, the authors determined that Japan's nuclearization would lead to its extreme isolation from both its allies and the rest of the international community. The study concluded that due to these constraints, the costs of developing an independent nuclear capability would far outweigh the one prospective and presumed benefit—less reliance on the United States for Japan's security needs.

The *1968/1970 Report* is the only known Japanese study of this scope and breadth on the nuclear weapons issue (there is speculation that other government studies may now either be under way or about to begin given the recent attention to this issue in the current Japanese environment). Despite the report's weighty conclusions against nuclear acquisition, many officials still did not want to formally or completely renounce the nuclear option.

At the same time that the study was being written, the Japanese government was debating whether to sign the NPT. The United States was strongly urging Japan to sign, maintaining that the U.S. nuclear umbrella would provide for its security. Many Japanese leaders, however, saw the treaty as fundamentally unfair in its basic charter. The Non-Proliferation Treaty allows the current members of the nuclear club to maintain their nuclear weapons status but prohibits any other signatory from joining the nuclear club. Vice Foreign Minister Takeso Shimoda told a press conference that "Japan cannot agree to such a big power-centered approach, implying as it does that the nuclear powers would not be required to reduce their capabilities or stockpile, while the non-nuclear powers would be barred . . . from having nuclear weapons."[18] Similarly, LDP Secretary General Takeo Fukuda said, "Liberal Democrats see the need to outgrow the 'nuclear allergy.'"[19]

Early in 1969, an internal policy planning study for the Foreign Ministry concluded that Japan should, even if it signed the NPT, maintain the economic and technical ability to develop and produce nuclear weapons in case the international environment deteriorated to the point that such a step became necessary. Japan finally signed the NPT in 1970 (but ratified it only in 1976), though only after both West Germany joined and the United States "promised not to interfere with Tokyo's pursuit of independent reprocessing capabilities in its civilian nuclear power program."[20] Despite the conclusions of the *1968/1970 Report*, the record indicates quite clearly that Prime Minister Sato and other LDP members wanted to preserve Japan's nuclear options.

Okinawa reverted to Japanese rule in May 1972, following a June 1971 agreement between Japan and the United States. According to the Three Non-Nuclear Principles, all nuclear weapons had to be removed from the island. The United States, affirming the Japanese non-nuclear position, completed this withdrawal by the end of 1972. Ironically, no Japanese leader had been more pro-nuclear than Prime Minister Sato, and yet, it was during his tenure that Japan formalized its non-nuclear position. Each successive Japanese administration has reaffirmed the Three Non-Nuclear Principles and Four Nuclear Policies. The nuclear debate lay largely dormant throughout the rest of the cold war.

End of the Cold War and the New International Security Environment

The 1980s saw the final death throes of the Soviet Union and the collapse of the cold war. The United States, under the leadership of Ronald Reagan, poured resources into a military buildup aimed at the Soviet Union, which among other consequences caused the Asia-Pacific region to increase in strategic importance as a theater of superpower competition. At the same time, Japan's economic might continued to grow as the country transitioned from a postwar industrial economy to one based on high technology and luxury goods. Japan's export-led growth caused increasing friction with the United States, which manifested itself in trade wars and American pressure on Japan to alter its protectionist policies. Nevertheless, the United States and Japan had few security differences, largely due to the perceived threat from the Soviet Union, and continued to reaffirm their alliance in their respective regional strategies and public pronouncements.

Yukihiko Ikeda recalled that he could not detect any nuclear ambitions among the Japanese military during his term as a defense minister in the late 1980s. "Ultimately, I think Japan could use nuclear power militarily for such purposes as nuclear submarines, and there might be a desire among the military for that in the future," Ikeda said. "But I think that they also believe Japan should keep her non-nuclear policy and that Japan will never actually possess nuclear weapons."[21]

In the immediate aftermath of the cold war, following the USSR's collapse, debate on the nuclear weapons issue in Japan remained largely mute. Most Japanese anticipated a new era of international peace, democracy, and good will. However, Korea remained divided, tensions between China and Taiwan persisted, and India and Pakistan continued their low-level conflict. These tensions kept Asians from fully experiencing the brief post–cold war euphoria that swept Europe. Nevertheless, the first major conflict of the post–cold war era did not occur in East Asia but in the Middle East, when Iraqi dictator Saddam Hussein invaded neighboring Kuwait. The United States, mustering an international coalition, went to the defense of the tiny but strategically important Arab country.

In Japan the Persian Gulf War led to much debate about the use of force in the post–cold war world, as the international community, particularly the United States, called "for Japan to support peacekeeping operations with more than its checkbook."[22] A fierce debate arose within the Japanese Diet, with the LDP forcing through the International Peace and Cooperation Law of 1992 against the firm opposition of the Japanese Socialist Party.[23] This law provided a framework for Japan to send troops overseas for participation "in international peace and relief efforts"—specifically, UN peacekeeping operations and international humanitarian relief operations. It stipulated five principles or requirements for these efforts: 1) existence of a cease-fire agreement; 2) consent of the host country; 3) impartiality of the operations; 4) withdrawal of Japanese forces if the government deems necessary; and 5) minimum use of force required for troop protection.[24] Under this new law, Japan was able to send troops to Cambodia as part of a United Nations peacekeeping operation, the first time the Japanese Self-Defense Forces (SDF) had been deployed abroad.[25]

Other international developments, which appeared to more directly threaten Japanese security, soon led to a revival of the nuclear weapons debate in Japan. In 1994 American intelligence discovered that the Democratic Peoples' Republic of Korea had a secret nuclear weapons development program. This crisis on the Korean Peninsula led to speculation in the United States and other countries that if the North Korean situation was not peacefully resolved, the Japanese might reconsider their policy of nuclear abstention. At the same time, tensions along the Taiwan Strait were also increasing. Over the course of the late 1990s, Japanese leaders and strategic thinkers came to perceive both North Korea's nuclear weapons program and the rapid modernization of China's nuclear weapons and other military capabilities as presenting a more dangerous and realistic threat to Japan than that which emanated from the Soviet Union during the cold war.

It was in the context of this increasingly disturbing environment that the Japanese Defense Agency conducted a secret investigation into Japan's nuclear option in late 1995. Although the full details of the thirty-one-page report have never been released, in 2003 the *Asahi Shimbun* obtained a copy of the report and revealed some of its findings. The study resoundingly reaffirmed Japan's non-nuclear status and outlined the numerous drawbacks that would result from Japan's nuclearization. In particular, the study found that Japan's acquisition of nuclear weapons would destroy the military balance in Asia and possibly cause an arms race with China, a nuclear South Korea, or an openly hostile North Korea. According to *Asahi*, the report said that "Japan would effectively destroy the basis for the Nuclear Nonproliferation Treaty; the reliability of the U.S. nuclear umbrella would be undermined and Japan would be viewed as distrustful of its military alliance with the United States; [and] neighbors would fear that Japan was taking a more independent defense policy stance."[26]

The report concluded that continued reliance on the U.S. nuclear deterrent provided Japan's best economic and security option. The authors argued that it would be prohibitively expensive for Japan to develop the infrastructure to produce nuclear weapons. In addition, if the country actually experienced a nuclear attack, its densely populated urban areas would be devastated. The study also asserted it was highly unlikely that the United States would allow North Korea to develop nuclear weapons.[27]

The report's conclusions may have influenced Japan's decision regarding whether to support an indefinite extension of the NPT, an issue that arose in 1995. The Clinton administration strongly pushed the Japanese government to endorse the treaty's indefinite extension, but Japanese leaders initially took an ambiguous position on the issue. "We thought it was better for us not to declare that we will give up our nuclear option forever and ever," recalled a former high-ranking Japanese government official on condition of anonymity.[28] Eventually, however, pressure from Washington and other governments led to Japan's supporting the indefinite extension.

But then two events in 1998 shocked the Japanese public and strengthened the hand of individuals and groups advocating that Japan at least reconsider if not reverse its policy of nuclear abstention. These advocates included conservative academics, some government officials, and a few influential industrialists (in addition to the very vocal nationalist organizations that prowl Tokyo's streets with bullhorns, spewing right-wing rhetoric).

First, in May 1998, India and Pakistan conducted back-to-back nuclear tests, formalizing their nuclear status. The perceived laxness that the international community showed in condemning the countries' nuclear adventurism troubled the Japanese. One reason the Japanese had decided to join the NPT in the early 1970s was that they had anticipated severe penalties for those states that defied the international consensus against further nuclear weapons acquisition.[29] In addition, the Japanese and other nations feared that India's development of a nuclear arsenal could spur a nuclear arms race with China. A Chinese military buildup would have much more potential for upsetting the delicate balance of power in Asia than the ongoing India-Pakistan conflict.

An even more disturbing event in 1998 was the launch of a North Korean Taepo Dong missile over Japan in August.[30] This demonstration of North Korea's ballistic missile capability led to an outcry among all sectors of Japanese society and caused some to call for remilitarization or nuclear weapons development. Fukushiro Nukaga, the chief of Japan's defense agency, said that "his government would be justified in mounting pre-emptive military strikes against North Korean missile bases."[31] Prime Minister Keizo Obuchi said that he was "extremely concerned" about the tests.[32] The Diet passed resolutions stating that the "actions of North Korea were imprudent and extremely dangerous, ignoring international common sense, and posed a serious situation for our national security."[33] It also unanimously passed a resolution of protest, and the Japanese government suspended both the talks on normalizing relations between the two countries and its food shipments to North Korea.[34]

The missile incident gave nationalist conservatives more prominence in the defense debate than at any time since the Sato administration in the 1960s. The conservative *Sankei* newspaper wrote in an editorial that "in order to counter such a threat, [Japan] has to establish a cold, merciless policy of power politics" in order to let the North Koreans "know that [Japan] has the option of attacking launch sites in North Korea in self-defense."[35] However, the general public still was reluctant to flirt with abandoning a well-established non-nuclear policy, and opinion polls at the time showed strong opposition to pursuing nuclear arms. For example, when Vice Defense Minister Shingo Nishimura said in a 1999 magazine interview that parliament "should consider the fact that Japan may be better off if it armed itself with nuclear weapons," it resulted in a public furor both in Japan and neighboring countries.[36] Other government officials described the comment as "extremely inappropriate," and then prime minister Keizo Obuchi called for, and accepted, Nishimura's resignation.

But the increased threat to Japan perceived to be emanating from North Korea, combined with worries about China's ongoing military buildup and the other concerns described below, continued to raise the issue of Japan's acquiring nuclear weapons. For example, in an interview with *Asashi Shimbun*, Deputy Chief Cabinet Secretary Shinzo Abe stated that Japan's possession of atomic bombs would not violate the constitution because "it does not necessarily ban the possession of nuclear weapons as long as they are kept at a minimum and are tactical."[37] Chief Cabinet Secretary Yasuo Fukuda subsequently said, in trying to clarify Abe's statement, that "'in legal theory' Japan could have intercontinental ballistic missiles and atomic bombs and that the Three Non-Nuclear Principles might change if the people believed Japan should go nuclear."[38]

Notwithstanding the resulting domestic and international backlash, Prime Minister Junichiro Koizumi said Fukuda's comments were only a "slip of the tongue" and "nothing serious."[39] Unlike Nishimura, Fukuda was not asked to resign. Instead, he renounced his comments in the Diet, saying that Japan's Atomic Energy Basic Law permitted Japan to use nuclear energy only for peaceful purposes. Koizumi also insisted, "My Cabinet will keep the non-nuclear weapon principles. Japan will not possess a nuclear arsenal because we have these principles. This is not even worthy of discussion."[40]

Despite these remarks, many in the Japanese public, which is still firmly behind the Three Non-Nuclear Principles, apparently believe that government officials continue to conduct secret talks on the nuclear issue much as they had done in the past. Koizumi himself implied that he agreed that Japan had the right to possess nuclear weapons when he added, "it is significant that although we could have them, we don't."[41]

Japanese leaders made additional pro–nuclear weapons statements in 2003. In August Fukuda said at a press conference that it would be possible for Japan to legally keep its nuclear option for the near future.[42] Abe, a rising political star from the ruling LDP, said in response to a question during a speech he delivered at Waseda University in Tokyo on March 13, 2003, that Japan could have nuclear weapons if they were small and defensive, a position that is gaining increasing traction among Japan's younger foreign policy elite.[43] Both Fukuda and Abe later explained that the Koizumi cabinet has no intention of developing nuclear weapons at present, but that future foreign policy makers should be able to decide whether or not to develop nuclear weapons. Other Japanese officials, including Prime Minister Koizumi, have repeatedly stressed that Japan will maintain its policy of nuclear abstention for the foreseeable future.[44]

Influential people outside the government also have called for Japan to reverse its policy of nuclear abstention. Terumasa Nakanishi, a professor at Kyoto University, insists that Japan now needs to possess nuclear weapons because the country cannot protect itself only with ballistic missile defenses (BMDs) or conventional weapons like Tomahawk cruise missiles.[45] A conservative opinion leader from Keio University, Kazuya Fukuda, supports Nakanishi's view. Fukuda maintains that the U.S. nuclear umbrella is an illusion and compelling reasons have arisen as to why Japan should have nuclear weapons.[46]

Main Factors Affecting Japan's Future Nuclear Weapons Policies

There are several current and future situations that could propel Japan along the path toward acquisition of nuclear weapons. Among these are an increase in the perceived external security threat emanating from

North Korea, the rise of a Chinese strategic and military power, concerns about the ability of successive U.S. governments to manage these threats in ways most beneficial to Japan, and the weakening of the international nonproliferation regime, despite vigorous Japanese efforts to bolster it.

Eroding Regional and Global Security Situation

During the last decade, both the Japanese public and their leaders have become increasingly concerned about the growing perceived threat to Japan from North Korea. Indeed, the most likely factor that could trigger a Japanese reconsideration of its nuclear weapons policy in the near term is the emergence of a nuclear-armed North Korea.

As already noted, North Korea's launch of a long-range Taepo Dong missile over Japan's mainland in August 1998 stunned the Japanese public. According to Matake Kamiya, "The shock that it gave to the Japanese was arguably comparable to the one the Soviet launching of Sputnik in October 1957 gave to the Americans. For most Japanese, the launching was the first occasion in the postwar period in which they really felt their country was being immediately threatened by a hostile external power."[47]

Besides the still experimental Taepo Dong, North Korea also possesses hundreds of shorter-range Nodong missiles that could also reach Tokyo and other Japanese cities. The Pyongyang government has warned Japan that it lies "within the striking range of" North Korea and therefore should behave well.[48] Japanese leaders have expressed repeated concern about North Korea's missile program. In March 2003, Shigeru Ishiba, director general of Japan's Defense Agency, even affirmed that the Japanese government could legitimately launch a preemptive strike against North Korea if government leaders had concluded that an attack against Japan was imminent.[49]

Ishiba's remarks reflect the potential devastation Japan could suffer from even a single North Korean missile if it were armed with a nuclear warhead. The CIA estimates that the North Korean government has made more progress toward developing nuclear weapons than any other potential proliferator.[50] During 2003 North Korean representatives acknowledged that they have abandoned their pledge not to develop nuclear weapons. Indeed, they claimed that they have reprocessed 8,000 spent plutonium fuel rods. Although such boasts remain unproven, U.S. officials estimate that North Korea's large-scale plutonium-reprocessing facility at Yongbyon could produce sufficient plutonium for approximately half a dozen bombs within twelve to eighteen months.[51] For years media reports have indicated that U.S. intelligence feared that North Korea already had developed one or two nuclear bombs in the early 1990s. The IAEA believes that Pyongyang recently produced sufficient plutonium to produce two additional bombs.[52] Analysts fear that unrestrained by a workable arms control regime, Pyongyang could conceivably develop tens of nuclear weapons—or more—by the end of the decade.[53]

The Japanese government has taken a number of steps to impede and reverse North Korea's nuclear ambitions. A favorite tool has been diplomacy. Prime Minister Junichiro Koizumi visited Pyongyang in September 2002 to convince North Korean leaders to refrain from additional missile testing. Koizumi and other Japanese officials repeatedly have joined with their foreign counterparts to issue joint declarations calling on North Korea to dismantle its nuclear weapons program "in a prompt and verifiable manner."[54] The government has stated, "Japan cannot accept, by any means, any development, acquisition or possession, test and transfer of nuclear weapons by North Korea."[55] Japanese representatives also actively participated in the August 2003 Six Party Talks that attempted to achieve settlement of the security problems on the Korean Peninsula.

Beyond diplomatic measures, the Japanese government has imposed economic sanctions against Pyongyang for its nuclear activities, such as supporting the decision by the Korean Peninsula Energy Development Organization to suspend heavy fuel oil shipments in November 2002. Japan also has participated in the Proliferation Security Initiative (PSI), which aims to prevent North Korea and other countries from importing or exporting materials related to weapons of mass destruction (WMD). A Japanese Coast Guard ship played a prominent role in the Pacific Protector exercise that took place in September 2003 under the PSI's auspices.[56] Prime Minister Koizumi also has promoted a series of bilateral and multilateral accords with other Asian countries designed to strengthen international efforts to interdict illegal transfers of WMD and missile-related materials. These initiatives have included calls for enhanced intelligence sharing and greater support for the PSI.[57]

Unfortunately, thus far the efforts of Japan and other countries have proven inadequate to ensure that North Korea does not develop a nuclear arsenal that could target neighboring states. If Japanese leaders conclude that North Korea has acquired the ability to launch nuclear weapons against Japan, they might feel compelled to develop their own nuclear arsenal to deter such an attack. Such a reaction would be even more likely if Taiwan or South Korea had already established a precedent by acquiring their own nuclear arsenals.

If the United States decided to attack North Korea in a preemptive strike without first gaining Tokyo's approval, Japanese leaders might no longer feel comfortable entrusting Japan's ultimate security to Washington, a situation that also might lead them to abandon the policy of nuclear abstention. Ironically, an absence of consultation in such a grave situation would likely provoke a deep rethinking of the benefits of the alliance regardless of whether U.S. military strikes against North Korea were ultimately successful. The risk of a North Korean attack on Japan in any military conflict on the peninsula would be significant because the United States would confront the demanding task of deterring or preventing North Korea from escalating the conflict at the same time that U.S. forces were pursuing a conventional military victory over the North Korean military. Finally, even Korea's peaceful reunification under South Korea's leadership might not avert Japan's nuclearization if the new Korean government insisted on maintaining its inheritance of nuclear weapons and ballistic missiles.

While ordinary people worry more about the danger posed by a nuclear North Korea, many Japanese leaders are ultimately more concerned about a potential long-term Chinese threat to Japan. A 2003 Defense Agency white paper observed, "China has been modernizing its nuclear and missile forces as well as its naval and air forces. Careful deliberation should go into determining whether the objective of this modernization exceeds the scope necessary for the defense of China, and future developments in this area merit special attention."[58] Ichiro Ozawa, president of the Liberal Party, was more blunt. In April 2002 he suggested that Japan might need to exploit its vast stockpile of plutonium to produce thousands of nuclear weapons to counter future Chinese aggression.[59] In fact, some members of the conservative camp are using the current situation with North Korea to beef up Japan's readiness and overall capabilities to cope with such a threat.

China is continuing to modernize its own WMD and ballistic missile arsenal, presenting an increasing threat to Taiwan, a de facto U.S. (and, by extension, Japanese) ally.[60] However, it is also true that these Chinese missile deployments are raising anxieties elsewhere in the region, including among Japan's strategic thinkers. In particular, given the mobile nature of these systems, there is a worry that these missiles could be used to blackmail Japan in some tense future diplomatic situation. In addition, Chinese technology firms persist in seeking to sell WMD-related material or technology to foreign buyers, some of which could be rogue regimes or nonstate actors hostile to Japan and the United States. Some

Chinese business entities are adopting increasingly sophisticated means to avoid detection—and U.S. sanctions.[61] While it is unlikely that this proliferative behavior would directly trigger a Japanese response, there is the potential for surreptitious Chinese nuclear activities to undermine the nonproliferation regime and thereby raise the risks of Japan rethinking its nuclear options.

The Chinese government's foreign policy ambitions will decisively affect the kind of challenge confronting future Japanese policymakers. A Chinese government satisfied with the status quo in East Asia would present less of a threat than a revisionist regime that sought to better its regional position, even at the risk of international disorder. Although the dispute is in abeyance, China and Japan continue to contest control over the Senkakaku (Diaoyutai) Islands, and the Japanese remain concerned about China's ambitions in the South China Sea. Even a Chinese government that focused its revisionist aims against Taiwan alone could trigger events that could lead to Japan's deciding to acquire nuclear weapons—especially if the United States had tried but failed to avert or resist a Chinese attack on the island.

Conversely, the Japanese also worry that in the future the United States might develop closer ties with China—the emerging economic and military leader of East Asia—than with Japan.[62] Anxiety over "Japan passing" has become a regular feature in Tokyo's preoccupations over a rising China, along with worries that China is beginning to replace Japan in American regional diplomatic priorities. Some Japanese fear that if these trends continue, a crisis in confidence could ensue. While it is today difficult to imagine a scenario that could lead to such a profound alienation between the United States and Japan, in the future such a development might prompt the Japanese to seek the independent means of defense that nuclear weapons would provide.

At some future point, a revitalized—or even regressing—Russia also could contribute to a Japanese rethinking of its security options. Russian-Japanese relations remain poor because of Russia's unwillingness to return to Japan the four islands constituting the Northern Territories. The dispute over the islands has prevented the two countries from signing a peace treaty formally ending their World War II–era conflict. Hopes that Japanese and Russian businesses could cooperate to exploit the riches of Russia's Far East have run aground against the unfavorable investment climate and high crime rate in the region.

Although former Russian president Boris Yeltsin told then Japanese prime minister Ryutaro Hashimoto in 1997 that Russia no longer targeted nuclear missiles at Japan, a future Russian government could easily reverse this policy.[63] The collapse of Russia's conventional forces since the Soviet period has also led Russian leaders to rely increasingly on nuclear weapons as their country's main defensive bulwark. For example, the current Russian government has renounced the Soviet policy against the first use of nuclear weapons. Recently, Russian officials have also asserted the right to launch preemptive strikes in response to imminent threats. From Tokyo's perspective, Russia's long-term role in the evolving international system remains uncertain, especially in a post-Putin era. Ironically, Russia's weakened military and the recent major Russian-American strategic arms reductions also make it more plausible for the Japanese to reason that they could develop a nuclear deterrent robust enough to survive a Russian first strike.[64]

A more pressing concern for the Japanese is the threat of international terrorism posed by Islamic fundamentalism in the wake of September 11, 2001. The threat of terrorism in Asia and elsewhere has provided the ostensible rationale for Japanese officials to introduce measures to enhance Japan's ability to contribute to international security efforts, even in regions far beyond Japan's borders such as Afghanistan and now Iraq. Although Japan had been methodically but intensively revising its approach to security for over a decade, the recent international security environment—including new terrorist threats and the potential for ballistic missile attacks—has catalyzed ongoing deliberations in the Diet over how to increase the nation's option to play a more active role to meet these new challenges.

As discussed above, in 1992 the Japanese Diet passed a law permitting the SDF to participate in UN peacekeeping operations. In 1995 the new National Defense Program Outline instructed the SDF to acquire the capabilities necessary to operate outside Japanese territory.[65] In 1997 the Japanese government announced revisions to the guidelines that governed defense cooperation between Japan and the United States. Among other things, the new guidelines specified that Japan would provide "rear area support" for American forces engaged in an East Asian military contingency.[66]

In 1999 Japan enacted legislation that allowed the government to conduct joint operational planning with the United States for contingencies that occurred outside its national territory "in situations in areas surrounding Japan that will have an important influence on Japan's peace and security."[67] The Anti-Terrorism Special Measures Law of 2001, which was renewed in 2003, enabled the SDF to dispatch warships to the Indian Ocean to provide logistical support (primarily at-sea refueling) for allied military operations in Afghanistan as part of Operation Enduring Freedom.[68]

In December 2002, the Prime Minister's Commission on Japan's Cooperation for International Peace recommended expanding the SDF's role in international peacekeeping operations. The Iraq Special Measures Law of July 2003 permits the government to deploy ground troops in Iraq to provide logistical support for the allied military campaign in that country.[69] As discussed below, the Japanese government also has shown increasing interest in cooperating with the United States to develop defenses to protect Japan from a ballistic missile attack from North Korea (and, perhaps in the not so distant future, China).

Thus far, the United States and other countries have supported Japan's increased involvement in global security affairs because they perceive these steps as compatible with Japan's assumed role within the Japanese-American security alliance and other international institutions. Such compatibility is not guaranteed, however, and future scenarios may see threats arise that the Japanese elite feel Japan can best manage outside the alliance. In any case, Japan's vigorous measures to manage these threats by abandoning past practices demonstrates the willingness of its leaders to institute major changes in Japan's security policies in situations where they perceive international circumstances so warrant. This capacity and willingness suggest that in the face of even more severe regional or global threats, the Japanese government might reluctantly feel compelled to also alter Japan's nuclear weapons policies.

U.S. Foreign and Security Policy

Although the credibility of the U.S. nuclear deterrence guarantee has never been tested (in the form of actual nuclear use) in the case of Japan, or any other country, it continues to lie at the heart of the security relationship between the United States and Japan. Indeed, the guarantee, and the Japanese-American security alliance in which it is embedded, provides the most important reason why Japan has not sought to develop an independent nuclear weapons capacity. Thanks to their continued faith in American foreign and security policy, successive Japanese administrations have refrained from fully developing the military potential commonly associated with a "normal" state (that is, having the potential to wage war for both offensive and defensive purposes).

If anything, Japanese-American security relations have become even stronger in recent years. For example, the Japanese have become increasingly supportive of U.S. ballistic missile defense efforts (at least in terms of defending Japan and the American forces based there).[70] In September 1998, Japan started a joint research and development program on theater BMD with the United States. At present, Japan's Defense Agency anticipates beginning to deploy a BMD system, consisting of ground-to-air Patriot Advanced Capability-3 missiles and an Aegis-equipped destroyer with Standard Missile-3 missiles, as early as fiscal year 2007.[71] In the meantime, Japan's government and private industry are collaborating with their U.S. counterparts on BMD research and development.

But the persistence of a Japanese-American alliance so robust that it can indefinitely dissuade Japanese leaders from acquiring nuclear weapons cannot be guaranteed. The alliance has been plagued by long-standing disputes on a number of issues. Americans have attacked what they see as Japan's protectionist trade policies, export-led growth strategies, and alleged "free riding" on the United States to manage international security problems. For their part, the Japanese have persistently worried about Washington dragging them into a military conflict against their wishes. Furthermore, since the advent of the alliance, prominent members of the Japanese elite have displayed discomfort with the way it seems to diminish Japan's independent weight in world affairs or circumscribes the Japanese government's ability to pursue its preferred policies on a number of important global issues.[72]

Some of Japan's most able and influential diplomats will privately complain that they have been treated like a second-class nation in the international arena, mainly because Japan does not have an "ultimate power" (that is, nuclear weapons). Some Ministry of Foreign Affairs officials confess they experience this treatment most strongly when U.S. officials exclude them from important decisionmaking processes. While most officials inside the ministry strongly uphold the importance of the U.S.-Japan alliance, some diplomats fear that the day will come when Japan can no longer rely on the United States, and they want Japan to be prepared to defend its interests in that eventuality.

The arguments of certain advocates of an independent Japanese nuclear weapons capacity resemble those employed by some West Europeans during the cold war. After the Soviet Union developed its own nuclear weapons and the means to deliver them against the American homeland, many European strategists came to doubt the credibility of the U.S. extended nuclear deterrence guarantee that lay at the foundation of the NATO alliance. They feared that the only way to avert a "decoupling" of America's and Europe's defense was for Western European countries to develop an independent nuclear capacity. These concerns played an important role in prompting Britain and later France to develop their own independent nuclear arsenals and induced U.S. leaders to take measures to enhance NATO's involvement in America's nuclear weapons policies. They also prompted the United States to deploy American intermediate-range nuclear forces in West Germany, Britain, and Italy.

For reasons similar to those of their European counterparts, some Japanese have doubted the United States would risk New York for Tokyo. Kumao Kaneko, former director of the Nuclear Energy Division of the Foreign Ministry, has written that the "United States would be highly unlikely to use its nuclear arms to defend Japan unless American forces in Japan were exposed to extreme danger."[73]

More recently, the crisis on the Korean Peninsula and the long-term rise of China also have caused some American officials to worry how foreign policy concerns are prompting Japanese leaders to reevaluate Japan's policy of nuclear abstention. During a hearing before the House International Relations Committee in June 2003, Under Secretary of State for Arms Control and International Security John Bolton warned that "the balance of opinion of those who have looked at the region carefully is that a nuclear capable North Korea could well produce a decision in Japan to seek a nuclear weapons capability."[74]

Vice President Richard Cheney has also touched upon the issue, saying that "the idea of a nuclear-armed North Korea with ballistic missiles to deliver those will, I think, probably set off an arms race in that part of the world, and others, perhaps Japan, for example, may be forced to consider whether or not they want to readdress the nuclear question."[75]

Senator John McCain said that "we should make clear to China and others the consequences of acquiescing to North Korea's nuclear ambitions, including Japan's emergence as a nuclear power."[76] Former secretary of defense William Perry also expressed his concern that if North Korea acquired nuclear weapons, Japan might also feel compelled to pursue the nuclear option.[77]

These sentiments reflect, in part, a genuine belief that a North Korean nuclear capability could prompt Japan to acquire a nuclear capacity of its own. However, such public statements have other motives, such as heightening China's anxieties in an effort to get Beijing to constrain Pyongyang, or even indirectly pressuring the Bush administration to engage more seriously in preventing North Korea from pursuing nuclear weapons.

A direct military confrontation between the United States and China could also prove disastrous for the Japanese-American alliance. More than likely, Washington would expect more assistance from Japan than Tokyo would be willing to provide—leading to recriminations on both sides. In addition, the Japanese could lose faith in America's ability to manage international security crises that could affect Japan's vital interests. An American failure to defend Taiwan against China could also lead Japanese leaders to reevaluate their reliance on the U.S. extended deterrence guarantee to ensure Japan's security.

Even the recent efforts by the U.S. Department of Defense, under Secretary Donald Rumsfeld, to revise America's global military posture have engendered anxiety in Japan and other countries. For example, when it became known that the Pentagon was considering withdrawing some U.S. military forces from South Korea, some South Korean officials indicated they were losing confidence in the U.S. security commitment to their country.[78] Former national security adviser Zbigniew Brzezinski warned that such actions could trigger not only Seoul but also Tokyo to consider a nuclear weapons option: "Conceivably, if we withdraw from South Korea, then South Korea either will have to defend itself somehow, in which case it may need nuclear weapons, and that would certainly further intensify pressure on Japan to respond."[79]

Japanese leaders also might lose confidence in the United States should Washington pursue an agreement with Pyongyang that seemed to ignore or downplay legitimate Japanese concerns. For example, a U.S. pledge never to attack North Korea could call into question America's ability to fulfill its extended deterrence guarantee to Japan should North Korea attack Japan directly. Masashi Nishihara, president of Japan's National Defense Academy, has warned:

A nonaggression pact would conflict with the Japan-US Security Treaty. A North Korea without nuclear weapons would still possess biological and chemical weapons and could use them to attack Japan. In such an event, the U.S. forces in Japan could not help defend Japan in accordance with their bilateral treaty, since the United States would already have promised not to attack North Korea. Tokyo could no longer rely on its alliance with Washington and thus might decide to develop its own retaliatory weapons.[80]

The Bush administration is well aware of these anxieties, however, and it is likely that the United States would only offer an assurance to Pyongyang that was carefully conditioned on North Korea not attacking the U.S. or any of its allies.

Breakdown of the Global Nuclear Nonproliferation Regime

The Japanese have long held that the best way to avert further nuclear proliferation is for the established nuclear powers to make substantial progress toward their own nuclear disarmament. It is easier for Japan to justify remaining non-nuclear if it looks like the nonproliferation regime is, on the one hand, reducing gradually the salience of nuclear weapons as an instrument of power and influence and, on the other, serving as an effective barrier to new entrants into the nuclear club.

Japan is concerned, however, by signs that the nonproliferation regime is eroding. Those signs include the slow pace of nuclear disarmament, the Bush administration's decision to consider developing new nuclear weapons with much smaller yields (which could make them more usable as well as more credible deterrent weapons), and Congress's refusal to ratify the Comprehensive Test Ban Treaty (long supported by the Japanese government and public), as well as the perception that there is little penalty associated with defying nonproliferation norms. Most disturbing for the Japanese has been the way North Korea was able to pursue a covert nuclear weapons program while nominally an adherent to the NPT. But the Japanese were also upset at the lackadaisical international response to the Indian and Pakistani nuclear tests of 1998. Japan and other countries also have become increasingly alarmed by Iran's nuclear ambitions.

Of course, the Japanese and other nations appreciate that American concerns about the ineffectiveness of the nonproliferation regime are not without foundation. Foreign Minister Yoriko Kawaguchi has said that "the most important task for nations today is to prevent threats to the safety of their people by keeping deadly and destructive weapons, whether chemical, biological, or nuclear, from falling into the hands of states that support terrorism or of the terrorists themselves."[81] Moreover, the Japanese government knows that its desire for nuclear disarmament must be balanced by the need for its main ally, the United States, to retain an adequate nuclear deterrent.

Still, Japan believes the regime is eroding and must be strengthened, lest an avalanche of nuclear weapons testing and development adversely affect Japan's interests. Tokyo's initial response has been to continue its efforts to shore up the existing nuclear nonproliferation regime through diplomacy and foreign economic assistance.[82] For example, in November 2002, Japan hosted the first meeting of the Asian Senior-Level Talks on Nonproliferation.[83] In addition, Japan has been a founding participant in the Proliferation Security Initiative, which seeks to promote international agreements and partnerships that would enable the concerned countries to interdict planes and ships suspected of carrying WMD, missiles, and their related equipment and technologies. But a perception that the regime had collapsed beyond repair could prompt Japan's leaders to conclude reluctantly that they, too, had to join the nuclear bandwagon.

Domestic Factors

As the only people to have had a nuclear weapon used against them, the Japanese have long maintained a pacifist stance when it comes to nuclear and military issues. Even with the current debate regarding constitutional reform and Japan's becoming a normal state (that is, remilitarizing), the Japanese public has not lessened its resistance to an independent nuclear capability. The depth of this antinuclear sentiment is such that only major changes in the international or domestic environment, and probably only a combination of such changes, could engender a domestic political environment more permissive toward Japan's acquiring nuclear weapons.

Domestic factors do exist, however, that could lead to such a development. For example, although broadly supportive of the Japanese-American alliance, the Japanese people have expressed discontent with some of its manifestations. A substantial portion of the Japanese public, for instance, opposes the American military presence in Japan and would like to see it much reduced or even eliminated entirely. Such feelings are especially prevalent on the island of Okinawa, where the American military occupies approximately one-sixth of the island and American troops repeatedly behave improperly in the eyes of the local population.

This sentiment could very well increase if the United States continues with its plans to integrate its East Asian military bases more deeply into the global war on terror (thereby making the bases in particular and Japan in general more likely terrorist targets) and sustains unpopular American military operations in the Middle East.[84] Likewise, should U.S. forces have to withdraw from the Korean Peninsula as a result of a decision by the government of either South Korea or a newly reunified

Korea, the Japanese government would find it hard to justify Japan's becoming the sole Asian country hosting American military bases. However, if Washington carried out a major reduction in the U.S. military presence without sufficient consultation with or approval of the Japanese government, it could be an inducement for Japanese leaders to reconsider a nuclear weapons option.

Political changes that occur for reasons unrelated to international developments also could prompt Japan to reevaluate nuclear options. For example, a hawkish political figure such as Shintaro Ishihara, the popular Tokyo metropolitan governor who said that Japan should be prepared to develop nuclear weapons if China continued to modernize its nuclear arsenal, could emerge as the leader of a future Japanese government.[85] Should this occur, the domestic barriers to Japan's acquisition of nuclear weapons would weaken.

Even without such an event, antinuclear sentiment among the Japanese public already is experiencing a secular decline as the victims of Hiroshima and Nagasaki—and the popular preoccupation with these attacks—gradually fade away.[86] In a July 2003 poll, 37 percent of the 1,436 respondents said that Japan should consider acquiring nuclear weapons if North Korea declared that it had them, too.[87]

There is also the delicate issue of Japan's anxieties about its future prospects. Once the proud citizens of a considerable global power, many Japanese now struggle with concerns over international irrelevance. The notion of "Japan passing" is more than an itinerary issue for foreign dignitaries visiting East Asia. It reflects a mindset that suggests an ebbing of influence in global politics brought on by domestic malaise. Endemic and growing Japanese regime pessimism could lead a future generation of leaders in Tokyo to consider acquiring the ultimate hedge against irrelevance and perpetual insecurity—nuclear weapons.

Finally, although public sentiment against nuclear weapons remains strong, its ability to fully inhibit the decisions of Japanese leaders should not be exaggerated. For many decades, despite its government's professed policy of nuclear disarmament, Japan has relied on the United States to defend Japan, even with nuclear weapons if necessary. Antimilitarism in Japan has not prevented the country from becoming the fourth-highest military spender in the world. Nor have antinuclear sentiments impeded Japan's extensive reliance on civilian nuclear power. Just as the Japanese people today appreciate that Japan has no choice but to rely on nuclear power to meet its energy needs, so in the future they might accept that international threats left Japan with no choice but to develop nuclear weapons.

Technological and Related Infrastructure Issues

Japan has often been described as a "virtual" nuclear weapons state because it possesses the scientific, economic, and technological infrastructure to rapidly develop a nuclear arsenal should the government decide to do so. (Other terms to describe Japan include a "para-nuclear" state and a country that practices "nuclear hedging."[88])

According to the Federation of American Scientists, "Japan could possibly produce functional nuclear weapons in as little as a year's time."[89] Analyst Ariel E. Levite maintains that for some time Japan has remained "within a few months of acquiring nuclear weapons."[90] Japanese scientists mastered the techniques of civilian nuclear power production many decades ago. As early as 1967, a secret Japanese study concluded that Japan could produce the material necessary to make an atomic bomb by extracting plutonium from its civilian nuclear power plants.[91] In June 1974, Prime Minister Tsutomu Hata told reporters, "It's certainly the case that Japan has the capability to possess nuclear weapons but has not made them."[92]

Since then, Japan has acquired a growing surplus of reactor-grade plutonium, now estimated at more than five tons, sufficient to manufacture hundreds of nuclear weapons.[93] Such reactive material could by itself be manufactured into a nuclear device, or it could be refined further into a higher grade more suitable for making bombs.[94] The Japanese also could produce, without much difficulty, weapons-grade uranium through standard enrichment techniques. As early as 1971, the quasi-governmental Japan Nuclear Cycle Development Institute began uranium enrichment operations using gas centrifuges at the Tokaimura Reprocessing Plant.[95]

Today, Japan has one of the most advanced and largest (ranking third in the world in terms of installed capacity) civilian nuclear power programs in the world.[96] Although the IAEA heavily scrutinizes the program, Japan could, in accordance with article 10 of the treaty, withdraw from the NPT with three months' notice by claiming that its "supreme interests" were at risk.[97] (Unlike Germany, Japan has not signed any other international agreements that explicitly renounce its right to develop nuclear weapons.[98]) Japanese concerns about their continued access to Middle Eastern oil likely will ensure a prominent place for nuclear energy in Japan for the foreseeable future.

Japan also has been a long-standing participant in space rocket launches. It launched its first earth-orbiting satellite in 1970 and has launched many commercial and research satellites since then. Recently, the launch of North Korea's Taepo Dong over Japan, combined with other disturbing international developments, prompted Japan to develop and launch, beginning in March 2003, its own surveillance satellites.[99] Their intelligence-gathering capabilities would prove invaluable for assisting with target selection and strategic and tactical warning should Japan pursue a nuclear arsenal. Several of Japan's current space launch vehicles could, with some effort, serve as the basis for developing long-range ballistic missiles capable of carrying nuclear warheads. From a technical perspective, these missiles ideally would be capable of being launched from a submarine, which would make them less vulnerable to preemption than if they were deployed in immobile, land-based silos, but Japan would need to develop and manufacture the required missile-carrying submarines. Given their extensive experience and capabilities with nuclear material and supercomputing, Japanese scientists presumably would not find it difficult to develop a reliable nuclear warhead even if they refrained from testing it. Similarly, both the Nippon Electric Corporation and IHI Aerospace are able to develop and manufacture reentry vehicles.[100]

The current protracted stagnation of the Japanese economy could serve as a barrier to Japan's undertaking an expensive program to develop a full-fledged operational nuclear arsenal. But Japanese leaders could make the sort of calculation that members of the Eisenhower administration reached decades earlier: that possessing nuclear weapons could allow Japan to spend less on its conventional military forces (though, obviously, they would not abandon Japan's policy of nuclear abstention just to realize such savings, given the much greater importance of the other potential costs and benefits such a decision would entail). In addition, should the Japanese-American alliance collapse, which is almost a prerequisite for Japan's pursuing the nuclear option, then Japan would no longer need to provide host-nation support for the U.S. troops based on Japan.

Although Japan has the economic and technological basis to develop a nuclear arsenal, it would require several months for it to develop the institutional infrastructure required for such a force. In particular, it would need to work out appropriate command and control procedures to govern the use of nuclear weapons. Important issues, such as who could authorize nuclear weapons use and under what conditions, would need resolution, as would both positive and negative launch controls and the content of Japan's nuclear doctrine more generally. As with the efforts required to modify its space rockets into ballistic missiles, however, such requirements would not present an insurmountable deterrent to a Japanese government that had decided it had to acquire nuclear weapons.

Implications for U.S. Foreign Policy

American policies toward Japan and other regions of the world will have the greatest impact on whether the Japanese decide to acquire nuclear weapons in the future. The United States can best avert such a development by pursuing three policies.

First, American officials must overcome any doubts among the Japanese about the credibility of the U.S. extended deterrence guarantee. As former Japanese prime minister Morihiro Hosokawa observes, "It is in the interest of the United States, so long as it does not wish to see Japan withdraw from the NPT and develop its own nuclear deterrent, to maintain its alliance with Japan and continue to provide a nuclear umbrella."[101] U.S. officials should reaffirm at every opportunity Washington's willingness to defend Japan against external threats.

In the near term, such reassurance will likely focus on the perceived threat from North Korea. Pyongyang's development of a nuclear arsenal represents the most immediate factor that could prompt Japan to develop nuclear weapons. Over the long term, convincing the Japanese of Washington's continued ability and willingness to defend them against a potential Chinese military threat may become a delicate American priority. Although a national missile defense system that provided protection solely to the United States might intensify Japanese concerns about a possible decoupling of Japanese-American security ties, the deployment of theater BMD in Japan could reinforce the American security guarantee against both North Korea and China, provided such a move did not accelerate their arms buildups.[102] Even more important, although changes in the U.S. global military posture may be warranted in light of ongoing political and technological developments, the continued deployment of substantial American military forces on Japanese territory would provide a very visible and very effective mechanism for demonstrating the credibility of U.S security guarantees.

Second, the American government must make clear its continued commitment to combating the proliferation of weapons of mass destruction. Vigorous counterproliferation measures such as the newly adopted Proliferation Security Initiative should be maintained and strengthened. But it is also essential to reassure the Japanese about Washington's commitment to preserve the NPT and reinvigorate the global regime and international institutions against nuclear weapons possession and use. Traditional arms control obviously presents only one tool to combat WMD proliferation, but its value as an instrument to reassure the Japanese and others strongly committed to nonproliferation norms should not be discounted. Policy continuity in this and other areas between U.S. administrations also would help counter concerns about American unilateralism and unpredictability.

Finally, and perhaps most controversially, American leaders and influential commentators both within and outside the government should never signal to the Japanese, even inadvertently, that they actually favor Japan's acquisition of nuclear weapons. Many Japanese appreciate that without U.S. approval or at least acquiescence, Japan would find it very difficult to proceed along the difficult path toward acquiring an operational nuclear arsenal. Although the temptation invariably arises to play the "Japan card" (that is, to warn that unfavorable international developments such as North Korea's creation of a nuclear arsenal might prompt the Japanese to acquire nuclear weapons) to frighten Chinese and Russian officials into more vigorously opposing North Korea's development of nuclear weapons or ballistic missiles, the long-term risks of such a stratagem outweigh the short-term negotiating gains.[103] The Japanese persist in looking to the United States for leadership in how to manage international security threats, and Americans should continue those responsible policies that have gained them their well-deserved role as stewards of international peace and security. This standing is perhaps most critical to maintain in Japan as East Asia confronts important political and security challenges here now and over the horizon.

Notes

1. For a comprehensive assessment of the factors that could induce a country that had previously renounced nuclear weapons to abandon its policy of nuclear abstention, see Kurt M. Campbell, "Nuclear Proliferation beyond Rogues," *Washington Quarterly*, vol. 26, no. 1 (Winter 2002–03), pp. 7–15.

2. Masakatsu Ota, "Will Japan Keep Renouncing Nuclear Weapons in the Coming Century?" Issue Brief 2, Program on General Disarmament, University of Maryland, July 2000 (www.bsos.umd.edu/pgsd/publications/pdf/issbrief2.pdf [February 2004]). See also the website of the Federation of American Scientists (www.fas.org/nuke/guide/japan/nuke [February 2004]).

3. For the text of this law, see www.jnc.go.jp/kaihatu/hukaku/english/library/ l-atomiclaw.htm [February 2004].

4. Ota, "Will Japan Keep Renouncing," p. 2. From Masumi Ishikawa, *Sengo Seijishi* (Iwanamishinsyo, 1995), pp. 217–63.

5. Nobusuke Kishi, *Kishi Nobusuke Kaikoroku* (Koseido, 1983), pp. 310–11; cited in Ota, "Will Japan Keep Renouncing," p. 3.

6. Nobumasa Akiyama, "The Socio-Political Roots of Japan's Non-Nuclear Posture," in Benjamin L. Self and Jeffrey W. Thompson, eds., *Japan's Nuclear Option: Security, Politics, and Policy in the 21st Century* (Washington: Henry L. Stimson Center, 2003), p. 80.

7. Yuri Kase, "The Costs and Benefits of Japan's Nuclearization: An Insight into the 1968/70 Internal Report," *Nonproliferation Review,* vol. 8, no. 2 (Summer 2001), p. 60.

8. Central Foreign Policy Files, "Your Meeting with Prime Minister Sato," memorandum for the president from the secretary of state, secret, January 9, 1965, box 2376, RG 59, National Archives, College Park, Md.

9. Ibid.

10. "Gist of White Paper on Defense," *Japan Times,* October 1970, p. 20.

11. The American policy of neither confirming nor denying the existence of nuclear weapons on board these ships helped the Japanese tolerate these visits.

12. They were also a primary factor behind the awarding of the Nobel Peace Prize to Sato.

13. Kei Wakaizumi, *Tasaku Nakarishiwo Shimzemuto Hossu* (Tokyo: Bungei Shunju, 1994), pp. 140–41, cited in Kase, "Costs and Benefits," pp. 59–60.

14. *Yomiuri Shimbun,* March 16, 1968.

15. Central Foreign Policy Files," State Department incoming telegram from Tokyo," confidential 267, January 14, 1969, box 2249, RG 59, National Archives, College Park, Md.

16. The title arises from the fact that the first part examining technical and economic issues was completed in September 1968, while the second part examining strategic and political issues was completed in January 1970.

17. Kase, "Costs and Benefits," pp. 57–58.

18. Press conference, Foreign Ministry, Tokyo, February 17, 1966, cited in Selig Harrison, *Japan's Nuclear Future* (Washington: Carnegie Endowment for International Peace, 1996), p. 7.

19. Ibid., p. 7.

20. Ibid.

21. Yukihiko Ikeda, interview by Tsuyoshi Sunohara, Tokyo, September 4, 2003.

22. Matthew J. Gilley, "Japan's Developing Military Potential within the Context of Its Constitutional Renunciation of War," *Emory International Law Review,* vol. 14, no. 3 (Fall 2000), p. 1681.

23. Ibid.

24. For the text of this law, see www.mofa.go.jp/policy/un/pko/pamph96/01.html [February 2004].

25. "Japan-US Security Treaty Should Entail Frank Expression," *Asahi Shimbun,* January 19, 2000.

26. "'95 Study: Japan and Nukes Don't Mix," *Asahi Shimbun,* February 20, 2003.

27. Ibid. See also Kenji Hall, "Japan Studied, but Ruled out, Developing Nuclear Weapons in 1995, Agency Says," *Associated Press,* February 20, 2003.

28. Japanese government official, interview by Tsuyoshi Sunohara, Tokyo, March 2003.

29. Joseph Cirincione, "The Asian Nuclear Reaction Chain," *Christian Science Monitor,* March 1, 2002.

30. This incident is described in Howard Diamond, "N. Korea Launches Staged Rocket that Overflies Japanese Territory," *Arms Control Today,* August–September 1998 (www.armscontrol.org/act/1998_08-09/nklas98.asp [April 2004]).

31. Jonathan Manthorpe, "Japan: A Return to Militarism," *Vancouver Sun,* September 14, 1998.

32. Eric Altbach, "Tokyo Protests North Korean Missile Test," *JEI Report: Weekly Review,* no. 34, September 4, 1998 (www.jei.org/Archive/JEIR98/9834w4.html [February 2004]).

33. Masako Fukuda, "Japan Calls Off Aid and Talks after North Korea Fires Missile," *Nikkei Weekly,* September 7, 1998.

34. "Announcement by the Chief Cabinet Secretary on Japan's Immediate Response to North Korea's Missile Launch," September 1, 1998 (www.fas.org/news/dprk/1998/901-2.html [February 2004]).

35. Cameron W. Barr, "North Korea's Missile Show Tests Japan's Tolerance," *Christian Science Monitor,* September 4, 1998, p. 11.

36. Kozo Mizoguchi, "Japanese Defense Official Resigns over Nuke Remarks," *Associated Press,* October 20, 1999.

37. *Asahi Shimbun,* June 12, 2002.

38. "A Reckless Pro-Nuclear Comment," *Japan Times,* June 7, 2002.

39. Ibid.

40. "Koizumi Denies Change in Non-Nuclear Policy Amid Reports of Officials Suggesting a Switch," *Associated Press,* May 31, 2002, cited in Eric Talmadge, "Controversy over Remarks on Japan Nuclear Option," *Disarmament Diplomacy,* no. 65 (July–August 2002) (www.acronym.org.uk/dd/dd65/65nr07.htm [April 2004]).

41. Ibid.

42. Press conference held at the Japanese prime minister's residence in Tokyo, August 6, 2003.

43. Katsuhisa Furukawa observes, "Abe simply meant to explain the purely legal interpretation of the Constitution, which was literally quite correct but politically very incorrect." See Katsuhisa Furukawa, "Nuclear Option, Arms Control, and Extended Deterrence: In Search of a New Framework for Japan's Nuclear Policy," in Benjamin L. Self and Jeffrey W. Thompson, eds., *Japan's Nuclear Option: Security, Politics, and Policy in the 21st Century* (Washington: Henry L. Stimson Center, 2003), p. 105.

44. See, for example, Koizumi's remarks as cited in Yuri Kageyama, "Japan Considers Nuclear Options," *Sun News*, August 10, 2003 (vol. 35, no. 8, p. 22), as well as during his press conference, held at the Japanese prime minister's residence in Tokyo, July 2003.

45. Terumasa Nakanishi, "Japan's Decision for Nuclear Armament," *Syokun*, vol. 81, no. 7, August 2003, p. 176.

46. Kazuya Fukuda, "Nuclear is the Only One Option for Japan?" *Bungeisyunjyu*, June 2003.

47. Matake Kamiya, "A Disillusioned Japan Confronts North Korea," *Arms Control Today*, May 2003.

48. Ibid., citing "KCNA Urges Japan to Behave with Discretion," *Korean Central News Agency*, April 15, 2003.

49. *Yomiuri Shimbun*, March 27, 2003.

50. David E. Sanger and William J. Broad, "Surprise Word on Nuclear Gains by North Korea and Iran," *New York Times*, November 12, 2003, p. A3.

51. See, for example, Sonni Efron, "Nuclear Waiting Game Called Risky," *Los Angeles Times*, October 3, 2003, p. 4, and Anthony Faiola, "N. Korean Report Spurs Debate on Credibility," *Washington Post*, October 4, 2003, p. A16.

52. David Sanger, "Intelligence Puzzle: North Korean Bombs," *New York Times*, October 14, 2003, p. A9.

53. Additional sources of tension between North Korea and Japan include North Korea's abduction of Japanese citizens, its deployment of spy ships in Japanese territorial waters, and its involvement in illegal activities, such as drug trafficking, within Japan.

54. Department of State, "Joint U.S.-Japan-ROK Trilateral Statement on North Korea," October 26, 2002 (usinfo.state.gov/topical/pol/arms/02102603. htm [February 2004]).

55. "Speech by Minister for Foreign Affairs Yoriko Kawaguchi to the Conference on Disarmament," September 4, 2003 (www.mofa.go.jp/policy/un/disarmament/conference/speech0309.html [February 2004]).

56. Takushi Ono and Yoshihiro Makino, "Japan Nervous as Star of WMD Exercise," *Ashahi Shimbun*, September 15, 2003.

57. Yomiuri Shimbun, "Koizumi to Ask for Anti-MD Vigilance," *Daily Yomiuri,* October 7, 2003.

58. See Sheila A. Smith, "Japan's Future Strategic Options and the US-Japan Alliance," in Benjamin L. Self and Jeffrey W. Thompson, eds., *Japan's Nuclear Option: Security, Politics, and Policy in the 21st Century* (Washington: Henry L. Stimson Center, 2003), p. 4, note 2.

59. Ibid., p. 4, note 4, citing "A Japanese Nuke: No Longer Unthinkable," *Business Week,* April 11, 2002.

60. Liu Wenyu, writing in the official municipal paper *Beijing Daily,* asserted that the new U.S.-Japanese defense guidelines "attempt to include Taiwan, a part of Chinese territory, within the scope of the U.S.-Japan Defense Cooperation." *Beijing Ribao,* September 25, 1997, cited in Kathleen J. Brahney, "U.S.-Japan Defense Cooperation Guidelines: Fears of a 'Provoked' China, a 'Remilitarized' Japan," *United States Information Agency Daily Digest of Foreign Media Reaction,* October 6, 1997 (www.fas.org/news/japan/97100601_rmr.html [February 2004]).

61. Susan V. Lawrence, "U.S. Presses China on Arms, Quietly," *Wall Street Journal,* October 30, 2003, p. A14.

62. Stuart Harris and Richard N. Cooper, "The U.S.-Japan Alliance," in Robert D. Blackwill and Paul Dibb, eds., *America's Asian Alliances* (MIT Press, 2000), p. 46.

63. "Russia Says It Will Stop Pointing Nukes at Japan," *Reuters World Service,* June 20, 1997, cited in "Russia to De-Target Japan," *Disarmament Diplomacy,* no. 17 (July–August 1997) (www.acronym.org.uk/dd/dd17/17jap.htm [April 2004]).

64. Mortin H. Halperin, *The Nuclear Dimension of the U.S.-Japan Alliance,* Nautilus Institute, July 9, 1999 (www.nautilus.org/nukepolicy/Halperin [February 2004]).

65. Peter J. Katzenstein and Nobuo Okawara, "Japan, Asian-Pacific Security, and the Case for Analytic Eclecticism," *International Security,* vol. 26, no. 3 (Winter 2001–2002), p. 159.

66. Jim Garamone, "U.S., Japan Announce Defense Guidelines," *American Forces Press Service,* September 26, 1997; see also "New US-Japan Defense Cooperation Guidelines," *Disarmament Diplomacy,* no. 19 (October 1997) (www.acronym.org.uk/dd/dd19/19guide.htm [April 2004]).

67. Harris and Cooper, "U.S.-Japan Alliance," pp. 38–39.

68. The details of the legislation are described in International Institute for Strategic Studies, *Strategic Survey 2002/3* (Oxford University Press, 2003), p. 255.

69. Current Japanese plans regarding such a deployment are discussed in David Pilling, "Japan's Troops in Iraq May Be Force for Change at Home," *London Financial Times,* December 12, 2003, p. 11.

70. David Fouse, "Japan Gets Serious about Missile Defense: North Korean Crisis Pushes Debate," *Asia-Pacific Security Studies,* vol. 2, no. 4 (June 2003).

71. Yomiuri Shimbun, "Government May Ease Procedure for Missile Defense," *Daily Yomiuri,* August 25, 2003.

72. On how such alliance management considerations circumscribe Japan's disarmament policies, see Motoko Mekata, "Words and Deeds: What Japan Should Do to Promote Nuclear Disarmament," *Disarmament Diplomacy,* no. 45 (April 2000) (www.acronym.org.uk/dd/dd45/45deeds.htm [April 2004]).

73. Kumao Kaneko, "Japan Needs No Nuclear Umbrella," *Bulletin of the Atomic Scientists,* vol. 53, no. 2 (March–April 1996), p. 46.

74. See Furukawa, "Nuclear Option," p. 107, note 20.

75. Richard Cheney, interview on NBC's *Meet the Press,* March 16, 2003.

76. A statement released by Senator John McCain on January 20, 2003 (mccain.senate.gov/index.cfm?fuseaction=Newscenter.ViewOpEd&Content_id=7 07 [February 2004]).

77. "Confronting North Korea," symposium held at Center for Strategic and International Studies, Washington, D.C., May 19, 2003.

78. For a description of the Bush administration's plans and how they might affect security dynamics in East Asia and elsewhere, see Kurt M. Campbell and Celeste Johnson Ward, "New Battle Stations?" *Foreign Affairs,* vol. 82, no. 5 (September–October 2003), p. 95.

79. Zbigniew Brzezinski, interview by Tsuyoshi Sunohara, Washington, D.C., January 16, 2003.

80. Masashi Nishihara, "North Korea's Trojan Horse," *Washington Post,* August 14, 2003, p. A19.

81. Yoriko Kawaguchi, "A Foreign Policy to Consolidate Peace," *Japan Echo* (April 2003).

82. These efforts are described in Yukiya Amano, "A Japanese View on Nuclear Disarmament," *Nonproliferation Review,* vol. 9, no. 1 (Spring 2002) (http://cns.miis.edu/pubs/npr/vol09/abs91.htm [April 2004]), and Michael J. Green and Katsuhisa Furukawa, "New Ambitions, Old Obstacles: Japan and Its Search for an Arms Control Strategy," *Arms Control Today,* July–August 2000 (www.armscontrol.org/act/2000_07-08/japanjulaug.asp [April 2004]).

83. Smith, "Japan's Future Strategic Options," p. 22.

84. The 1994 sarin gas attack, perpetrated by the fanatical Aum Shinrikyo religious cult, already has heightened Japanese fears of a devastating terrorist attack on their soil.

85. Ishihara's remarks appear in Furukawa, "Nuclear Option," p. 106.

86. Nobumasa Akiyama, "The Socio-Political Roots of Japan's Non-Nuclear Posture," in Benjamin L. Self and Jeffrey W. Thompson, eds., *Japan's Nuclear Option: Security, Politics, and Policy in the 21st Century* (Washington: Henry L. Stimson Center, 2003), p. 90.

87. The poll was conducted by VOTE.co.jp.

88. The first term appears in an essay at the Federation of American Scientists'

website (www.fas.org/nuke/guide/japan/nuke [February 2004]). The second term is used in Ariel E. Levite, "Never Say Never Again: Nuclear Reversal Revisited," *International Security,* vol. 27, no. 3 (Winter 2002–2003). Levite defines "nuclear hedging" as "a national strategy of maintaining, or at least appearing to maintain, a viable option for the relatively rapid acquisition of nuclear weapons, based on an indigenous technical capacity to produce them within a relatively short time frame ranging from several weeks to a few years" (p. 69). He argues that "Japan provides the most salient example of nuclear hedging to date" (p. 71).

89. Federation of American Scientists, "Japan Special Weapons Guide: Nuclear Weapons Program" (www.fas.org/nuke/guide/japan/nuke [February 2004]).

90. Levite, "Never Say Never Again," p. 72.

91. Furukawa, "Nuclear Option," p. 104.

92. *Kyodo News Service,* June 17, 1974, cited in Halperin, *Nuclear Dimension.*

93. Dan Plesch, "Without the UN Safety Net, Even Japan May Go Nuclear," *Guardian,* April 28, 2003 (www.guardian.co.uk/print/0,3858,4656463-103677,00.html [April 2004]). It would require only seven to eight kilograms of plutonium to build an atomic bomb of equivalent strength to the one that exploded in Nagasaki in 1945.

94. For a discussion of how Japan could use reactor-grade plutonium to construct a nuclear explosive, see www.globalsecurity.org/wmd/world/japan/nuke.htm [February 2004].

95. *Japan: Technical Paths to a Nuclear Deterrence Background: Questions and Answers* (Arlington, Va.: CENTRA Technology, December 2003). Since 1981 the Tokaimura plant also has been reprocessing spent plutonium from Japan's light-water reactors, making mixed oxide fuel in the process (Ibid., p. 7).

96. For a comprehensive listing of the governmental and commercial organizations in Japan involved in the country's civilian nuclear power program, see *Japanese Nuclear Energy Related Organizations* (Arlington, Va.: CENTRA Technology, December 2003).

97. Japan has signed both the IAEA standards agreement and the Additional Protocol.

98. However, Japan has signed bilateral safeguard agreements with the United States and five other major nuclear suppliers. These bilateral accords, which provide backup safeguards on transferred materials and technologies should Japan withdraw from the NPT, could present a greater barrier to any Japanese nuclear ambitions; see Furukawa, "Nuclear Option," p. 103.

99. International Institute for Strategic Studies, *Strategic Survey 2002/3,* p. 261.

100. *Japan: Technical Paths,* p. 23.

101. Morihiro Hosokawa, "Are U.S. Troops in Japan Needed? Reforming the Alliance," *Foreign Affairs,* vol. 77, no. 4 (July–August 1998), p. 5.

102. Japanese concerns about China's possible response to Japan's BMD efforts are discussed in Ken Jimbo, "Rethinking Japanese Security: New Concepts in Deterrence and Defense," in Benjamin L. Self and Jeffrey W. Thompson, eds., *Japan's Nuclear Option: Security, Politics, and Policy in the 21st Century* (Washington: Henry L. Stimson Center, 2003), p. 37.

103. For a discussion of this stratagem, see Ted Carpenter, "Options for Dealing with North Korea," Foreign Policy Briefing 73 (CATO Insitute, January 6, 2003), and Charles Krauthammer, "The Japan Card," *Washington Post,* January 3, 2003. Carpenter writes: "U.S. officials should inform Pyongyang that, if the North insists on crashing the global nuclear weapons club, Washington will urge Tokyo and Seoul to make their own decisions about acquiring strategic deterrents" (p. 4). Analyst Katsuhisa Furukawa observes: "Ironically, however, it is precisely these U.S. arguments about Japan's nuclear scenario, not necessarily the North Korea nuclear threats per se, that triggered Japan's debate on its nuclear option. Indeed, U.S. arguments suggested to a small number of extremists in Japan that the acquisition of nuclear weapons could possibly be Japan's alternative national security policy. Even more surprising, many Japanese who argue in favor of Japan's nuclear argument completely mistake America's open discussion about Japan's nuclear option as a signal of America's tacit encouragement for Japan's nuclear armament" ("Nuclear Option," pp. 108–09).

CHAPTER 10

South Korea:
The Tyranny of Geography
and the Vexations of History

JONATHAN D. POLLACK
MITCHELL B. REISS

Situated on an eastern outcrop of the Eurasian landmass, the Korean peninsula lies at the strategic intersection of great power competition among China, Japan, Russia, and, since the late nineteenth century, the United States. At various times, Korea has been viewed as a dagger pointing at the heart of Japan and as a land bridge into the invasion routes of China and the Russian Far East. Not surprisingly, the history of the peninsula has been characterized by repeated conflict, invasion, foreign occupation, violence, and dictatorship. Many manifestations of past struggles continue into the present. Northeast Asia encompasses four of the world's six largest armies and (including the United States) three declared nuclear weapons states, as well as an undeclared nuclear power in North Korea. Stability has been elusive and, even when present, far from assured. The "Land of Morning Calm" has been anything but.

For the past fifty years, the Korean nation has been divided at the waist, a lasting legacy of the Korean War and the subsequent confrontation

Mitchell B. Reiss prepared an initial version of this chapter before joining the U.S. Department of State as director of the Office of Policy Planning in August 2003. Jonathan D. Pollack undertook a longer revised version. Both authors assume full responsibility for its content. The judgments in this essay represent the personal opinions of the authors and should not be attributed to the Department of State, the Department of Defense, or the Naval War College.

between North and South. The two Koreas present starkly different paths of political, economic, and social organization and wholly distinct approaches to international politics. The Republic of Korea (ROK) and the Democratic People's Republic of Korea (DPRK) continue to inhabit separate worlds. It is difficult to imagine more sharply divergent development models than those pursued by the two Koreas, a fact made more remarkable by the peninsula's ethnic and linguistic homogeneity and well over a millennium of unified dynastic rule. South Korea's economic dynamism and democratic pluralism stand in marked contrast to the destitution, totalitarianism, and cult of personality in the North. They are squared off in what is arguably the last major flashpoint of the cold war.

Neither Korean state has ever been reconciled to permanent partition of the peninsula. North Korea has pursued its goal of reunification by trying to undermine, intimidate, and psychologically and militarily overwhelm the South by conventional and unconventional means. This strategy has encompassed a half century of unrelentingly hostile propaganda, periodic acts of terrorism, commando infiltrations, and, not least, forward deployment of a million-man army that places Seoul within easy range of the North's heavy artillery. Pyongyang has complemented these forces with covert chemical and biological weapons programs and a flourishing ballistic missile program that has also become a principal source of hard currency earnings for North Korea through export sales. In the late 1980s, Pyongyang added a covert nuclear threat by separating enough weapons-grade plutonium for one or two bombs, according to U.S. intelligence. Toward the end of the 1990s, it secretly expanded its nuclear weapons potential by purportedly acquiring uranium enrichment technology. In early 2003, it shredded all of its international nonproliferation commitments, becoming the first country ever to withdraw from the Nuclear Non-Proliferation Treaty (NPT). It also resumed its nuclear weapons activities at Yongbyon and (according to some sources) threatened to export bomb-grade material and nuclear weapons.

Since the end of the Korean War, Seoul has responded to North Korea's political and military threats by three principal means. First, it has deterred renewed military attack by the North through a close alliance with the United States, which has deployed major military forces on the peninsula and provided a security guarantee to the ROK ever since the armistice agreement of 1953. This commitment has implied an American willingness to use nuclear weapons to deter renewed warfare and defend South Korea, if needed. Second, the ROK has maintained very large conventional forces to counter any potential attack by the North. Third, South Korea has periodically sought to open political and diplomatic channels to the DPRK, at first secretly, but subsequently in far more open fashion. The results of these latter efforts have proven highly vexing to the ROK, but this has not dissuaded successive leaders from repeatedly exploring these avenues.

In the late 1990s, the ROK embarked on its most ambitious effort to date to seek reconciliation with the North, when President Kim Dae Jung offered peaceful coexistence and massive infusions of economic and humanitarian aid to the DPRK. The "sunshine policy" culminated in Kim Dae Jung's June 2000 visit to Pyongyang and the first-ever summit between leaders of North and South. Despite such unconditional generosity, Pyongyang refused to reciprocate these gestures and initiatives, only begrudgingly agreeing to limited, periodic interactions with the South. The North cynically exploited these exchanges to extort money and food from the ROK, yet at the same time sought to bypass Seoul politically by expanding ties with the United States and Japan, while insisting that it had to shield its people from any "ideological contamination." Indeed, South Korean critics of the sunshine policy argue that a strategy designed to transform the DPRK had the perverse effect of changing attitudes in the South but not in the North.

Notwithstanding the profound differences in the strategies and goals of the two Koreas, both leaderships have sought to limit the role of outside powers. There is an enduring frustration among Koreans on both sides of the thirty-eighth parallel that they are not free agents but have been repeatedly constrained by the roles of larger powers. However, their respective approaches differ sharply. The North defiantly maintains an exceptionalist mythology, insisting that it alone is the authentic embodiment of Korean nationalism. By contrast, the South has pursued a more gradualist approach, allowing for the incremental development of ties between the two states, with the South still buttressed by a substantial U.S. security commitment. In recent decades, the ROK's economic and industrial capabilities have outstripped those of the North by ever wider margins. Seoul has come to believe that it will be increasingly able to shape the contours of reconciliation and national unification, thereby enabling Korea to assume a leadership role in East Asian and global politics.

But how? Even as Seoul believes that realization of larger goals is within its grasp, history to many in the ROK appears to be repeating itself. South Korea can easily envision outside powers once again determining its security environment and controlling its destiny, all to its perceived disadvantage. A nuclear-armed adversary in the North would, at the very least, enhance Pyongyang's leverage in future inter-Korean relations; at most, it might lead to military conflict or, longer term, a chain reaction of proliferation by other countries in East Asia. Scenarios that fall somewhere in between, such as pressuring North Korea through the imposition of multilateral sanctions, might trigger acute instability and an outpouring of refugees that could destabilize the South's economy and overwhelm its capacity to deal with such a crisis.

In addition, the Korean-American alliance is experiencing major strain. As collective memories of the Korean War fade and as the ROK's past backwardness and dependence on American power steadily recede, a younger, more self-confident generation of South Koreans believes that their country should strive to assume its rightful place in the international politics of East Asia. Divergent threat assessments of North Korea, along with friction from accidents and incidents involving U.S. troops based on Korean soil, have also contributed to growing alliance tensions. In the view of many South Koreans, the U.S. determination to seek the definitive elimination of the North's nuclear weapons capabilities (and, perhaps, of the DPRK itself) makes Washington a greater threat to peninsular security than Pyongyang.

With a shifting strategic balance on the peninsula and an uncertain security environment in Northeast Asia, South Korea's future stability and prosperity seem far from assured. Will a nuclear-armed North Korea try to extract concessions from a weaker and thus more pliant ROK? Will the United States, confronting more immediate challenges in the Persian Gulf and Southwest Asia, further a process of disengagement from the peninsula, leaving the South to fend for itself? Will the North's internal contradictions ultimately prove fatal, with final collapse presenting Seoul with new burdens and unprecedented responsibilities? In the event of the disintegration of the DPRK, will a newly reunified Korean state find itself dominated by its more powerful neighbors, China and Japan? Under such circumstances, some South Koreans may again conclude that nuclear weapons—or, at least, preservation of a nuclear weapons option—are necessary to ensure the country's autonomy and national destiny.

That said, a decision to acquire or pursue nuclear weapons development would not derive from threat perception alone and would not be made by accident or afterthought. For states that contemplate such a consequential step, the ultimate judgment would be shaped by a complex mix of political and security calculations; by the interplay of domestic attitudes, bureaucratic competition, and scientific capabilities; and, perhaps most fundamentally, by the symbolic meaning and strategic value that leaders attach to possession of such capabilities.[1] As one scholar has observed, "every known nuclear weapons program . . . has been a *dedicated* program, with facilities largely designed and procured for the purpose of developing a weapon. No country with nuclear weapons has gotten them by lurching absentmindedly out of a peaceful nuclear power program."[2]

The South Korean case amply illustrates the relevance of all the above judgments. To assess these considerations more fully, this chapter explores Korea's scientific and technological capabilities, the country's nuclear history, and whether changes in national identity and collective security perceptions might again lead the ROK to pursue nuclear weapons development.

Capabilities and Constraints

The Republic of Korea undoubtedly possesses the industrial infrastructure and manufacturing base to underwrite an indigenous nuclear weapons program. It boasts one of the most dynamic, technically sophisticated economies in the world. The ROK ranks eleventh in the Organization for Economic Cooperation and Development's ranking of gross domestic product per capita and is widely considered the most digitally advanced country in the world. Led by its *chaebol*, it has world-class industries in computer chips, semiconductors, and precision machine tools and markets a variety of globally recognized brand-name products.[3]

South Korea has long pursued the peaceful uses of nuclear power as a means to address its energy insecurity (it has no significant oil or gas deposits and only limited anthracite coal deposits) and as a source of status and prestige. It joined the International Atomic Energy Agency (IAEA) in 1957 and created an Office of Atomic Energy two years later. A small research reactor went critical in 1962, and Seoul began work on its first commercial nuclear power reactor, Kori 1, in 1970. This reactor was subject to an IAEA safeguards agreement that Seoul had signed two years earlier. Under a 1975 agreement with the IAEA, all of South Korea's present and future nuclear activities were covered by relevant international safeguards. South Korea has never had any uranium enrichment or spent-fuel reprocessing capability, although it tried, unsuccessfully, to purchase reprocessing technology in the mid-1970s. It imports low-enriched and natural uranium for its reactors from France, the United States, Russia, and China. All spent fuel is currently stored at the reactor site where it is produced.

By the mid-1980s, South Korea had developed two broad nuclear power initiatives: first, to standardize power plant design and second, to achieve technical self-reliance. In 1987 the South Korean nuclear industry entered into a ten-year, comprehensive technology transfer agreement with Westinghouse to meet the goal of technical self-reliance. In 1997 this agreement was expanded and extended for another ten years.[4] These commitments reflected deeply held convictions within the South Korean research and development community that the ROK needed to build and enhance core technical competencies across a wide range of dual-use nuclear technologies, so as to ensure against future uncertainties related to nuclear fuel supply. Senior South Korean nuclear scientists during the early and mid-1990s regularly bemoaned the ROK's lack of independence in nuclear fuel production, compared with Japan's far greater technological autonomy. These scientists characterized U.S. oversight of the ROK's nuclear activities as highly restrictive, thereby denying Seoul its longer-term goal of enhanced technical autonomy, including indigenous pursuit of an enrichment capability as a source for fuel for the South's nuclear reactors.[5] Notwithstanding such perceived restraints, the ROK's accomplishments in nuclear power during the latter half of the 1990s and continuing into the early twenty-first century have been highly impressive. By the end of 2003, South Korea had nineteen operational nuclear power reactors, with another nine under construction or on order.[6] The ROK derives almost 40 percent of its overall energy needs from nuclear power, placing it among the top five users of nuclear energy in the world.[7] Seoul also plans to become a leading international vendor of nuclear technology in the twenty-first century.[8]

Despite this impressive engineering base and technological infrastructure, it would be no easy matter for South Korea to develop nuclear weapons. Previous estimates of the time needed to complete a weapons program severely underestimated the technical barriers.[9] The extreme secrecy required for a covert program would also be far harder to maintain in the current democratic environment than what prevailed during the era of military dictatorship. The greatest obstacle would be obtaining the required fissile materials, either weapons-grade plutonium or highly enriched uranium. South Korea does not possess the indigenous capability to produce either type of bomb-grade material, although research breakthroughs (notably, in pilot production of high-speed centrifuges for isotope separation) have been reported in South Korean publications. Although South Korea could attempt larger-scale manufacture of the sophisticated equipment required for fissile material production, the ultimate success of such a home-grown effort would be far from assured and would entail a sustained, massive commitment of financial and manpower resources. A more likely route, therefore, would be for Seoul to import reprocessing or uranium enrichment technology from abroad.

The political and institutional barriers to such transfers, however, are quite daunting. In recent decades, the leading nuclear industrial countries have informally banded together in a Nuclear Suppliers Group to control international trade in this area. The transfer of sensitive technologies is monitored closely, and any request by a South Korean firm or end user for reprocessing or uranium enrichment technology would trigger alarm bells abroad, especially in Washington. If South Korea sought to repeat an earlier attempt at a nuclear option, it is far more likely that Seoul would explore a clandestine route to avoid detection, trying to exploit the network of black market suppliers. The ROK would still need to invest years of effort, at great risk of exposure by foreign suppliers or by its increasingly rambunctious mass media, before it could acquire the infrastructure needed to produce the material for a bomb. Even then, it would require additional time before it could develop workable, deliverable nuclear weapons.

During the period between a political decision to undertake a nuclear weapons program and actually obtaining a nuclear arsenal, the ROK would also encounter acute political and security vulnerabilities. A decision could provoke a U.S. withdrawal of political and military support, and South Korea would likely confront the vocal opposition of various nearby powers, including both China and Japan. Seoul would be without its staunchest ally, one armed with unmatched conventional and nuclear forces, and at the same time, the ROK might still be confronted by a hostile and aggressive DPRK.

However, despite the daunting risks and obstacles, South Korea launched a dedicated covert program in the early 1970s, when its scientific, industrial, and economic base was far weaker than at present. Although many details remain obscure, it is instructive to examine this history and whether the experience of thirty years ago provides lessons and insights into future ROK behavior.

A Nuclear-Armed South Korea: First Attempt

In the late 1960s and early 1970s, forces beyond South Korea's control redefined the strategic environment in East Asia, largely to Seoul's disadvantage. The single most important factor was the changing role of the United States. With the Vietnam War taking an increasingly heavy toll on American lives and treasure, Washington decided to reduce its direct engagement in the region. On July 25, 1969, with no advance warning to America's Asian allies, President Richard Nixon announced that "as far as the problems of internal security are concerned, as far as the problems of military defense . . . the United States is going to encourage and has a right to expect that this problem will be increasingly handled by, and the responsibility for it taken by, the Asian allies themselves.[10] Known as the Nixon or Guam Doctrine, the United States was telling its allies that they had to become more self-reliant in defense matters.

Washington turned this rhetoric into reality by abruptly withdrawing the Seventh Infantry Division from the ROK in mid-1971, over the sharp objections of President Park Chung Hee. From Seoul's perspective, the timing could hardly have been worse. At that time, the DPRK, already a formidable military adversary, was significantly outspending the ROK on defense.[11] The troop withdrawal followed a series of feeble American responses to major provocations by the DPRK, including a brazen commando raid on the Blue House in January 1968 in an attempt to assassinate President Park; the seizure of the U.S.S. *Pueblo* two days later, followed by the long imprisonment of its crew; and the North's shooting down an American EC-121 reconnaissance plane in April 1969 over the Sea of Japan, with the loss of all on board. In conjunction with the steady withdrawal of U.S. forces from Vietnam, the U.S. disengagement raised questions about Washington's reliability as an ally prepared to defend the ROK.

The stunning and unanticipated Sino-American rapprochement of 1971–72 further fueled South Korea's feelings of insecurity. In February 1972, President Nixon visited China and signed the Shanghai Communiqué. The practical consequence of this document was to marginalize Taiwan's status, which Seoul saw as particularly ominous. The American accommodation with China appeared to condition Washington's continued support for Taipei on Beijing's acquiescence and restraint.[12] The parallels between Taiwan and the ROK were readily apparent. Both regimes were products of civil wars, loyal devotees of American interests since the end of the 1940s, outposts holding forth against communist adversaries, and allies of the United States for over two decades. As Park Chung Hee made abundantly clear to U.S. officials, if Taiwan now found itself abruptly and unexpectedly compromised by its long-term benefactor, could South Korea be far behind?

In response to these growing security anxieties, President Park decided to undertake a secret nuclear weapons option under the tight control of the Blue House. In 1970 the ROK established the Agency for Defense Development (ADD), which openly conducted research and development to modernize the ROK military, and the more secretive Weapons Exploitation Committee, which was a "covert, ad hoc governmental committee responsible to the Blue House for weapons procurement and production."[13] This committee made a unanimous recommendation to President Park to proceed with nuclear weapons development.[14] The entire program was maintained with utmost secrecy. In late 1973, the ADD completed a long-term plan for development of nuclear weapons; the program was expected to take six to ten years, with an estimated cost between U.S.$1.5 billion and $2 billion.[15] According to one South Korean official who purportedly discussed the project with President Park Chung Hee, a team of more than twenty scientists assigned to the program reported personally to the president one or two times per month on the research results.[16]

Obtaining special nuclear material remained Seoul's largest technological hurdle. To remedy this deficiency, South Korea entered into negotiations with France to purchase a spent fuel reprocessing facility, with Belgium for a mixed-oxide reprocessing laboratory, and with Canada for a heavy-water (CANDU) reactor, which would more readily allow the secret diversion of plutonium-laden fuel rods than would light-water reactors. But South Korea's activities had not gone unnoticed by the United States, which suspected Seoul of launching a clandestine nuclear weapons program. Washington was increasingly alert to clandestine nuclear efforts following India's "peaceful nuclear explosion" in May 1974. The American embassy in Seoul was instructed to learn more about the ROK's weapons programs, and a young CIA case officer was given the assignment. Within three months, he had recruited a disaffected South Korean nuclear physicist who had been dragooned into working on the secret program.[17]

Washington brought both indirect and direct pressure to bear upon Seoul to forsake its nuclear weapons ambitions. It intervened with Paris, Brussels, and Ottawa to head off any sales of sophisticated nuclear technology to South Korea. The United States pressed Seoul to ratify the Non-Proliferation Treaty, and it threatened to terminate all civilian nuclear energy cooperation with the ROK.[18] Even more fundamentally, the United States threatened to end the bilateral relationship with the ROK. As U.S. ambassador to the ROK Richard Sneider warned President Park in late 1975, "Far more than our nuclear support is at stake here. . . . If the ROKG proceeds as it has indicated to date, [the] whole range of security and political relationships between the U.S. and ROK will be affected."[19] Faced with the imminent abandonment of its ally and well before realizing the goal of an independent nuclear arsenal, the Blue House terminated the project, with the United States reaffirming its security commitments to the ROK.

Following President Carter's election in 1976 and the new administration's plan to withdraw U.S. ground forces from the peninsula, Seoul sought to resume its nuclear weapons activities. The renewed effort was focused more on acquisition of nuclear materials and development of indigenous technologies that could enable future pursuit of a nuclear capability, rather than an outright renewal of the covert weapons program. But heightened U.S. scrutiny compelled the ROK to restrict these activities to civilian nuclear development; American officials never found convincing evidence of a revived covert program.[20] However, an ROK official subsequently claimed that President Carter had been prepared to cancel an Export-Import Bank loan of close to $300 million for the Kori-2 reactor program unless the ROK ceased suspicious research and development activities. This same source also alleged that many of the key ADD personnel associated with the nuclear weapons program did not retire or were not terminated until as late as December 1982. This official asserted that President Chon Tu-hwan took more definitive steps to dismantle the ROK's nuclear weapons potential in exchange for explicit U.S. recognition of the results of the coup that brought Chon to power in 1980.[21]

Fear of abandonment by an inconstant United States was the primary motivation for Seoul's attempts during the 1970s to acquire nuclear weapons. In the South's highly pessimistic assessment, the United States could remove its nuclear umbrella and security commitment just as unilaterally and unexpectedly as it had announced the Guam Doctrine and the withdrawal of the Seventh Infantry Division. South Korea feared a U.S. retreat from Asia more deeply than other Asian countries because it had witnessed, up close, the consequences of faltering U.S. support and retreat in South Vietnam, despite having committed 50,000 troops to the Vietnam War.[22] South Korean president Park interpreted the Guam Doctrine and related developments as "a message to the Korean people that we won't rescue you if North Korea invades again."[23] To counter abandonment, it sought nuclear armaments.

However, the ROK also responded to its mounting concerns about U.S. support by undertaking high-level contact with the leaders of the North. In the early 1970s, the DPRK had already been hinting at its interest in direct talks with officials from the South. These overtures resulted in multiple rounds of talks between the Red Cross organizations of the two countries during 1971 and 1972, with the leaders of both delegations being senior North and South Korean intelligence officers. These exchanges led to the May 1972 visit to Pyongyang of Lee Hu Rak, Director of the Korean CIA and among the most powerful figures in the ROK. In an extraordinary late night meeting with North Korean leader Kim Il Sung, the two antagonists both bemoaned that their behavior was often dictated by the major powers: the Sino-American accommodation was at least as much a blow to Kim Il Sung as it was to Park Chung Hee. Lee Hu Rak argued that "unification should be achieved by ourselves without interference of the four powers [the United States, China, Japan, and the Soviet Union]." Kim, in agreement, stated: "Let us exclude foreign forces. Let's not fight. Let's unite as a nation. . . . Big powers and imperialism prefer to divide a nation into several nations."[24]

This discussion and a return visit to Seoul by a senior North Korean official culminated in the North-South Joint Statement of July 4, 1972. This document provided, at least in broad outline, the basis for potential accommodation and national integration. Although its premises have yet to be realized more than three decades later, it created a "baseline" to which both Koreas have repeatedly returned in subsequent efforts at reconciliation. Though it remains more aspiration than achievement, the commitment to a "Korea only" accommodation conveys the deep impulse in both Koreas to pursue an autonomous route to national integration, irrespective of their profound ideological cleavages and military threats directed against one another. This impulse has been particularly marked when the two sides have voiced specific grievances about the role of outside powers, leaving both Koreas vulnerable to manipulation and control.

Such beliefs help explain the ROK's secret pursuit of a nuclear weapons program in the 1970s, and the far more enduring efforts by the

DPRK to build a nuclear weapons capability. In Kim Il Sung's reasoning, a nuclear option, or at least the credible appearance of one, afforded the best guarantee that the North could not be blackmailed or coerced by any outside power. Indeed, as Moscow and Beijing in the late 1980s and early 1990s steadily distanced themselves from their past relations with Pyongyang and cemented ever closer ties with Seoul, the nuclear program assumed far greater salience for the North Koreans, even if it was nominally justified as a means of countering U.S. military threats. A nuclear weapons program had the added virtue of opening the door to direct high-level negotiations with the United States while retaining an unambiguous political, military, and psychological advantage over its ever more economically robust—but militarily inhibited—southern neighbor. These lessons were in all likelihood not lost on the ROK.

A Nuclear-Armed South Korea: A Second Attempt?

Could comparable calculations by Seoul convince South Korea to reconsider its non-nuclear commitments? At first blush, this prospect seems highly remote and would have to derive from an extremely unlikely sequence of events. In the 1970s, Park Chung Hee ruled the South with an iron fist and in absolute secrecy. The ROK was a highly authoritarian, military-dominated regime that remained hugely dependent on U.S. political and military support. The South today is a vibrant, if still highly turbulent, democracy enjoying decades of extraordinary economic achievement and near-universal diplomatic recognition, increasingly close ties with China, fuller relations with Russia and Japan, and an increased self-confidence about Korea's place in the world.

Despite mounting concerns in 2002 and 2003 about the DPRK's renewed pursuit of a nuclear weapons capability and an enhanced ballistic missile program, prevailing sentiment in the ROK no longer perceives the North as a major military threat. The South appears intent on accommodation rather than confrontation with the DPRK. Generational attitude changes reflect an extraordinarily idealized view of North Korea that is starkly at odds with decades of confrontation and ideological hostility between Seoul and Pyongyang. Indeed, much to the consternation of American policymakers, many South Korean officials seem intent on transcending or denying the belief that the North still represents a major threat to the ROK. This phenomenon has led to increasing South Korean disaffection from the United States, and vice versa, weakening the alliance bonds that have sustained bilateral ties for a half century.

Thus, despite some superficial parallels with the 1970s, the emergent dynamics in the ROK point to different imperatives and possibilities. A decision by the South to fully pursue strategic autonomy, including renewed pursuit of a nuclear weapons option, would be fraught with enormous consequences and risks. We therefore need to examine the major factors that could shape ROK attitudes and policies over the longer term, quite possibly in paradoxical and unanticipated ways. Rather than posit specific paths or scenarios that might result in renewed pursuit of nuclear weapons, we will explore five major policy considerations that are likely to shape the ROK's longer-term national security strategy: 1) the shifting contours of the U.S.-ROK alliance; 2) changing South Korean threat perceptions about the North; 3) the ROK's growing accommodation and alignment with China; 4) the outcome of the renewed North Korean nuclear crisis, in particular the fate of the DPRK's nuclear assets and weapons potential; and 5) the aftermath and consequences of the potential end of the Pyongyang regime, with particular attention to the North Korean nuclear legacy over which the ROK would likely assume custodial control. We will then offer conclusions on the likely implications of peninsular unification for the ROK's nuclear weapons policies.

The Korean-American Alliance in Upheaval

Despite the dangerously high concentrations of military power in both the North and South, the Korean peninsula has been largely stable for the past fifty years, without any resumption of full-scale hostilities. This is in significant measure explained by the long-term presence of U.S. ground, air, and sea forces committed to the defense of the ROK. Together, the United States and South Korea have successfully deterred military threats from the DPRK, an arrangement that both countries have codified through the Mutual Defense Treaty of 1954. South Korea has provided a forward base for U.S. forces in East Asia and, in conjunction with American forces in Japan, an anchor for the U.S. presence in the western Pacific. For South Korea, the United States has provided a shield behind which it has thrived economically and matured politically. By all measures, this has been an enormously durable and successful relationship.

In recent years, however, significant fissures have raised serious questions about the durability of the alliance. A "push-pull" dynamic has developed, with elements of South Korean society wanting to push the United States away and some American voices, predominantly but not exclusively concentrated in the Pentagon, wanting to pull back from the traditional U.S. commitment to Korea. The inherent inequalities in U.S.-ROK alliance relations, which have long alienated many in the South—including close supporters of security ties—are also increasingly evident. A once-solid relationship is now experiencing severe strain.

This weakening of the alliance is hardly surprising. For the past five decades, the United States and South Korea have stood shoulder-to-shoulder in maintaining a robust military deterrent against the DPRK. At the same time, all of the major regional actors since 1953 have supported the status quo of a divided Korea. Given the growth of its own power, North Korea's precipitous economic decline, and the ROK's ever stronger international position, Seoul resents any characterizations of continued dependence on the United States or any presumption that it must automatically defer to American preferences. As South Korea has changed and as regional politics and security have undergone major flux, the traditional rationale of the alliance is being called into serious question.

U.S. and South Korean interests, while overlapping in many respects, are far from identical. Although the latent strains have been evident for several decades, some of these major differences are increasingly manifest under the Bush administration. There is growing tension between America's global security interests in the post–September 11 world and the ROK's more peninsular focus. Washington and Seoul have very different assessments of the military threats posed by North Korea, especially the implications of its nuclear weapons program. In short, different responsibilities have created different interests. At the same time, Korea's democratization has triggered growing popular frustration and resentment within the ROK over the asymmetries in the U.S.-ROK alliance, with Seoul the subordinate actor.

Recent developments in Korean-American military relations have highlighted this increasing divergence of interest. Traditional earnests of the American commitment to Korea have either disappeared—the last U.S. tactical nuclear weapons were withdrawn from Korea in the early 1990s—or are in motion—the redeployment and looming reduction of U.S. "boots on the ground" in the South. In early 2003, the Pentagon, with little if any prior consultation with its South Korean ally, announced plans to redeploy the Second Infantry Division from just below the demilitarized zone (DMZ) to south of the Han River. The United States viewed this redeployment as part of a more general reconfiguration of U.S. forces to ensure a more "capabilities-based" approach to its global force structure, in accordance with the recommendations of the Quadrennial Defense Review.[25]

Several principal factors help explain the U.S. decision to redeploy its major combat units on the peninsula. First, U.S. defense planners argue that the time is long overdue for Korean forces to assume increased responsibility for the country's defense, even though senior officials in the ROK contend that major redeployment decisions in the midst of the renewed North Korean nuclear crisis send the wrong message to Pyongyang. Second, the Bush administration asserts that the forward deployment of U.S. forces is increasingly irrelevant to military realities on the peninsula. U.S. planners no longer believe that either country should be devoting major resources to a replay of the first Korean war. Washington contends that North Korea would employ its missile, artillery, and special forces to bypass the traditional invasion corridors and directly target major cities and military facilities throughout the southern half of the peninsula. The redeployment is therefore designed to limit U.S. vulnerabilities in a future conflict and—in conjunction with a major strengthening of South Korean forces—to exploit U.S. technologies and operational concepts to undermine North Korean capabilities.

Third, and most important, U.S. planners believe that American forces may be needed much more elsewhere, especially given the expectation of open-ended demands on U.S. forces deployed to Iraq, Afghanistan, and elsewhere in the Persian Gulf and Southwest Asia. In this view, American forces must become much more flexible and agile, able to redeploy on very short notice to distant theaters. Under prevailing circumstances, the Second Infantry Division remains a fixed asset, committed exclusively to deterrence and defense on the peninsula. The redeployment and reconfiguration of U.S. forces would enable their transformation into far more mobile combat units geared to a much wider array of prospective contingencies, not simply to peninsular missions. The United States therefore envisions a much less singular U.S. security role in Korea and (very likely) appreciable reductions in the American military presence on the peninsula over the coming decade. Although a reduced U.S. footprint will also reduce public resentment in the ROK of a highly visible U.S. security presence, ROK security planners express growing unease, since they fear that they will be left exposed and ill prepared to deal with future military threats. They also fear that a major withdrawal of U.S. forces will leave South Korea surrounded by more powerful neighboring states.

In addition, South Korean defense planners view the redeployment as removing an American "trip wire" that would guarantee immediate U.S. involvement in any clash with Pyongyang, thereby decoupling American's security from that of the South.[26] The ROK sees the impending repositioning of U.S. forces as creating a clear "killing field" below the DMZ and north of Seoul in anticipation of preemptive American military strikes against the North. With these steps, the United States accomplished the seemingly impossible feat of raising Seoul's fears of abandonment and entrapment *simultaneously.*[27] Such anxieties constitute the ultimate culmination of decades of South Korean dependence on the United States and of cumulative resentments this has generated over the years.

The domestic context of the Korean-American alliance has also changed greatly. South Korea, as befits one of the world's most advanced industrialized countries, is both more assertive and less deferential to American wishes. A series of events, some trivial, some serious, has fueled rising Korean nationalism, the dark side of which erupts periodically as anti-Americanism. Among the more trivial were blaming the United States for disqualification of a South Korean speed skater (by a non-American official) at the winter olympics. Other claims were more substantive, such as the poor public treatment of President Kim Dae Jung during his visit to Washington in March 2001, the alleged strong-arming of Seoul into buying American-made F-15 fighter jets, and resentment over perceived unfairness in the Status of Forces Agreement. The deaths of two schoolgirls in a road accident involving an American military vehicle in June 2002 were judged by an unforgiving South Korean public as more serious still.

Public protests against the United States in reaction to these events are surface symptoms of deeper, generational shifts occurring in South Korea. Memories of the Korean War have faded as the older generation has disappeared from the scene, giving way to a younger generation that dwells on far different memories of the United States, including the Kwangju massacre and U.S. support for repressive military regimes.[28] The influence of the "386 generation"—those currently in their thirties, college-educated in the 1980s, and born in the 1960s—has grown and will grow further as it moves into more powerful positions in the universities, government, and media. Polling data bear out these generational differences, with majorities of Koreans in their twenties and thirties holding unfavorable views of the United States, versus the favorable views held by those in their forties through seventies.[29] In addition, this younger generation has provided strong support for the sunshine policy under President Kim Dae Jung, later renamed the peace and prosperity policy after Roh Moo Hyun was elected president in December 2002.

For this generation, and perhaps for South Korean society as a whole, engagement with North Korea has become virtually irreversible. As observed by Kim Kyung Won, a leading ROK strategic thinker and former ambassador to the United States,

> It disturbs me that North Korea is no longer seen as a threat to us by a certain percentage of the South Korean people. . . . The fact that they have a nuclear program is not sinking in. The danger we face from this is that we may be falsifying reality, thinking that our safety is assured. That weighs on the debate over the U.S. military presence. If the South Koreans perceive no threat, there may very well be more questions over whether the U.S. should be here at all."[30]

The growing risk for the United States is that increasing numbers of Koreans will perceive the United States as being on the wrong side of history, preventing reunification of North and South, and denying Korea its rightful place in the sun.[31] To assess these possibilities further, we need to turn attention to changing ROK views of future inter-Korean relations, and how these could shape future attitudes toward nuclear weapons.

ROK Attitudes and Policies toward the North

To what extent might the growing strains in U.S.-ROK relations replicate the circumstances and pressures of the early 1970s? Would the simultaneous fear of abandonment and entrapment lead to a backlash against the U.S. military presence and jeopardize the alliance, leaving the South without a nuclear-armed ally? If the ROK found itself without a reliable nuclear guarantee, what are its prospective strategic options? The answers to these questions depend critically on the evolution of Korean nationalism and on future ROK domestic politics, and how both influence Seoul's policy calculations.

There are two predominant strains in Korean nationalism, and they predict very different outcomes. The predominant voice is from the political left, which became politically dominant during the presidency of Kim Dae Jung and seems even stronger under Roh Moo Hyun. The underlying impulse is to mute or dispute assessments of the North Korean threat, which many South Koreans now view as a rationalization for the military-dominated politics of the past. A more benign view of the

DPRK military threat envisions little need for a nuclear deterrent because the North's military capabilities could not possibly be seen as threatening the ROK. (A comparable attitude is evident in the resistance of the ROK political left to U.S. proposals for ballistic missile defense.) To some degree, large segments of the South Korean public already share these beliefs, regarding the North more with pity than with fear.[32] This view is also partially reflected in recent ROK assessments of the declining North Korean conventional threat, which clash markedly with the view of U.S. Forces Korea that there has been no appreciable degradation of North Korean military capabilities, notwithstanding the DPRK's precipitous economic decline in the 1990s.[33]

Some of the manifestations of changing domestic attitudes are evident in ROK reactions to the renewed North Korean nuclear crisis, to be reviewed further on in this chapter. There has been a lack of outrage in the South to the North's shredding of its international nonproliferation commitments, including the 1992 North-South Joint Declaration on the Denuclearization of the Korean Peninsula. Among some South Koreans, this reflects a belief that the North would never attack the South due to bonds of blood and family—"we're all Korean."[34] For others, it is explained by the ROK outsourcing its security to the United States for the past fifty years, preventing Seoul from coming to grips with the DPRK military threat. Some U.S. analysts assert that a ROK version of the Stockholm syndrome has set in. By this logic, since the ROK can never fully count on the U.S. commitment, then it must propitiate the North to give it as little reason as possible to feel threatened. Open-ended accommodation with the North thus becomes a form of reinsurance.[35]

Such thinking suggests, without explicitly making the case, two longer-term possibilities: a lasting North-South accommodation whereby a "reassured" North would preclude Pyongyang's need for a nuclear weapons capability, with Seoul willing to defer a full nuclear reckoning until the North received binding security assurances and related economic compensation; or tacit ROK acceptance of North Korean weapons capabilities, on the expectation that a unified Korean state would ultimately inherit them. For understandable reasons, no ROK government official gives public voice to either alternative. However, Roh Moo Hyun's 2003 Armed Forces Day address renewed a pledge, first voiced by Park Chung Hee and periodically reiterated by the ROK's leadership ever since, to "achieve self-reliant national defense within the next ten years." He went on to state that

I intend to lay the foundations for such self-defensive capabilities. It is beyond question that . . . an independent nation should have enough strength to defend itself on its own. The Republic is now the twelfth strongest economy in the world. . . . If a country with such potential cannot have a self-reliant national defense, it will not be able to hold its own in the international community [and] our people will be ashamed."[36]

Neither Roh's remarks nor the above two scenarios posit a *current* need for the ROK to pursue a nuclear weapons capability; indeed, President Roh's vision of a self-reliant defense force was not matched by a corresponding commitment of the requisite resources to fulfill such a pledge. However, his remarks reflect an unspoken assumption that an indirect strategy will ultimately enable a unified Korea to decide whether true strategic autonomy will be required, without any need to address this possibility at present.

The traditional conservative nationalist position is now a much weakened force in South Korean domestic politics, corresponding closely to the steady decline in the role of the uniformed military as a political force and the ROK's demographic transition. But the political right remains a potent actor in electoral politics and in some major media. It has yielded significant ground to Kim Dae Jung and Roh Moo Hyun on policies toward the North, though it severely criticizes both presidents for an idealized, naive view of the DPRK threat that Pyongyang continues to exploit. The principal voices defending the alliance with the United States are also found in conservative circles. Even though some observers raise major objections to U.S. heavy-handedness, they see few alternatives to continued close ties with the United States, both at present and following unification. Thus the nationalist right believes that the ROK must accommodate the impending shifts in U.S. defense strategy on the peninsula. At the same time, the political right wants to ensure that Seoul's defense needs are clearly addressed in any such changes and that perceived political imbalances in the alliance are rectified in return for the ROK's consent to looming policy changes. The political right also supports U.S. efforts to achieve North Korean denuclearization.

Notably absent from the political right's views is any consideration of a renewed nuclear weapons option.[37] The clear assumption is that the ROK must avail itself of the opportunity to modernize its conventional forces in line with the U.S. plans for military transformation. Over time this would enable the ROK to reduce the major manpower burdens imposed by its very large conventional forces—especially the ground forces—and begin to shift attention to modernization goals for a post-unification environment. Such steps would be deemed appropriate to ensure that the ROK remains an essential partner in U.S. regional security strategy over the longer term.

If there are advocates of a "Gaullist" position in the ROK, their voices are not heard, at least not at present. Indeed, against whom would such a hypothesized nuclear force be directed? Would it be an attempt to achieve notional strategic equivalence with the North, on the assumption that the DPRK's nuclear capabilities will persist and that the United States might ultimately expect the ROK to be fully responsible for its own defense? Some Korean officials, for example, have long envisioned the need for an upgraded ROK missile capability able to reach major targets in the North, even if restricted to conventional warheads. In the late 1990s, the ROK pressured the United States to permit an increase in the range of the Hyonmu, the South's indigenous short-range ballistic missile, from 180 to 300 kilometers. Such an enhanced range would approach but not exceed the guidelines under the Missile Technology Control Regime, although the ROK is not a signatory to it. At the time, U.S. officials voiced concern that the Hyonmu might possess an inherent capability to extend its range beyond 300 kilometers, creating the prospect of a future offensive missile capability.[38] Despite such concerns, the United States ultimately consented to ROK acquisition of the U.S. version of a 300-kilometer missile, with the ROK currently planning to deploy 110 of these missiles against targets in the North.[39]

But the enhancement of the ROK's missile capabilities might be viewed by some as ultimately facilitating the pursuit of larger strategic goals. Might an enhanced South Korean missile capability be directed against Japan, so as to provide the ROK a power advantage against Tokyo, even though such an action would likely trigger Japanese moves in the same direction? Would it be seen as protecting South Korea against future American actions perceived as threats to the ROK's vital interests? Might it be seen as preserving a nuclear weapons option under unspecified future conditions? None of these questions receives a public airing in South Korea, nor do they arise in private conversations with U.S. security experts. If some on the political right support greater strategic ambitions, including nuclear weapons, their advocacy remains deeply recessed at present and would presumably have to await acute reversals in the country's political and strategic fortunes before being revealed.

But even the nationalist right knows that the ground has shifted, both within ROK politics and in the ROK's larger international environment. The singular fact is that the post–cold war era is enabling the ROK to transcend its predominant focus on the DPRK threat and fashion a much more potent regional role, most notably in relations with China.

The Chinese-Korean Strategic Accommodation: Planning for the Longer Term?

The transformation of Chinese–South Korean relations over the past decade reflects the profound changes in the ROK's security environment and in the country's longer-term strategic and diplomatic options. Although more conservative circles in the ROK express continued wariness about pursuing overly close ties with Beijing, the changes in Chinese–South Korean relations have shifted the center of gravity in Seoul's external policies. The South's growing rapprochement with China is evident at multiple levels: in politics and diplomacy; in economic ties and investment; in China's growing popularity in the educational and career choices being made by younger Koreans; and in security ties between the two leaderships. There is also a perceived congruence of interests between China and the ROK with respect to approaches to the North Korean nuclear issue, a topic to be reviewed in the next section.

Although these altered circumstances have enhanced China's leverage and room for maneuvering between the two Koreas, the implications for ROK security calculations are also very significant. China's ever increasing cultivation of economic, political, and security ties with Seoul has been hugely validating to the ROK. Beginning tentatively in the mid-1980s and accelerating dramatically over the past decade, Beijing's strategic orientation toward the peninsula has shifted in remarkable ways, redounding to Seoul's clear advantage. Throughout most of the cold war, Beijing was never prepared to put its relations with Pyongyang at risk for the potential gains of opening doors to Seoul. China consistently treated the ROK as little more than an appendage of American power. These circumstances are now almost entirely reversed. China's 1991 decision to endorse simultaneous entry of both Koreas into the United Nations, followed a year later by the opening of full diplomatic relations with Seoul, conveyed unambiguously that China would no longer sacrifice its larger international interests for the sake of its increasingly circumscribed ties with Pyongyang.

The policy momentum set in motion by these decisions accelerated dramatically over the course of the 1990s and has continued to advance ever since. Beijing's readiness to bypass the North for the sake of larger goals and opportunities with the South convinced leaders in Seoul—and increasing numbers of ordinary South Koreans—that China might even one day supplant the United States as the ROK's primary great power benefactor. This changed relationship has manifested itself most profoundly in the economic arena, although Seoul believes it will have growing political consequences as well. In 2001 China became the ROK's leading investment destination; in 2002 it surpassed the United States as the ROK's leading export market; and in 2003 China for the first time emerged as the ROK's leading trading partner, with both governments announcing a target of $100 billion (U.S.) in two-way trade no later than 2008.[40]

To be sure, the ROK's shifting economic center of gravity and its growing deference to Chinese interests are not without potential liabilities. Some South Koreans believe that the ROK has overvalued its accommodation with China, perhaps in a misguided belief that Beijing can ultimately induce Pyongyang to undertake genuine coexistence and collaboration with Seoul. Others may believe that China is laying the groundwork for an "ROK-centered" unification of the peninsula, even though Beijing has demonstrated little interest in moving toward that goal. However, with or without unification, China now occupies a distinctive position on the peninsula, being the only external power that seems able to interact credibly with both Seoul and Pyongyang. At the same time, Seoul sees its longer-term security goals closely aligned with those of China, with both countries voicing a clear preference for designing post–cold war security arrangements for Korea as a whole. As early as August 1999, in the first-ever visit to Beijing by a senior ROK military official, then minister of national defense Cho Sung Tae spoke openly of the ROK's commitment to "a new regional peace structure," one also sought by Beijing. Minister Cho also stated, in remarks subsequently disavowed by senior officials in Seoul, that the future status of U.S. forces on the peninsula would be determined "in consultation with neighboring countries."[41] His remarks prefigured what is now incontestable: it is virtually inconceivable that the ROK leadership would ever consent to the use of Korean bases as potential strategic platforms for military contingencies directed against China.

The tenor and tone of ROK-Chinese security consultations have been enhanced greatly since the late 1990s, with senior political and military officials in Seoul increasingly comfortable in their interactions with Beijing. These ties have been especially evident in the context of the renewed

North Korean nuclear crisis. The symmetry between ROK and Chinese views of the nuclear crisis seems especially notable. Both increasingly characterize the risks of instability or war as outweighing the dangers posed by a nascent North Korean nuclear weapons capability. Seoul took note of China's singular role as advocate and host of the 2003 multiparty consultations in Beijing, first among the United States, China, and North Korea in April 2003 and then with the addition of Japan, Russia, and the ROK in August 2003 and February 2004. In contrast to U.S. policy, China and South Korea both urge Washington to offer explicit security assurances to the North, without which neither Beijing nor Seoul believes a political breakthrough is possible. At the same time, leaders in Seoul seem unconcerned that China's ever larger diplomatic role might marginalize Seoul or might lead Beijing to disregard the South's strategic claims.

The manifestations of these changes are increasingly evident in Korean public opinion surveys as well. The steady decline in U.S. favorability ratings correlates closely with increasingly positive evaluations of China. According to nationwide opinion polls and focus groups conducted by the U.S. Department of State, by July 2002, 43 percent of those interviewed deemed China's "basic values" as similar to those of Korea, as compared to 15 percent for the United States. Additional findings from the survey indicated that 54 percent of the population expected China to be the ROK's closest economic partner over the next five to ten years, while only 14 percent of those interviewed selected the United States for that role.[42] Shifts in positive, neutral, and negative views of China are also correlated closely with age groups: the younger the age cohort, the more favorable the views held of China.[43]

To be sure, these shifts in policy and public perceptions have all been expressed in the context of severely strained but still undiminished security relations with Washington, and at a time when nationalism of the left has been increasingly dominant in ROK politics. Should the U.S. military appreciably reduce its military presence on the peninsula or even opt to disengage entirely, the "era of good feelings" in ROK-Chinese relations could quite possibly subside, especially if the ROK were to then see itself as overly enveloped in the shadow of Chinese power. For now, however, the ground continues to shift between Beijing and Seoul, and these changes do not seem ephemeral, especially for younger Koreans. The presumption of China as a partner of choice for South Korea—and, quite possibly, *the* partner of choice—reflects ineluctable geographic, economic, and political realities. Should the ROK continue to lean to China's side and increasingly perceive a sustainable, mutually reinforcing basis for ever closer relations, the South's leadership will be less likely over time to accommodate U.S. strategic preferences. This is abundantly evident in the renewed North Korean nuclear crisis, to which we will now turn.

The North Korean Nuclear Program

The renewal of North Korea's efforts to develop a covert nuclear weapons capability has introduced major new uncertainties into the regional security environment and the ability of all involved powers to achieve the definitive dismantlement and cessation of the North's program.[44] Although the United States is currently pursuing six-party talks aimed at securing North Korea's complete and verifiable denuclearization, the prospects for diplomatic success are problematic at best. The U.S. and North Korean policy agendas remain widely divergent. Pyongyang continues to insist on various bilateral security pledges and economic commitments from Washington as conditions for relinquishing its nuclear deterrence power. The United States asserts that it will only consider security assurances as part of a multilateral process, further conditioned by the DPRK's unambiguous, irreversible commitment to forgo its nuclear weapons capabilities.

The United States has been able to assemble a consultation process with China, Russia, Japan, and the ROK, but agreement within this group is tentative and conditional at best. Indeed, among the four states participating in this process with Washington, the South Korean government has registered the sharpest dissents from U.S. strategy. It is not at all clear what Seoul proposes as an alternative course of action to induce Pyongyang to forgo its nuclear weapons activities, but the ROK seems almost congenitally opposed to all but the most conciliatory of strategies toward the North. This begs the issue of whether, in the final analysis, the ROK is genuinely intent on North Korean denuclearization, thereby engendering suspicions in various quarters that the South does not object to such a program provided that it remains covert rather than overt.

There are three prospective strategy options to constrain or eliminate the North Korean nuclear weapons program; all entail major liabilities and uncertainties, and one would entail acute military risks. The first path is negotiation and engagement, through which security assurances would be provided to the North in return for the DPRK's readiness to return to the nonproliferation regime and to definitively eliminate its nuclear weapons activities. Such an approach would presumably result as well in new security arrangements in and around the Korean peninsula. There are major doubts about the feasibility of such an approach, and the United States is unalterably opposed to renewed compensation of the North for its defiance of previous nonproliferation commitments under the Agreed Framework of 1994. At the same time, verification arrangements for such a process remain hugely problematic; it might not be possible to establish definitively that the North has fully declared its extant inventory of materials, weapons, and facilities. The United States and all other parties would then have to address how much residual nuclear ambiguity, if any, they would be prepared to accept.

Such possibilities are increasingly recognized by U.S. intelligence. In an August 2003 assessment prepared for the Senate Select Committee on Intelligence, the intelligence community concluded for the first time that North Korea's cumulative covert efforts precluded the need to test a device to validate the design of a simple fission weapon: "We assess that North Korea has produced one or two simple fission-type nuclear weapons and has validated the designs without conducting yield-producing nuclear tests. Press reports indicate North Korea has been conducting nuclear weapon-related high explosive tests since the 1980s in order to validate its weapon design(s). *With such tests, we assess North Korea would not require nuclear tests to validate simple fission weapons.*[45]

In responding to a related query from the same committee, the Defense Intelligence Agency has acknowledged its inability to verify various North Korean claims, in particular those associated with its renewed plutonium production and reprocessing activities:

North Korea expelled IAEA observers from its nuclear facilities at Yongbyon, and it has restarted operations of its 5Mwe nuclear reactor. We cannot confirm North Korea's claims that it [has] reprocessed nearly all the nuclear fuel that was removed from this reactor around the time of the signing of the Agreed Framework. We do not have precise information on activities at Yongbyon, but North Korea's threat that additional plutonium for new weapons has been or will be removed from the used fuel is real.[46]

These judgments raise the highly unsettling spectre of North Korean nuclear weapons production that is both unconstrained and, in the absence of a renewed agreement, unverifiable. They apply with even greater force to activities under way at undeclared locations.

The second strategy for constraining or eliminating the North Korean nuclear weapons program is containment and isolation. This approach posits that there are no realistic circumstances under which North Korea would be prepared to definitively abandon its nuclear weapons program; hence the United States and other powers must proceed on the assumption that Pyongyang is determined to build a nuclear weapons capability and deploy it operationally. Any delays or uncertainties in North Korean nuclear deployments are presumably explained more by limitations in technology, materials, and infrastructure rather than by Pyongyang's readiness to negotiate away these capabilities. The premise of the second path is that it is essential to limit, by all available means, any presumed security gains that North Korea would seek to achieve through its nuclear program. This would entail far more vigorous efforts at deterrence and defense—especially missile defense—with surrounding countries, and heightened emphasis on new multilateral approaches, such as the Proliferation Security Initiative, to interdict wherever possible any shipments of materials or technologies associated with weapons of mass destruction (WMD).[47]

An additional component of this approach would be to curtail any meaningful economic links between North Korea and neighboring states. This would clearly require the active collaboration of both China and South Korea, and it is not at all clear whether either would be fully prepared to implement such measures. A third facet of this strategy would be to seek UN Security Council sanctions against North Korea, to which China would likely accede only with great reluctance and only following protracted efforts to water down the language of any resolutions. Some advocates of containment and isolation believe that such a strategy would lead to the ever increasing marginalization of the DPRK and might even ultimately result in the disintegration of the North Korean state. It remains highly doubtful, however, that North Korea's collapse could be engineered short of the most coercive of strategies. Indeed, one of the principal liabilities of this approach is that it would be accepting the inevitability and irreversibility of a declared North Korean nuclear weapons capability, triggering the most severe of consequences for the regional security environment and dealing a severe blow to the nonproliferation regime as a whole.

The third prospective strategy would entail unilateral measures by the United States to forcibly eliminate North Korean nuclear capabilities. A coercive strategy would be predicated on the belief that the overt possession and deployment of nuclear weapons by North Korea, including the potential transfer of nuclear materials or completed weapons to third parties, poses an unacceptable danger to the vital security interests of the

United States, as outlined in the White House's National Security Strategy report of September 2002 and related documents.[48] Although there is no reason to conclude that such an option is under active consideration at present, it cannot be definitively ruled out, especially if Washington concluded that the estimated inventory of North Korean nuclear weapons was approaching unacceptably high levels. The liabilities of such a strategy seem self-evident. Given the uncertainties and unknowns concerning the location of North Korean fissile materials and any completed weapons, there is no assurance that the use of force would achieve its desired objectives. At the same time, any major attack on the DPRK would almost certainly prompt major North Korean retaliation against South Korea—especially against U.S. forces in the ROK—and against Japan, thereby creating the prospect of a full-scale regional war. Even if such a preventive or preemptive attack were to achieve its stated goals, it would very likely lead to acute instability throughout Northeast Asia and would also likely result in the dissolution of the U.S.-ROK alliance.

There is every reason to believe that there would be unrelenting South Korean opposition to any U.S. consideration of military action against the North. This is not simply a byproduct of recent political shifts in ROK politics. President Kim Young Sam's unambiguous opposition to any U.S. military actions during the 1993–94 nuclear crisis provides some highly relevant precedents. Despite President Kim's deeply held antipathies toward North Korea (his mother was killed by North Korean forces during the Korean War), he fiercely rejected any suggestion of potential U.S. military moves against the Yongbyon nuclear complex. When President Clinton conveyed to President Kim in mid-1994 that the United States would not preclude the use of force against the DPRK, Kim chastised the American leader in exceedingly sharp terms: "You are trying to fulfill your objectives by fighting war in our country. . . . [Y]ou would never be allowed to start bombing on our soil."[49] In his memoirs, President Kim reports a separate conversation with President Clinton that conveys Kim's unambiguous opposition to war:

> As long as I am the president, I would not mobilize any one of our 600,000 troops. The Korean Peninsula must never become a battle-field. If war breaks out, a large number of servicemen and civilians would be killed both in the South and in the North; the economy would be totally devastated; and foreign capital would fly away. You [President Clinton] might be able to bomb [the North] from the

air, but then the North would immediately start firing artillery shells against major cities in South Korea. An uncountable number of people got killed in the Korean War, but the modern weaponry is much stronger. No war is acceptable. I cannot afford to commit a crime against our history and our people.[50]

Kim's words bespeak a deeply held animosity among Koreans of all political persuasions toward any U.S. actions that would put the ROK's success and well being at risk. Such sentiments, if anything, are more strongly felt today than at the time of the earlier nuclear crisis. Taken to their logical conclusion, they suggest the ROK's readiness to sever alliance ties with the United States and, quite possibly, to reach a separate understanding with leaders in Pyongyang that would seek to inhibit any U.S. use of force.

Barring extraordinary policy changes on the part of North Korea, no available option affords certain success, and all entail varying degrees of uncertainty and risk. Option one would require major concessions and compromises by the United States that it is unprepared to make, and it may not definitively achieve the desired results. Option two would encompass very high political costs; it could also easily fracture the nominal consensus that prevails at present among the United States, China, Russia, Japan, and South Korea. An isolation and containment strategy might also prove very leaky, with Pyongyang's immediate neighbors ultimately unprepared to accept the risks and consequences of imposing the most severe of additional hardships on the North Korean people.[51] Option three would entail the most acute of dangers and risks, with equally problematic prospects for success. Short of the unambiguous display of North Korean nuclear capabilities and other especially egregious actions by Pyongyang (though perhaps not even then), leadership and public sentiment in Seoul would be almost viscerally opposed to either of the latter options.

Indeed, depending on the ultimate fate of the North Korean system, all three strategies could spawn longer-term consequences that might *increase* the risks of future proliferation that they were designed to prevent. Under all three scenarios, an ROK successor state could potentially inherit the residual nuclear capabilities and scientific competence possessed by the DPRK. In addition, we cannot preclude the prospect of a future North-South political understanding that leaves the North's nuclear weapons potential intact. In the event of an as yet undefined political agreement between the two Koreas, the North's nuclear weapons

capabilities might even be papered over or deferred for future consideration. The question would then be whether the leadership of a unified
Korea might decide to retain such capabilities or develop some of its own.

The ROK as Nuclear Inheritor

North Korea's extant nuclear capabilities and its uncertain prospects
for survival as a state create a unique situation with respect to South
Korea's longer-term nuclear intentions. Unlike all the other abstainers
featured in this volume, the ROK would inherit the nuclear infrastructure,
materials, and expertise that a collapsed rival state would leave behind—
or at least assume a temporary custody over these capabilities. Depending
on the size and scale of this nuclear legacy and the circumstances attending the disintegration of the DPRK, there might well be an enormous
temptation on the part of the ROK to retain all or some portions of such
a capability.

Much would also depend on whether the end of North Korea were to
occur amidst major violence and potential armed conflict or if it unfolds
in less convulsive fashion. A more "orderly" DPRK departure from the
international scene would presumably allow for full, early involvement of
the IAEA—or design of a separate multinational arrangement—to
locate, secure, dismantle, and monitor the North's surviving nuclear
holdings. As in the case of Iraq, the post-collapse period would entail
extensive efforts, presumably overseen by the Korean successor state, to
locate the North's WMD assets, including opportunities to interview
those directly associated with the nuclear program. Conversely, a more
abrupt collapse would necessitate rapid actions by South Korean forces,
with or without U.S. support, to secure relevant facilities, including
undeclared sites long suspected of involvement with the nuclear weapons
program. Although the United States and China would be keenly interested in the outcome of this process, it is far from certain that the ROK
would be prepared to permit full international access in this search. This
possibility alone suggests the need for early consultations and understandings among all involved parties and relevant international agencies
over procedures and potential crisis management mechanisms. The
cumulative experiences of other instances of denuclearization, notably in
the former Soviet Union and in South Africa, would be especially pertinent
in this regard.

However, a focus on detailed operational concerns obscures the larger
context of Korea's nuclear future. Would a unified Korean successor state

characterize itself as a satisfied or frustrated middle power? What would be the state of alliance relations with the United States before the final end of the North Korean system? Would prevailing sentiment within the ROK still remain reasonably well disposed toward long-term collaboration with the United States, or would the alliance have been largely supplanted by alternative political and security mechanisms? Would the North and South have achieved substantial economic interdependence before such an event? Would the ROK have been "center stage" in the process leading to the end of the North Korean state, or would the South Korean population perceive itself—rightly or wrongly—as again marginalized and shunted aside by larger powers? Korea's ultimate attitudes toward nuclear weapons could very likely turn on such questions.

If Unification Occurs

Most hypotheses about South Korea's renewed interest in nuclear weapons focus on a volatile combination of vulnerability, historical grievance, economic power, technical proficiency, and national assertiveness. Despite the current growing resentment of American dominance, any renewed interest in nuclear weapons seems likely to emerge fully after unification rather than before it. A future Korean leader might view nuclear weapons development, or retention of the DPRK's nuclear legacy, as the surest means to achieve equivalence with surrounding major powers— and perhaps especially with the United States. Such capabilities would presumably guarantee that Korea would not be victimized or manipulated by outside forces; the ROK would never again be viewed as a shrimp among the whales. As noted previously, however, the ROK's current strategic predicament is only tangentially reminiscent of the 1970s. The one clear parallel is resentment and anger at Korea's fate being controlled by the United States. Successive ROK leaders who otherwise have little in common—Park Chung Hee, Kim Yong Sam, and Kim Dae Jung—have chafed at American diktats when push came to shove. Each in turn was compelled to make concessions and compromise deeply valued goals while still trying to preserve as much strategic autonomy as possible.

Many Koreans characterize their history as an unbroken chain of victimization perpetrated by more powerful international forces to whom they were forced to submit. Unlike the partition of Germany, the twentieth-century division of the Korean peninsula did not derive from aggression directed against neighboring states, but rather from the predatory actions of Japan upon Korea and the subsequent division of the peninsula into American and Soviet zones of control. Koreans frequently speak of the concept of *han*, which one scholar defines as an attitude of "unredeemed resentment."[52] Such anger and frustration have frequently been directed at Japan, but it is also focused on any foreign forces judged responsible for national division. To some Koreans, it is an easy transition from such enmity to a belief that foreign forces will always conspire to keep Korea divided and weak.

It is thus impossible to understate the emotional and psychological magnitude of Korean unification for the leaders and people of the peninsula. As Don Oberdorfer has observed, the Shilla Kingdom maintained continuous, unified control over the peninsula from the consolidation of the kingdom's rule in 668 A.D. until Korea's penetration and subjugation by various imperial powers toward the end of the nineteenth century. In the eyes of the Korean people, the twentieth century thus constituted an aberration and humiliation in Korea's long dynastic history: first the country became a Japanese colony, it was subsequently divided into rival Soviet and American occupation zones, and since 1948 it has existed as competing regimes in the North and South.[53] Regardless of the precise circumstances that might attend unification, the de facto and de jure reconstitution of Korean sovereignty under a single political entity would be a singular event in Asian international politics.

But how would a unified Korean state define its security expectations in relation to its immediate neighbors and toward more distant powers, especially the United States? There is as yet no certain way to anticipate or predict such circumstances. A regional security arrangement that is inclusive and mutually acceptable to all relevant states might well diminish the perceived necessity for large-scale, fully autonomous military capabilities, especially nuclear weapons. As Derek Mitchell has observed:

> A unified Korea would likely have no interest in WMD development or deployment as such an act would likely spur a regional arms race and create tensions with the international community, especially the United States, over nonproliferation. This calculation will ultimately depend on the state of the regional security environment at the time of unification, including the status of Korea's alliance with the United States as well as the confidence in the U.S. nuclear umbrella, Korea's relationship with Russia and China, and whether or not Japan develops nuclear weapons.[54]

However, in the event that the North's nuclear capabilities persist in one form or another before unification, it seems highly unlikely that a "normal" Northeast Asian security order would have emerged in the interim period. A residual or declared North Korean nuclear weapons capability would not be conducive to building collaborative security arrangements in intervening years. Under such conditions, the impulse to seek or continue national advantage through independent strategic capabilities could prove irresistible to a unified Korea, barring domestic transitions across the region that obviated the need for such capabilities.

Threat perception alone, however, would not define the strategic universe of a unified Korea. Korea's standing in a multipolar East Asia—that is, still sandwiched between far more powerful neighbors—could either inhibit or stimulate the country's strategic expectations and needs. For example, if, as seems very likely, the burgeoning accommodation between the ROK and China is further enhanced in coming years, the incentives of a unified Korea to maintain a close but subordinate strategic position with China would almost certainly be maintained and quite possibly be strengthened even further. Devoid of a compelling strategic imperative, a unified Korea armed with nuclear weapons could undermine its relationships with neighboring major powers as well as the United States. The question would be whether a unified Korea would deem nuclear weapons a strategic necessity, without particular regard for American, Chinese, Russian, or Japanese preferences.

Despite the widely held belief in Korea's historical insularity (the "Hermit Kingdom"), Korean traditional statecraft and strategy also demonstrate a capacity to adapt to existing power realities. For example, two concepts existed simultaneously during the Chosun dynasty: *sadae*, literally serving the great, and *kyorin*, neighborly relations. *Sadae* presumed strategic deference to a superior outside power so as to ensure autonomy and security for the Korean state; it applied to Korea's relations with China and its accommodation to a Sinocentric world order. *Kyorin* applied to relations with Japan, with an assumption of equality maintained more at arm's length, thereby connoting a lesser importance attached to relations with Japan as compared to China.[55] Traditional statecraft might not be wholly relevant to present or future scenarios, but it highlights Korea's realistic appreciation of how larger power realities could continue to define its strategic choices.

In the final analysis, Korea's strategic path will derive more from collective national identity than from extrapolations based on prevailing security perceptions. Would the prevalence of *han* persist in Korean culture? How might Koreans reconcile, or even rationalize, perceived historical grievances and frustrations with the actual circumstances of national unification? Is it inevitable that unredeemed resentment find expression through military means, including nuclear weapons? Or might Korea's internal maturation in future years produce an outcome less freighted with memories of past victimization? Such questions cannot be definitively answered. But Seoul's future strategies will be influenced pivotally by ongoing realities and by how Korea's leaders and the mass public perceive and evaluate efforts to address existing security concerns.

For Korea there can be no definitive escape from geography or history. Whether these circumstances are ultimately viewed by the people of Korea as tyranny or opportunity remains to be seen. The question is how geography and history might ultimately shape a unified Korea's longer-term national identity. Despite the seeming appeal of a nuclear capability, it could prove irrelevant or self-defeating to the interests of a unified Korea. Even under unification, it will always be a smaller power surrounded by four major actors, three with significant nuclear arsenals. But the relative power asymmetries would be altered under conditions of unification. If Korea were to unify at present, the successor state would have a population of more than 65 million people and an imposingly large military force: at prevailing active force levels, the combined capabilities of the ROK and DPRK would exceed the manpower levels of all global military establishments save those of China.[56] Such military strength would clearly be disproportionate to the needs of a unified Korean state, but it highlights the country's latent power potential.

The ultimate disappearance of a hardened, ideologically committed adversary in the North would be an enormous vindication for the ROK and for the very different path it has followed in pursuit of national development and security. Might the cessation of national division, with final victory belonging to the Korean state that had decided to forego pursuit of nuclear weapons, convince Korea's citizens that such weapons afford neither security nor international standing? Or might the Korean people, emboldened by the end of more than a century of national division and humiliation, see nuclear weapons as essential to the nation's standing and security in a still-hostile world? The answers to these questions will reveal much about Korea's longer-term strategic destiny and will be equally pivotal in defining regional security as a whole.

Notes

1. For a fuller exploration, see Scott D. Sagan, "Rethinking the Causes of Nuclear Proliferation: Three Models in Search of a Bomb," in Victor A. Utgoff, ed., *The Coming Crisis: Nuclear Proliferation, U.S. Interests, and World Order* (MIT Press, 2000), pp. 17–50.

2. Richard K. Betts, "Universal Deterrence or Conceptual Collapse? Liberal Pessimism and Utopian Realism," in Victor A. Utgoff, ed., *The Coming Crisis: Nuclear Proliferation, U.S. Interests, and World Order* (MIT Press, 2000), p. 57.

3. For a somewhat dated, but still useful, examination of "Korea, Inc.," see Jung-en Woo, *Race to the Swift: State and Finance in Korean Industrialization* (Columbia University Press, 1991). See also Alice Amsden, *Asia's Next Giant: South Korea and Late Industrialization* (Oxford University Press, 1989).

4. "Korea's Nuclear Strategy," *Westinghouse World View*, August 2002, p. 8.

5. For a detailed discussion of the views of ROK nuclear scientists, see Foreign Broadcast Information Service (FBIS), "South Korea's Emerging Nuclear Potential," FBIS Special Memorandum 96-10002 (Washington, February 22, 1996), especially pp. 1–8.

6. World Nuclear Association, "Nuclear Power in South Korea," March 2004 (www.world-nuclear.org/info/info.htm).

7. World Nuclear Association, "World Nuclear Power Reactors 2001–2002 and Uranium Requirements," December 2002 (www.world-nuclear.org/info /info.htm).

8. Uranium Information Center, "Nuclear Power in South Korea," Briefing Paper 81 (Melbourne, November 2003).

9. For example, writing in 1983, Ha stated that "technological barriers to nuclear proliferation in Korea either already have been or soon will be overcome." Young-sun Ha, *Nuclear Proliferation, World Order and Korea* (Seoul National University, 1983), p. 145. A decade later, another assessment concluded that "in extreme circumstances, that option could be exercised by crash development of a crude nuclear device in about nine months." See Peter Hayes, "The Republic of Korea and the Nuclear Issue," in Andrew Mack, ed., *Asian Flashpoint: Security and the Korean Peninsula* (Canberra: Allen and Unwin, 1993), p. 53.

10. "Informal Remarks in Guam with Newsmen," July 25, 1969, *Presidential Papers of the United States: Richard M. Nixon, 1969* (Government Printing Office [GPO], 1971), p. 549.

11. See the annual issues of the International Institute for Strategic Studies, *The Military Balance*, from this period.

12. For a comprehensive reconstruction of the U.S.-China negotiating record, see Alan Romberg, *Rein In at the Brink of the Precipice: American Policy toward Taiwan and U.S.-PRC Relations* (Washington: Henry L. Stimson Center, 2003).

13. House Committee on International Relations, *Investigations of Korean-American Relations*, report of the Subcommittee on International Organizations, 95 Cong., 2 sess. (GPO, 1978), p. 79. This document is sometimes referred to as the Fraser Report, after the subcommittee's chairman, Representative Donald Fraser.

14. Ibid., p. 80. For the fullest treatment of this subject, see Sung Gul Hong, "The Search for Deterrence: Park's Nuclear Option in the 1970s," unpublished manuscript provided to the authors. See also Joseph A. Yager, "The Republic of Korea," in Joseph A. Yager, ed., *Nonproliferation and U.S. Foreign Policy* (Brookings, 1980), pp. 47–65; Mitchell Reiss, *Without the Bomb: The Politics of Nuclear Nonproliferation* (Columbia University Press, 1988), pp. 78–108; and Don Oberdorfer, *The Two Koreas—A Contemporary History*, revised and updated version (Basic Books, 2002), pp. 68–74.

15. Hong, "Search for Deterrence," p. 9. A 1975 U.S. government interagency study concluded that the ROK "could develop [a] limited nuclear weapons and missile capability within ten year time frame." National Security Council, "ROK Weapons Plans," memorandum to embassy, Seoul, March 3, 1975 (declassified May 16, 1997).

16. See the remarks of ROK National Assemblyman Kang Chong-sung in relation to an ongoing parliamentary investigation of the ADD, in *Hangkuk Kyongje Sinmun*, October 6, 1995, as cited in FBIS, "Emerging Nuclear Potential," p. 10.

17. Interview with former U.S. government official, Washington, December 2002. According to a knowledgeable American official, South Korea never anticipated that the United States would discover its nuclear program; it had intended to announce its nuclear weapons status to Washington as a fait accompli. Interview with former U.S. government official, Washington, January 2003.

18. See Robert Gillette, "U.S. Squelched Apparent S. Korea A-Bomb Drive," *Los Angeles Times*, November 4, 1978, p. 1. This threat included the termination of U.S. loans and grants that subsidized South Korea's civilian nuclear energy development, including the training of South Korean engineers and technicians.

19. "ROK Nuclear Reprocessing," telegram from Embassy Seoul to the Secretary of State, December 10, 1975, MLF MR case no. 96-146, document no. 53, cited in Hong, "Search for Deterrence," p. 17.

20. Hong, "Search for Deterrence," pp. 22–23.

21. See the remarks of Representative Kang Chong-sung, as cited in FBIS, "Emerging Nuclear Potential," p. 10.

22. Interview with former U.S. government official, Washington, January 2003.

23. Oberdorfer, *The Two Koreas*, p. 13.

24. Ibid., pp. 15, 23–24.

25. "American Forces in South Korea—The End of an Era?" *Strategic Comments*, vol. 9, no. 5 (July 2003), p. 1.

26. The most succinct example of coupling was a colloquy between Sir Henry Wilson and Marshal Ferdinand Foch, as recounted by Barbara W. Tuchman. Wilson: "What is the smallest British military force that would be of any practical assistance to you?" Foch: "A single British soldier—and we will see to it that he is killed." Barbara Tuchman, *The Guns of August* (Macmillan, 1979 ed.), p. 68.

27. These terms were coined by Glenn Snyder, "The Security Dilemma in Alliance Politics," *World Politics*, vol. 36, no. 4 (July 1984), pp. 461–95. See also Michael Mandelbaum, *The Nuclear Revolution: International Politics Before and After Hiroshima* (Cambridge University Press, 1981), pp. 147–75.

28. Derek Mitchell is undertaking a fuller examination of changing South Korean attitudes toward the U.S.-ROK alliance in a project at the Center for Strategic and International Studies.

29. James Marshall, "South Koreans See Two Faces of America," Office of Research Opinion Analysis (Department of State, October 17, 2002), p. 2.

30. Kim is quoted in Anthony Faiola, "What Do They Want in South Korea? Unification!" *Washington Post*, September 8, 2003, p. A1.

31. See Kurt M. Campbell and Mitchell B. Reiss, "Korean Changes, Asian Challenges and the U.S. Role," *Survival*, vol. 43, no. 1 (Spring 2001), pp. 53–69.

32. According to one Korean analyst, the sunshine policy undermined the twin pillars of Koran society: anticommunism and a pro-U.S. foreign policy. Stephen Kim, "Korea," in *Proliferation Challenges after Iraq* (Washington: Woodrow Wilson International Center for Scholars, December 2003), pp. 6–9.

33. See, for example, Chaiki Song, "A Decade of Economic Crisis in North Korea: Impacts on the Military," KIDA Paper 3 (Seoul: Korea Institute for Defense Analysis, October 2003). Song estimates that the North Korean economy shrunk on average by 4.5 percent between 1990 and 2002, with the overall level of economic production now at 45 percent of the 1990 baseline. The downturn in the military economy has been somewhat less (64 percent of the precrisis level), with military spending declining to two-thirds of its previous level. Song sees an "overall decline" in North Korean ground forces, with naval and air force capabilities remaining "stagnant." He concludes that the accelerated military buildup of the latter half of the 1980s has slowed appreciably. However, he acknowledges continued increases in the North's production of long-range and self-propelled artillery, multiple-rocket launchers, and ballistic missiles, underscoring the DPRK's growing reliance on asymmetric military capabilities rather than ones premised on major conventional assaults akin to those undertaken during the Korean War. This shift in North Korean strategy (including the expectation of severe damage to the ROK's industrial infrastructure) has presumably contributed to the increasing wariness in the ROK of any consideration of coercive options against the North.

34. This consanguinity sentiment surfaced in South Korea in the past few years in the form of a runaway bestseller, *The Rose of Sharon Has Blossomed*, in

which North Korea shares its nuclear weapons with the ROK to defeat the Japanese. The book was subsequently made into a movie and an opera.

35. These attitudes bear comparison with widely held Western European views of the Soviet Union voiced during the 1980s. On this issue, consult Josef Joffe, *The Limited Partnership: Europe, the United States, and the Burdens of Alliance* (Cambridge, Mass.: Ballinger Publishing Company, 1987).

36. Speech of President Roh Moo Hyun on Armed Forces Day, Seoul, Ch'ongwadae, Foreign Broadcast Information Service, KPP20031001000067, text in English, October 1, 2003.

37. A 1995 survey of 1,787 active duty military personnel reported that 49 percent of the officers believed that South Korea needed to develop the scientific capability to build nuclear weapons but should refrain from manufacturing them, and that 47.5 percent believed that the ROK "needs to make nuclear weapons in consideration of the country's history." Only 1.3 percent of those surveyed believed that U.S. nuclear guarantees obviated an independent deterrent, and 2.2 percent voiced no opinion. The survey, "A Study of the South Korean Military in the 21st Century," was reported in the *Sisa Journal*, October 19, 1995, as discussed in FBIS, "Emerging Nuclear Potential," pp. 11–12. We are unaware of any comparable survey of serving officers undertaken since that time, so it is impossible to offer definitive judgments about whether equivalent attitudes persist at present. The absence of any serious public discussion of this highly sensitive issue in recent years very likely attests to the declining political role of the uniformed military, as compared to its more prominent voice in setting national security policy in previous decades. It may also reflect a shift in attitude among serving officers, with lesser proportions perceiving the need for explicit pursuit of a nuclear weapons program, though the desire to retain the potential for such a program may well persist, even if it is unfulfilled at present.

38. Jonathan D. Pollack, "The Changing Political-Military Environment: Northeast Asia," in Zalmay Khalilzad and others, *The United States and Asia— Toward a New U.S. Strategy and Force Posture* (Santa Monica, Calif.: RAND Corporation, MR-1315-AF, 2001), pp. 123–24.

39. "South Korea to Deploy Longer-Range Missiles This Month," *Yonhap News Agency*, November 3, 2003.

40. Christine P. Brown, "Korea's Trade: Increasingly Looking to Asia," *Korea Insight*, vol. 5, no. 11 (November 2003), p. 1; James Brooke, "China 'Looming Large' in South Korea as Biggest Player, Replacing the U.S.," *New York Times*, January 3, 2003, p. 10.

41. Pollack, "The Changing Political-Military Environment," p. 122.

42. Marshall, "Two Faces of America," p. 8. For comparable findings in an elite opinion survey, see William Watts, *Next Generation Leaders in the Republic of Korea: Opinion Survey Report and Analysis* (Washington: Potomac Associates, February 2002).

43. Jae Ho Chung, "South Korea between Eagle and Dragon," *Asian Survey*, vol. 41, no. 5 (September-October 2001), p. 784.

44. For more detailed assessments, see Jonathan D. Pollack, "The United States, North Korea, and the End of the Agreed Framework," *Naval War College Review*, vol. 56, no. 3 (Summer 2003), pp. 11–49; and International Crisis Group, *North Korea: A Phased Negotiation Strategy*, Asia Report No. 61 (Washington/Brussels, August 1, 2003).

45. Central Intelligence Agency, "Responses to the Questions for the Record Regarding the 11 February 2003 DCI Worldwide Threat Briefing," submitted to the Senate Select Committee on Intelligence, August 18, 2003, 108 Cong. 1 sess. See posting at www.fas.org/irp/congress/2003_hr/021103qfr-cia.pdf [February 2004], p. 144. Emphasis added.

46. Vice Admiral L. E. Jacoby, Director, Defense Intelligence Agency, "Worldwide Threat Hearing 11 February 2003," response to questions from Senate Select Committee on Intelligence, June 30, 2003, 108 Cong. 1 sess. See posting at www.fas.org/irp/congress/2003_hr/021103qfr-dia.pdf [February 2004], p. 209.

47. The Proliferation Security Initiative, or PSI, was first proposed by President Bush in a speech in Warsaw in May 2003. The PSI is a multilateral effort to intercept any shipments of contraband materials and technologies (with particular attention to WMD materials and missile equipment and technologies) via air, land, and sea. See, in particular, House International Relations Committee, "U.S. Efforts to Stop the Spread of Weapons of Mass Destruction," testimony of John R. Bolton, Under Secretary for Arms Control and International Security, June 4, 2003, 108 Cong. 1 sess., and Department of State, "Proliferation Security Initiative: Statement of Interdiction Principles, fact sheet (September 3, 2003).

48. White House, *The National Security Strategy of the United States of America* (September 2002), and *National Strategy to Combat Weapons of Mass Destruction* (December 2002).

49. Sung Deuk Hahm, ed., *Gim Yeong Sam Jeongbu-ui Seonggong-gwa Silpae* (The Kim Young Sam Government: Its Success and Failure) (Seoul: Nanam, 2001), p. 37, as cited by Narushige Michishita, "North Korea's 'First' Nuclear Crisis," *Journal of Strategic Studies*, vol. 26, no. 4 (December 2003), p. 58.

50. Kim Young Sam, *Gim Yeong Sam Daetongryeong Hoegrog* (President Kim Young Sam's Memoirs) (Seoul: Joseon Ilbosa, 2001), pp. 315–16, as cited in Michishita, "'First' Nuclear Crisis," p. 58.

51. International Crisis Group, *North Korea: A Phased Negotiation Strategy*, pp. 25–26.

52. Victor Cha, "Japan's Grand Strategy on the Korean Peninsula: Optimistic Realism," in Henry D. Sokolski, ed., *Planning for a Peaceful Korea* (Carlisle, Pa.: U.S. Army War College, Strategic Studies Institute, February 2001), pp. 229–32. As characterized by Gary Rector, a writer and editor who is among the few U.S. citizens to become a naturalized ROK citizen, "*Han* is anger and resentment that

builds up, and at the same time a feeling of frustration or a feeling of desires that are unfulfilled. So resentment, frustration, and longing are lumped together." Philip Gourevitch further elaborates its meaning, based on discussions with a cross-section of Koreans from north and south: "[*Han* has] a cumulative nature, the steady accretion of a pattern of lesser injuries into one large and abiding sense of woundedness. Humiliation is a key ingredient of *han* . . . [which combines] the self-mockery of the self-loving who are all too aware of their weakness. It is touted as a keenly Korean emotion because it recognizes the contradictions of the Korean experience: traditionally, the intense nationalism and yearning for purity, so close to German ideas of *volk*, coupled with an overwhelming experience of victimhood, and for the past fifty years, the bitter reality of national division. *Han* at its tenderest is melancholic and wistful, and in its darker forms militant and vengeful; in either case it is freighted with dissatisfaction and the temptation of extremism." Philip Gourevitch, "Letter from Korea—Alone in the Dark," *New Yorker*, September 8, 2003, p. 74.

53. Oberdorfer, *The Two Koreas*, pp. 3–5.

54. Derek J. Mitchell, "A Blueprint for U.S. Policy toward a Unified Korea," *Washington Quarterly*, vol. 26, no. 1 (Winter 2002–03), p. 126.

55. Our thanks to Steven Park for highlighting these distinctions. For further discussion, see James B. Palais, *Politics and Policy in Traditional Korea* (Harvard University Press, 1975), and Andre Schmid, *Korea between Empires, 1895–1919* (Columbia University Press, 2002).

56. According to the International Institute for Strategic Studies (IISS), the current active duty levels of various military forces are as follows: China, 2,250,000; the United States, 1,427,000; India, 1,325,000; North Korea, 1,082,000; Russia, 960,600; and South Korea, 686,000. The aggregate number for both Koreas would therefore be 1,768,000. IISS, *The Military Balance, 2003–2004* (London, October 2003), pp. 18, 89, 136, 152, 160, 161.

CHAPTER 11

Taiwan's Hsin Chu Program: Deterrence, Abandonment, and Honor

DEREK J. MITCHELL

Faced with strong pressure from the United States and the International Atomic Energy Agency (IAEA) throughout the 1970s and 1980s, Taiwan finally renounced its nuclear program in 1988.[1] No indications exist today that Taiwan authorities are revisiting this decision.

Among nations that have decided to reverse their decision to develop nuclear weapons, however, Taiwan may be unique in facing only one clear and ever-present external threat: that from mainland China, across the Taiwan Strait. The People's Republic of China (PRC) and Taiwan remain in a tense stalemate left over from the Chinese civil war, which continued (as a cold war) even after the communist party's victory on the mainland in 1949 and the Nationalist government's ensuing escape to this offshore island. Taiwan's current assessment of its security environment is based solely on the threat from its massive neighbor 100 miles west across the Taiwan Strait.[2]

A dispute over sovereignty persists, ostensibly over who rules China, but increasingly over the sovereign identity of Taiwan itself. In many ways, the divide between the two sides is widening with time. As the generation that fled the mainland passes away, fewer and fewer people on

The author would like to thank Carola McGiffert, Andy Peterson, and Kristine Schenck for their assistance in the drafting of this chapter.

Taiwan feel a personal connection to the mainland, which, coupled with the development of democracy and liberalization of Taiwanese society over the past fifteen years, has led to growing assertions of Taiwan nationalism separate from China.

China is quite aware of this phenomenon, exacerbated by the rise to power in Taiwan of a political party whose charter and history are dedicated to Taiwan's independence. China contends its policy remains one of "peaceful reunification" under a "one country, two systems" formula (like that undertaken with Hong Kong). However, it continues to assert its right to use force to resolve this impasse—to bring this "renegade province" back to the "motherland"—and has engaged in a systematic military buildup to do so through deployment of ballistic and cruise missiles across the strait and procurement of advanced naval and air capabilities (largely from Russia).

Indeed, the Taiwan issue is enormously sensitive to the Chinese. China's history is dominated by the theme of unity and division, and its culture traditionally has equated national power and dignity with national unity. Whether through systematic political indoctrination or cultural tradition, the notion of recovering Taiwan to fulfill China's national honor and dignity is today deeply ingrained in the psyche of even the most progressive Chinese citizen. Under such circumstances, no Chinese leader can be perceived as weak on Taiwan, let alone "lose" Taiwan, and survive politically.

Taiwan's consideration of its security, including the development of nuclear weapons, occurs within this single, fundamental context of sovereignty—and vulnerability—in relation to its Chinese rival across the Taiwan Strait. A corollary theme that runs through the island's security perceptions has been a fear of abandonment, particularly by the United States, and the necessity of insurance should the world turn its back on the island.

When Taiwan formally launched its nuclear program in the 1960s, the United States, United Nations, and most of the leading countries of the world recognized the island's government as the legitimate representative of China. The United States was bound by a formal defense treaty to protect Taiwan and provided a nuclear umbrella over the island to deter PRC aggression. The PRC, on the cusp of its devastating Cultural Revolution and at odds with the Soviet Union, was largely an international outcast.

Many in Taiwan understood nonetheless the dangers of being exclusively reliant on one country's protection and on the good will of an international system that, for ideological reasons, favored an island of 20 million people over a nation of 1 billion. In fact, the PRC's 1964 nuclear test reminded the small island of its keen vulnerability and precarious situation as the mainland gained in military strength and strategic importance. Taiwan recognized that the world could not ignore a nuclear-armed People's Republic of China forever, regardless of sentiment or ideology, and that it could not rely on the international community indefinitely for political or other support.

Indeed, Taiwan's insecurities were borne out by developments in the 1970s. In 1971 the United Nations recognized the PRC as the legitimate sovereign of China and expelled the Nationalist regime on Taiwan from its seat. The shock of President Nixon's 1972 visit to Beijing and growing U.S.-PRC strategic rapprochement further alarmed Taiwan. Finally, Taiwan viewed the sudden normalization of U.S.-PRC relations in 1979 as a deep betrayal, proving to many in Taiwan that the United States could not be entirely trusted. The 1982 Sino-U.S. Communiqué that followed shortly thereafter, which ostensibly committed the United States to reduce its arms sales to Taiwan over time, only reaffirmed Taiwan's sense of insecurity and discomfort with the direction of U.S. policy and commitment toward the security of the island.

Successive U.S. administrations, from Johnson to Reagan, worried about Taiwan's nuclear ambitions and monitored the situation closely in partnership with the IAEA. The United States recognized the tense peace that reigned over the Taiwan Strait, and no U.S. administration, regardless of its support for Taiwan, reveled in the prospect of these tensions escalating into a nuclear standoff. By the time of Jimmy Carter's administration, a highly suspicious program—one that involved nuclear research reactors that conducted little research, doctored fuel rods, discrepancies in declared and IAEA-inspected spent fuel rods, and multiple attempts to acquire plutonium reprocessing facilities—had been revealed and was being shut down. Nonetheless, in the late 1980s, a defector's revelation of another clandestine nuclear program demonstrated the continued determination of Taiwan (or at least its leader, Chiang Ching-kuo) to fulfill its nuclear ambition. This time, under *continued* pressure from Washington, the island nation more conclusively dismantled its program.

Information about the origins and development of Taiwan's nuclear program during this period remains murky. Aside from the odd memoir, current and former Taiwan officials, even today, are reluctant to discuss the nature of the program and continue to treat it as a sensitive, if not embarrassing, topic of conversation. They reassure questioners that Taiwan's nuclear ambitions and program are a thing of the past, that the human and physical infrastructure for such a program are today greatly diminished, if not dismantled.

However, given its history, some have called Taiwan a "virtual proliferant," a nation that could quickly restart its nuclear program if it decided to do so.[3] If this assessment is valid, it leads to the following questions: how viable, technically and politically, is such an option; how quickly could Taiwan reconstitute its nuclear weapons program; and under what circumstances would Taiwan make such a fateful political decision? An examination of the history of Taiwan's aborted nuclear programs may provide some clues to the answers.

History of Taiwan's Nuclear Program

Taiwan opened its first nuclear reactor at National Tsinghua University in 1956.[4] However, it is generally considered that Taiwan did not launch a full-scale nuclear program until after 1964, in reaction to the PRC's first nuclear test. Taiwan feared nuclear intimidation, if not outright attack, by the mainland and also saw its international prestige decline. Indeed, a nuclear PRC may have challenged the government on Taiwan where it hurt the most: on the question of who were the keepers of China's historical great-power status.

Taiwanese authorities urged the United States to respond to the Chinese program by bombing PRC nuclear installations. When the Johnson administration refused and conditions across the strait worsened, Taiwan actively began to consider an indigenous nuclear program—reportedly in the form of a $140 million proposal from the defense ministry's Chungshan Institute of Science and Technology in 1967.[5]

The decision to pursue a nuclear weapons program appears to have been made by only a handful of senior advisers around then president Chiang Kai-shek, most notably his son Chiang Ching-kuo, who was then the director of the Science Development Advisory Committee but would later become minister of defense and ultimately succeed his father as president. Whether Chiang Kai-shek himself authorized Taiwan's nuclear weapons program or, as some suggest, Chiang Ching-kuo acted without his father's knowledge is still subject to debate.[6] Regardless, Taiwan's one-party, authoritarian government facilitated such a sensitive and fateful decision. No independent media existed, and security decisions were reserved for a tight clique on an island that was governed under martial law. It was therefore relatively easy to keep secret a nascent nuclear weapons program, although evidence and security leaks seeped out of the system over time.

Taiwan's nuclear weapons program was dubbed the "Hsin Chu" Project.[7] The program was placed under the authority of the Institute of Nuclear Energy Research (INER) and the Chungshan Institute, the military research and development center that had developed the original proposal. The project consisted primarily of procuring and operating a heavy-water reactor, a heavy-water production plant, a reprocessing research lab, and a plutonium separation plant.

As usual with clandestine nuclear weapons projects, the program began quietly through legal means in keeping with international law. The General Electric Corporation built Taiwan's first nuclear power plant, and Taiwan shopped around for additional nuclear materials, ostensibly for research purposes.[8] Germany finally agreed, with U.S. acquiescence, to sell Taiwan a nuclear reactor in 1967. Over the course of the next decade, INER would purchase nuclear equipment, supplies, and expertise not only from the United States and Germany but also from Canada, France, South Africa, and other nations. An early overture to Israel turned up empty, although what Taiwan sought from Tel Aviv at the time is uncertain.[9] Meanwhile, as it was subsequently learned, U.S.-supplied plutonium intended for civilian research ultimately was diverted to Taiwan's clandestine weapons program.

In 1968 Taiwan (as the Republic of China) joined the Non-Proliferation Treaty. The IAEA immediately began negotiating a safeguards agreement to treat the "Republic of China" explicitly as a non-nuclear weapons state. These discussions were short-circuited in 1971 when the United Nations, and thus the IAEA, transferred its official recognition to the PRC. Although some creative individuals within the Taiwan establishment later would suggest that international acceptance of the PRC as a nuclear weapons state allowed Taiwan to assume similar status under the "One China" concept, the United States, Taiwan, and the IAEA ultimately agreed in 1971 that an existing trilateral nuclear agreement dating from the late 1950s—the Nuclear Cooperation Agreement—would form the basis in the future for safeguards on Taiwan's nuclear program. Under the agreement, any nuclear materials that Taiwan acquired would be treated as if they came from the United States and thus be subject to restrictions in their application under U.S. law. The United States therefore became the ultimate legal guarantor of Taiwan's non-nuclear status—facilitated by IAEA inspections.[10]

At home, in an effort to shield its nuclear ambitions, Taiwan placed its nuclear program under the authority of a civilian agency, the Atomic Energy Council. Nonetheless, a senior military officer responsible for overseeing the nuclear weapons program at the Chungshan Institute served concurrently on the board of the Atomic Energy Council, a suspicious overlap that ensured military oversight of nuclear energy affairs.[11]

The same officer later assumed leadership of INER as that institute came under suspicion during the 1970s. INER operated adjacent to the Chungshan Institute, and observers noted that nary a fence divided the two institutes. Traffic flowed constantly and suspiciously between them.[12] In 1969 INER purchased from Canada a small heavy-water research reactor, which became operational in 1973, and procured equipment for facilities to produce, reprocess, and experiment with uranium and plutonium. The institute developed a fuel fabrication plant and secured approximately 100 metric tons of natural uranium from South Africa, much more than was necessary to serve the research reactor. Over time, U.S. officials came to recognize that INER served primarily to facilitate Taiwan's procurement of elements to produce plutonium.[13]

Some confusion remains over what reprocessing capacity Taiwan had acquired during this period. The United States turned down a Taiwan request for a relatively large reprocessing facility in 1969. A similar French deal also failed, but a French company may have provided a relatively small facility.[14] Strong U.S. opposition curbed German provision of equipment and nuclear materials for a reprocessing plant in 1972–73.[15] However, INER developed other smaller reprocessing facilities: one with the help of a Norwegian scientist and another as part of its "hot laboratory" adjacent to the research reactor.

Throughout the decade, the United States monitored Taiwan's nuclear program and put increasing pressure on the Taiwanese government to renounce any nuclear ambitions or risk losing U.S. support for its nuclear power program. Initial IAEA inspections were faulty at best, with poor equipment and underperforming inspectors; nonetheless, by the middle of the decade, the agency determined that INER's activities were suspicious enough to require closer examination. The U.S. embassy in Taipei reported in 1973 that "the lack of a research program [for the research reactor] has caused considerable comment among Chinese and foreigners" and noted that the "hot lab" under construction was apparently meant to

serve as a pilot reprocessing facility to produce small quantities of plutonium each year (later clarified to be about 300 grams).[16] The CIA concluded by 1974 that Taiwan was apparently working toward a nuclear
weapons capability and would be capable of producing a nuclear weapon
within approximately five years.[17]

Suspicions continued into early 1976 after a *Washington Post* report
suggested that ten fuel rods with about 500 grams of plutonium were
unaccounted for. IAEA inspectors also discovered a laboratory for handling plutonium fuel and a furnace for producing plutonium metal, a
form of plutonium virtually never used in civilian programs. The laboratory operated with U.S.-supplied plutonium, and thus the agency insisted
that the facility undergo regular inspection.

In the middle of the year, the IAEA conducted a baseline assessment of
Taiwan's nuclear material, upgraded its surveillance system, and measured
spent fuel to check against Taiwan's declarations to ensure none had
been diverted. The agency found discrepancies but could not determine for
certain whether Taiwan had diverted fuel rods for reprocessing. Meanwhile, the *Washington Post* reported soon afterward that U.S. intelligence detected signs of secret reprocessing, although U.S. officials
subsequently denied this.[18] Regardless, the signs were ominous concerning Taiwan's intentions, and the United States began to press Taiwan
hard to resolve the matter conclusively.

In September 1976, new Taiwan president Chiang Ching-kuo promised
through a diplomatic note that Taiwan would not acquire its own reprocessing facilities or engage in any activities related to reprocessing. The
United States responded with thinly veiled threats that to do otherwise
would damage U.S. nuclear cooperation at a time when U.S. uranium
was essential to the function of Taiwan's expanding number of nuclear
power plants.[19]

Nonetheless, subsequent revelations raised concerns even further.
These discoveries included doctored fuel rods for potential use in smaller
reprocessing facilities and a secret gate obscured within a spent fuel pond
through which fuel rods could surreptitiously be diverted. At this point,
an outraged United States insisted that Taiwan shut down its research
reactor and allow scientists from Los Alamos to conduct a thorough
study of fuel rods in its core. The study validated the declared irradiation
history of fuel rods in the reactor core, establishing a baseline to protect
against future diversions, but it did not settle questions about past diversions. In 1977 the United States insisted that Taiwan dismantle its hot lab

and most of its reprocessing facilities (some were converted to other purposes) and return U.S.-supplied plutonium. Such requirements seemed to take care of international concerns at the time over Taiwan's nuclear program.[20]

The United States also insisted on monitoring more closely INER's research reactor. This involved both converting the reactor so that it would produce much less plutonium in spent fuel and transferring the fuel out of the island. Beginning in 1985 and over the next several years, about eighty kilograms of such plutonium was returned to the United States under this agreement. Another two kilograms reportedly remain in Taiwan under tight safeguards.[21]

Taiwan Tries Again: 1987–88

Despite successfully derailing Taiwan's nuclear weapons program in the mid-1970s, the United States and the IAEA remained wary of its nuclear intentions under President Chiang Ching-kuo. Among President Jimmy Carter's foremost concerns upon recognition of the PRC and termination of defense commitments to Taiwan in 1979 was how to deter Taipei from developing nuclear weapons as a substitute for U.S. defense support. Indeed, in 1987, shortly before Chiang's death, INER suddenly and quietly began building a multiple hot cell facility in violation of its 1976 commitments. The United States discovered it in 1988 after receiving a tip from a Taiwanese defector. Although no plutonium had yet been separated at the facility, U.S. intelligence officials estimated that Taiwan was within a year or two of developing a nuclear bomb.

The defector, Colonel Chang Hsien-yi, was a U.S. informant who had served as INER's deputy director and worked on Taiwan's secret nuclear program. In 1987 Colonel Chang smuggled to the United States classified documents that extensively detailed Taiwan's plans to produce a nuclear bomb.[22] Confronted with U.S. spy satellite data and under intense pressure from the United States, Taiwan agreed to terms that were designed to end conclusively and verifiably its nuclear weapons program, including a written guarantee from new president Lee Teng-hui to President Reagan that Taiwan would end its nuclear program and close the research reactor.[23] The forty-megawatt research reactor was shut down for conversion into a light-water reactor that was more proliferation resistant. The United States suspended shipments of heavy water, and Taiwan subsequently returned its remaining heavy water to the U.S., thereby disabling the reactor. Taiwan also agreed to a ban on any research that could be applicable to weapons development. Overall, Taiwan's 1988 commitment to the United States went beyond those obligations mandated by the Nuclear Non-Proliferation Treaty.

Since 1988 Taiwan's official position has been that it will not apply its scientific know-how to build nuclear weapons. This position was reiterated by then defense minister Tang Fei to the media on January 5, 2000, when he stated that the "ROC government would never develop nuclear arms."[24] Tang claimed Taiwan lacked the ability to produce nuclear weapons, and the country's legislators reinforced that position, claiming that as Taiwan had halted all research work on nuclear weapons, it did not have the technical skills necessary to produce a weapon from nuclear material.[25] However, some observers are still not convinced.

Taiwan's Nuclear Program: Then and Now

The story of Taiwan's nuclear capabilities today is mixed. Some argue persuasively that Taiwan has dismantled its weapons facilities irrevocably, while other experts claim that if Taiwan changed its mind and decided again to develop nuclear weapons, it could do so quickly, perhaps within a year or two.

When Taiwan agreed to fully dismantle its nuclear weapons program almost a quarter of a century after it was launched, it was almost entirely the result of U.S. pressure, as well as recognition that the risks of such a program—particularly to its relationship with the United States—would outweigh the rewards. If the United States had not intervened, could Taiwan have developed a nuclear weapons capability during this time?

There is general consensus that Taiwan did not possess much separated plutonium, although its scientists were well trained in how to turn plutonium into metal, as well as in explosive technology. A former senior defense official, Hau Pei-tsun, asserted in his autobiography that Taiwan had achieved a controlled nuclear test reaction by the late 1980s, a critical step in the production of nuclear weapons.[26] It would have taken a few more years and most likely more imports of nuclear technology and materials, but Taiwan could have become a full-fledged nuclear power if allowed to proceed.

That said, despite its clear nuclear weapons ambitions and capabilities of the past, Taiwan has several technical and practical obstacles to quickly becoming a nuclear power today. First, according to experts,

Taiwan is in far worse shape today in terms of materials and processing capability than it was fifteen years ago when it renounced its nuclear program and shut down its largest research reactor and its reprocessing facilities. The research reactor is now reported by outside sources to be entirely clean, a hollow shell disassembled in the presence of U.S. and IAEA observers, with key components buried and only the fuel pond—and spent fuel—remaining inside under keen IAEA observation. All Taiwan power reactors are dutifully inspected quarterly. An informed U.S. source confirms that Taiwan possesses less than two kilograms of plutonium and less than two tons of uranium, leftovers from 1988 that are closely monitored by the United States and the IAEA. The island today lacks uranium enrichment or spent fuel reprocessing capabilities. Its facility for handling plutonium has been dismantled. Observers confirm that INER itself is out of the fuel cycle business, does not do nuclear material handling, has ended its nuclear research programs and light-water reactor fuel development work, and focuses today instead on the job of developing alternative energy sources.

Second, the scientists who led Taiwan's nuclear program have retired or passed away, reportedly including the two most capable nuclear engineers of their day. While technical know-how has assuredly been preserved for a new generation of Chungshan Institute scientists and technicians, they have not had the opportunity to engage in practical training in the field. Indeed, Taiwan observers note that young engineers are not interested in pursuing such work, viewing it as irrelevant and not "career-enhancing."[27] Taiwan scientists claim that a whole new generation of nuclear scientists would need to be "nourished," requiring a substantial investment of money and time.[28] U.S. monitors note that technicians have not been maintaining their expertise in the relevant areas of nuclear physics, including solvent extraction chemistry, uranium fuel fabrication and reprocessing, uranium purification, and related aspects of chemical engineering, for example. Were technicians indeed pursuing such training, these monitors contend, it would be detectable.

Furthermore, over the past decade, Taiwan's nuclear program became the first "substantial" (defined as involving big power reactors) program to become subject to the additional protocol to the IAEA Safeguards Agreement instituted after the Iraq war. Beginning in 1996, the protocol expanded the range of items subject to IAEA inspection from "nuclear material" to "nuclear-related activity," a much broader scope that severely restricts a nation's ability to cheat.

Indeed, inspectors report that they have had no major issues concerning the safeguard regime on Taiwan. At the same time, the U.S. State Department and Taiwan participate in the "Joint Standing Committee on Civil Nuclear Cooperation," a confidence-building measure that promotes health and safety in civilian nuclear use and includes elements that ensure the island meets its nuclear obligations stemming from integration of U.S. nuclear components. In addition, the United States continues to enjoy consent rights to all nuclear material in Taiwan under the 1950s-era Nuclear Cooperation Agreement.

Nonetheless, the most important ingredient of a nuclear weapons program is political will. Sources in Taiwan have asserted that if the political will were there, "existing weapons-grade material could be weaponized in three to four months. If Taiwan were abandoned by the United States . . . it would take no more than a year to build a reprocessing plant for the plutonium that might be burned at a fast rate in its civilian nuclear power reactors."[29] The country still maintains a hot cell facility, and in support of a highly enriched uranium program—which would be relatively difficult to detect and highly concealable, particularly given Taiwan's extensive mountain facilities—Taiwan has the capability to wind fibers, has produced rare-earth magnets, and maintains critical laser capabilities that could be applied to the effort. It is uncertain whether Taiwan has centrifuge enrichment capability, but it would not be difficult to acquire if needed. In other words, much of the basic technology already exists on the island; it needs only a political directive to be put into motion.

Revisiting Nuclear Weapons: Political Constraints

The key constraints to Taiwan revisiting its nuclear weapons program are ultimately political rather than technological. First and most significant among these is mainland China's past assertion that nuclearization of Taiwan would serve as one of its criteria for launching an attack on the island.[30] While China has claimed that its nuclear weapons are not aimed at Taiwan, it insists that Taiwan's development of a nuclear capability would "menace [the] mainland's security and stability in the Asia-Pacific region. . . . The mainland will not use nuclear weapons against its own compatriots, but it will also not allow Taiwan to produce nuclear weapons to menace the mainland."[31] Thus in its search for the ultimate deterrent to attack from the mainland, Taiwan may, in fact, provoke it.

In addition, in today's Taiwan, maintaining a secret nuclear weapons program is theoretically possible but much less likely, given the robust media, open society, and relatively transparent governance that has taken hold since the transition to democracy on the island in the late 1980s. Rapidly departing are the days when the Taiwan military or a small clique within the political establishment could make dramatic decisions about Taiwan's security with impunity and in the shadows. Legislative oversight is growing, and military budgets are receiving unprecedented scrutiny. "Black budgets" still exist for selected military development and procurement, but whether a program of such controversy and sensitivity, with such drastic security implications, could remain concealed among a select number of political, military, scientific, and engineering coconspirators is difficult to imagine in today's Taiwan. Indeed, the record of the past thirty years demonstrates that even the authoritarian system had difficulty in this regard.[32]

The division between political and military societies in Taiwan today also serves as a constraint against reconsideration of the nuclear option. While the Taiwan military was intensely loyal to the Chiang clique and the Nationalist Party in the past, today it is an open secret that the military is less enamored with the ruling Democratic Progressive Party (DPP). Given Taiwan's modern history as the home of the exiled Republic of China, the military has traditionally been dominated by "Chinese," with ties to those who escaped the mainland in 1949. They therefore tend to be suspicious of the policies of the predominantly Taiwan-born DPP, which formed as a party dedicated to Taiwan's independence from China.

The military would thus be doubly opposed to a nuclear weapons program, particularly under the DPP. As a largely "Chinese" institution, its members tend not to support independence or policies that would promote it, which a nuclear program might seem to do. (It should be noted that neither do they necessarily support immediate unification, at least while the Communist Party dominates China.) Furthermore, the military would certainly not support any policies that it believes would force it into combat with China. One of those policies would be development of a nuclear weapon. As a result, the military, an essential component of any nuclear development strategy, would likely be inclined to undermine any such policy, whether through strategic leaks or through its continued influence within the political system. "Taiwanization" of the military over time might help erode this obstacle, but in the near term, the likelihood that Taiwan's military could be induced to go along with a nuclear plan is uncertain at best.

Furthermore, although the independence-minded radical wing of the DPP may arguably be the most tempted to proceed with a nuclear weapons program, the party as a whole has championed non-nuclear policies, both civilian and military. President Chen Shui-bian ran successfully on this platform in 2000, and the prospect of building a fourth nuclear power plant on Taiwan remains a sensitive political subject for his party (indeed, his first prime minister resigned over the issue). A strong antinuclear constituency still exists in Taiwan, both in the general public and the Legislative Yuan (parliament). Thus any moves to improve or upgrade Taiwan's nuclear facilities, for instance, would be heavily publicized and face strong public opposition, perhaps disrupting the relative political balance that exists today on the island.

Of course, any evidence that Taiwan had resumed a nuclear weapons program would almost certainly elicit strong U.S. opposition—at least under the political conditions that prevail at the start of the twenty-first century. The United States has a thirty-year record of seeking to prevent Taiwan from going nuclear and of upholding the nonproliferation regime in East Asia. Allowing Taiwan to proceed with a nuclear weapons program would fundamentally undermine the credibility of the U.S. international nonproliferation effort.

No less important, the United States has asserted its opposition to provocation from either side of the Taiwan Strait, as it has substantial interest in keeping the region peaceful and stable. Taiwan's development of a nuclear weapons capability could well be seen as a provocation, pulling the United States into a cross-strait conflict. The United States has asserted and demonstrated its willingness to assist Taiwan in defending itself from unprovoked aggression but is obviously not interested in picking a fight with China, and it would not look kindly on unilateral action by Taiwan that could lead the United States into a war with a large nuclear power. The United States would likely retaliate forcefully against such an action by freezing, if not cutting, its defense assistance to the island. Thus Taiwan could jeopardize the support of the one nation critical to its political and military defense.

In addition, the United States might impose sanctions whose impact would be quickly felt. Taiwan's nuclear plants account for 20 percent of the island's total electricity needs, and all their fuel comes from the United States; a cut-off would bite substantially into Taiwan's economy and society.

Another consideration is the increasingly significant issue of Japan's support for Taiwan's defense. Japan (particularly Okinawa) serves as an important launching point for any U.S. defense of Taiwan in the event of cross-strait hostilities. Indeed, Taiwanese are unique in looking back with some fondness on their history under Japanese colonialism. As a result, within Japanese society there is a growing appreciation for Taiwan—its democracy, economy, and popular culture—and growing antipathy and resentment toward Japan's traditional rivals on the mainland. At the same time, however, Japan also has a historic antipathy toward nuclear weapons— what some have called a "nuclear allergy"— as a residue of World War II. Should Taiwan decide to pursue a nuclear weapons capability, particularly in the absence of a decision by Japan to do likewise, it could jeopardize this important and growing source of support, both political and operational.

Revisiting Nuclear Weapons: Inducements

Although the above-mentioned constraints are significant, it is not difficult to imagine circumstances where Taiwan might reconsider the nuclear weapons option. One scenario concerns the overall security situation and military balance across the strait. U.S. Department of Defense reports have indicated that while China and Taiwan have maintained a kind of dynamic equilibrium militarily, the former's current modernization efforts—including procurement of advanced weaponry, particularly from Russia, and deployment of increasingly lethal and accurate ballistic and cruise missiles directed at Taiwan—are tilting the balance increasingly toward China over time.[33]

As this military gap widens, Taiwan may feel increasingly vulnerable and unable to count on U.S. protection during the critical early stages of a conflict. It may decide that it needs its own decisive weapon to even the balance. Indeed, even short of nuclear weapons, Taiwan strategists today are increasingly considering the need to develop an "offense defense" plan—entailing deployment of surface-to-surface missiles capable of striking the mainland—to serve as a partial deterrent (and counterstrike force) to a Chinese attack. The addition of a nuclear component to this strategy is not necessarily an illogical extension of this independent deterrent concept. Furthermore, as China's economy continues to grow rapidly and Taiwan's slows, a nuclear weapon may be a more cost-effective (if risky) option when compared with the expense of the myriad conventional weapons, such as submarines and missile defense, that Taiwan will need to consider over time.

A related scenario would be a perceived reduction in the overall U.S. defense commitment to the island. As indicated, the United States remains unique in its commitment to Taiwan's defense. Should such a commitment recede—or be perceived as receding—dramatically, Taiwan authorities, as they have in the past, may feel they have little choice but to consider drastic options, including the nuclear one.

It is conceivable that at some point the U.S. position on nuclearization of Taiwan could also become muddier. Influential U.S. proponents of Taiwan "self-determination" (read: independence) could loudly and forcefully assert that Taiwan has the right or indeed ought to have a nuclear deterrent. As some have done with respect to Japan, they might note that Taiwan is a responsible free-market democracy that simply seeks to protect itself from coercion by its big brother across the strait.

Then there is the argument that North Korean development of a nuclear weapons capability would inevitably lead to a domino effect in the region, inspiring Japan, South Korea, and then Taiwan to follow suit. The direct linkage is weak in the unique case of Taiwan, but there could be an indirect impact by decreasing the stigma against nuclear weapons that exists both within the region and in Taiwan itself. Such a scenario may also allow Taiwan's external supporters in the United States to argue more convincingly that the nonproliferation regime has collapsed in East Asia and that democratic Taiwan deserves to follow suit to protect its interests, even if separate from other regional calculations.

Finally, a combination of domestic politics and a perceived opportunity regarding China in the next several years might stimulate a reconsideration of the nuclear option. Some believe that the prospect of holding the 2008 Olympic Games in Beijing will constrain China's international actions before that time, creating an opportunity for the more radical, independence-minded elements within Taiwan to push the nuclear issue.[34] Although it seems unlikely, such dynamics cannot be ruled out, particularly in relation to other trends in cross-strait political and military affairs.

Conclusion: The Future of U.S. Credibility and the "Nuclear Card"

Factors in each of the "inducement" scenarios described above can be detected in Taiwan's original decision to pursue development of nuclear weapons. It began in the 1960s in the aftermath of the 1964 Chinese test, when Taiwan perceived a capabilities and prestige gap. The decision gained momentum during a period of growing isolation—epitomized by its expulsion from the UN in 1971—and perceived lessening of U.S. commitment to its security. The latter was based on the reduction in U.S. troop levels in Asia as the Vietnam War concluded, the prospect that U.S.-PRC normalization would lead to severing of Taiwan's mutual defense treaty with the United States, and the possibility of a reduction in—if not termination of—U.S. arms sales.

Taiwan's decision to acquire nuclear weapons in the 1980s also arose in a context of positive trends in U.S.-China relations and growing insecurity over the U.S. commitment to Taiwan, particularly in the aftermath of the 1982 Sino-U.S. Communiqué, which held out the prospect of declining future arms sales to the island. Taiwan's decision to revisit its nuclear program during that decade may also have reflected, perhaps, the last-chance ambition of the Chiang clique to fulfill a long-time dream.

And during the previous decade, echoes of these same dynamics can again be detected in the comments and activities of Taiwanese authorities. After China test-fired missiles near the Taiwan coast in 1995, Taiwanese president Lee Teng-hui told the legislature that Taiwan should consider restarting its nuclear weapons program—a statement from which he backed down just a few days later after U.S. government protests. In 1998 independence-minded legislator Parris Chang of the DPP stated bluntly that "if Taiwan were to perceive no alternative guarantee to its security and a possible sell-out of Taiwan by the U.S., the motivation to go nuclear would be there."[35] In 1999 then vice president Lien Chen stated that Taiwan should develop its own long-range surface-to-surface missiles, which many believed would be produced as potential delivery systems for nuclear weapons.

These statements occurred in the context of two trends, at least as Taiwan perceived them at the time. The first was evidence of an increasing threat from China. Indeed, when China attempted to use military coercion to influence Taiwan, as happened in 1995 and 1996, Taiwan responded with increased nuclear rhetoric. The second trend was a "decline" in U.S. support for Taiwan as President Clinton attempted to repair the U.S.-China relationship. During his 1998 visit to China, President Clinton's pledge to abide by the "Three No's"—a policy statement explicitly restricting U.S. support for Taiwan's sovereign rights internationally—reinforced a growing feeling in Taiwan of vulnerability and abandonment.[36] Only two years earlier the United States had responded to Chinese missile tests and increasing coercive pressure toward Taiwan by sending the Seventh Fleet toward the Taiwan Strait; yet some on Taiwan, remembering past shocks in 1972 and 1979, worried that deterrence across the strait was weakening and began to wonder once again about the U.S. security commitment to the island.

Despite such general concerns, in the current political and security environment, Taiwan has more reasons to continue to forego nuclear weapons than to revisit the matter seriously. The U.S. defense commitment is still firm, and the aversion to proliferation in the region—particularly among its key allies, the United States and Japan—remains equally strong. Pursuit of a nuclear weapons program would cost Taiwan the support of the United States and the rest of the international community at a time when it is more dependent than ever on them for its economic, energy, and security needs. And China's detection of a nuclear weapons program on the island would extract an even greater price in terms of Taiwan's security. Although China no longer explicitly lists the presence of nuclear weapons on Taiwan among its criteria for attack, the warning is surely assumed.

What ultimately forced Taiwan to forego nuclear weapons development in the past is still a factor today: Taiwan's dependence on the United States. Although Taiwan may view a nuclear option as insurance against possible future U.S. abandonment, such a program could make this scenario a self-fulfilling prophecy. Gerald Segal, a former professor at the International Institute for Strategic Studies in London, heard precisely this fear from Taiwanese leaders during a visit in 1998, as he argued that a nuclear strategy may "give the United States an excuse to throw Taiwan to the Chinese wolves."[37]

Nonetheless, Taiwan may decide to maintain a degree of uncertainty about its nuclear intentions over time, in an attempt to increase cross-strait deterrence. In the late 1990s, as aggressive Chinese rhetoric waxed and U.S. support seemed to wane, Taiwan politicians did not hesitate to remind both major powers that Taiwan could seek an independent road. This "nuclear card," according to Segal, is meant to send a message to the United States not to abandon Taiwan, and to the PRC to beware of pushing the island too hard.

Although Taiwan is not developing nuclear weapons and has apparently dismantled the physical, if not the human, infrastructure with which it sought to develop them in the past, it would not take long for this island nation to resume the development process should internal or external conditions prove compelling. Taiwan's nuclear expertise is dormant but advanced and may be reengaged, given a political consensus.

The gradual shift in the conventional military balance across the strait is perhaps the most compelling concern that may cause Taiwan's leadership to change its perspective: as Taiwan's defense planners find themselves less and less able to defend against a quick and devastating attack from the mainland, a nuclear "trump card" may gain more appeal.

In the past, a strong, stable, and cooperative U.S.-Taiwan security relationship has served as the best antidote to both an attack from the mainland and development of a Taiwanese nuclear weapons program. It must be maintained as a necessary component of continued stability in the area. However, in the face of advanced and growing Chinese capabilities, this stabilizing dynamic could weaken, as the United States may not be in a position to provide credible protection against a "quick-strike, quick-resolution" mainland strategy. If this is coupled with a deterioration of the nonproliferation regime in East Asia, from the activities of North Korea or others, and an increasingly assertive Taiwanese nationalism at home, traditional constraints against a Taiwan nuclear weapons program may lose their power.

Notes

1. For the purposes of clarity and simplicity, "Taiwan" is used in this chapter to represent the sovereign entity on the island of Formosa during the period addressed in the study. In fact, the regime on Taiwan formally—and constitutionally—considers itself to represent the "Republic of China," a remnant of the Chinese civil war.

2. It may be argued that reports in early 2004 that al Qaeda has put Taiwan on its list of attack targets, given the island's support of the United States in Afghanistan and Iraq, may force the Taiwan government to focus also on this potential threat to its homeland security in coming years.

3. David Albright and Corey Gay, "Taiwan: Nuclear Nightmare Averted," *Bulletin of the Atomic Scientists,* vol. 54, no. 1 (January–February 1998).

4. This section benefits greatly from Albright and Gay, "Taiwan."

5. Ibid.

6. In a 1998 interview, Wu Ta-you, a member of Taiwan's National Security Council at the time, claimed Ching-kuo acted behind his father's back. See Albright and Gay, "Taiwan." On the other hand, a National Taiwan University professor, Hsu Cho-yun, told U.S. embassy personnel in 1966 that the president himself was the primary driver. See U.S. Embassy Taipei, "Indications GRC Continues to Pursue Atomic Weaponry," airgram 1037, June 20, 1966, in William Burr, ed., National Security Archive Briefing Book No. 19, "New Archival

Evidence on Taiwanese 'Nuclear Intentions,' 1966–1976," accessed online at www.gwu.edu/~nsarchiv/NSAEBB/NSAEBB20/ (hereafter citations from this Briefing Book will be referred to as Burr, "New Archival Evidence"). More evidence is required to decide conclusively on this point.

7. "Hsin Chu" refers to the city just south of Taiwan's capital, Taipei, where National Tsinghua University is located.

8. There are conflicting reports about the date on which the plant opened. The Center for Nonproliferation Studies at the Monterey Institute states that the power plant opened in 1965 (see the Nuclear Threat Initiative's Taiwan Country Profile at www.nti.org/e_research/profiles/Taiwan/index.html [March 2004]). Other articles suggest that GE built the power plant in 1967 (for example, see William Ide, "How the U.S. Stopped Taiwan's Bomb," *Taipei Times,* October 14, 1999, at www.taipeitimes.com/News/local/archives/1999/10/14/6401 [March 2004]).

9. U.S. Embassy Tel Aviv, "More of Nationalist Chinese Atomic Experts Visit to Israel," airgram 810, March 24, 1966, in Burr, "New Archival Evidence."

10. These inspections were initially rather weak, but they were strengthened subsequently, particularly after Taiwan's nuclear weapons program was revealed. They continue to be conducted at a more junior level than normal for the IAEA for political reasons—related to China's demand that Taiwan be treated as a non-state actor by international organizations.

11. Albright and Gay, "Taiwan." Ironically, the officer, General Tang Chun-po, argued privately to President Chiang Kai-shek against Taiwan developing a nuclear weapons capability, but he was overruled. According to internal U.S. reports at the time, Tang contended that developing such a capability would be "impractical." Regardless of his private objections, General Tang subsequently continued to play a critical role in the island's nuclear weapons development program. U.S. Embassy Taipei, "Indications GRC Continues to Pursue Atomic Weaponry," airgram 1037, June 20, 1966, in Burr, "New Archival Evidence."

12. Albright and Gay, "Taiwan."

13. Ibid.

14. Ibid.

15. Embassy Taipei to State Department, "ROC Decides against Purchase of Nuclear Reprocessing Plant," cable 828, February 8, 1973. It should be noted that President Nixon during this period was focused on developing his new relationship with the PRC as part of his global strategy against the Soviet Union and on extricating the United States from the Vietnam War. He was highly opposed, to say the least, to a Taiwan nuclear program that would undermine his grand strategy.

16. Embassy Taipei to State Department, "Chung Shan Nuclear Research Institute," cable 1197, February 24, 1973; and State Department to Embassies in Taipei and Tokyo, "ROC Nuclear Research," cable 51747, March 21, 1973, in Burr, "New Archival Evidence."

17. Albright and Gay, "Taiwan."

18. Ibid. Albright and Gay cite Edward Schumacher, "Taiwan Seen Reprocessing Nuclear Fuel," *Washington Post*, August 29, 1976, p. A1.

19. Ibid.

20. State Department Memorandum of Conversation, "ROC Nuclear Energy Plans," November 18, 1976, in Burr, "New Archival Evidence."

21. A U.S. judge in a December 1991 ruling ordered the transfer to stop on environmental grounds. The Department of Energy would be required to challenge the court order. Upon examination, the U.S. government determined that the appeal would be too costly, requiring a new environmental impact statement, and unnecessary given the adequate safeguards over Taiwan's nuclear program. It is unlikely that the final two kilograms will ever be transferred back to the United States.

22. Colonel Chang himself was smuggled out of Taiwan by the CIA and reportedly lives today in Virginia.

23. "Former Top General Reveals Secret Nuclear Weapons Program," *China Post*, January 6, 2000, p. 1. The article reports on information revealed in an autobiography by former chief of general staff and premier Hau Pei-tsun in 2000. The article also cites Hau as noting that Taiwan leaders assumed that Chang Hsien-yi was not the only CIA asset involved in the nuclear weapons program and that concern over a possible crisis in relations with Washington served as the determining factor in Taiwan deciding to finally terminate its nuclear ambitions. Regarding the written guarantee sought by President Reagan from President Lee, Hau quotes Reagan envoy David Dean as being told by Reagan, "If (Lee) doesn't put his signature on this within a week's time, don't bother coming back."

24. "Taiwan Will Not Develop Nuclear Arms: Defense Minister," *Central News Agency* (Taiwan), January 5, 2000.

25. Ibid.

26. "Former Taiwan Military Chief Details Nuke Weapon Program," *Japan Economic Newswire*, January 5, 2000.

27. Interview with former senior CSIST official, Taiwan, May 7, 2002.

28. Ibid.

29. Gerald Segal, "Taiwanese Officials Hope Subtle Nuclear Campaign Will Force U.S. to Reaffirm Security Umbrella," *Asian Wall Street Journal Weekly Edition*, August 10, 1998, pp. 16-17. It should be noted that this claim may be exaggerated for deterrent effect (see subsequent discussion). For their part, Taiwan engineers claim that it would take "eight to ten years" of concentrated effort to rebuild Taiwan's nuclear weapons development capacity, both human and physical. The true time frame is likely somewhere in between, though probably sooner than later. Interviews with former CSIST official and mid-level engineer, Taiwan, May 7, 2002.

30. In 1998, as rhetoric escalated in Taiwan regarding revisiting the nuclear option, the Chinese Communist Party's Central Committee, reportedly under

"strong" pressure from the military, added development of nuclear weapons as a third inducement—along with Taiwan independence and foreign intervention—for the mainland to attack Taiwan. According to a news report, the mainland leadership would announce this new criterion when Taiwan's nuclear development reaches a "critical stage" in order to check development of both nuclear weapons and "carrier tools" (presumably missiles). See "PRC Announces 3rd Reason for Use of Force," *Sing Tao Jih Pao* (Hong Kong), November 10, 1998, p. A7 (Foreign Broadcast Information Service–Asia and Pacific). This rationale for a Chinese attack on Taiwan was accepted as Chinese policy within the international community, although subsequent public documents, including periodic defense white papers, failed to include this criterion. Indeed, cross-strait observers since the early 1980s have assumed, apparently through official PRC leaks, that Taiwan's development of nuclear weapons was on the mainland's list of criteria for an attack on the island. However, locating an explicit PRC statement or document from this period stating such has been elusive.

31. Ibid.

32. One of the more recent and dramatic examples of the complications of modern Taiwan security occurred in August 2003 when Taiwan media revealed that a technician at the Chung Shan Institute was arrested and charged with helping transfer strategic high-tech products and leaking sensitive classified information, reportedly including Taiwan's missile defense development, to mainland China. This episode is only the latest embarrassment for Taiwan's internal security system. "Taiwan steps up anti-spy measures," *Taiwan News,* August 8, 2003 (http://etaiwannews.com/Taiwan/2003/08/08/1060305408.htm [March 2004]).

33. See Department of Defense annual reports to Congress from fiscal year 2000 through 2003, on the military power of the PRC.

34. Kevin Platt, "To Get Attention in Taiwan, Put Nukes in Your Election Campaign," *Christian Science Monitor,* August 27, 1999, p. 7. In the course of the country's 2000 presidential campaign, a fringe party, the Taiwan Independence Party, argued that Taiwan should acquire nuclear weapons and become the world's eighth nuclear power.

35. Segal, "Taiwanese Officials Hope."

36. The "Three No's" include "no support for Taiwan independence; no support for "Two Chinas" or "One China, One Taiwan"; and no support for Taiwan membership in international organizations that require statehood. Long enunciated in private as U.S. policy, President Clinton provided the first public U.S. endorsement of the formulation in response to an academic's question at an open forum in Shanghai in October 1998.

37. Segal, "Taiwanese Officials Hope."

PART 3

Prospects for a Nuclear Future

CHAPTER 12

Avoiding the Tipping Point:
Concluding Observations

KURT M. CAMPBELL

ROBERT J. EINHORN

When the editors of this volume first proposed this project to Carnegie Corporation of New York over three years ago, examining why and under what circumstances countries might reconsider their nonnuclear bargain, it seemed an interesting and important topic but not an especially urgent one. Events over the intervening time period, as well as the results of the extensive research contained in several of the country case studies, have disabused us of our earlier assessment.

During the cold war, the dominant security preoccupation and paradigm of governments and analysts alike was the threat of mutual annihilation in a U.S.-Soviet nuclear exchange, not the spread of nuclear weapons capabilities to additional states or subnational groups. By the end of the cold war, only the five original nuclear powers had overt capabilities, three "threshold" countries had undeclared capabilities, and several countries were clandestinely pursuing a nuclear option. The lid had been kept on although it had not been sealed. President Kennedy's dire predictions of a world with fifteen, twenty, or even twenty-five nuclear powers had not materialized.

The authors are grateful to research assistant Austin Carson, Center for Strategic and International Studies, for his valuable assistance in writing this chapter.

But changes in the international security system since the end of the cold war have created an environment more favorable for nuclear proliferation. These developments include the erosion of the security alliances that existed in the bipolar world; the accelerating diffusion of sensitive enabling technologies; the emergence of rogue states with ambitions to acquire weapons of mass destruction (WMD); the increasing salience of regional instabilities in South Asia, the Persian Gulf, and Northeast Asia; and the appearance of terrorist groups with apocalyptic agendas.

There were welcome developments over the course of this period: the nuclear renunciations by South Africa, Argentina, Brazil, and by three of the inheritors of the former Soviet nuclear arsenal stand as significant achievements in international efforts to roll back nuclear capabilities. However, there were worrisome developments as well. In particular, the 1998 nuclear tests by India and Pakistan inflicted severe damage on the nonproliferation regime, especially because the penalties imposed on the newly self-declared (and demonstrated) nuclear powers were modest and short lived. Although the United States imposed sanctions in the immediate aftermath of these tests, within six months Washington started lifting them. Within a few years, more penalties were relaxed. In recent years, Washington has embarked upon a deep strategic engagement of India aimed at elevating relations between the two countries, accompanied by a significant easing of restrictions on weapons sales and technology transfers. Would-be proliferators no doubt took notice of the mild international consequences for breaching the nuclear ramparts.[1]

The 1990s witnessed the further spread of WMD-related technologies. A growing number of countries acquired biological and chemical weapons as well as ballistic missiles and other systems that could deliver WMD. International networks of "rogue" states assisted by shadowy commercial entities now evaded multilateral export controls by trading these illicit technologies surreptitiously among themselves.[2] These weapons not only extended the lethality and reach of their possessors, but the stigma surrounding these unconventional weapons of mass destruction also contributed to their unsettling psychological impact, thereby perversely making them all the more attractive for some countries to acquire.

The new century saw a further erosion of the nonproliferation regime. It opened with Iraq continuing to defy UN Security Council resolutions and excluding UN inspectors. In October 2002, North Korea admitted to a secret uranium enrichment program, thereby confirming its violation of the 1994 Agreed Framework and triggering a downward spiral of events that included the restarting of its frozen nuclear facilities, expulsion of International Atomic Energy Agency (IAEA) inspectors, withdrawal from the Non-Proliferation Treaty (NPT), and threats that it might provide a "physical demonstration" of its nuclear capabilities and actually export nuclear weapons.[3] In mid-2002 an Iranian dissident group revealed that Iran was constructing two sensitive nuclear facilities out of sight of the IAEA, the international body responsible for verifying its safeguards agreement. Subsequent investigations by the IAEA showed that Iran had made alarming headway in its nuclear program and had committed numerous violations of its nonproliferation commitments in the process. Revelations from Afghanistan and elsewhere have indicated that the al Qaeda terrorist group has actively sought to acquire nuclear weapons and other WMD for over a decade.[4] Terrorist movements with global reach, the proliferation of WMD, and the breeding grounds provided by failed states have created a dangerous confluence of security threats in the early twenty-first century. Individual governments and multilateral institutions are today straining to cope with these threats. In this environment, it is no wonder that some countries—even responsible states with long non-nuclear traditions—might consider, or reconsider, nuclear weapons as a guarantor of their security.

Given the basic questions that have arisen about the effectiveness of international efforts to curb proliferation, we began this study with a concern that we might be edging—or perhaps even hurtling—toward a world of more and more nuclear-armed countries, possibly including states other than the usual nuclear suspects. Indeed, rather than focus our attention on the front lines of the current battle against the spread of WMD, involving the rogue states and al Qaeda–like groups, we concentrated our research efforts and analysis on countries that many years ago renounced nuclear weapons. Our collection of country studies asks the simple question: what might motivate these long-time nuclear abstainers to reconsider their atomic abstention? By studying this group of compliant (as far as we can tell) NPT parties—rather than countries that have all along sought nuclear capabilities or only recently relinquished them—we determined we would gain a better appreciation of just how durable, or fragile, the global nonproliferation regime may be and in the process gain a better understanding of the long-term policies that will be needed to strengthen it.

Findings from the Case Studies

The countries studied vary widely in terms of their domestic political situations, technical capabilities, regional relationships, and international security outlooks. Not surprisingly, these states also differ in terms of the likelihood that they might reconsider a nuclear option in the future—from Germany (where it is difficult to construct a plausible scenario in which Germans would reconsider nuclear abstention) to, say, Taiwan (where one or two not unrealistic developments could trigger a decision to again consider the pursuit of nuclear weapons). But there are also many similarities among the case studies, especially in the kinds of factors that might drive countries to seek independent nuclear deterrent capabilities. A discussion of the impact of these factors follows, but an important conclusion from our research is that in most of the cases studied, it would take a combination of highly threatening and mutually reinforcing factors—a "perfect storm"—to set in motion the momentous decision to reverse a non-nuclear course and initiate the pursuit of a nuclear weapons capability.

Regional Security Environment

For virtually all of the countries studied, the main factor that could motivate a decision to pursue nuclear weapons would be an acute regional security threat. The threat most likely to drive such decisions would be the acquisition of a nuclear weapons capability by a neighboring hostile state—in particular, North Korea or Iran. Conversely, stopping Iran and rolling back North Korea could make an enormous contribution in reducing proliferation incentives.

While *new* nuclear powers would create the greatest pressure for rethinking past decisions to forgo nuclear weapons, some of the countries studied would also be driven by more threatening capabilities and policies from rivals that already possess nuclear weapons. Prominent examples of this include the possible reactions of Taiwan and Japan to China's growing military capabilities or the responses of Syria and Egypt to Israel's possibly becoming a declared nuclear power.

The authors of the case studies note that the desire for prestige and political clout could also conceivably play a role in inducing some countries to reconsider their policies of nuclear abstention. For example, Syria might envision nuclear weapons as a way to assert its domestic legitimacy or pan-Arab credentials, although it is hard to see why the Syrian government would risk the possible military consequences of being caught attempting a nuclear breakout, especially given the precedent of Iraq. However, the cases suggest that prestige factors would carry much less weight than traditional security considerations for most of the states studied, and in none of the countries would the motivation of prestige alone trigger a reconsideration of nuclear weapons options.

U.S. Foreign and Security Policy

Given the unprecedented power and influence of the United States today, what it says and does will have a significant impact on the nuclear behavior of individual countries. For example, although a severe new security threat (especially a new nuclear threat) would strongly motivate a country to reconsider its nuclear renunciation, such a threat probably would not be sufficient to elicit this reaction if the country has an American security guarantee that is not perceived to be weakening. Thus as long as the U.S. nuclear umbrella remains credible and U.S. relations with Japan and South Korea remain strong, even a nuclear-armed North Korea would not necessarily lead these two countries to decide to acquire nuclear capabilities of their own.

The case studies suggest that the perceived reliability of U.S. security assurances will be a critical factor, if not *the* critical factor, in whether such countries as Japan, Saudi Arabia, South Korea, Taiwan, and Turkey reconsider their nuclear options. It is noteworthy that both Taiwan and South Korea became most interested in pursuing nuclear weapons programs in the mid-to-late 1970s, a time when the United States appeared to have adopted a policy of security disengagement or detachment from East Asia following the humiliation of the Vietnam War. (Germany, which currently does not face a serious threat to its security, has the luxury of having both a U.S. nuclear guarantee and close ties with other nuclear weapons states through NATO and the EU.)

Besides the question of American security guarantees, the state of U.S. bilateral relations with individual countries will influence their nuclear decisions. The case studies illustrate how in the past, fears of alienating Washington were a major inducement to U.S. friends and allies to refrain from the pursuit of a nuclear arsenal. The more countries value their relationship with the United States—for the political, economic, or other benefits they derive from it—the higher will be the perceived costs associated with embarking on a nuclear weapons program. However, if relations with Washington become strained (as they are in the cases of Egypt,

Saudi Arabia, South Korea, and Turkey) or if new governments assume power that are not interested in good relations with the United States, the disincentives against going nuclear could weaken.

The Bush administration's more muscular counterproliferation strategy—potentially involving the use of preemptive or even preventative military force—is unlikely to have a direct impact on the nuclear decisionmaking of most of the countries studied because they have generally favorable relations with the United States (with the exception of Syria) and therefore do not see themselves as targets of American coercion or attack. But to the extent that the U.S. strategy is seen as influencing the nuclear programs of potential adversaries like North Korea, Iran, and Libya, it may have an indirect but critical effect on the threat perceptions and nuclear choices of these heretofore abstaining countries.

The Bush administration's counterproliferation strategy already seems to have produced significant results in terms of diminishing prospects for pursuing nuclear options, at least in the case of some former rogue states. Whether or not Iraq's nuclear program was active or even existent on the eve of the U.S. invasion, it is now clearly dead for the foreseeable future. In addition, the toppling of Saddam probably influenced Colonel Muammar Gadhafi's apparent decision to abandon his WMD programs. The timing of Libya's overtures to British and U.S. officials strongly suggests that fear of preemptive military action played a significant role in the internal decisionmaking process, although other motivations (for example, boosting a devastated domestic economy and stemming growing unrest among unemployed youth by reintegrating Libya into the international community) were presumably also at work.[5]

On Iran and North Korea, the jury is still out. North Korea's participation in the six-party talks and Iran's signing of the IAEA Additional Protocol and the suspension of its enrichment activities were positive developments and would not have been possible in the absence of strong U.S.-led pressures. But whether the threat of military force or regime change will eventually motivate those two countries to abandon their nuclear options rather than cling to them more tightly remains an open question. Indeed, it is the central question and conundrum in matters associated with current proliferation challenges facing the United States and the international community.

One of the more controversial aspects of the Bush administration's WMD strategy is its desire to increase U.S. options regarding the development, testing, and use of U.S. nuclear forces. This policy includes exploring new low-yield nuclear weapons and "bunker busters," opposing the Comprehensive Test Ban Treaty, shortening lead times to resume nuclear testing, and reserving the right to use nuclear weapons to respond to or prevent chemical weapons or biological weapons attacks. Proponents say that enhancing U.S. nuclear options will allow the United States to field a modern, credible nuclear force that will not only deter proliferators from using WMD against the U.S. and its allies but will also dissuade would-be proliferators from pursuing WMD programs in the first place. Opponents say that the administration's policies, by enhancing the perceived importance and utility of nuclear weapons, will increase the likelihood that other countries will try to acquire them.

Despite the attention this issue has received internationally and in the United States, the case studies suggest that Bush administration policies to continue improving the U.S. nuclear arsenal will have little or no *direct* effect on the nuclear choices of others—either to stimulate them to acquire nuclear weapons or to discourage them from doing so. Furthermore, U.S. nuclear gluttony—the allegation that the United States has not sufficiently reduced its vast stockpiles of nuclear weapons and therefore failed to live up to its NPT "bargain"—is also judged to have little immediate relevance in the complex decisionmaking surrounding those choices. Most of the nuclear decisions in our case studies are driven primarily by regional security considerations in which the characteristics of U.S. nuclear capabilities play at most only a minor role. To the extent that U.S. nuclear capabilities are a factor—either because a country depends on a U.S. nuclear umbrella or fears U.S. nuclear coercion or attack—it is very unlikely that the country's behavior will be affected by any distinction it may perceive between older and newer U.S. nuclear designs (or by the size of the U.S. nuclear arsenal). In reality, the behavior of most countries will be influenced not by their perceptions of the specific qualities of the U.S. nuclear arsenal (old or new, large or small) but by their judgment of the willingness of the United States to bring its unprecedented *conventional* military superiority to bear—either on their behalf or in opposition to them.

Global Nuclear Nonproliferation Regime

Although U.S. policies regarding the development, testing, and use of its nuclear weapons are unlikely to have a direct or immediate impact on the nuclear choices of the countries studied, they may well affect their perceptions of the long-term viability of the nonproliferation regime. Non-nuclear states have an important stake in a healthy global regime that encourages nuclear abstinence. A world in which the goals of the NPT are being fulfilled—where existing nuclear arsenals are being reduced, parties are not pursuing clandestine nuclear programs, nuclear testing has been stopped, the taboo against the use of nuclear weapons is being strengthened, and in general, the salience of nuclear weapons in international affairs is diminishing—helps reinforce their non-nuclear status.

However, if the nonproliferation regime is widely seen as eroding, a few of the nuclear abstainers may perceive this development as a threat—not necessarily an immediate one that would prompt them to launch a nuclear weapons program, but a longer-term threat that could lead them over time to begin hedging their bets. Signs of erosion could include a more robust posture on the part of established nuclear powers toward the military utility of nuclear weapons, clandestine nuclear weapons programs by NPT parties in violation of their obligations, the continued presence of some states outside the NPT regime, and the failure of the international community to make NPT violators pay a sufficient price for flouting nonproliferation norms. This handful of nuclear abstainers may calculate that an eroding nonproliferation regime would exert an ever-weakening grip on its members and lead more of them over time to believe they could cheat or withdraw with impunity. Fearing future defections from the regime, even countries that currently have no nuclear aspirations may feel compelled to rethink their nuclear options so as to avoid being the last to join a rapidly enlarging nuclear club.

The case studies suggest that pessimism has indeed grown in recent years about the future of the nonproliferation regime. The expectation that nuclear weapons will become a more, rather than less, important feature of global security calculations could make Japan and Egypt, for example, increasingly uncomfortable with their non-nuclear status. Several of the countries studied assessed that the international community's relatively mild and short-lived reactions to the 1998 Indian and Pakistani nuclear tests may have reduced the perceived penalties for going nuclear. Counteracting that expectation, presumably, will be the message sent by the Iraq war, Iran's opening to more intrusive IAEA inspections under growing international pressure, and Libya's very public renunciation of WMD.

Concern about the future of the nonproliferation regime is unlikely to be a decisive factor in the nuclear choices of any of the countries studied, but in combination with other factors, especially acute regional security threats and worries about the continued viability of American security guarantees, it could play a significant supporting role. Of course, the critical test of whether the nonproliferation regime is succeeding or failing will be whether additional countries become nuclear powers. In this respect, the fates of North Korea and Iran will be crucial. If the nuclear programs of both of those countries can be thwarted (especially now that the nuclear ambitions of former rogue Iraq have been put to rest), much of the pessimism surrounding the nonproliferation regime we have witnessed in recent years could well be reversed or at least halted.

Technological Availability

Another critical factor affecting the nuclear choices of the countries studied is the availability of the technologies, equipment, human expertise, and materials required for nuclear weapons, and the ability of a would-be nuclear power to integrate these ingredients into a successful nuclear weapons program. For quite some time, the conventional wisdom has been that once a political decision has been made to acquire nuclear weapons, the technical hurdles are relatively quick and easy to overcome. However, despite the continued if not accelerating dissemination of scientific knowledge, technological expertise, and engineering competence, the technical barriers to developing nuclear weapons remain formidable.

The key bottlenecks are the facilities needed to enrich uranium or separate plutonium, which require technologies that most countries cannot produce indigenously. Several of the countries studied are years away from having the nuclear infrastructure to produce fissile materials, either by enriching uranium to weapons grade or separating plutonium from spent fuel. For Saudi Arabia, an indigenous nuclear infrastructure capable of supporting a nuclear weapons program is simply out of reach for the foreseeable future. For others (for example, Egypt, Syria, and Turkey), acquiring such an infrastructure would take at least three to five years and probably much longer. Investigations of Libya's nuclear program in the wake of Gadhafi's December 2003 renunciation of WMD suggest that, for countries without advanced technical and industrial infrastructures, acquiring the materials and equipment to produce fissile materials may be a lot easier than integrating that input into an effective weapons program.[6] Even for a technologically advanced country, such as a "virtual nuclear weapons state" like Japan, proceeding from a well-developed civil nuclear energy and space launch program to an effective deliverable nuclear weapons capability could take years.

However, unforeseen revelations in Iraq—involving greater than expected nuclear strides discovered after the first Gulf war and less than expected capabilities after the second—as well as the surprising headway made by Iran in its uranium enrichment program point to the profound limitations of U.S. intelligence when it comes to making precise judgments about progress along the nuclear acquisition curve. Contributing to this problem has been the growth of stealthy black market procurement networks of brokers, intermediaries, and front companies as well as the preference of several countries that have recently sought nuclear weapons for technologies (mainly centrifuge enrichment) that are easier to conceal than the production capabilities widely favored decades ago (plutonium production reactors and reprocessing facilities). So technological hurdles remain, but our ability to know where a country actually is along the path of nuclear development may often be limited.

Domestic Factors

The case studies also demonstrate the importance of domestic factors in nuclear decisionmaking. A leading academic theory postulates that democracies do not wage war on one another, and the weight of historical evidence appears to support this contention. It is less clear what impact the adoption of democratic institutions has had on a state's desire to acquire nuclear weapons. The evidence from the case studies is rather mixed. In South Korea and Taiwan—both of which pursued secret nuclear weapons programs under authoritarian governments before the United States discovered their plans and forced them to stop—democracy exerts real constraints on the ability of both governments to pursue nuclear weapons. Not only does an aggressively free media make it much harder to keep a program secret, but public opinion in those countries would oppose the acquisition of nuclear weapons. The same can be said for public sentiment in Japan and especially Germany, where politicians appreciate that advocating the acquisition of nuclear weapons would be deeply unpopular.

An interesting and somewhat problematic finding of the study is that Egypt, for one, remains non-nuclear in part because it is *not* a democracy. Strong, autocratic leaders now essentially aligned with the West have determined that nuclear weapons are not in Egypt's national interest and have made these decisions stick despite continuing and widespread dissatisfaction with the country's continued non-nuclear status. Free elections in Egypt (and perhaps in Saudi Arabia and Syria one day) could conceivably bring to power leaders who might be responsive to populist, nationalistic public pressures to acquire nuclear weapons.

Another domestic factor that could also come into play in the complex calculus surrounding a decision to embark on a nuclear path is a society's perception of its own vitality, both in terms of regional comparisons and domestic measurements. For instance, certain trends in Japan—including societal aging, growing structural unemployment, anxieties surrounding future economic prospects, comparisons with a rising China, the now-painful and dashed memories of Japanese economic might in the 1980s—have, taken together, produced a widespread malaise in Japanese society that reflects deepening feelings of pessimism about the future. This sense of failure to fulfill historical national missions (or myths) could contribute to a national psychology that seeks an ultimate guarantor against perceived external threats and mounting signs of domestic decay. These phenomena might also manifest themselves among failing authoritarian regimes in the Middle East and, coupled with heightened regional security concerns, could trigger a dangerous domestic dynamic leading to nuclear reconsideration. While nuclear weapons status has often in the past been associated with visions of greatness and rising fortunes, it could in the future be seen by declining societies or regimes as a hedge against irrelevance or a guarantee of survival in a dangerous world that is passing them by.

Approaching the Tipping Point?

At the outset of this study, we asked ourselves whether the world was approaching a nuclear tipping point—the point at which momentum toward a world of many nuclear powers became overwhelming and irreversible. The case studies suggest that a "group dynamic" may indeed play a role in nuclear decisionmaking. The nuclear abstainers are mindful of the nuclear activities and choices of other countries in the aggregate, especially of those that are neighbors or potential adversaries. If they judge that others will remain non-nuclear, they are more likely to be content with the nuclear status quo, and only a strong stimulus, such as an acute new security threat, is likely to shake their non-nuclear convictions. Their natural reluctance to embark on what could be a risky and unpredictable course is reinforced by a sense that if they opted for nuclear weapons, they would be alone and vulnerable to tremendous pressures.

But if the abstainers see others moving to acquire nuclear weapons— and especially if they perceive that the penalties that would be incurred would be tolerable—then the factors that might trigger a reconsideration of nuclear options might not have to be as compelling. States that might otherwise see insurmountable obstacles to going nuclear could be more inclined to take comfort in numbers (or, perhaps more accurately, discomfort in numbers) and reconsider their nuclear options. Rather than go full speed ahead toward a nuclear weapons capability, some might consider an intermediate course of hedging their bets by acquiring the nuclear infrastructure that would leave open the option to proceed with a full-blown weapons program in the future. It is these intermediate steps, rather than a headlong pursuit of nuclear weapons, that we judge in most cases to be the more likely near-term choice for countries deciding to abandon the non-nuclear status quo.

Whatever path countries may take toward the tipping point, we are almost certainly not there yet—in fact, we do not appear to be close. Indeed, a welcome overall conclusion from the case studies explored in this volume is that the global nonproliferation regime may be more durable and less fragile than has sometimes been suspected or feared. Worrisome developments in recent years have given rise to a widespread concern that a world of more and more nuclear powers is essentially inevitable—that JFK's nightmare vision had only been postponed, not avoided. To be sure, the risks of further proliferation are very real. But despite widely held feelings of pessimism about the regime itself, our focus on the individual cases in the study reveals that it is not so easy to reverse longstanding decisions to forswear nuclear weapons. The evidence suggests that there is a hidden robustness in the fraying fabric of the global non-nuclear compact.

Policy Recommendations

The following policy recommendations are aimed at reducing the likelihood that today's nuclear abstainers will reconsider their options and at strengthening the nonproliferation regime in general. Beyond these specific policy steps, however, we want to stress the general importance of paying closer attention to the nuclear choices of states that have renounced nuclear weapons and of giving a higher priority to trying to ensure that they continue to do so. Governments and outside experts concerned with nuclear nonproliferation typically have focused enormous efforts on countries such as Iraq, North Korea, and Iran that appeared to pose the most immediate risk of proliferation, and they have devoted much less attention to countries that genuinely gave up nuclear weapons long ago. While our study indicates that the nonproliferation regime may be less fragile than is often thought, it also suggests that we cannot take continued abstinence for granted in the case of several crucial states. In pursuing the full range of political, security, and economic relations with each of the abstainers, the United States and other champions of nonproliferation should give special attention to the need to strengthen their incentives for remaining in the non-nuclear camp and their disincentives for reconsidering their nuclear choices.

Stop Iran and North Korea from Going Nuclear

The case studies show how the continued pursuit of a nuclear arsenal by Iran could induce Syria, Saudi Arabia, Egypt, and Turkey to revisit their policies of nuclear abstention. Similarly, if North Korea—which already has a robust regional ballistic missile delivery capability—retains and builds up its nuclear capability, this could increase pressures on Japan, South Korea, and even Taiwan to develop their own nuclear weapons. Stopping Iran and rolling back North Korea would therefore remove a compelling reason why most of the countries studied might reconsider their approach to possessing nuclear weapons. After the successful examples of nuclear rollback in Iraq and Libya, moreover, stopping Iran and North Korea would greatly reduce pessimism about the health of the nonproliferation regime more generally.

Although Iran has signed the Additional Protocol and agreed to suspend enrichment and reprocessing activities, it does not yet appear to have made a fundamental decision to abandon its nuclear weapons ambitions. The United States—by continuing to work closely with the Europeans, Russians, and the IAEA—must induce Iran's leaders to conclude that they can only realize their national goals, including political and economic reintegration into the international community, by unambiguously renouncing a nuclear weapons capability. Iran's current suspension of its sensitive nuclear fuel cycle activities should be made permanent, and Tehran should verifiably dismantle its existing fuel cycle facilities, including those related to uranium enrichment. In return, Russia, the United States, and the Europeans should provide multilateral assurance that as long as Iran fulfills its nonproliferation obligations, it will receive nuclear fuel and related fuel cycle services for any nuclear power reactors that it builds. In addition, the United States should take steps to convince Tehran that while the U.S. stands on the side of those who favor freedom and democracy in Iran, American policy will not actively promote regime change.[7]

North Korea presents a harder challenge. It is far from certain that, at this stage, Pyongyang would be prepared to abandon its nuclear weapons program, no matter what inducements the international community dangled before it. Still, the stakes are so great that its stated readiness to relinquish its nuclear arsenal must be put to the test at the six-party negotiating table. The basic elements of a deal (that is, the verified, complete, irreversible, and phased dismantling of North Korea's weapons program in exchange for security assurances, removal of remaining sanctions, energy and other forms of assistance, and normalization of relations between Pyongyang and Washington) are already well understood by all parties involved.[8] Of course, any such bargain would have shortcomings. In particular, the international community would not have watertight confidence that North Korea was complying with its obligations and that it had forsaken all of its clandestine nuclear activities. But the alternative—trying to build multilateral support to pressure North Korea until it either capitulates or collapses—is much less likely to prevent Pyongyang from amassing a substantial nuclear arsenal. Not the least of the downsides of that alternative is that it could create one of the prime conditions for nuclear reexamination by several of the states discussed in these pages.

In dealing with Iraq, the first of the three members of the so-called axis of evil, the Bush administration decided that the preventative use of military force was necessary. In North Korea and Iran, however, military options have not been viewed as very promising. In the case of North Korea, this has been because intelligence about the locations of DPRK nuclear assets and facilities has not been good enough to permit effective targeting and because of the prospect that North Korea could respond to any U.S. military attack with conventional artillery and rocket barrages that would cause massive casualties in South Korea. In the case of Iran, uncertainty about the ability to target and decisively set back Tehran's nuclear program has also been a factor, but the main reasons for not giving the military option serious consideration have been the judgment that the military and political costs of an invasion would be prohibitively high (especially after the difficulties that arose in the aftermath of the Iraq operation) and the belief that political evolution in Iran could increase the likelihood of a diplomatic solution.

The Bush administration's reluctance so far to use military force in North Korea, Iran, and Libya—notwithstanding the heavy emphasis on preemption in its 2002 National Security Strategy and the abundant evidence that each has actively pursued nuclear and other WMD programs—suggests that the military instruments of counterproliferation policy will be suitable only rarely. In very few real-world situations will opportunities exist for "clean," decisive, Osirak-type military strikes.[9] In the absence of timely and accurate intelligence, proximately deployed military assets, and the support (or at least acquiescence) of key neighboring states, the preemptive use of force will usually be militarily impractical.[10] Beyond questions of practicality, the anticipated political, military, and economic consequences of initiating the use of force will often tip the balance against military preemption.

The Bush administration and its critics will continue to debate whether the "demonstration effect" of the military invasion of Iraq has encouraged other states to give up or hold onto (and perhaps even accelerate) their nuclear weapons programs. As suggested above, Gadhafi's decision to confess and abandon Libya's WMD programs seems to have been motivated—at least in part—by a fear of what the Bush administration might have had in store for him. However, it is probably too early to judge the net impact of Iraq on the calculations of leaders in Pyongyang and Tehran. But the Bush administration and its critics seem to agree that even though military force will be appropriate for addressing proliferation challenges only in a limited set of circumstances, it makes little sense to rule out military options altogether. After all, it is very hard to know how rogue-state leaders assess the likelihood of military attack by the United States. Military options that, from a U.S. perspective, would be highly risky and undesirable may appear credible to such leaders and have some positive influence on their nuclear decisionmaking.

In any event, whatever one thinks about the value of military attack options in dealing with particular proliferation challenges, it seems clear that some form of pressure, or disincentives, will be necessary if satisfactory solutions to such problems as Iran and North Korea are to be achieved. Iran would not have agreed last fall to sign the IAEA Additional Protocol or to suspend enrichment and reprocessing activities without the credible threat that continued failure to cooperate would result in a finding of noncompliance by the IAEA board, referral to the United Nations, and eventually Security Council sanctions. Nor would North Korea have agreed to multilateral, six-party talks in the absence of a strong U.S.-led campaign that threatened diplomatic pressures and possibly coercive economic measures.

But pressure alone is unlikely to work, either in North Korea or Iran. Both countries have made major, long-term commitments to acquiring nuclear weapons. Getting them genuinely to forswear nuclear weapons at this stage will require not just the threat of very harmful consequences if they persist but also the prospect of a much brighter future if they reverse course. In particular, that will require measures that provide the two governments confidence that by giving up nuclear weapons, they will not be jeopardizing their national security. Positive outcomes on North Korea and Iran are far from assured, especially in the former case. But if diplomatic solutions are to be reached that reliably end the nuclear ambitions of those countries, they will surely involve a combination of international pressures and inducements—carrots and sticks.

Although the Bush administration's chest-thumping articulation of its strategy to counter WMD proliferation gave many observers the impression that it would be relying heavily on unilateral, military policy tools, it has in practice pursued a much more differentiated approach: military force without an international consensus in the case of Iraq, multilateral pressures and diplomacy in the case of North Korea, secret contacts and the promise of better bilateral relations in the case of Libya, and reliance on international institutions and European-led diplomacy in the case of Iran. The administration has recognized that in dealing with countries that have actively sought nuclear and other WMD capabilities, no cookie-cutter approach will suffice; it is necessary to tailor U.S. policies to the particular circumstances surrounding each case. The same is true in dealing with the nuclear abstainers, the countries whose nuclear choices will be strongly influenced by success or failure in Iran, North Korea, Iraq, and Libya.

Alleviate Security Concerns

With the exception of Syria, all the countries covered in this study derive substantial security benefits from their association with the United States. Some (Germany, Japan, South Korea, Turkey) are formally allied with the United States through bilateral or multilateral (that is, NATO) security treaties; one (Taiwan) has received commitments in the form of U.S. legislation and presidential policies; another (Saudi Arabia) has relied on informal understandings and close defense cooperation; and still another (Egypt) has been an intimate partner of the United States in regional peace arrangements and bilateral security ties. These various security relationships with the United States have been instrumental in each country's nuclear calculus. Indeed, in the cases of South Korea and Taiwan, the historical record suggests that perceived erosion in the reliability of security guarantees from the United States can dramatically change the calculation of the costs and benefits of remaining non-nuclear.

In the period ahead, questions may arise about the continued value of the U.S. factor in the security equations of a number of the countries studied. In response to fundamental changes in the international security environment since the end of the cold war—especially the demise of the Soviet threat to Europe, the spread of WMD and other asymmetrical military capabilities, the emergence of failed states and militant Islamic movements, and the growth of well-financed, capable terrorist networks operating on a global basis—the United States is now proceeding with a massive overhaul of its force deployments overseas. As U.S. forces are reconfigured and repositioned to meet the evolving requirements of the war on terrorism, friends and allies (including some whose perceptions of the terrorist threat and prescriptions for dealing with it differ from those of Washington) may wonder whether these changes are fully consistent with their own security priorities. For example, many South Koreans, including strong supporters of the U.S.–South Korean alliance, are troubled by plans to relocate U.S. troops away from the demilitarized zone and out of Seoul, especially while the impasse over North Korea's nuclear program remains unresolved. Japanese are speculating about how U.S. force realignments in Korea and elsewhere will eventually affect them. In Southwest Asia, while U.S. forces are now heavily committed to stabilizing and rebuilding Iraq and Afghanistan, major questions exist about the future of America's military presence in the region.

Beyond the uncertainties surrounding the redeployment of U.S. forces overseas, several other current developments create the potential for increased confusion and insecurity among some U.S. friends and allies. The Bush administration's tendency to rely on ad hoc "coalitions of the willing" rather than on established alliance relationships and structures has raised questions about the future of those alliances. In Taiwan the surprisingly rapid warming of Sino-American relations after September 11 and blunt warnings from Washington that Taipei should not tinker with the status quo in cross-strait relations may be prompting some Taiwanese politicians to re-think the amount of support they can expect to receive from the United States. In South Korea sharp differences with Washington over policy toward North Korea; a dramatic reorientation of economic, political, and cultural ties with China; and a major shift in public opinion against the United States (especially among young people) have all contributed to a weakening of mutual confidence and trust, especially between the White House and the Blue House. In Egypt and Saudi Arabia, the rulers in Cairo and Riyadh continue to retain the support of the U.S. government, but they may be wondering whether the American public's dissatisfaction with their governments and its growing desire to press for far-reaching political and societal reform in their countries will lead to an estrangement with the United States and a reduction in the support they can expect to receive for their security. In the minds of the Turkish people and their leaders, Turkey's place in Europe and its institutions remains unsettled, while uncertainty about the future role of NATO and its relationship to embryonic European defense arrangements may pose worrisome questions about whom Turkey can depend on in the future to help it meet its security needs.

To reduce the likelihood that today's nuclear abstainers will rethink their nuclear options in the future, the United States must do what it can to address such concerns. Undertaking new U.S. security obligations—for example, extending formal security guarantees to Egypt or Saudi Arabia or expanding U.S. commitments under the Taiwan Relations Act—is hardly realistic, either politically or practically, especially given the high priority that will be assigned in the period ahead to stabilizing Iraq as well as the concern that U.S. forces may already be stretched too thin. The focus should instead be on bolstering existing security alliances and defense arrangements, alleviating as much as possible the strains that have developed in certain key bilateral relationships, and in general maintaining (and in some cases restoring) confidence in the reliability of the United States as a security partner.

Addressing the security needs of U.S. friends and allies will often involve tangible forms of reassurance. For example, the U.S. decision to spend $11 billion to modernize American forces in Korea can help persuade Seoul, especially in light of concerns about the repositioning and possible reduction of those forces, that the U.S. remains committed to South Korea's security. Maintaining a sizeable but discreet U.S. military presence in the Gulf region, even after the eventual stabilization and drawdown of forces in Iraq and Afghanistan, will signal to friends in the Middle East that the U.S. will stay heavily invested in promoting stability in the area. Continuing robust cooperative defense relationships with friendly states—including conventional arms transfers, training, exercises, and contingency planning—will provide concrete evidence of U.S.

support and reduce their incentive to acquire nonconventional military capabilities. In this connection, U.S. cooperation with East Asian and Middle Eastern partners in theater missile defenses could help address concerns about nuclear and missile threats from North Korea and Iran, and could help minimize pressures for pursuing independent nuclear deterrent capabilities. In recent years, interest in missile defenses has grown rapidly in Japan, which has embarked on a program of joint research with the United States, and in Turkey, which has discussed missile defense with both the United States and Israel.

However, bolstering the confidence of nuclear abstainers in the reliability of U.S. security assurances requires more than tangible support. It is essential, especially as the United States transforms its worldwide force structure, that Washington go out of its way to consult closely with friends and allies whose interests are affected to explain the rationale for the adjustments, to accommodate any requests that it reasonably can, and to demonstrate that the changes do not erode the U.S. security commitment. In the case of the repositioning of U.S. forces in Korea, more harm was done to U.S.–South Korean alliance relations by the peremptory manner in which decisions made in Washington were presented to the Korean allies than by the content or even the timing of the moves.

In dealing with the abstainers, the United States should not wait until the specter of nuclear reconsideration arises. It should instead anticipate possible problems and try to head them off with preventative diplomacy. In anticipation of the unwelcome prospect that North Korea will persist in pursuing a nuclear weapons capability, the United States should begin consulting privately now with its South Korean and Japanese allies on how to cope with that contingency without them having to acquire independent nuclear deterrent capabilities. Similarly, discreet discussions should be held with Seoul about the possibility that a nuclear-armed North Korea would some day collapse and be absorbed into South Korea and that a reunified Korea would inherit the DPRK's nuclear arsenal. Well before that contingency arises, the United States should seek a commitment from South Korean authorities that in exchange for a continued American security assurance, a reunified Korea would give up its nuclear inheritance and remain a non-nuclear weapons state. Preventative diplomacy could also be useful in the case of Turkey. In discussions involving NATO, the European Union, and Turkey about future defense structures and missions and about Turkey's place in the evolving European architecture, the United States should be conscious of the importance of ensuring that

Ankara remains confident enough about its security situation to maintain its non-nuclear course. And with an eye to keeping Egypt in the non-nuclear camp, we should encourage Israel not to do or say anything in the nuclear realm—such as publicly declaring or testing its nuclear capability—that could generate pressures in Egypt for pursuing a nuclear option.

Raise Barriers to Nuclear Acquisition

Discouraging the abstainers from reconsidering their nuclear choices requires not just addressing the reasons they might want nuclear weapons—that is, the demand side of the equation. It also means focusing on the supply side—in other words, making it more difficult for them to acquire the materials, equipment, and technology needed to pursue a nuclear weapons program.

One of the welcome findings of this study is that acquiring the necessary infrastructure to produce nuclear weapons is not as quick and easy as is often assumed. A long-time abstainer contemplating nuclear reversal may face a formidable series of technical and practical hurdles. Such a country also knows that if and when its intention to pursue nuclear weapons became known or even suspected, it could come under immense international pressure to abort the effort. Unless it believes the goal can be achieved in a relatively short period of time and unless it figures it can conceal its intentions until the goal is nearly within reach (and thereby minimize its exposure to international pressures), it may well calculate that the path ahead toward nuclear weapons is too risky. To reduce the likelihood that nuclear abstainers will reconsider, the United States and other supporters of nonproliferation should therefore do whatever they can to make the path from abstention to nuclear weapons appear as daunting as possible—time consuming, expensive, uncertain, subject to detection, and potentially even dangerous.

A problem in this connection is that the NPT itself can give non-nuclear states legal cover to get far down the path toward a nuclear weapons capability under the guise of a civil nuclear energy program. Specifically, as long as NPT parties are prepared to place their nuclear activities under IAEA verification, the treaty allows them to acquire uranium enrichment and reprocessing capabilities (fuel cycle capabilities) that not only can be used to produce fuel for nuclear reactors but also could be used to produce fissile cores for nuclear bombs. Claiming that its program is strictly for peaceful purposes, a party can pursue such fuel cycle capabilities openly and legally. But once the facilities are completed and operational, the party can legally invoke the NPT's withdrawal provision and leave the treaty, evict IAEA inspectors, and proceed directly to building nuclear weapons. Or it could adopt a hedging strategy—pursuing a peaceful energy program for the time being, while keeping its options open to break out of the NPT at a future time. Either way, having already acquired the necessary nuclear infrastructure—the most time-consuming, expensive, and technically challenging part of a nuclear weapons program—the country would need only a relatively short period of time after "breakout" to build nuclear weapons and would therefore be minimizing its period of exposure to international pressures.

Iran hoped that the world would buy its story that its large uranium enrichment program was intended only to provide fuel for nuclear power reactors. But faced with broad skepticism about that claim, charged by the IAEA with numerous violations of its nonproliferation obligations, and confronted with unified international pressure and the prospect of UN Security Council sanctions, Iran was forced to agree to a suspension of its enrichment activities. It is not yet clear whether the suspension will become permanent or Iran will resume its enrichment program when it believes the pressure has died down.

Brazil presents a very different case. Like Iran, it intends to have its own uranium enrichment capability; its facility is planned to begin operations next year. But unlike the case of Iran, there is no evidence that Brazil is pursuing nuclear weapons. With the change from military to civilian rule, it abandoned its nuclear weapons program and later joined the NPT in 1998. Still, especially given its earlier military nuclear aspirations as well as its refusal to thus far adhere to the IAEA's Additional Protocol, Brazil's stated intention to proceed with its enrichment program inevitably gives rise to international speculation that, at a minimum, Brazil has begun to hedge its bets—creating an option for the future, even if it has not decided to resurrect its old weapons program. If Brazil, an NPT party in good standing, is seen as hedging its bets, others might well be inclined to follow.

The Iran case and, to a lesser extent, the Brazil case demonstrate the risk associated with allowing additional independent fuel-cycle facilities. At the same time, non-nuclear NPT parties in good standing should be able to receive—indeed under article 4 of the treaty have the right to receive—the peaceful benefits of nuclear energy. Fortunately, it is possible to square this circle. States can acquire nuclear reactors for power generation, but instead of acquiring the sensitive fuel cycle facilities to make and process their own fuel, they can buy fuel from foreign suppliers and send it back to them after it is irradiated.

Various approaches have been put forward for discouraging the spread of independent nuclear fuel cycle capabilities without discouraging the growth of nuclear power. Under one such approach, supplier states would agree not to transfer nuclear fuel cycle facilities or related equipment and technology to anyone, and they would agree to sell nuclear reactors and associated equipment and technology only to those countries that have verifiably renounced the acquisition of their own fuel cycle capabilities. Moreover, to assure those countries that they would not be subject to future supply cutoffs, the supplying governments would commit to providing fuel cycle services (supply of fresh reactor fuel and repossession of spent fuel) at commercial or in some cases even subsidized rates to any recipient country joining and abiding by the arrangement.[11] A similar proposal for discouraging independent nuclear fuel cycle capabilities was advanced by President Bush in his speech at the National Defense University on February 11, 2004.[12]

Non-nuclear states genuinely interested in reaping the benefits of nuclear power would have an interest in taking advantage of such arrangements and forgoing expensive, independent fuel cycle facilities in favor of reliable, cost-effective fuel cycle services. However, states seeking nuclear weapons could be expected to try to acquire fuel cycle equipment and technologies from suppliers that either failed to join the arrangement or were prepared to violate it. Strong pressures and possibly international sanctions would therefore have to be brought to bear on supplying governments that were unwilling to participate in or abide by the arrangement and possibly also on recipients that tried to circumvent it in order to obtain sensitive technologies.

The United States should begin soon to build international support for such an arrangement designed to prevent the spread of fuel cycle capabilities to additional states. Building a strong international norm against the proliferation of such capabilities, even under international safeguards, would not only raise the barrier to a state wishing to pursue nuclear weapons quickly and directly, but it would also make it harder to pursue a hedging strategy of acquiring a dual-use nuclear infrastructure and holding open the option for breakout at a later date. It would therefore lengthen the perceived lead time before a nuclear aspirant could present the world with a fait accompli and would make the option of embarking on a path toward nuclear weapons look more complicated and less attractive.

Beyond seeking to discourage the spread of overt fuel cycle capabilities, the United States and other states should do everything they can to strengthen nuclear-related export controls—both national systems of control and multilateral export control regimes—to prevent aspiring nuclear powers from surreptitiously getting the technical wherewithal they need. The nature of clandestine nuclear procurement has changed dramatically over the last decade. In the past, a country seeking nuclear weapons would direct its own nationals (officials or private citizens) to buy the necessary ingredients from foreign governments with few scruples about nuclear exports or from foreign firms willing to manufacture and export the desired goods in circumvention of controls in their countries. Such relatively simple patterns of procurement continue, but they have now been supplemented by large, secretive networks of brokers, middlemen, scientists, engineers, manufacturers, and front companies that operate in many countries around the world, often in jurisdictions with weak controls, and that are run by shady characters of various nationalities. While the U.S. government has long been aware of black market operations in the nuclear procurement field, information provided by Libya to U.S., British, and IAEA officials about the assistance it received from Pakistani scientist A. Q. Khan's illicit network indicated that these operations are far more extensive and sophisticated than anyone had imagined.[13]

Drawing on lessons learned from debriefings in Libya, the IAEA's investigation of Iran's procurement efforts, and Pakistani authorities' interrogation of A. Q. Khan, U.S. and other national export control authorities, as well as multilateral export control groups such as the Nuclear Suppliers Group, should review and strengthen their controls. In addition to focusing hard on certain critical technologies (especially centrifuge enrichment, the fuel cycle technology of choice for today's aspiring nuclear powers), these national authorities and multilateral groups must act aggressively to thwart and eliminate the nuclear black market. This will require strong international cooperation, not only to develop new legal and policy tools but also to enforce them.

It will not be enough to work with the forty or so countries, many of them advanced industrialized states, that are members of the multilateral suppliers groups. The revelations from the Libyan case demonstrate that many black market activities—including manufacture of components, assembly, transshipment, and technical consulting services—take place outside the jurisdictions of countries that belong to the multilateral groups. The United States and other strong supporters of nonproliferation will have to make a major effort in the period ahead to persuade countries in Southeast Asia, the Middle East, and elsewhere that may play a substantial role in the illicit nuclear trade—whether as brokering, manufacturing, or transshipment centers—to adopt the necessary controls and, just as important, to devote the necessary energy and resources to enforcing them effectively. The U.S., European, and Japanese governments already have programs in place to assist less developed countries in establishing national export control systems. In light of what has been learned recently about clandestine procurement efforts, these programs have to be stepped up substantially.

Recognizing that the task of acquiring and building indigenous nuclear fuel cycle capabilities may be expensive, protracted, and require more skilled manpower than is available internally, some countries interested in obtaining nuclear weapons might prefer the shortcut of purchasing or stealing already produced nuclear weapons or weapons-usable nuclear material. While such a path to nuclear weapons has the drawback of limiting the size of a country's arsenal to the amount of nuclear material it can get its hand on, it may well suffice for a country seeking only a few bombs for deterrence, blackmail, or terrorist purposes. Under the Nunn-Lugar threat reduction programs, the United States over the last decade has devoted well over $7 billion to addressing this threat by assisting Russia and other former states of the Soviet Union to secure, account for, dismantle, and eliminate former Soviet weapons of mass destruction and related materials and infrastructure. A significant part of these programs involves finding useful civilian work for former Soviet weapon scientists to reduce their incentives to peddle their expertise to hostile states or terrorist groups. In June 2002, the United States got substantial help from its G-8 partners in pursuing these cooperative threat reduction programs. At their annual summit, the G-8 leaders agreed to a "Global Partnership" in which they would collectively raise $20 billion over ten years (half from the United States and the other half from the remaining G-8 members) to secure and eliminate nuclear and other sensitive materials, primarily in Russia.

But while the U.S. Nunn-Lugar and now the G-8 Global Partnership programs have accomplished a great deal, much work remains. The process of enhancing physical security at nuclear materials sites in Russia is moving too slowly. Only about 40 percent of the sensitive nuclear material covered by the U.S. Department of Energy's materials protection program has so far been subject to even basic security upgrades. The

"Megatons to Megawatts" program to blend down highly enriched uranium from Soviet nuclear weapons into low-enriched fuel for nuclear power reactors has worked well, but the program (which has blended down less than 50 percent of the 500 tons covered in the United States-Russian agreement) should be accelerated. Moreover, there are still about 130 nuclear research reactors operating with bomb-grade uranium at potentially vulnerable sites in over forty countries. The U.S., Russia, and other interested countries should intensify current efforts to remove highly enriched uranium from such sites and convert the reactors to operate on low-enriched fuel that cannot be used in weapons. The $20 billion pledged by the G-8 countries in 2002 is far short of what is needed. That figure should be considered a floor, not a ceiling.

It is clear, moreover, that the former Soviet Union is not the only potential source of materials, equipment, and expertise that could be used in a nuclear weapons program by a state that had previously renounced a nuclear capability. Acute concerns have arisen in recent years, for example, about whether Pakistan's nuclear weapons and materials are under adequate physical controls and especially about the role played by Pakistani nuclear scientists in sharing nuclear equipment and expertise with such governments as Iran, North Korea, and Libya. Discreet assistance should be offered to Pakistan to help it ensure the protection of its nuclear assets from theft or seizure, and the government of Pakistan must be urged in the strongest terms to institute procedures and controls to ensure that no Pakistani-controlled nuclear technology will be transferred to foreign or other unauthorized hands in the future.

Efforts to interdict shipments of WMD- and missile-related equipment can also have an inhibiting effect on states contemplating the nuclear option. Not only will successful interdictions impede particular nuclear programs, but the existence of an increasingly robust and broadly supported interdiction capability can send a signal to potential nuclear aspirants that if they opt to pursue nuclear weapons, the way ahead may be fraught with difficulties, embarrassment, and even dangers. Indeed, the deterrent effect of such an interdiction capability may be at least as important as the interdiction operations themselves because, given the need for timely, accurate intelligence about illicit shipments as well as a range of other practical requirements, it is likely that successful interdiction operations will occur only rarely.

The Bush administration's Proliferation Security Initiative (PSI), a multination cooperative effort to interdict WMD-related cargoes at sea, on land, and in the air, deserves strong support. Building on the initiative's eleven original, like-minded participants, the administration is picking up support from a growing number of countries. Gaining the support of China and Russia will be especially important, given their geographic locations near countries of proliferation concern and their roles as potential sources of nuclear materials and related technologies. So far, in part to help build broad international support for the initiative, the United States and its PSI partners have taken the relatively cautious approach of operating through existing national and international legal authorities and not pushing the legal envelop very much. Given the nature of the threat and the need for powerful tools to counter it, it may now be time to seek expanded legal authority, perhaps through the UN Security Council or other means.

In addition to raising technical barriers to nuclear acquisition—by discouraging development of independent fuel cycle capabilities and making procurement of the necessary materials more difficult—it is also important to create political obstacles. As discussed above, one path to a nuclear weapons capability is to acquire a nuclear infrastructure legally under the guise of a civil nuclear energy program and then to leave the NPT by invoking its withdrawal provision. To make this path less attractive, steps should be taken to discourage NPT parties from invoking the withdrawal provision. For example, experts believe that under existing international law, a party cannot legally withdraw from a treaty that it is violating. Under that standard, North Korea would not have a legal right to free itself of its NPT obligations. In addition, the international community may want to discourage parties from withdrawing from the NPT even if they have a legal right to do so. In this connection, a Security Council resolution might state that under certain circumstances, a withdrawal from the NPT could constitute a threat to international peace and security that would require the council to meet and consider an appropriate response. While the legal and policy implications of such approaches require further study, the idea of discouraging NPT parties from leaving the treaty should be pursued.

Strengthen Verification, Intelligence, and Analytic Capabilities

One way of dissuading non-nuclear states from going nuclear is to make them appreciate that if they decide to pursue a nuclear weapons program covertly, there is a good chance they will get caught, and caught early enough to ensure that they will be brought under intense international pressure for a sustained period of time. U.S. intelligence capabilities and the intelligence services of various U.S. friends and allies will play a critical role in detecting signs of clandestine nuclear programs. While the precise capabilities of U.S. and friendly intelligence agencies will not be known to a state considering a covert nuclear program, such a state is likely to have a healthy respect for those capabilities and perhaps to err on the side of caution when it considers the pros and cons of proceeding covertly.

The NPT's international verification system, carried out by the IAEA, is another deterrent to a non-nuclear state embarking on a clandestine nuclear program. Questions have frequently been raised about the ability of the IAEA to detect a clandestine program that a safeguards violator has taken pains to conceal. Critics note that Iraq's pre-1991 nuclear weapons program escaped IAEA detection, that an Iranian dissident group rather than the IAEA disclosed the Natanz enrichment plant, and that the IAEA was unaware of Libya's enrichment program before Gadhafi's revelation. The IAEA defends itself by pointing out that covert programs at an early stage (like Libya's) are very difficult to detect, that even the United States was surprised by Iran's enrichment program at Natanz, and that the IAEA does not have sophisticated intelligence-gathering means of its own and must rely on intelligence cooperation with key members like the United States.

Perhaps the IAEA's strongest argument is that it has only recently received the powerful verification tools it needs via the Additional Protocol, which requires its parties to provide comprehensive data about their nuclear activities and submit to much more intrusive on-site activities, including environmental sampling, than was permitted under the traditional safeguards agreements. The problem is that only eighty states have signed the Additional Protocol, and it has entered into force for only about half of those.[14] Iran and Libya have now both signed the Additional Protocol and have pledged to act as if they were bound by it, even before ratification. Only time will tell if the protocol becomes an effective means of detecting and deterring clandestine nuclear activities. In the meantime, the United States should press hard for the broadest possible adherence to it.

However effective the IAEA and its protocol turn out to be, the United States will inevitably rely primarily on its own intelligence-gathering and analytic capabilities to provide early warning of disturbing developments in the proliferation area. With early warning, timely steps can be taken, diplomatic or otherwise, to head off a problem before it becomes unmanageable. Proliferation-related activities must therefore remain near the top of the U.S. intelligence community's list of collection priorities.

A related finding of this study is that the United States and other key governments need a better understanding of the internal factors that could propel a country toward nuclear weapons. The study on Japan, for example, revealed that there has been more internal consideration of the nuclear option than is commonly thought. Our research also indicated that decisionmaking in authoritarian countries such as Syria and Saudi Arabia was even more opaque. Given the importance of domestic factors in driving nuclear choices and given uncertainties about who will govern key states of the Middle East in the years ahead, there is a pressing need for a more finely tuned appreciation of the attitudes of key individuals, institutions, and political movements toward the nuclear issue.

Reduce the Salience of Nuclear Weapons

There is no indication that controversial policies of the Bush administration regarding nuclear weapons—such as its plans to research new low-yield nuclear weapons and bunker busters and its opposition to the Comprehensive Test Ban Treaty—have had a direct impact on deliberations regarding the acquisition of an independent nuclear capability in any of the countries studied. But these polices have heightened an impression worldwide that the current American government believes nuclear weapons are essential security tools that will play a continuing if not increasing role in international affairs. The danger is that if Washington is perceived to be preparing for a world in which nuclear weapons will remain important, other governments will also feel a need to alter their policies to prepare for such a world.

The United States should forgo the marginal advantages it sees in further refinements of its nuclear capabilities and pursue policies aimed at reducing the salience of nuclear arms.[15] A long-term strategy to devalue the role of nuclear weapons in the international system is fundamentally in American interests. The United States is the world's strongest conventional power with no real peer military competitor in sight. Indeed, this military-industrial supremacy is likely to remain unchallenged for well into this century. The single greatest danger facing the United States today and for the foreseeable future is that another country or nonstate actor might use a nuclear device against a major American city. Reducing the salience and significance of nuclear weapons in the global security environment is profoundly in American strategic interests.

Staying away from the Tipping Point

In examining the health of the global nonproliferation regime through the prism of countries that had long ago renounced the acquisition of nuclear weapons, the authors of this volume found, not surprisingly, a mixture of positive and negative developments. The discouraging signs were not hard to find—the persistent efforts of states like North Korea to obtain a nuclear capability, the ability of would-be nuclear powers to procure sensitive goods and technologies on the black market, a widespread foreboding about the erosion of the global nonproliferation regime, and deep concerns about regional disorders, catastrophic terrorism, and other destabilizing trends in the international system. But offsetting these gloomy signs, to some extent, were a number of encouraging developments: the movement of two long-standing nuclear aspirants (Iraq and Libya) from the nonproliferation "loss" column to the "win" column, a growing readiness by the international community to combine more assertive counterproliferation policy instruments (for example, the PSI) with more traditional institutional arrangements like the IAEA and the multilateral export control groups, and in general a greater recognition, perhaps in the wake of September 11, that the risks of rampant proliferation were unacceptable.

Another encouraging finding of the study—more apparent when one focuses on the nuclear choices of individual countries than on the macrolevel of the regime—is that decisions to renounce nuclear weapons are not so easy to reverse. Countries do not drift casually toward a nuclear weapons capability. Achieving such a capability requires strong leadership and a major commitment of energies and resources over a sustained period of time. Embarking on a nuclear weapons program after a lengthy period of abstinence would require a new aspirant to overcome years of non-nuclear inertia, both political and technical. Our research indicates that while a wide range of regional, international, and domestic factors might trigger internal debate within nuclear abstaining governments about their nuclear options, the threshold for triggering a decision to pursue nuclear weapons, either immediately or by establishing the technical base to permit a future decision, is rather high, usually requiring a combination of several stressful factors—again, the perfect storm.

The conclusion we draw is that while the prospect of additional countries acquiring nuclear weapons remains very real, there is nothing inevitable about it. Indeed, it is not inconceivable that the tide of proliferation can be stopped and even turned back to some extent. What that would require is not just the vigorous pursuit by the international community of policies tailored to meeting today's evolving proliferation challenges; it would also require a change in attitude and expectations. It would mean resisting the proliferation pessimism that has arisen in recent years and instead resolving that the stakes are so high that nothing short of the goal of arresting nuclear proliferation altogether should be acceptable. Moreover, it would require the United States, which has the largest stake in the outcome and the greatest ability to influence it, to show strong leadership—working closely with partners and institutions whenever possible, acting boldly and independently whenever necessary, and thereby moving the international consensus in the direction of taking firm, decisive steps.

We can take some comfort in the study's conclusion that while the tipping-point phenomenon may be an apt metaphor for the process of proliferation, we are neither at the tipping point nor destined to reach it. But there is something very troublesome about this metaphor: movement toward the tipping point starts very slowly, picks up speed, and then becomes swift and irresistible. At the earliest stages, movement is barely discernible. By the time the tipping process becomes readily identifiable, it may be very difficult to stop. So are we now in a state of proliferation equilibrium, with the balance level and stable? Or are we sliding imperceptibly toward the tipping point? We honestly do not know. What we do know is that keeping safely away from the tipping point will require the international community to act with unity, imagination, and strength. And it should act now, before it's too late.

Notes

1. The effect these tests had in stimulating further WMD proliferation is discussed in Paul Bracken, *Fire in the East: The Rise of Asian Military Power and the Second Nuclear Age* (HarperCollins, 1999).

2. For analysis of how this new form of transnational commerce in WMD among rogue states, terrorists, and international criminals is challenging the established nonproliferation regime, see Guarav Kampani, "Second Tier Proliferation: The Case of Pakistan and North Korea," *Nonproliferation Review*, vol. 9,

no. 3 (Fall-Winter 2002), pp. 107–16; Bob Drogin and Jeffrey Fleishman, "Banned Arms Flowed into Iraq through Syrian Firm," *Los Angeles Times*, December 30, 2003; and Paul Kerr, "Intelligence Chiefs Paint Grim Picture of Proliferation," *Arms Control Today*, March 2003 (www.armscontrol.org/act/2003_03/proliferation_mar03.asp [March 2004]).

3. See International Crisis Group, "North Korea: A Phased Negotiation Strategy," *Asia Report*, no. 61 (August 1, 2003), pp. 12–13.

4. David Albright, *Al Qaeda's Nuclear Program: Through the Window of Seized Documents,* Special Forum 47 (Berkeley, Calif.: Nautilus Institute, November 6, 2002) (www.nautilus.org/fora/Special-Policy-Forum/47_Albright.html); and Arnaud de Borchgrave, "Al Qaeda's Nuclear Agenda Verified," *Washington Times*, December 10, 2001, p. A14. For additional information on al Qaeda's pursuit of WMD, see Daniel Benjamin and Steven Simon, *The Age of Sacred Terror* (Random House, 2002).

5. For an argument that the Bush administration's strategy of prevention in Iraq and elsewhere induced Libyan leader Muammar Gadhafi to abandon his WMD program, see Tod Lindberg, "A Policy of Prevention," *Washington Times*, December 30, 2003, p. A17; for the case that international sanctions had a greater effect, see Ray Takeyh, "Sanctions, Not Threats, Forced Libya to Yield," *Long Island Newsday*, December 30, 2003.

6. Joby Warrick and Peter Slevin, "Libya's Disclosures Put Weapons in New Light," *Washington Post*, March 2, 2004, p. A1.

7. Such a proposal is adumbrated in Richard Weitz, "Averting a Nuclear-Armed Iran," *In the National Interest*, October 1, 2003 (www.inthenationalinterest.com/Articles/Vol2Issue38/Vol2Issue38WeitzPFV.html [March 2004]). See also Geoffrey Kemp, "How to Stop the Iranian Bomb," *In the National Interest*, no. 72 (Summer 2003), pp. 48–58; Ray Takeyh, "Iranian Options," *In the National Interest*, no. 73 (Fall 2003), pp. 49–56; and Richard Weitz, "Averting a Nuclear-Armed Iran," *In the National Interest*, October 1, 2003 (www.inthenationalinterest.com/Articles/Vol2Issue38/Vol2Issue38WeitzPFV.html [April 2004]).

8. For detailed discussions of the provisions of any such deal, see Victor D. Cha and David C. Kang, *Nuclear North Korea: A Debate on Engagement Strategies* (Columbia University Press, 2003); and Michael E. O'Hanlon and Mike M. Mochizuki, *Crisis on the Korean Peninsula: How to Deal with a Nuclear North Korea* (McGraw-Hill, 2003).

9. In 1981 an Israeli air force bombing raid destroyed the French-supplied Osirak nuclear reactor in Iraq, setting back Iraq's nuclear weapons program for a considerable period of time.

10. For a discussion of the difficulties associated with employing a strategy of preemption to counter or roll-back WMD proliferation, see Robert S. Litwak, "The New Calculus of Pre-emption," *Survival*, vol. 44, no. 4 (Winter 2002),

pp. 53–79. Also see Walter B. Slocombe, "Force, Pre-emption and Legitimacy," *Survival*, vol. 45, no. 1 (Spring 2003), pp. 117–30.

11. Ashton B. Carter and others, "Good Nukes, Bad Nukes," *New York Times*, December 22, 2003, p. A31.

12. President George W. Bush, "Bush's Speech on the Spread of Nuclear Weapons," transcript in *New York Times*, February 11, 2004.

13. Warrick and Slevin, "Libya's Disclosures Put Weapons in New Light."

14. President Bush called for wide adherence to the Additional Protocol in his speech on February 11, 2004 (cited above). He proposed that only states that have joined the Additional Protocol be allowed to import equipment for their nuclear programs.

15. On the general advantages accruing to the dominant state from the pursuit of moderate security policies, see G. John Ikenberry, *After Victory: Institutions, Strategic Restraint, and the Rebuilding of Order after Major Wars* (Princeton University Press, 2000).

About the Authors

Kurt M. Campbell is senior vice president and director of the International Security Program, and holder of the Henry A. Kissinger Chair in National Security at the Center for Strategic and International Studies (CSIS). In addition to his CSIS duties, he is the director of the Aspen Strategy Group, a contributing writer to the *New York Times,* and frequent on-air essayist for National Public Radio's *All Things Considered.* He has also been a consultant to ABC News. Previously, Campbell served in several capacities in government, including as deputy assistant secretary of defense at the Pentagon from 1995 to 2000, as a director on the National Security Council in 1994, as deputy special counselor to the president for NAFTA on the White House staff, and as a White House fellow (class of 1992–93) at the Department of the Treasury. Campbell was also associate professor of public policy and international relations and assistant director for the Center for Science and International Affairs at the John F. Kennedy School of Government at Harvard University. As a reserve officer in the United States Navy, he served on the Joint Chiefs of Staff and the Special Advisory Group to the Chief of Naval Operations. He is the author or editor of several books, including *To Prevail: A Strategy for the War on Terrorism,* as well as a contributor to numerous journals, magazines, and newspapers. He is a member of the International Institute for Strategic Studies and the Council on Foreign Relations.

Robert J. Einhorn is a senior adviser in the CSIS International Security Program, where he works on a broad range of nonproliferation, arms control, and other national security issues. Before coming to CSIS, he served in the U.S. government for twenty-nine years. From November 1999 to August 2001, he was assistant secretary for nonproliferation at the Department of State, where he was responsible for nonproliferation of nuclear, chemical, and biological weapons, missile delivery systems, and advanced conventional arms. In that capacity, he was the principal adviser to the secretary of state on nonproliferation matters, oversaw U.S. participation in the multilateral nonproliferation export control regimes, and represented the United States in nonproliferation discussions and negotiations with a wide variety of countries in East Asia, South Asia, the Middle East, and Europe. Einhorn was deputy assistant secretary for nonproliferation in the State Department's Bureau of Political-Military Affairs from 1992 to 1999 and a senior adviser in the department's policy planning staff from 1986 to 1992. He served at the U.S. Arms Control and Disarmament Agency (ACDA) from 1972 to 1984, where he dealt with strategic arms issues, nuclear testing limits, chemical and biological weapons constraints, nonproliferation, and other security issues. From 1982 to 1986 he represented ACDA in the START talks. In August 2001 Secretary Colin L. Powell presented him with the Secretary of State's Distinguished Service Award. Einhorn has authored several publications on strategic nuclear issues, arms control, and nonproliferation. He is a member of the Council on Foreign Relations and the International Institute of Strategic Studies.

Leon Fuerth has served in government for thirty years, including positions in the State Department, House and Senate staff, and the White House. Most recently, he was Vice President Gore's national security adviser for the eight years of the Clinton administration, where he served on the Principals' Committee of the National Security Council, alongside the secretaries of state and defense and the president's national security adviser. During Gore's years in Congress, Fuerth also advised him on national security issues. Before beginning his work on Capitol Hill in 1979, Fuerth spent eleven years as a foreign service officer. After retiring from government service at the end of the Clinton administration, Fuerth served as the J. B. and Maurice C. Shapiro Professor of International Affairs at George Washington University from January 2001 to January 2003. He is currently a research professor of international affairs at GWU and leads Forward Engagement, a program for the study of long-range policy analysis.

Ellen Laipson became president and CEO of the Henry L. Stimson Center in April 2002, after a twenty-five-year career in the U.S. government. Her work has focused mainly on the Middle East and South Asia. She last served in government as vice chairman of the National Intelligence Council (1997–2002), where she comanaged the interdisciplinary study *Global Trends 2015*. Previously she served at the U.S. mission to the United Nations, as director for Near East and South Asian Affairs at the National Security Council, and as a specialist in Middle East and North African affairs at the Congressional Research Service (1979–90). She currently serves on the boards of the Asia Foundation and the Education for Employment Foundation.

Thomas W. Lippman, an adjunct scholar at the Middle East Institute, is a Washington-based author and journalist specializing in U.S. foreign policy and Middle East affairs. He is the author of *Inside the Mirage: America's Fragile Partnership with Saudi Arabia,* as well as three other books. A former Middle East bureau chief and former diplomatic correspondent for the *Washington Post,* Lippman wrote extensively about nuclear security and proliferation issues in the 1990s. He is also a member of the Council on Foreign Relations.

Jenifer Mackby is a fellow at the Center for Strategic and International Studies, where she works on nonproliferation and European projects. Previously she served as secretary for the verification work of the Comprehensive Nuclear-Test-Ban Treaty Organization in Vienna, after being responsible for the negotiations on the Treaty and for the Group of Scientific Experts in Geneva. As a senior political affairs officer in the United Nations, Mackby handled outer space issues, the Nuclear Non-Proliferation Treaty review conferences, Biological Weapons Convention meetings, the Special Commission on Iraq, a government expert study on nuclear weapons, the Environmental Modification Treaty review conference, and a committee on South Africa's Nuclear Capability. She has written for the *New York Times, Newsweek,* the *Bulletin of the Atomic Scientists,* and other journals, and recently coauthored *The Final Test,* a history of the Nuclear Test Ban Treaty negotiations.

Derek J. Mitchell is senior fellow for Asia in the International Security Program at CSIS. He was appointed to the Office of the Secretary of Defense as special assistant for Asian and Pacific affairs in July 1997, and subsequently as director for regional security affairs from 1998 through 2000 and senior country director for China, Taiwan, Mongolia, and Hong Kong from 2000 to 2001. During his term at the Department of Defense (DoD), Mitchell also served as country director for Japan and senior country director for the Philippines, Indonesia, Malaysia, Brunei, and Singapore. He was the principal author of the DoD's 1998 *East Asia Strategy Report*. Before joining the DoD, Mitchell served as senior program officer for Asia and the former Soviet Union at the National Democratic Institute for International Affairs in Washington, D.C. In the fall of 1992, he served as logistics and operations manager for the United Democratic Campaign field program in California (Clinton-Gore, Boxer, Feinstein), and he was personnel director for field operations during California Campaign '88 (Dukakis-Bentsen), the first field program ever organized in California for a presidential campaign. In 1989 Mitchell worked as a copyeditor at the *China Post,* the largest English-language daily newspaper in Taiwan. From 1986 to 1988, he served as assistant to the senior foreign policy adviser to Senator Edward M. Kennedy in Washington, D.C.

Jonathan D. Pollack is professor of Asian and Pacific studies and chairman of the Strategic Research Department at the Naval War College. He has published extensively on China's political-military strategy, U.S.-China relations, the international politics of East Asia, U.S. policy in Asia and the Pacific, Korean politics and foreign policy, and East Asian technological and military development. His latest studies include *Strategic Surprise? U.S.-China Relations in the Early Twenty-First Century;* recent articles in *Asia-Pacific Review, Korea National Defense University Review, Naval War College Review, Strategic Comments, Orbis,* and *Asian Survey;* and chapters in *The China Threat—Perceptions, Myths, and Realities,* in *George W. Bush: A Midterm Assessment,* and in *U.S. Strategy in the Asia-Pacific Region.* He is presently preparing studies of ballistic missile development and ballistic missile defense in East Asia; U.S. strategic reassessments in the Asia-Pacific region; and Chinese regional security strategy alternatives.

Mitchell B. Reiss is with the Reves Center for International Studies at the College of William and Mary, Williamsburg, Virginia. He was formerly director of the Reves Center and dean of international affairs, professor of law at the Marshall-Wythe Law School, and professor of government in the Department of Government at William and Mary. Prior to this, Reiss helped to establish KEDO (the Korean Peninsula Energy Development Organization), a multinational organization created to address weapons proliferation concerns in North Korea. His responsibilities there included serving as chief negotiator and as general counsel. His government service includes positions in the National Security Council at the White House, and as a consultant to the U.S. Arms Control and Disarmament Agency, the State Department, the Congressional Research Service, and the Lawrence Livermore and Los Alamos National Laboratories. Reiss has also been a guest scholar at the Woodrow Wilson International Center for Scholars and has worked as an attorney at the firm of Covington and Burling. He is the author of *Bridled Ambition: Why Countries Constrain Their Nuclear Capabilities* and *Without the Bomb: The Politics of Nuclear Nonproliferation,* and has contributed to nine other volumes and written over fifty articles on international security and arms control issues.

Walter B. Slocombe was, from May to November 2003, senior adviser and director for security affairs (national security and defense) in the Coalition Provisional Authority for Iraq. He had served as under secretary of defense for policy from September 1994 to January 2001. Before becoming under secretary, he was principal deputy under secretary for policy from June 1993 and, pending confirmation for that post, a consultant to Secretary of Defense Les Aspin from January 1993. In earlier DoD service, he had been deputy under secretary for policy planning from November 1979 to January 1981 and principal deputy assistant secretary for international security affairs from January 1977 to November 1979. In both jobs, Slocombe served concurrently as director of the DoD task force on the Strategic Arms Limitation Talks (SALT). From January 1981 until he returned to the Defense Department in 1993, he was a partner in the firm of Caplin and Drysdale, where he had been an associate from 1971 to 1974 and partner from 1974 to 1977. At the firm, his practice had been in the fields of bankruptcy litigation, defense trade, tax litigation, and tax-exempt organizations. After graduating from law school, Slocombe clerked for United States Supreme Court Justice Abe Fortas in the October 1968 term, worked briefly as a special assistant in the Office of Economic Opportunity Legal Services Office, and served on the National Security Council staff in 1969 and 1970, working on strategic arms control, nuclear issues, and intelligence analysis policy.

Tsuyoshi Sunohara is a visiting fellow in the International Security Program at CSIS. Previously he was the chief correspondent in the Washington Bureau of *Nikkei News,* covering the White House, the Pentagon, and the State Department from 1999 to 2003. From 1996 to 1997, Sunohara served at the *Nihon Keizai Shimbun* as chief correspondent for the Japanese Ministry of Foreign Affairs. He has also been a correspondent for *Nikkei News* in Washington and chief correspondent for business affairs for the *Nihon Keizai Shimbun.* From 1986 to 1987, Sunohara was a visiting fellow in the Advance International Reporting Program at the Columbia University Graduate School of Journalism.

Index